How to Start and Operate a Mail-Order Business

JULIAN L. SIMON
University of Illinois, and
Julian Simon Associates

McGRAW-HILL BOOK COMPANY
New York Toronto London Sydney

HOW TO START AND OPERATE A MAIL-ORDER BUSINESS

For Rita

Preface

The primary purpose of this book is to teach newcomers to the mail-order business what they need to know to make money in mail order.

By "newcomers" I mean those of you who want to start a business from scratch. I also mean businessmen who now sell retail or through salesmen, and who want to utilize the mail-order selling method to increase their profits or to expand their operations.

The step-by-step organization of the book is tailored to newcomers to mail order. It tells you what to do first, second, and third. It teaches you exactly how to proceed from one stage to the next, until you are reaping the profits you want.

Choosing a product is the first and crucial decision you must make; hence we tackle that problem first. I show you the real "professional method" that is the secret of the big operators who find one profitable product after another.

This book teaches the *business* of mail order and the *business decisions* a mail-order man must make. This is unlike previous books about mail order, all of which have concentrated on how to write advertising copy. But copywriting and artwork skills are worthless to a mail-order man unless he can make sound decisions about what to sell and where to sell it.

Furthermore, art and copy talent can be obtained from advertising agencies and free-lance specialists. There are no specialists to help a mail-order man with his *business* decisions. That's what this book is designed to do.

The second purpose of the book is to collect in one place the important facts and data that will be of interest and help to experienced mail-order men. I've tried very hard to separate *proved* facts from mere opinions and old wives' tales, not always an easy task.

The third purpose is to describe mail-order selling to students of business, especially those interested in small business. More than any other business, a mail-order business can use the basic ideas of economics and statistics. Therefore the mail-order business can be a model for people in other kinds of businesses. Furthermore, students will gain by the how-to-do-it approach, I believe, even if they have no intention of going into mail order.

How to Use This Book

Begin by flipping through the book. Study the table of contents. Browse around to find out just what is in the book, and where. Read Chapter 2, "What Is the Mail-Order Business?" to give you some background on the industry you want to enter.

Then *study* Chapters 3 ("The Professional Method of Finding Products") and Chapter 4. If you are already in another line of business, those chapters will help you evaluate your product for mail-order selling. If you are starting from scratch, Chapters 3 and 4 will make it relatively simple to solve the problem of what to sell *profitably*. And you don't even need to have a bright idea!

Make no mistake about it, Chapters 3 and 4 are the key to the mail-order business. They teach newcomers to select products in the same way the biggest operators do. Read Chapters 3 and 4 again and again, and then begin to follow the instructions. If you *really* want a mail-order business you must follow through the steps in those chapters.

Once you are satisfied that you have selected one or more salable products, read Chapter 5 to make sure that your products may be sold by mail. Then Chapter 6 on mail-order strategies will help you prepare a road map for the sale of your products. Chapter 6 will also direct you to the other chapters in the book that will be most helpful in solving your particular problems. Your further study will depend upon your choice of type of business, product, and general strategy.

Anyone who has completed eighth grade and has a knowledge of arithmetic has enough education to understand the ideas in this book. Nevertheless, some of it may seem hard going sometimes. And I say, let it be a little difficult. If a reader is not smart enough or hard-working enough to plow through this book, he is probably not smart or diligent enough to make money in mail order.

(It is sad but true that a dullard or a lazybones will not make money in mail order any more than he will in farming or selling or running a flower shop. The sooner some of the dreamy fortune seekers quit kidding themselves, the better for all.)

Mail order requires specialized knowledge, which this book will help you gain. The ignorant beginner who *intends* to stay ignorant is surely wasting his time and money. Even those who tackle the business with plenty of intelligence and energy may get hurt until they learn what mail order is all about.

There are two important sources of knowledge about mail order.

You must learn from *both* these sources. The first source is your observation of other mail-order businesses. Chapter 3 tells you how and what to observe. A unique advantage for the beginner is that it is easier to learn the inner workings of a mail-order firm than any other type of firm. You don't need to work there or spy on them. All you need to do is to watch their advertisements. Almost everything important about the running of a mail-order business is revealed in its advertising.

Books and articles about mail order are the second source of mail-order knowledge. This book rounds up for you most of the important general mail-order knowledge. But you must also read other books. Buy or borrow as many of the books I mention as you have time to read. It will be the best investment you can make in your mail-order future.

There are two important reasons for reading what other writers have written about mail order: (1) some books cover specialized aspects of mail order that I cannot cover here; and (2) you must constantly refresh your memory. Even the old-time professionals never stop their mail-order education.

Don't let the length of this book scare you. You don't need to read many chapters right away. Instead, you will refer to them as you need them. And when you are operating successfully and you need some answers, you will curse me because the book is too short and doesn't contain everything.

Here's a piece of general advice. Get to know people who are already in the mail-order business. You will soon learn which mail-order businesses are in your area. Call the owners, and ask if they will talk with you. Don't be shy; tell them what you want. Probably they will be hospitable. The mail-order business is a lonely one, and mail-order men, like everyone else, like to give advice. If you seem intelligent and willing to listen, they'll be glad to spend some time with you, to your great advantage.

How This Book Is Written

The *general* advice in the book about how to proceed step by step to build a mail-order business is based on my own experience in mail order. Business economics and marketing provide the background theory.

The *specific* facts include my own data, plus whatever I have been able to glean from every book I could lay my hands on. It is paradoxical that the mail-order business lives on statistical information, yet very little data about mail order has been compiled. That is why I have collected every *fact* about mail order I could find.

The casual reader may grow impatient with such apparent trivia as a list of recommended abbreviations of state names. But any one such trivial point might be worth more than the price of the book to a new or old mail-order operator. There are no schools in which to learn the mail-order trade, and it is not easy to get a job in someone else's establishment in order to learn the procedure. Mostly, mail-order men learn by costly experience. If we can do anything here to reduce that cost of experience, I consider it a good cause.

Many of these specifics in the book are "only common sense." But the application of common sense takes time. Time costs money and mistakes cost money. Let's hope this book saves you both, and starts you on the path to profit and pleasure.

It is time to thank Mr. Gil Totten for teaching me how to think about advertising at the beginning of my career, and Mr. Joseph Phelan for his demonstration by example that an artist can and should think hard and straight about business problems.

Mrs. Jan Schick typed this manuscript with a maximum of efficiency, intelligence, and accommodation, all of which I appreciate. My mother, Mrs. Philip M. Simon, cheerfully typed the first draft of the manuscript, braving the worst of the dangers of a treacherous handwriting. Mr. Lawrence Miller gave helpful assistance in the final stages of preparing the manuscript, and wrote Appendix B.

The following people graciously read chapters of this book, and made helpful comments from their expert knowledge:

Mr. Paul Barris, Chapter 5 and others
Mr. Orlan Gaeddert, Chapter 18
Professor Glen Hanson, Chapter 19
Professor John Maguire, Chapters 14, 15
Professor Jack Sawyer, Chapter 18
Mr. Victor Schwab, Chapters 13, 16
Mr. Morton J. Simon, Chapter 5
Dr. Robert Wolfson, Chapter 18

Julian L. Simon

Contents

1

The Possibilities of Mail Order

Who Can Make Money in Mail Order? • *Is There Room in Mail Order?* • *Can You Start Part-Time?* • *Can You Still Make a Fortune in Mail Order?* • *Can You Make a Nice Living Without Much Capital to Invest?*

WHO CAN MAKE MONEY IN MAIL ORDER?

A little government booklet on establishing a mail-order business says:

> With a little determination and sagacity, the average person can easily master the principles of selling by mail. A principal requirement is good common sense and a mind made up to build a business . . . As well suited for women as for men . . . Age only a secondary consideration . . . Advanced schooling helpful, but not essential.[1]

True enough! But let me add, loud and clear and repeatedly, so no one can miss it: *mail-order success is only a dream to most people who get interested in it.* Fast-money mail-order "deals" fan the delusion of quick, easy fortunes. But few people who come to mail order have the necessary characteristics to make a go of it.

Robert Baker[2] checked eighty-seven advertisers and found that only ten were advertising five years later. He also found that only 27 percent of 500 advertisers had run ads the previous year. He states that more than half of mail-order operations lose money.

Baker's figures are interesting, but not very scientific. He probably checked advertisers in the "shelter" magazines (*House Beautiful,* etc.), the riskiest ventures in mail order. Still, what he says is helpful in pulling you down from the clouds.

And why should the mail-order business be easy? It is probably the most desirable business in the world to be in. ("Make Your Own Hours," "Work Home," "Small Capital," etc.) As with all good things, the fight to get a piece of it will not be easy.

The government booklet is right in saying that you don't need to be brilliant or well-educated to succeed in mail order. Many remarkably successful operators had little formal schooling. And some of the smartest professors at the world's great universities have made suggestions to me at parties ("I have a great idea for mail order") that would make them go broke in no time at all.

The successful mail-order operators have studied mail order and know it inside out. That's about all the education they need. The professors are as ignorant of mail order as you are of their specialties of topology or the sociology of medicine.

IS THERE ROOM IN MAIL ORDER?

In case you worry about "competitive conditions," read this squib written *sixty years ago* in 1900: "Of course it is not so easy to succeed in the mail-order business now [1900], as it was a few years ago, when there was much less competition. This is especially true in case the business is started and conducted along the same lines as followed by scores of other mail dealers."[3]

Many, many fortunes have been made since then, and even more will be made in the future. In fact, the prospects in mail order now are probably better than ever.

In mail order, more than in any other business, you must be able to go it alone. You must be able to do without people with whom to talk things over. There is no boss, of course. But there is also no competitor nearby, nor any face-to-face customers, or salesmen coming by to sell you. And unlike a doctor or lawyer or plumber who goes into business for himself, you can't just sit in your office until something happens. Nothing will happen until you make it happen.

So—you need real gumption and self-reliance. This is one reason why a part-time start may be wise. While you have an outside job, you have financial and social support to keep you going.

CAN YOU START PART-TIME?

One of the great advantages in starting up a mail-order business is that you *can* start part-time. There is no store to open in the morning, no interference with your present job.

Furthermore, it is usually *smart* to start part-time. Mail order is a rough, tough business, and you can't learn it overnight. Learning will be much less painful if your livelihood, and that of your family, doesn't depend on immediate success.

And you have an *advantage* if you start part-time. As you will learn later, one of the important skills in mail order is to be able to move fast on the basis of skimpy evidence. The part-time operator doesn't need to move so fast, and therefore he can move more surely. His slower pace helps keep him from making wrong and expensive guesses.

Some mail-order ventures can *continue* to be part-time profitable hobbies. A special skill that you can sell by mail—bookbinding, for example—can be a perfect mail-order product.

Or, you can run a small mail-order business as a hobby if you spend some time developing an item for which there is a limited appeal. (Successful items with wide appeal cannot remain small. Big competitors will find you out, horn into the field with their versions of the product, and steal your market.)

An example of a limited-market ad: "CIGARETTES—Make 20 plain or filter-tip for 9¢. Facts free . . . " That ad has appeared almost word for word for years—an unquestioned profit-maker. But because of the small size of the operation (the ad runs in only a few magazines) and small profits, it can continue relatively safe from competition.

CAN YOU STILL MAKE A FORTUNE IN MAIL ORDER?

Sears, Roebuck and Montgomery Ward are not the only great success stories in mail order. Fortunes have also been made in recent years. Examples include Hudson Vitamin, Spencer Gifts, Sunset House, and many more.

It *is* possible to pyramid your winnings and get rich fast in mail order because you can increase your market tremendously in a great hurry. A retail store can increase its patronage only slowly. It takes time for its reputation to become known and for customers to become steady patrons. In mail order, however, if you find a very profitable item, you can spread into a great many media practically overnight. You can quickly increase the amount of space bought and profit made.

Furthermore, the high profit margin above the product cost for most mail-order products means that you can earn a huge return on your investment if your advertising is successful. As an example, read this letter from a Los Angeles advertising agency specializing in mail-order advertising to *Golf World:*

> Enclosed is our check in the amount of $195.89 to cover the full page ad for the XXXXX Book Co., less agency discount and 2% discount. This was the ad on the book, *XXXXX*, by XXXX. We thought you would be interested in knowing that as of this date the ad has pulled exactly 1187 orders.
>   Sincerely,

If XXXXX's figures are correct—this letter was sent out by *Golf World* to help boost space sales, and you should therefore give credence to it only with caution—these are my guesses as to the profit results of the ad:

```
1,187 orders in 3 weeks
1,187 orders estimated after first 3 weeks
2,374 × $2.98 = gross revenue.....................................  $8,074.52
  Less: Advertising.......................................  $  195.89
    Estimated cost of books, shipping, etc..............   1,600.00
    Total cost..............................................          1,795.89
    Gross profit...........................................          $6,278.63
```

Needless to say, this ad probably will not pull as well in other media. Successes like this one are all too rare.

On the other hand, it is no snap to make a fortune in mail order. Competition is keen. If you show signs of doing well, competition finds it easy to imitate you and cut into your market. And once you are really in business, you face all the problems of any other business: personnel, stock, housing, taxes, and the rest. Bankruptcies and reorganizations of several large mail-order firms should convince you that mail order is no easy-magic way to make money.

R. H. Macy went into the mail-order business in a big way for a while. But eventually Macy's got out.

Furthermore, you can't make a huge fortune unless you have capital to use as leverage. Even if you *know* you have a tremendous winner, you must have cash or credit to purchase stock, advertising, and printing. Even if your winner is terrific, you can't make a fortune in a hurry just by plowing back earnings. By the time you have a respectable stake your competition will have swamped the market.

CAN YOU MAKE A NICE LIVING WITHOUT MUCH CAPITAL TO INVEST?

There are many small mail-order businesses, netting their owners a nice living, that started from scratch with practically no capital (a few hundred dollars, maybe). Many of these businesses originally depended upon some special skill or knowledge of the owner: hat restoring, playing cards for collectors, bee supplies. Many of these businesses were built slowly, as customers were gained and kept. There is a cosmetics firm in California that all my many aunts have bought from over the last thirty-five years, since one of them visited the store in 1927.

These small mail-order businesses that make nice livings yet neither grow big nor die off usually are too small to attract much competition. But "small" could mean an income of $25,000 per year.

Some of these successful small firms are tied to retail or manufacturing operations. The people who successfully sell wrought-iron furniture by mail probably could not survive if they had built solely as a mail-order business.

Other small mail-order businesses scratch out a specialized corner in a profitable market—perhaps by straight price appeal. There are several successful operators who operate this way in the photographic supplies market. But take my word for it: this is a rough way to make money. The competition is extremely tight, and woe to the inefficient.

Still, the mail-order business has a wonderful advantage for a fellow who wants to go into business for himself; it is relatively cheap to get into business long enough to find out whether your plan is profitable. To open up and test out a restaurant may require $20,000 and two years. You can test most mail-order products for $50 or $500, though $5,000 may be necessary to test a large, repeat-order business.

This is the long and short of it: mail order is a terrifically desirable business, and it has many advantages. Because it is so desirable it is also very competitive and tough. And trying to find "one great item" is not the way to solve the problem, as we shall explain later.

2

What is the Mail-Order Business?

Why Do People Buy by Mail? • *How Big Is Mail Order?*
• *Is Mail Order Growing?*

When we talk about "the mail-order business," we mean all businesses
that deal with customers at a distance, without face-to-face selling. We
also include the appropriate departments of firms that do *some* business
at a distance, e.g., the mail-selling and telephone-selling activities of
department stores.

The product itself need not be *delivered* by mail, of course. A tractor
can be sold through mail order and delivered by railroad.

Firms that sell over the telephone resemble mail-order businesses, too.
The selling techniques they use are like mail-order techniques, those
of direct mail in particular.

Businesses that sell through agents recruited by mail are in the mail-
order business, too. Fuller Brush started that way. In 1913 Fuller used
tiny classified ads in *Popular Mechanics* magazine.

When you think of mail order, you probably think first of Sears,
Roebuck and Montgomery Ward, the correspondence schools, and book
and record clubs. But don't forget the magazines, from *Life* and *Look* to
the *Journal of Marketing*, all of whom sell subscriptions by mail. Magazine
subscription sales are perhaps the biggest mail-order operation of all.
They account for 9.6 percent of all the direct mail that is sent out each
year in the United States. (Next come general mail-order houses with
4.5 percent, book publishers with 3.4 percent, and newspaper publishers
with 3.4 percent. But don't forget that direct mail only takes in a *part*
of the mail-order business.)[1]

And keep in mind the fancy foods, prescription eyeglasses, artist's

6

supplies, auto accessories, motors and generators, chemicals, and the hundreds of other categories of goods sold effectively by mail (see Appendix I).

It is important that when you think about possibilities for your mail-order business, you should *not* restrict yourself to those products narrowly thought of as "mail-order products." Remember that there is *some* truth in the old saying that "if it can be sold, it can be sold by mail." And if you already have a business of your own of almost any kind, you should consider doing some of your business by mail—even if you only hang up a sign that says "Packages Mailed Anywhere in the World," as the candy and novelty shops do, or "Meals To Go" if you run a restaurant. (Later we shall discuss your choice of product at length.)

WHY DO PEOPLE BUY BY MAIL?

Some people genuinely like to buy by mail. Many get a thrill from waiting for the postman to bring their packages of goodies. But most people buy through mail order because a mail-order merchant makes them an offer of merchandise or price that no store nearby can match, or because no salesman calls on them in person to sell the product. Mail-sold novelty goods are seldom available in nearby stores. Marriage books are available in book stores but can be bought by mail without embarrassment.

Very little mail-order merchandise competes on a price basis with merchandise sold through nearby stores. Actually, selling by mail is an *inefficient* and *expensive* sales technique. Except for Sears and Monkey Ward, staple merchandise sold over the counter in a retail store is cheaper than it can be sold by mail. The retail merchant can operate on a gross margin of 60 percent down to 20 percent, while mail order usually operates on a margin of 60 percent and up.

But mail order can usually compete very well on products for which a salesman makes *outside* calls for the firms selling the item. The cost of an outside sales call may be anywhere from $3 to $25, and sales can often be made by mail at considerably cheaper cost than that.

The Small Business Administration classifies mail-buyers this way:

(1) Those interested in novelties. They want something different from their neighbors. These people look over magazines for items that appeal to them. Frequently they find products, relatively inexpensive, of novel appearance and design.

(2) Those pursuing a hobby or some particular line of interest. Included here are such groups as home gardeners, stamp collectors, how-to-do-it enthusiasts, and many others.

(3) Those who buy by mail as a matter of convenience. They find it easier to buy by mail, and especially so if they live in a location removed

from adequate shopping facilities. Often they send away for merchandise to benefit from a wider selection. They fill much of their staple goods needs in this way.

(4) Those who buy by mail purely for what they consider a price advantage. They look over mail-order catalogs and also the advertisements of stores in their area or farther away to make comparisons and selections in the same manner that women shop for bargains in the local stores.[2]

HOW BIG IS MAIL ORDER?

We cannot make a reasonable estimate of how much merchandise is sold by mail each year, because so much mail-order business is done by firms whose primary business is not by mail, or by firms that don't think of themselves as being in the mail-order business. There are no government indices that measure the amount of business done by mail.

These figures may help you, though:

• Estimates of business done by *strictly* mail-order firms range upward from $4 billion. My *guess* is that a truer estimate of *all* business done by mail would be at least five times that high, $20 billion. If we include advertising-stimulated telephone sales, which are really a form of mail order, the estimate might be $30 to $50 billion, though I have absolutely no factual basis for this guess.

• *Time*[3] estimated $30 billion in sales from direct mail alone. *Direct Mail*,[4] which is more likely to be accurate, revises *Time's* figures downward, figuring $200 million being spent for list rental, which implies $9 billion in sales from direct mail. This estimate probably includes some sales made through channels other than mail order.

• In 1940 the Federal Trade Commission[5] estimated the sales of the direct-sale and mail-order *book* business to be $20 to $25 million.

• Robert Baker[6] added up the cost of *space* in a November issue of *House Beautiful* as $300,000. That's just one issue (though a big one) of one magazine. And the value of the goods sold from those ads was necessarily many times that figure.

• *Klein's Directory*[7] lists about 2,500 well-established *novelty* firms who operate *primarily* by mail. That list does not include most part-time operators, or businesses who sell primarily through other channels of distribution.

• A recent research study showed that about one out of ten retail stores in Minneapolis do a "significant" amount of business by mail.[8]

• According to Stanley I. Fishel[9] there are about "10,000 individual mail-order advertisers using the shopping sections" in the various magazines. And certainly there are many types of mail-order businesses— perhaps most of them—that never use shopping sections.

• Of the 33,859 bulk-mailing permits active in a recent year, 14,813 were used to obtain mail orders for products, and another 9,484 were used to obtain prospects for salesmen. There are probably at least as many additional firms that do not use bulk mail.[10]

IS MAIL ORDER GROWING?

Most observers note strong upward trends for mail order and forecast a bright future. A 1960 article[11] about mail-order catalog operations in Great Britain found a 15 percent yearly growth from 1950 to 1960, a very bright situation indeed.

And many huge corporations indicate that they believe mail order has a bright future. Only recently J. C. Penney, Singer Sewing Machine, Bell & Howell, and Grolier have moved into new mail-order operations. Some marketers even believe that in the future automobiles will be sold largely from catalogs by mail order.

On the other hand, the "shelter" magazines (including *House Beautiful, Better Homes & Gardens,* etc.) show a steady decline in mail-order pages since just after World War II. These magazines are major media for novelties. This decline could be the result of many factors and does not necessarily indicate a decline for mail order. For instance, increased catalog selling could account for a decline in space advertising.

Expenditures for direct-mail *advertising* rose from $803 million in 1950 to $1,933 million in 1962,[12] and a large proportion of direct mail is mail-order advertising. Increased costs of postage, printing and other expenses must be taken into account, however.

Most signs point to a very, very promising future for mail-order selling.

3

The Professional Method of Finding Products

Types of Mail-Order Marketing • "The Method"
• Theory behind "The Method" • Step by Step—
How to Find and Evaluate Successful Products •
Buying a Business

Chapters 3 and 4 are absolutely the most crucial in the book. Read them through several times. Be sure you are familiar with everything that is within them.

Everyone who has ever dreamed the American dream even a little bit wants a nice, cozy mail-order business for his own. Preferably he'd like a mail-order business he can run with his left hand, from his hammock, and between fishing trips.

The sad truth is that if you ever do find a dream product that sells like hotcakes, at a fantastic profit, the dream won't last much longer than it takes you to quit your steady job and get used to easy living. Competition will pour in so fast, squeezing your profit margins, that you'll be half drowned before you know it.

But that sad truth can also be your key to success in mail order. That's what this chapter is all about.

TYPES OF MAIL-ORDER MARKETING

Before you go looking for a mail-order product, you had better decide which general type of operation you are interested in. These are the important types.

One-shot Items

This is everyman's idea of the mail-order business. You advertise in magazines or by direct mail, and you either sell enough of the advertised product right from the ad to make a profit, or you lose money.

The advantage of a one-shot product is, first, that you know *immediately* whether you succeed or fail. You don't pour money into a business for a year before finding out it won't work. The one-shot product also gives you back your investment in the shortest possible time. This means that one-shot items have the greatest get-rich-quick potential.

But one-shot items are also the toughest, most competitive business in all the world. It is easy for *you* to get into business, and it is just as easy for your imitators, who will jump in just as soon as they detect you are making a pile—a fact that is hard to conceal in mail order.

As Paul Bringe says,

> If you are in a business where every new customer brings an immediate profit *you are in a dangerous business.* The fast buck boys will be swarming in on you soon. There are few who have the courage to invest in future customers—and that's just what makes such an investment a wide open opportunity for the man who looks ahead.[1]

Not only do successful one-shot items draw direct competition, but they also get indirect competition. The catalog houses like Spencer Gifts, Sunset House, and Walter Drake leap on any inexpensive novelty sold through mail-order advertising, and they insert the item into their catalogs. The cost of selling through a catalog is considerably less than one-shot selling costs, and therefore you can't stand catalog competition for long. Furthermore, catalog merchants can saturate a market.

You never really build a *business* when you sell one-shot items. You do not have a loyal clientele who come back and back just as long as you are in business. The one-shot merchant's business is dead three months after he runs his last ad. His entire business is in his head.

There are two types of one-shot items: (1) the explosive fads that sell furiously in full-page ads till the market is saturated and (2) the one-shot staples. The staples never have a big enough market to make big ads pay off, but some of them go on and on, year after year, in 1-inch, 2-inch, and 3-inch ads.

What is generally true of one-shot items is especially true of the explosive fads. If you really are looking for a quick million, that's where to cast your eye. But beware the fantastic odds even if you are a thoroughly experienced mail-order man. Note also that even if you hold a patent on an item, there isn't one product in ten years that will support a whole mail-order business. It takes many items to do that. The one-shot dealer is constantly discarding old products.

Correspondence Courses and Other High-priced Inquiry-and-Follow-Up Propositions

Correspondence courses are like one-shot items in this respect: you expect to make only a single sale to the customer. But correspondence courses are different from inexpensive one-shot products in most other respects.

Correspondence courses and other high-priced merchandise are never sold directly from display advertisements, and they seldom are sold from a cold-canvass direct-mail piece. Instead, they are sold by a series of letters sent to people who have been made to inquire for information by display ads.

Furthermore, correspondence courses cannot usually be bought wholesale by you. They require careful and expensive preparation by the firm that sells them by mail. Other high-priced merchandise also usually requires more work to obtain supplies than does low-priced merchandise.

For these reasons, it is not quite so easy to put this type of merchandise on the market. And therefore the successful operator won't be swamped so quickly with imitating competitors, and his profits are sheltered for a while.

Repeat Lines

Most mail-order businesses that are successful for a long time sell a product that the customer buys again and again: cigars, uniforms, office supplies, etc. Invariably, they "lose money" on the first order from the ad, but they make their profit on the second or tenth sale to the customer.

The strength and the weakness of a repeat-line mail-order business is that it requires more capital and more courage to get started. It takes more time and money before you can tell whether or not you're going to make a success. You can't cut your losses as quickly in a repeat-line business as you can with one-shot items.

But because you must risk more to get into business, you have greater protection from competition once you're established. It is just as tough for *them* to get in. Furthermore, your customers are an ever-growing asset that your competition can't reach. The customer list *is* your business, and no one can ever take that away from you.

Repeat-line businesses are also more profitable, I believe. A rule of thumb is that the harder and more costly it is to break into a line of business in which some firms are operating profitably, the higher the profits will be once you have broken in.

The General Catalog Business

This section is about Sears, Roebuck, of course, and also the novelty catalog people like Spencer Gifts, Sunset House, Walter Drake, Breck's, and several others.

Forget this type of business. At least for now. That's my best advice for all newcomers to mail order.

Mail Order through Agents

Many firms that employ house-to-house canvassers as their sales force recruit their men exclusively through mail-order ads in magazines and newspapers. Firms selling Christmas cards, cosmetics, fire extinguishers, and shoes are good examples. The agents and the firm never meet in person. All business between them is done by mail.

You are not likely to tackle this aspect of mail-order unless—through other outlets—you already sell a product that is adaptable for this type of mail-order operation. And that's another long story that we won't tell here.

Commercial and Industrial Products

Some commercial products are sold by firms who sell only by mail. Office supplies are an example. But a good deal of mail-order sales of commercial and industrial products is by manufacturers or wholesalers who sell through a sales force, also.

One-shot Items Will Be Our Examples

Throughout the book we shall talk mostly about one-shot items, but *only* because they make the clearest examples and demonstrations of mail-order techniques. *Everything* that applies to finding a good one-shot item applies to repeat lines and other aspects of mail order. And I *strongly advise* that you try to build a business not based on one-shot, sold-from-the-ad products.

"THE METHOD": TAKE OFF YOUR THINKING CAP

Proof First. Before telling you what "The Method" is, I'll try to *prove* it to you with real examples. And I'll try to ram the lesson home by making you work through the experience.

Below you will find display advertisements A and B and classified ads C, D, E, and F. Each advertisement is for a different product. Your problem is to decide (1) whether A or B brought in more dollars and (2) which two of the four classified ads did best.

All the ads were written by the same copywriter, so you need not concern yourself with the *quality* of the ads. A and B appeared in the same issue of the *National Enquirer,* and the ad that did better had by far the worse position on the page. C, D, E, and F all appeared in *Popular Science* classified. The classifications they ran under were not the crucial factor.

Advertisement A

$2.98 CONTRAPTION
SQUELCHES SOUND
OF TV COMMERCIALS

Mad at loud, nasty TV commercials? Now with AD-SQUELCH you can shut up those advertisers that annoy you.

AD-SQUELCH is a brand-new contraption that allows you to shut off, & turn on, TV sound right from your chair. The picture stays on. Works with any TV set made in U.S. Hangs out of sight when not in use.

To install AD-SQUELCH on your set, first open the back with All-model screwdriver included in kit. Then make two connections that a 7-year-old child can do in 3 minutes. That's all!

Complete AD-SQUELCH contains everything necessary to equip your set, plus simple, step-by-step, illustrated directions.

Lean back & enjoy your TV without extra-loud, unpleasant commercials. Send $2.98 to-day to XXXXXXX...................
............AD-SQUELCH mailed postpaid same day order received. Complete Satisfaction Guaranteed or Money Refunded.

Tear Out and Mail To-day

Advertisement B

SMOKING STOPS
IN 7 DAYS
OR MONEY BACK!

Cigarette smokers live 7.4 years less than non-smokers, on the average! Tobacco causes not only lung cancer, but also more heart disease, bronchial disease, and even premature births. That's why a tremendous number of doctors have quit smoking recently.

Now you, too, can break the cigarette habit. A brand-new product, DENICOTOR Lozenges, helps you stop or reduce smoking. DENICOTOR is absolutely safe, contains no harmful drugs.

Just suck a DENICOTOR each time you feel cigarette urge, until desire leaves you completely.

DENICOTOR is guaranteed to help you quit smoking, or your money back, no questions asked. Send $1 for 7 day supply (16 day supply for heavy smokers $2) to: XXXXXX Dept. Shipped postpaid same day order received.

Tear Out and Mail To-day

Advertisement C

"MAKE YOUR OWN WILL." Forms, Instruction Booklet $1. (Guaranteed!)

Advertisement D

HARMONICAS. Excellent imported chromatic harmonica now only $3.95. Satisfaction guaranteed. Catalog free.

Advertisement E

"HOMEBREWING..Beers..Wines!" Instruction Manual $1. (Guaranteed!)

Advertisement F

"SECRETS of Poker and Dice." Tested book teaches winning in honest games. Odds. $1. (Guaranteed!)

Made your decisions? These are the answers:

B outpulled A by a ratio of 15 to 1. A was one of the most complete fiascos of all time, while B was a success. (Actually, the paper's typographer set up B in a terrible format. The ad did well *despite* the bad typography.)

C and E were profitable ads. D and F would have to have pulled three to four times as much as they did to become really profitable.

Unless you know the mail-order business, it is unlikely that you picked the winners. But any experienced mail-order man would probably have got them all right—*without thinking hard, and without guessing.* He would *know* for sure.

The mail-order man's secret is this: he would recognize that B, C, and E offer products that have been, and are now, sold successfully by mail. He knows that they are sold successfully because he has seen ads for them repeated again and again over long periods of time. But A, D, and F are not now being offered repeatedly by anyone.

The principle of the theory is: *Do what is being done successfully.*

The first corollary of that principle is: *Never innovate, never offer really new products.* It's as simple as that.

The second corollary is: *Offer your product in a similar manner and in exactly the same media as the innovator,* at least until you know the situation intimately. At that time you may test new copy against the old, and you can use additional media to *add* to your schedule.

The words of authority never *prove* anything. But the words of a man who has demonstrated success can be very persuasive. So I quote John

D. Rockefeller: "When you hear of a good thing—something already working for the other fellow—don't delay but get in while you can."

THEORY BEHIND "THE METHOD"

The artist in you that thrills to novelty, boldness of thought, and "creativity" will point to the good new ideas that have made men rich. The examples you will give are true and well known. But the number of men who have sunk big chunks of their lives into schemes that failed badly is not known. And the failures vastly outnumber the successes. Few of us can afford the time that it takes before rare success turns up for us. (Don't forget that each man who backs a losing scheme is always quite sure he has a winner. But, of course, the losers are not as smart as you are!)

It may be true that the total *amount* made by winners exceeds the *amount* lost by losing schemes. This would explain why large corporations can afford to try many new schemes. But only large corporations have the time and money resources to wait till a great many tries bring in the inevitable profit.

Furthermore, most operating companies do not gamble on totally new ideas. Their innovation is limited to products that are extensions of their existing line.

John Howard writes:

> [That formulation of such a policy is] often precipitated by an unfortunate experience with a new product, is illustrated by the experience of the Solar Aircraft Company. In 1939, its sales were $500,000, but by 1945, because of the war demand for heat-resistant engine components for jet airplanes, sales skyrocketed to approximately $30 million. At the end of the war, with its war-time market largely eliminated, the company began to look for new products through buying small companies. After some serious mistakes with such products as steel burial caskets, picture-film development machinery, dairy machinery, milk pails and garden furniture, it now formulated the guide "new products that are related in some way to high-temperature materials and their fabrication." Although general in nature the criterion is probably quite useful.[2]

Another example from *Time*:

> Ever since Ford introduced its highly successful four-seater Thunderbird in 1958, Detroit has been speculating on when General Motors would bring out a competitor. Buick ended the speculation last week when it unwrapped its big-fendered Riviera hard-top, which is firmly dedicated to the G.M. principle that if you have to join 'em, beat 'em.

Only one U.S. automaker is bucking the '63 trend toward sporty prestige cars—American Motors. But being different is how American Motors makes its money. However, its '63 Classic and Ambassador models have shed their maiden-aunt look for more flowing and graceful "Detroit" lines.[3]

Howard also quotes the American Machine and Foundry Company as saying, "Don't plunge into a new venture without first finding a man who has lived successfully in the market you are about to serve."[4]

The quotations teach that intimate knowledge of the market gives a firm a tremendous advantage in the odds. (There are, of course, other reasons of efficiency that also restrict innovation to products within the general line.)

My personal experience should help prove what I have said. This is the story of how I learned this secret.

Before I went into mail order, I had a fine college education, service in the Navy as an officer, plus experience working in one of New York's top advertising agencies selling by direct mail and in the advertising promotion department of a huge Madison Avenue publishing house. I received the degree of Doctor of Philosophy in Business Economics. Furthermore, I had been an advertising consultant to, among others, one of the biggest department store chains in the United States.

Then I decided to go into the mail-order business for myself. I read every available book, but found little to help me. I talked with everyone I could find, some of the smartest and most successful people in the country. I asked each one of them what I should sell.

Finally, I had a list of four major product lines to try. And I went full steam ahead!

Sounds like I was perfectly prepared, doesn't it? Maybe you can guess what happened—a complete *bust!*

One after the other, the products proved unsuitable for mail order. I hadn't lost much money. (I didn't have much to start with.) But I was bewildered and discouraged. Where should I go from here?

But I knew that *some* operators had the knack of finding successful products. So I went back and studied the operations of the most successful mail-order dealers. I studied them, and studied them, and studied them until . . . *Finally I knew.* I had found out what the top money-making mail-order men—many of *whom had never finished high school*—knew all along.

And it was so easy! How I regretted the time I had wasted. All my education and experience did me no good in learning the secret of "The Professional Method." In fact, even now I have trouble convincing professor friends of mine that the secret is real—that is, until I show them the *results.*

Why This Unpleasant Business Principle Holds True

The principle says that brilliant and artistic thinking is of little use in this aspect of business. Sad but true. Psychologists tell us that the best administrators do not have "creative" minds. The best businessmen do not generate new ideas. They choose between the ideas suggested by others.

But note that the standards and goals of business are very different from those of art and scholarship. Innovation for its own sake has value in art and science. If a painting or a story fails in every other way, mere innovation gives us some pleasure and wins some praise for the artist. The same goes for a wonderfully imaginative but wrong-headed theory in the sciences. But the yardstick in business is simply how well the idea works and how much it makes.

So if you're looking for an outlet for your creativity, stay away from the mail-order business. You'll save yourself money and frustration.

The *first reason* why the copycat principle works so well is that both the mail-order industry, and business as a whole, do a great deal of trial-and-error experimentation. Much of this experimentation is carried on by people highly qualified to do it. All this trial-and-error investigation makes it highly unlikely that a single innovation by a nonprofessional will find a wide and profitable market.

Your chances are better when the innovation requires specialized knowledge, such as that of a chemical engineer or of an airplane pilot or of a biologist. But anyone can dream up a new kind of can opener. The chances against your making a fortune with a new kitchen gadget are astronomical.

The *second reason* why copycat works is the outsider's lack of information. The newcomer to mail order doesn't know what has been tried and found to fail. He doesn't know what the market needs. And the newcomer doesn't have information with which to project the profit potential of a totally new product.

The *third reason* why copycat works is *especially* true in the mail-order business. The first fellow to sell a product has very little advantage over those who follow him. He has less advantage than in almost any other line of business because it is so easy and cheap for mail-order competition to duplicate his product and his advertising. The "barriers to entry" of his competitors are low indeed. So the time advantage of the leader is only a matter of months. That's why the one-shot mail-order business is such a toughly competitive field.

The *fourth reason* why the copycat principle works is also peculiar to mail order. A mail-order campaign is remarkably open to inspection by all who care to look. Reading all the likely magazines, and checking the mail sent to major mailing lists, will tell you much of what you need to know about a competitor's campaign. There is little in the way of trade secrets that the leader can keep hidden. What he learned by the sweat of his brow and costly experimentation, all others learn free and at ease.

And *fifth*, the copycat even has an *advantage* over the leader. The leader had to bear the cost of testing until he found the most effective copy and the media that would pay out. The copycat then follows as closely as consistent with business ethics. He can explode into a great many media just as soon as he has tested his copy, and this means that he will reach peak volume much faster than the innovator did.

It may be that the market is too small for both of you, though this is true much less often than you would imagine. Perhaps you have developed better copy or a better offer than the leader, and are able to force him out. But if your test ads are well done and your results are still borderline, you'd better seek another product.

The only advantages the leader has over his imitators are: (1) he has already developed tested copy, and he has information about the relative performance of the various media; and (2) his development costs are "sunk," so that, in a true economic sense, his cost for future operations will be less than that of the followers. Like any other lower-cost producer, the leader can last longer in a struggle than can the higher-cost producers.

Those are the reasons why the best mail-order product for you to market is a presently successful product. The same reasons also show that the media you should expect to use are exactly the media used by the leader. You will first use the media that the competition uses most heavily—in terms of space, or frequency—because those are the media in which his (and your) payout will be greatest.

STEP BY STEP—HOW TO FIND AND EVALUATE SUCCESSFUL PRODUCTS

The first step to finding successful products is to get hold of a copy of *Standard Rate & Data*, "Consumer Magazine and Farm Publication" section, and write to every magazine listed in it with circulation over perhaps 100,000 in these classifications: Men's, Romance, Women's, Sports, Almanacs, Mechanics and Science, Motion Picture, Fraternal, Religious and Denominational, Exposure, Fishing and Hunting, Gardening, Newspaper-distributed Magazines, Health, Home Service and Home, TV and Radio, Veterans, Business and Finance, plus every single farm magazine. There are other mail-order media, but these will do for a start. Give yourself a company name, and write to each magazine for a sample copy and a "rate card." A postcard will do the job except for *Esquire* and two or three other snobbish magazines.

If your local library is too small to have *Standard Rate & Data,* and if you can't borrow a copy from a local advertising agency, use the list of magazines and addresses in Appendix I.

Look through each magazine you receive, and for each one make notes on an index card of the types of products sold in it. You should be learning that there are hundreds of magazines you have never seen in all your well-bred, high-thinking life. And those magazines of which you are not aware are probably the best mail-order media of all. They carry a tremendous proportion of the one-shot products we are using as our examples here. For goodness sake do not limit yourself to the Home Service magazines. Much of the advertising they carry is amateurish and unsuccessful, and much more is of products and lines that are tough for a newcomer to mail order.

Keep your eye on the classified sections, too. There is much to be learned from classified.

Next, go to a back-date magazine shop, and buy 100 back copies of *Popular Science, Workbasket,* farm magazines, *House Beautiful,* and low-life men's and women's magazines—especially the latter. Not only are the "gray matter" low-life magazines important, but you can't find them in any library.

Now you should begin reading ads in earnest. Don't try to form conclusions. Just look and look and look at all kinds of mail-order ads. At first you will think there are 100,000 products on the market. But soon the various ads will become familiar. Then you will recognize the addresses of some companies offering several different products.

You are making progress when you recognize *most* of the ads you see. And you have learned almost enough when you can recognize the layout styles of the important mail-order firms. By that time you will know that there are relatively few products and advertisers on the market, and even fewer big and successful companies that have been around for several years.

Of course, the successful products are the ones that you recognize as appearing again and again over a period of years, and in a great many magazines. The most successful among the successful are those that even run in the slow summer months.

(Why do once-successful products disappear? Some go off the market because the Federal Trade Commission or the Post Office Department finds them fraudulent or deceptive. Others, some full-page-ad products, may exhaust their fads after a while. Many do not really disappear, but reappear intermittently.)

Next, get acquainted with the direct-mail mail-order offers. Get a few friends to save all the direct mail they get. Write to every single free offer, or offer of information, that you come across in the magazines, especially one full issue of *House Beautiful.* This means writing for *hun-*

dreds of catalogs and offers. And try to find some products you want to buy or try by mail. Get your wife to buy some things by mail (not from Sears) that she wanted anyway. Don't be afraid to accept offers of a free trial, or offers to refund your money if you're not satisfied. You'll get your money back, just as you'll give it back once you're in the mail-order business.

Important: Use a different set of first initials in the name you sign, for each firm you write to, and keep a record of which initials went where, and on which date. Then record which offers you receive addressed to which initials, and the date. Your initial code will then teach you which lists are rented to whom, very important information later on. The card below is an example from our files.

```
        G. H. SMITH

    Sent to
        Miles Kimball Company, Sep 1, 1962. HOUSE BEAUTIFUL
    Rented by:
        Publishers Clearing House. Jan 21, '63.
        American Home Magazine
        Saturday Evening Post, Mar 31
        Publishers Clearing House. July 18

                    etc.
```

Study the direct-mail offers the same way you studied the magazines.

Then write to several mailing-list brokers who handle mail-order-buyers lists. (Pay no attention to *compiled* lists.) Try these firms that advertise "Free Catalog":

Abbott National Mail Services, Inc., 41–26 Queens Blvd., Long Island City, N.Y.
Ahrend Associates, Inc., 601 Madison Avenue, New York, N.Y.
Dunhill International List Co., Inc., 444 Park Avenue South, New York 16, N.Y.
Book Buyers Lists, Inc., 363 Broadway, New York, N.Y.

Names of other list brokers, some of whom have catalogs, are in big-city and New York classified phone directories.

Study the lists being offered for rent, and the *size* of the lists. This will give you further information on the number of firms in any line (even though the firm names are not given), and the amount of business they do in the various products. These data will also be important later on when you try to estimate the profit potential for various product lines.

All this time you should be watching the mail-order section of your Sunday newspaper, examining the magazines that come into your hands, and keeping a sharp ear for mail-order offers on the radio.

Appendix J in the back of the book contains a long sample list of successful mail-order lines.

BUYING A BUSINESS

Buying an already going mail-order business is another way to get started, of course. Chapter 22 discusses that subject in detail.

4

Which Products Are Best for You to Sell?

Profit-Potential Estimate • How Much Investment Will It Require? • Is the Product Strictly Legal? • Developing Markets: How to Make a Slow Horse Run Fast • Specialty and Novelty Products • Why Is a Profitable Mail-Order Product Profitable? • If You Already Control a Product and Want to Sell It by Mail . . . • Testing the Potential of the Product Line You Choose

By now you should have started making a list of products that you know are being sold successfully and that might be possibilities for you. Our job in this chapter is to narrow that list down to the five, one, or no product(s) that are right for your interests, your capital, your background, and your energies.

PROFIT-POTENTIAL ESTIMATE

One of the most important factors that you must consider when choosing a product is its profit potential. It is not enough that you can make a high *percentage* of profit on your advertising investment. You must also be able to invest enough money in advertising so that the *total profit* return is great enough for your desires, and great enough to repay your investment of energy and time in organizing the project.

For example, this ad has run for over 30 years, month after month, practically without change: "Earn money evenings, copying and duplicating comic cartoons for advertisers." Ordinarily, any ad running for many months will draw competitors, like flies to honey. But the cartoon-duplicating ad runs in only a few classified sections, and hence, no matter how profitable each ad might be, the total profit each month will not amount to much. This may explain why there is no competition.

Of course, if there is no competition, it may also mean that there is only room for one firm. It may be that the market cannot be widened with new kinds of product offers, by finding new media, or by using display ads.

Cardmaster ads for hand postcard duplicators are another example of a long-running ad that has probably drawn little competition because of a too-restricted market. Cardmaster does use display ads, however, which puts it in a much bigger profit class than cartoon duplicating. Or it may have the market to itself because it can obtain the merchandise cheaper than anyone else can. But that would be unusual.

Many more of these limited-profit product situations occur in specialized and trade markets.

What you seek, then, is a product that can generate enough *volume* so that it can also generate considerable profit. You can estimate a product's market, and its volume and profit potential, by searching out the media where the product's ads presently appear. Add up the dollars spent for space in a given month, and you will have an underestimate, because you will never manage to find all the insertions.

Estimating the volume of a product sold by direct mail is much harder, because you have no easy way of determining how many and which mailing lists they are using. This is one more good reason why the beginner should stick to magazine advertising until he has some experience.

HOW MUCH INVESTMENT WILL IT REQUIRE?

You must make an estimate of the expenditure of time, energy, and money required for developing the product and the campaign to sell it by mail. Then compare the time-and-energy expenditure to the estimated profit to see if the profit is worth the investment of your time.

For example, selling a law-study course may be profitable and interesting to you. But unless you can think of a shortcut, the development of the course and the backup texts will require vast resources of time and money.

To sell wallet-size photo duplicates, you need either photographic equipment or a connection with a firm that will do your processing. A photographic plant may well cost more than you want to invest, and lining up a reliable connection may be difficult to arrange.

Remember, though, that the greater the costs in time and money for you to get into a particular line, the harder it is for future competitors to get in, too. So a hard-to-begin product line may offer you some protection and security.

IS THE PRODUCT STRICTLY LEGAL?

A large proportion of one-shot mail-order items advertised at any one time are close to the line of legality, some on one side of the line, some on the other. Sooner or later many will be forced out of business by the Federal Trade Commission or the Post Office, while others will be assaulted by the Better Business Bureau.

What is legal and what is illegal is discussed in the next chapter. In brief, you will remain on safe ground if:

1. The buyers get from you exactly what even the most gullible of them expect to get.

2. If the customers don't feel gypped.

3. If every word and picture you put in your ad is true in spirit as well as in letter.

4. If your product is neither pornographic nor obscene.

5. If the product is not a lottery or gambling scheme of any kind.

6. If it is not a "chain" scheme in which your customers make money by doing the same thing you do.

Be especially careful of drug products, and of plans and equipment designed to make money for the purchaser.

There are two good reasons why you should not imitate others in venturing to the edge of what is legal:

1. The experienced shady mail-order operators, together with their legal advisors, have spent a long time learning what they can get away with. Even then, the biggest of them have been caught and thrown in jail. As an inexperienced newcomer, you're the guy that is *sure* to get hurt.

2. Perhaps more important, you may be surprised to find that you have a powerful conscience when you least expect it. Before carrying out a sharp scheme, you may feel, like P. T. Barnum, that it's a game to fleece the suckers that are born every minute. But after the deal is done, you may feel a terrible remorse and guilt that you never anticipated. This has wrecked many a man.

Don't laugh at what I say as being naive. I warn you: don't take a chance. Sell a product you can respect, in a manner you will not be ashamed of.

HOW LONG TO MAKE MONEY?

If you settle on a repeat-business item—as I hope you will—you must also think about how *long* it will take for your customers to return you a profit, and what else can be sold to them. The longer it takes to get into the black ink, and the greater the capital you need to start, the greater the risk you are taking, *and* the more valuable and secure your business if all goes well.

DEVELOPING MARKETS: HOW TO MAKE A SLOW HORSE RUN FAST

You *may* be able to increase the size of the market and force the volume of a product much higher than your competitors have managed to do. In this section we shall discuss ways of developing proven products. But heed this warning: do *not* count on expansion potential when you estimate the size of a product's market, unless you are already a highly skilled mail-order man.

These are some ways you can develop or increase the size of a market:

1. *Advertise classified products in display advertising.* Some firms who advertise in classified have insufficient skill, initiative, or capital to push out into display, and an enterprising firm can take advantage of this. For example, coin catalogs have been successfully sold in classified for years. Starting in 1961 (I believe), a big operator began selling coin catalogs in full-page ads in dozens of magazines, spending hundreds of thousands of dollars in advertising. But this operator is the country's "leading" seller of such items. Few others have the skill and know-how to move so quickly.

But—many of the firms who use classifieds are wise birds who *also* use display, or who have found out from hard experience that display advertising won't work for their purposes.

2. *Another way to increase a market is by personalizing items with the customer's monograms or initials.* This is actually a special case of increasing a market by improving the desirability of the product offer. But be careful—personalizing can be costly.

3. *Search through old magazines (ten to forty years old) for products that were once sold successfully but that outlived their fads.* Sometimes you can bring these products back to life. But sometimes their market has died with them because times have changed and Americans no longer are interested in the product.

4. *Find successful mail-order products in English magazines and transplant the ideas to this country.* Again, be careful: Englishmen and Americans are very different in many ways.

5. *Sell a product similar to existing products.* If one outfit successfully sells a franchised business to clean rugs, you might consider selling a franchised business to clean walls.

6. *Upgrade a successful book or short correspondence course.* The "Little Blue Books" of Emanuel Haldeman-Julius represent a gold mine of tested mail-order material. The subject matter of many of the books he

sold for 5 cents (and his family still sells for 15 cents) can be amplified and upgraded into full-scale mail-order successes. (But be sure not to copy his material!) Write for a catalog to Girard, Kansas, and read Haldeman-Julius' book *The First Hundred Million*,[1] the best book ever written on the technique of choosing and selling books by mail order.

SPECIALTY AND NOVELTY PRODUCTS

Despite everything I have said up until now, you are going to be interested in novelty and specialty products. Since that's the way it is, I'll tell you about a success story and how it was done. But remember that there are few success stories like this one.

Leslie Creations[2] is a Philadelphia firm that sells several hundred thousands of dollars of merchandise each year at a nice profit—new specialty and novelty products like record racks, bar accessories, novelty lamps, small pieces of furniture, and other home accessories.

Most of the merchandise is sold from direct-mail pieces, and all of it is drop-shipped direct from the supplier. Leslie carries no merchandise and runs his business from his home.

Leslie finds items for his seventy-two-product brochures in these ways:

Trade Shows. Stationery, Gift, Housewares, Premium and Hardware Shows.

Major Trade Publications. *Housewares Review, Hardware Age, Gift & Tableware Reporter, Incentive, Gift & Art Buyer.*

Other Trade Publications. Small electronics magazines, for example.

Selecting profitable items is an *art* that comes only with experience. After years in the business, Leslie still picks almost as many wrong items as right ones.

After Leslie decides on the items in which he is interested, he checks on the wholesale price from the manufacturer, and he finds out whether the manufacturer is willing to drop-ship reliably and guarantee satisfaction and safe delivery. The wholesale price is usually 44 percent or less of the retail price. Retail prices are in the range of $4.95 to $20. If he can't find a supplier who will give him a reasonable price, Leslie contacts manufacturers who may duplicate the item at lower cost. He says there are several manufacturers who specialize in that kind of work.

Each issue of his brochure catalog carries about half repeat items from the last brochure. Leslie either tests new items in the *New York Times Magazine*, or directly in the brochure.

The basic brochure style is a single sheet 11 by 17 inches, without an envelope, printed in black and white, both sides, plus order coupon and envelope. Leslie formerly was an artist, and preparing the brochure demands a high order of advertising talent. Such talent can be hired, of course.

Leslie apparently develops new customers for his list both from display ads and from renting lists that are highly suitable for his operation.

Sounds easy, doesn't it? Sure Leslie makes money. But for every Leslie who has made it big in the mail-order specialty business, there must be a hundred people who have failed because they do not have a good nose for specialty mail-order items, or because they could not handle the advertising and business end.

Another success story is that of Sunset House. Leonard Carlson started the business on a shoestring in 1951, and now grosses an estimated $12 million per year.[3]

WHY IS A PROFITABLE MAIL-ORDER PRODUCT PROFITABLE?

I have already argued that at first you should never ask or answer this question. All you should need to know is that an item *is* already a good seller for someone else. Forget about *why* it is, or is not, a good mail-order item.

Nevertheless, if you stay in the mail-order business for a while, or even if you don't, you will probably get involved in the unprofitable practice of considering whether an untried mail-order product will be a winner.

This idea should help you to understand mail-order products: except for novelty, repeat, and catalog items, most items that can profitably be sold by mail can also be sold profitably by an *outside* salesman. Those items that are sold *within* stores will *not* make a mail-order profit.

This is the reasoning behind the idea: outside selling and mail-order selling are both expensive methods to sell goods, figured as a proportion of sales. Only those items that continue to support a high markup are good for mail order.

Repeat-order and catalog mail-order businesses have a much lower cost of selling, because the largest expense is making a *new* customer.

Here are some questions you can ask yourself about a product, if there is no competition to guide you:

1. How many media (or, for direct mail, how many lists) do I expect to be able to use profitably?

2. Are these media large?

3. How much will it cost to stock the product and prepare the advertising?

4. Will I be able to use only tiny ads, or bigger ads also?

If the product falls into one of the following classes, it has a very *poor* mail-order prospect:

1. Standardized and branded goods, unless you can offer a substantial price advantage.

2. Goods whose characteristics are hard to communicate in ads, e.g., perfume and high-style women's dresses.

3. Goods sold on a small profit margin, e.g., coffee and food (except gourmet food).

4. Goods that don't lead to profitable repeat sales.

If you are considering a product to be sold through sales agents, consider John Moran's checkoff list of the requirements of an agent-sold item:[4]

1) Must appeal to agent.
2) Must appeal to agent's customers.
3) Little investment for agent.
4) Not seasonal.
5) No choice of size or color (but shoes do well, and dresses).
6) Light weight.
7) Easy for agent to carry samples.
8) Not obtainable in stores.
9) No breakage or spoilage.
10) 100% or more commission.

IF YOU ALREADY CONTROL A PRODUCT AND WANT TO SELL IT BY MAIL . . .

Few people who start in mail order from scratch would decide to sell airplanes or farms. But if you are already in one of those businesses, you may decide that you can increase your volume by mail-order selling.

Remember: we are *not* talking about ordinary direct mail that so many firms use to *help* them close deals. We're talking about mail-order deals in which the customer is first contacted with printed material, and in which the whole transaction takes place without face-to-face meeting.

Businesses that may not be practical to *begin* purely for a mail trade may be very profitable to expand by mail. The art-supplies business is a good example. You would require a stock of perhaps $100,000 to back up a mail-order business—expensive indeed. But if you are already a large retail dealer in art supplies, you already bear the cost of the stock, and you do not need to charge any of that cost to the mail-order operation as you would if you sold by mail only.

Lamps, rugs, and advertising specialties are other examples of the same principle.

There is still another good reason why an established retailer or manufacturer may find it profitable to develop a mail-order operation. Mail-order advertising can stimulate the sale of goods through regular outlets, too. Book publishers often find that a mail-order campaign will increase sales of books in stores by between 100 percent and 400 percent. This means that the mail-order sales campaign can bring back *mail-order* sales far less than its cost and still be very profitable.

If you already sell a product, these are some of the factors to consider when you decide whether to market your product through mail order:

1. Do any of your competitors sell by mail? If they do, your problem is almost solved. If they don't, don't let their example stop you.

2. How many customers do you have who *now* buy from you only by mail? If you already have a good many people or firms on your books who have moved to other parts of the country, or whom you never see, and who still buy from you, then you probably have a product that lends itself to mail order.

3. These rules of thumb may be helpful:

• Is it light in weight per dollar of sales price? Mailability is very important if you are to obtain a profitable return. Books are ideal because of the cheap postage rate they enjoy.

• Can you get a high markup on the cost to you? Three-to-one is a familiar formula, but there are too many situations to which it does not apply. Don't be hamstrung by the formula.

• Is it a product that is not readily obtainable in stores near most consumers?

• Can the sales appeal be communicated on paper? Perfume is hard to sell by mail because prospects want to smell before they buy.

• Will you have to offer credit? It is generally true that you must offer credit if the sales price is over $10 or $20. Do you have the capital and the organization to offer terms?

• Do outside salesmen sell your product? Examples: insurance, industrial equipment, commercial supplies. All are sold both by outside salesmen and through mail order.

• Is your product a regular seller year after year? The effort and money necessary for a mail-order campaign are often too great for a novelty item that will soon have no market.

Finally, you must determine whether or not your product will sell by mail by actually *testing* it. But since you already sell the product, you have the great advantage of knowing your product and what aspects of it appeal to customers. Furthermore, you also have stock to fill test orders with. The next section and Chapter 18 tell you how to make the necessary tests.

TESTING THE POTENTIAL OF THE PRODUCT LINE YOU CHOOSE

Never think that you have "found a product line" until you have successfully tested the product, the offer, and the copy. Until then, all you have is an idea, and it is exceedingly unwise to invest much time or energy in a product line that is only at the idea stage.

The actual mechanics of testing are fully described in Chapter 18. But these points are relevant here:

1. *It is customary to run test advertisements before you have the merchandise.* This allows you to beat a cheap and hasty retreat if your

ad doesn't pull. Return the money and letters as "Out of Stock." This may not be the nicest practice in the world, but it is sanctioned by the practice and public utterances of such trade leaders as Bennett Cerf.

One of the great virtues of mail order is that you *can* put your toe into the business and test it fully without getting in up to your neck. This is not the case with any other kind of business I know of.

2. *Mediocrity of results is the most likely test outcome.* Chances are you'll get neither a runaway winner or a dud. The professional is the fellow who can tinker with a so-so proposition and make a winner of it.

3. *Failure of an ad can mean that the product or the offer or the copy is at fault.* But a clear failure is *most likely* to be the fault of the product.

A Closing Note

Now I'm going to sound like a fortuneteller . . . The best way to find a good mail-order product is to *have another* good mail-order product already. This isn't just double talk. It's my guess that any successful mail-order man has a file of a dozen good products that he doesn't have time or capacity to develop at the moment, or that are too big or too small for him to tackle.

What this should mean to you, however, is the importance of getting into business with *some* product. Even if your first product is not tremendously profitable, it will at least lead you to evaluate other products, and that is the way you will find better products.

So—think of your first venture as an investment in getting into business. And if you're willing to work on a thin margin, almost *any* already proved product will do for you. You can then compete successfully because you won't be charging for salary or overhead, or demanding a profit margin, as your established competition will be. You can't go on that way for very long, of course, but it's a way to break in.

5

What You May, and May Not, Do in Mail Order

Why Is the Law So Important in Mail Order? •
What They Used to Get Away with • *What Is a
Racket?* • *Special Products You May Not Sell by
Mail* • *Penalties for Illegal Acts* • *How to Check on
Legality*

Don't, DON'T, *DON'T* skip this chapter. Don't make the mistake of thinking that it doesn't apply to you. Sooner or later—probably sooner —you will have reason to understand why I make this appeal so strong.

A quick example to make you see how important this chapter is: I might have advertised this book by saying, *"You, too, can earn money in mail order"* or *"Make $10,000 yearly in mail order."* I would not have used those headlines for two reasons:

First, I know they will get me in trouble with the law; and second, I would feel badly about misleading some people about how easy it is to make money in mail order.

But if I *had* used those headlines, some legal agency (probably the Federal Trade Commission) would have jumped on me sooner or later. No matter what the legal outcome, I would be caused trouble, and aggravation, and a big money loss.

I am *not* a lawyer, and I have *not* studied the law of mail order carefully. Therefore, what I say here is not legally precise or perfectly accurate. It does not deal with the subtleties that are the very essence of legal practice. I shall try to tell you in *businessman's* terms how I think the law affects you as a mail-order businessman.

32

If you have *any* doubts whatsoever about the legality of a plan of action, refer *immediately* to *The Law for Advertising and Marketing* by Morton J. Simon.[1] (No relative, we have never even met.) If you can't find a *definite* answer there, you can either consult one of the sources mentioned below (if you are a good researcher), or you should see a lawyer. Don't make a move until you are sure the move is within the law.

WHY IS THE LAW SO IMPORTANT IN MAIL ORDER?

An unscrupulous or overzealous operator can cheat the public more successfully (until the law stops him) in the mail-order business than in almost any other line of trade, for several reasons.

Unlike a retail store owner, the seller of one-shot items does not depend upon the goodwill of satisfied customers. He has his money whether or not the customer grumbles. A satisfied customer does him no more good than an unsatisfied customer.

Even unconditional guarantees do not remedy the situation. Many dissatisfied customers will not trouble themselves to wrap and ship a piece of shoddy merchandise to get back one, two, or three dollars.

A dissatisfied customer of a local store will tell his or her neighbors about being cheated. Not only will the store's business suffer, but the store owner will have to face the loss of his personal reputation among his neighbors. Someone may even punch him in the nose.

But the dissatisfied mail-order customer has no way of getting back at the unscrupulous mail-order operator—except reporting him to the authorities. And the mail-order man's neighbors seldom know the exact nature of his business. So this important community control of a business-man's actions does not exist in mail order.

The mail-order seller has great control over what the buyer knows about the product. The buyer cannot ask sharp questions of the seller or examine the merchandise carefully. The advertisement tells the buyer exactly what the *seller* wants him to know, and nothing more. This increases the possibility of a cheated customer.

That's why you *must* know about what you can and can't do in mail order.

And it's not just dishonest people who get into legal trouble in mail order. Anyone can get carried away with his desire to make a sale.

WHAT THEY USED TO GET AWAY WITH

The majority of mail-order operations are, and always have been, respectable. They are respectable because many of them sell repeat items that demand a satisfied customer, because of the law, and because of the conscience and ethics of most mail-order men.

But sixty and more years ago when mail order was a brand-new way of doing business, the law did not have sufficient remedies against hanky-panky. The laws that worked to regulate face-to-face business dealings were inadequate to deal with business at a distance by mail. And so, sharp operators ran wild.

Verneur E. Pratt[2] told the following stories:

> One ad, for example, offered a "Steel Engraving of George Washington" for 50 cents. The copy beneath the headline described the excellence of the engraving, the beautiful, deep, rich color used, and the fact that the paper was deckled on all four edges. In return for his 50 cents, the buyer received a two-cent stamp.
>
> Another well-known example was that of the "Patented Cigarette Roller" that rolled with equal ease either round or oval cigarettes. It was made entirely of metal, heavily nickel-plated, with only one moving part. It fitted the vest pocket and was so simple that it could not get out of order. In return for $1.00 the buyer received a three-inch nickel-plated spike. The instructions read: "Lay either a round or oval cigarette upon the table, pushing the spike directly behind it, upon doing which you will find the cigarette to roll easily and with almost no effort."
>
> Every statement in the copy was true. The individual merely placed his own interpretation upon it, and his curiosity as to how the device would roll the cigarettes led him to part with his dollar bill.
>
> In the advertisement for the "Patent Potato Bug Killer" stress was laid on the fact that "$1 equips you to kill all the potato bugs in a ten-acre field." In return for the dollar, two little slabs of wood were sent, accompanied by ironically elaborate instructions as to how to pick the bugs off the vines with fingers, laying them down on one slab, pressing the other firmly down upon the bug, and thus quickly and efficiently extinguishing its life.
>
> Another mail-order ad was headed "$3.95 for this 5 piece Wicker Set." The illustration showed a handsome, sturdy wicker table, a settee, two straight-backed wicker chairs, and a rocker. The copy, after extolling the virtues of the materials used, guaranteed the set to be "exactly like the illustration." When the set arrived, the discomfited buyer found it to be in truth exactly the same size as the illustration.

And sixty years ago, Samuel Sawyer related this yarn.[3]

> A manufacturing concern, in Connecticut, produced an interesting little novelty in the form of a sun-dial enclosed in a watch-case. It was the same size as a gentleman's watch and when the case was opened, revealed the dial by which time could be determined from the sun, in the good old-fashioned way of our forefathers. This article was produced and supplied at wholesale for a few cents to any concern that wanted to buy.
>
> One New Yorker conceived a bright idea. He had an illustration made of the article in such a manner that anyone who glanced at it could

naturally say it represented a nice watch. Then he prepared an advertisement describing "the new timekeeper; warranted for twenty years, not to get out of order" and called it a timekeeper, which was true enough, and by the general language of his announcement led the reader to believe that a watch could be obtained with a subscription to a cheap periodical . . .

People showered their complaints upon the police and postal authorities, but as there was really nothing in the advertisement which described the article as a watch, the authorities were afraid to undertake legal action . . . No misstatement in language could be found by the district attorney and no prosecution ever went very far, but the promoter of the scheme was compelled to submit to columns of unpleasant newspaper exposures . . .

WHAT IS A RACKET?

By now the situation has changed drastically. As always, the law may be slow, but it eventually finds ways to deal with injustice. Today, practically any shady mail-order proposition is within the long reach of one or another branch of the law.

The law covers a lot of ground. For example, telling the literal, technical truth is *not* enough. You may be in the wrong for what you *don't* say; for example, you must reveal that imported goods are made abroad, in most cases.

You may fall into the clutches of the law because your ad *suggests* an untruth, even if it doesn't say it. And you can err by hiding the truth away in small print or big words, or in many other ways.

Fraud, false advertising, and deceptive advertising constitute the likeliest problem you must avoid. Here are some general guides:

• "Fraud" means "taking money under false pretenses," but almost anything that a jury thinks is a "racket" will qualify to get you into jail.

• Your advertisement must not fool even "gullible" people, or "ordinarily trusting people." The test is not what a *university graduate* would find in an ad, or even a "reasonable man." If you fool any substantial portion of *your public,* you are in the wrong. And what counts is not your actual words, but what people believe after they have read your ad.

Some kinds of exaggeration may be permissible, however. You could probably get away with saying that a cheap dress is "the most beautiful dress in the world." But that probably would not be successful advertising practice.

• Good intentions on your part *may* save you from going to jail—if you can prove your good intentions—but they will *not* prevent the Federal Trade Commission from shutting down your operation. That is sufficiently painful, and sufficiently costly, so that you should make every effort to prevent its happening.

• Your advertisement *can* be illegal even though the customer is not obviously injured. For example, if you get him to write for full further information by misleading him, you are outside the law even though the information you send is perfectly truthful in describing the product. An example is advertising a correspondence course in a "Help Wanted" column.

• Whether or not your ad is legitimate is *not* obvious from the content of the advertisement itself. Other evidence may be necessary. For example, perhaps you advertise that your correspondence course on bicycle repairing will teach people how to earn $5 an hour. Whether the ad is legitimate depends upon how many bicycle repairmen make $5 per hour, and how many graduates of your course actually do so.

The best way to learn what is legitimate and what is not is to read the weekly Federal Trade Commission report, and the monthly Post Office Enforcement Report. Write your Congressman to ask for them.

Here are some specific things to watch out for:

• Medical and drug products usually need valid *scientific* proof that they will work. Testimonials from satisfied users are not enough to prove that your product relieves a disease. Many diseases go away by themselves and your product may get false credit in the user's mind. You need *clinical* evidence, scientific *experimentation,* or *chemical* evidence, furnished by qualified people.

Recently the Federal Trade Commission suppressed a business that sold a plan to increase height, though the seller claimed to have scientific evidence of the *possibility* of doing so.

• Be triply careful of such words as "cure," "banish," and "remedy" when selling drugs. See the literature mentioned at the end of the chapter for further information.

• You can't use a company name that includes such words as "Laboratory," "Manufacturer," "Refiner," etc., unless you really perform those activities. And names that suggest nonprofit organizations, such as "Institute" and "Bureau," are highly suspect.

• Guaranteeing a refund to dissatisfied customers probably does not keep you safe from the charge of defrauding your customers. (I say "probably" because the law does not seem to be clear on this point.)

• Phony prices are illegal. For example, you can't say "formerly sold at $10.98" unless a *substantial number* were really sold at that price. However, there is no restriction on your charging as high a price as you like for anything you sell.

• Testimonials must be true. Any statement you quote from a customer must be as correct as if you made the statement yourself.

Here goes an unlawyerlike statement of how you can test whether your advertisement or offer is free of fraud or deceptive advertising. You are safe if:

1. Your customers get from you exactly what the most gullible of them expect to get.

2. If the customers don't feel "gypped."

3. If every word and picture in your ad is true in spirit as well as in letter.

A customer can be dissatisfied without feeling "gypped." For example, a month after buying from you his taste may change, and he may no longer like the style or design of your product. He won't be happy, but he won't feel cheated.

A customer may also be dissatisfied at some later time because he comes across an opportunity to buy for less. He will then be dissatisfied, but our society generally recognizes that it is not theft to charge as much as the traffic will bear, as long as you stick to the truth.

It may help you evaluate the honesty of your offer if you consider the information that the potential consumer *needs* to evaluate your offer. The less information about the product he has to start with, the more responsibility you have to inform him completely.

As examples, compare selling fabric by the yard to women sewers, and selling a patent medicine. As long as you don't lie about the quality, width, pattern, or type of yarn in the fabric, women sewers have plenty of knowledge to decide whether your offer is what they want. Furthermore, as soon as they receive and examine the goods, they can tell whether you really told them the truth. So you can take some liberties in puffing the beauty and quality of your merchandise.

But the potential consumer of a patent medicine is neither a scientist nor a doctor. He has no way of testing whether your medicine will help him, or even whether it is any good for anyone. He does not understand the difficult and subtle scientific tests of a drug's efficacy, and he can easily be swayed by misleading evidence. He may believe testimonials of people who *thought* the medicine helped them, without considering that many patients get well even if they only take sugar pills.

Furthermore, the consumer may not have sufficient information to evaluate your product until long *after* his purchase. Correspondence courses and money-making plans are good examples: the purchaser must often try them out for quite awhile before he finds out whether they are helpful or worthless.

Sawyer[4] long ago wrote accurately about what is and is not legitimate:

> To explain what I mean, let me give you a few brief examples. First I write this lying statement:
> *"Our stogies are made of pure Havana tobacco."*
> That's a lie because the stogies are made of Virginia tobacco.
> Here is a sample of evasion that might be used if deemed necessary:
> *"Smoke some of our stogies, then smoke the best 15 cent Havana cigar you can buy and we believe you will like our stogies better."*

That's an ingenious evasion. You've probably become so used to Virginia tobacco that it suits you better than Havana and you assume that everyone else will think likewise. Some persons might criticise your opinion, but nobody can successfully accuse you of deceiving if you train yourself to believe what you suggest. The first statement may bring you to jail, the second never can. In fact, this very expression would tend, by psychological operation, to lead a person to think the same as yourself (after he had smoked a box of stogies at one cent each) that they tasted better than Havanas.

I repeat, tell the exact truth whenever and wherever you can. If you feel that it is necessary to your success to make a strong statement, use ingenuity and don't put yourself in a position where you can be proved a downright liar under cross-examination.

To cover the principal argument of your ad, and yet tell the strict truth without the slightest bother from your conscience as to black or white lying, you can say:

Our stogies are made of Virginia tobacco and after smoking a box of them, we believe you will continue their use, even though you have been accustomed to smoking 15 cent Havanas.

. . . . The same idea will apply to any commodity. I have simply undertaken to show the difference between a deliberate lie, a unique and legal evasion, and an ingeniously told actual truth. Even the statement I have given as truthful is as a salted and buttered baked potato compared to a raw potato, but the advertiser who cannot at least write up his goods with some enterprise, better try another line of trade.

Times are different now, though, and much of what got by when Sawyer wrote would not pass muster now.

SPECIAL PRODUCTS YOU MAY NOT SELL BY MAIL

Lotteries. Straightforward gambling schemes are forbidden, of course. But also be careful of any "contest" idea, because many of them are found to be forms of lotteries.

Pornographic and Obscene Literature, Films, etc.

Birth-control Information and Devices. (But recently I have seen several ads of this kind, and they have run long enough to make me think there may have been a change in the policies of government agencies.)

"Chain" Schemes. These are many money-making plans in which your customer is taught to make money in the same way you do. Example: you sell him a plan to sell the same plan to other people. These schemes are illegal.

"New Drugs." This includes all drugs that are not standard, well-accepted medical remedies. You may not sell "new drugs" without special permission from the Food and Drug Administration.

PENALTIES FOR ILLEGAL ACTS

Several agencies of the Federal or state governments can jump on you, and they each have different procedures and penalties. Your likeliest sources of trouble, in this order, are:

Post Office Department. Postal inspectors have the power to arrest you with the probability of trial and jail. However, first offenses of a minor nature, by basically honest people, are often handled with a Fraud Order. This is an order from Washington to your local post office to stamp "Fraudulent" on incoming mail and return it to the sender.

Postal inspectors also have the authority to suppress your illegal business by getting you to sign a statement that you will go out of business, and authorizing the post office to stamp "Refused. Out of Business" on the mail and return the mail to the senders.

Federal Trade Commission. After giving you a chance to state your case, and to appeal it, the Federal Trade Commission can order you to cease your illegal practice. No penalty is attached to most cease-and-desist orders, but if you violate the order, you may be fined. Some orders—e.g., those against dangerously false drug advertising—may carry an immediate penalty.

Food and Drug Administration. This organization has the power to stop you, or to fine and jail you, for false statements on the *labels* of drugs, cosmetics, and foods. Under some circumstances, advertising may be considered a label.

State Fraud Commissions. Most states have bodies with police power over advertising. However, they are less likely to be heard from than the Post Office or Federal Trade Commission.

Though not a government agency, the National Better Business Bureau has the power to hurt you. It can collect information about an operation they believe is illegal or unfair, and disseminate that information to media in which you wish to advertise. The media might then refuse to accept your advertising.

Pay attention to this: even if a doubtful scheme does not land you in jail, the effects can be disastrous. This is what you can lose:

1. You can lose the lawyer's fees to fight your case. Even in the unlikely event that you come out clean, it will take you a long time to make up what you have to pay your counsel.

2. You can lose the heavy investment of time, energy, and money required to set up a going business. Nothing could be more discouraging than to slave and spend, until finally you see a neat profit coming in, only to have to close up shop by order of the law. This is a losing proposition no matter how you look at it.

3. You can lose your self-respect, and your pleasure in the mail-order business. Don't shrug your shoulders at this. Many a good man has found out to his terrible regret that what seemed like a prank wound up a terrible burden on his conscience. Don't think you can play footsie with the public without coming to feel guilty and losing your esteem for yourself. Few happenings can cause more misery and unhappiness.

HOW TO CHECK ON LEGALITY

Here are some ways to find out if your offer is legal.

Don't Assume that What Others Do Is Legal. Some of the advertisements you see will eventually be squelched by the authorities. Others are by very slick operators who know the law well, employ smart lawyers, and are not frightened of going to jail. If you try to imitate them, you will either play too safe and make no money, or go too far and land in trouble.

Use Your Common Sense about whether Your Offer and Advertisement Are Honest. Show the ad to friends and ask them what they think it means. If they are misled by the ad, rewrite it.

If you are ashamed to show the ad to friends because of your good name, then the offer is probably shady and illegal.

Get Information. Write to the Federal Trade Commission and ask for their weekly "News Summary." Write to the Information Service of the Post Office and ask for their monthly bulletin on "Enforcement Action— Fraud and Mailability." Do this today, and by the time you are ready to go into business, you will have learned a great deal about what is legal and what is not.

Call or write the National Better Business Bureau, 230 Park Avenue, New York, New York. Ask if they have had any complaints about the concerns who will be your competitors.

You may request opinions about the legitimacy of your product, your offer, or your advertisement from the Federal Trade Commission, the Food and Drug Administration, or the Attorney General of the United States, all in Washington. Make sure that your request is routed to the appropriate addressee. Do *not* ask your local postmaster for an opinion. He is prevented by regulation from doing anything more than referring you to the appropriate section of the regulations.

Check with a Lawyer. Try to find a lawyer who has experience with advertising and marketing problems. If you select a general practitioner, he may appreciate your referring him to the sources in the book below.

Read and Research. Refer to *The Law for Advertising and Marketing* by Morton J. Simon[1] and the *Advertising Truth Book*, which Simon wrote for the Advertising Federation of America.[5] If you are a good researcher and know your way around a law library, you may also want to consult these references:

Trade Regulation Reporter, a Commerce Clearing House publication.
Do's and Don'ts in Advertising Copy, National Better Business Bureau.
"The Regulation of Advertising," *Columbia Law Review,* vol. 56, p. 1018, November, 1956.
Postal Frauds and Crimes, Mack Taylor (1931).
"Trade Practice Rules for the Subscription and Mail Order Book Publishing Industry," Federal Trade Commission, Sept. 3, 1940.

Carefully read the statement in Appendix D, from the 1954 Federal Trade Commission Annual Report. It is a good summary of what you can and cannot do.

6

Strategies of Mail-Order Selling

Which Media to Use for Your Test? • Direct Mail versus Display Advertising • The Advantages and Disadvantages of Classified Advertising • Selling through Agents versus Other Mail-Order Methods

By this time I assume you have selected a product. Either it is a product that you already sell at retail, or a product you decided upon after following the procedure in Chapters 3 and 4. If you have not yet decided on a product, you should go back and follow the instructions in Chapters 3 and 4.

But you're not in business yet! You won't *really* be in business until you have tested a particular ad for your product in one or more media—and obtained successful results!

The greatest thing about the mail-order business is that you can reserve final judgment until you have the best possible evidence for your decision to go full steam ahead. You can't know whether a retail store or other kind of business will succeed until you have invested $5,000, $15,000, or $50,000. But in mail order you hold back all but $50 or $500 of your stake till you almost *know* your business will succeed.

You can't get off so cheaply if you choose to sell a line of repeat-order goods, or a line of catalog items. In that case, you must test not only the pull of your original ads, but also the subsequent reorders from your customers. Chapter 15 tells you how to calculate. In any case, your original ad or mailing will not break even on repeat-order goods. The amount you "lose" on that first ad is your investment in the customer list which will form the backbone of your business.

42

Selling by inquiry–and–follow-up requires somewhat more investment than a one-shot item. One of the biggest correspondence-course operators budgets $20,000 to test a new correspondence course; $10,000 of that is for the writing of the course, and $10,000 is for testing ads. But if you have time and the knowledge to do your own work, you can get by with far, far less. The *out-of-pocket* expense to me in setting up a correspondence course of mine was much less than $500.

Selling through agents also requires more testing investment than one-shot sales, but less than a catalog business.

Our problem now is to spend your $50 to $500 wisely, so that you can get a positive test. We must draw up a blueprint for your mail-order selling effort. We want to make the blueprint as successful as we can, right from the start.

The three most important decisions you must make are decisions about:

1. The *type* of media to use, and the *specific* media in which you will place your test ads.
2. The proposition you will offer.
3. The copy and layout of your ad.

At the test stage, the order of importance of the decisions is the same as in the list above.

WHICH MEDIA TO USE FOR YOUR TEST?

If you choose a product that is already being sold by several competitors, your choice of media in which to test is obvious. Advertise in exactly the same magazines the competitors advertise in *most frequently*, and with the *biggest ads*. That's where the best chance of success is.

Some mail-order men advise against testing in the very best media. They say that you are likely to get inflated expectations of how your product will sell. They have a point in their argument.

But I believe in trying the very best media first, because even if you have only a mild success there, and can never improve your technique, you have found a *small* profit anyway, a profit you can tap again and again.

Besides, it is much less painful to test various offers and copy if you make a couple of bucks at the same time, instead of having to shell out of your pocket for the test.

If your product is *not* being sold by mail by competitors, then choose media in which *similar* products are advertised. If you intend to sell garden furniture, go where other furniture or garden advertisers are— maybe magazines like *House Beautiful*, or the garden section of *The New York Times*.

If you have a new correspondence course to teach a skilled trade, go where other trade correspondence courses are—maybe magazines like

Popular Science, or the *Adventure Men's Group* magazines, or *Specialty Salesman.*

If you have a new type of low-cost insurance offer, try the mailing lists used by advertisers of auto insurance, casualty insurance, and life insurance. A good list broker can steer you to those lists.

Still in the dark? If your product is so different from anything else on the market (and it should *not* be), you may not even know whether to use direct mail, display advertising, or classified advertising. The following sections will teach you the advantages and disadvantages of the three basic mail-order media.

You may use radio, matchbook covers, and other exotic media—but only *after* you are successful in the basic types of selling channels.

Radio has been successful for some types of promotions, especially those that can tie in the ad with editorial content. A health program can produce a lot of inquiries for vitamin catalogs. Disk jockeys can sell hit-record deals. (The White House outfit sold up a storm of "18 Top Hit Records" with a fifteen-minute radio show that they packaged for the stations they used.)

But radio requires extremely tight day-to-day control. If you don't stop commercials as soon as they stop pulling, you can lose a wad of dough.

Match covers are used a great deal by correspondence schools. They also seem to be profitable for stamp companies and address-label offers. Any offer with wide enough appeal should at least consider match covers. The big problem is that you can't test for less than a few thousand dollars.

Radio, match covers, and other such media should not be used for initial testing of a product offer.

If you sell a line of goods by catalog, there are two ways you can test whether an item should become a permanent part of your catalog—or as permanent as anything can be in the mail-order business.

1. Throw a 2-inch or 3-inch ad into mail-order media with which you are well acquainted—perhaps *The New York Times Magazine*—for a quick test. After several such tests of different items, you will learn what a set of results in that medium indicates about the probable pull of the items in your own catalog.

2. Or, run the product in one edition of your catalog. This is the fairest test of all, of course. Its only disadvantage is the time it takes to obtain results.

DIRECT MAIL VERSUS DISPLAY ADVERTISING

When Should You Use Direct Mail? The answer is *not* "always," as some beginners in mail-order think. In fact, direct mail is not the first medium you should think of for products. I think you should first consider whether your offer will sell profitably in display ads. If it seems to be a tossup between display and direct mail, try display first. Here are reasons for trying display first:

1. Testing is cheaper in display. For $100 total cost for space *and* preparation, you can often get an accurate idea of whether a product will succeed. But preparation costs alone, for the simplest direct-mail piece, will be many times as expensive.

2. Testing is also more *informative* in display. Some magazines are very general in appeal, partly because of their huge circulation—Sunday supplements and the "shelter" magazines, for example. Unless your offer is very specialized, you can rest assured that poor results in a very general medium are not due to an idiosyncrasy of the medium, as might often be the case with lists.

Use direct mail if your competitors use it. Their success promises your success. That is the basic logic of this entire book.

Use direct mail if you can shoot at prospects with a rifle instead of a shotgun. (That is the favorite metaphor of the direct-mail enthusiasts.) If your product has much greater appeal for some groups of people than it does for others, and if your potential customers can be identified by any external characteristics and a list of them is available, then you should use direct mail.

For example, if you want to sell a course on raising children, any general magazine *may* be satisfactory. If you sell a book on Catholic religious instruction, Catholic magazines deliver the audience you want. But if you sell a teaching device of special interest to priests who head Catholic schools, you will use direct mail (unless Catholic educators also have their own magazine).

Compiled lists are the most specialized of all. Lists of mail-order buyers are not so specialized except with reference to the product they bought originally. A list of customers who buy cheese by mail is tremendously specialized for another cheese company (which isn't likely to be able to rent the list). It is much less specialized for gift sellers, though it may nevertheless be a very profitable list for them.

Industrial and commercial lists are very specialized, of course. Businesses that sell to a particular industry will generally use both direct mail and the trade magazines. But direct mail is far more essential to them. Trade-magazine space costs are very high compared to consumer magazines, and that narrows the gap between display and direct-mail costs.

Direct mail is also more flexible for the form of the copy message, the timing of the message, the addressee of the message, and the length of the message. It is also much more satisfactory for repeat-order businesses. Office supplies are a favorite product sold by direct mail to *many* industries and trades. Economic information services are another very successful direct-mail product to businesses.

Any *particular* nonfiction book is an extremely specialized item. Few books on special topics in anthropology or mathematics are likely to have a wide general audience. There is seldom a magazine circulation that corresponds perfectly with the focus of the book—even an anthropology or mathematics journal, though they may be good media, anyway. Furthermore, the publisher can do the necessary *complete* selling job only in direct mail. That's why publishers of specialized nonfiction use direct mail so much.

Use direct mail only if you expect to get at least $10 out of the average customer, including all future purchases—$25 may be a more sensible figure. These estimates are based on

1. The minimum costs to get a mailing into the mail (perhaps $70 to $100 per thousand, in 1964) and

2. The highest rates of response you can possibly expect in any large-scale mailing.

An example: Correspondence-course sellers seldom are willing to pay more than $1, $1.50, or $2 at most, for inquiries from display ads. But to get inquiries that cheaply from direct-mail solicitation, they would need to obtain a response of almost 10 percent—very unlikely, indeed.

But if you can afford a much higher inquiry cost and if the specialized prospects cannot be obtained through magazines, direct mail might be a good bet.

You are more likely to use direct mail to develop new customers if you sell a "repeat item." Repeat items obviously produce more revenue in the long run than if the customer never buys again, and therefore a new customer is worth more to you. In fact, if you sell a repeat item, you usually expect to "lose money" on the first order (if you count in the cost of developing the customer, as you should).

Repeat-item catalog houses use direct mail to solicit for all orders subsequent to the first, of course.

Use direct mail when you have a story to tell that is too long and complicated for a display ad. Use direct mail when your product requires illustration, especially in color. There are virtually no limits to the methods you can use to tell your story in direct mail.

Catalogs are an example of a form of *material* that can be carried by direct mail but not in magazines.

Sometimes you don't want the whole world to know about a special proposition you are offering to some part of your market. Magazine publishers, for instance, sell some subscriptions at full price and others at a cut rate. If they offered cut-rate deals in display ads, no one would ever renew a subscription at the full rate. That is one reason magazine publishers use so much direct mail.

The relative privacy of direct mail provides *some* screen from the prying eyes of your competitors. The display advertiser does business in a fishbowl, and is often eaten by predatory cats.

Direct mail can search a limited geographical area for customers, and a periodical cannot. A manufacturer of fire alarms developed a lovely small-area technique. First he saturates a town to develop leads for his "sales engineers." Then he circularizes the immediate *neighbors* of each family that buys, telling the neighbors to ask the fellow who purchased what he thinks of the fire-alarm system. This follow-the-leader method helps instill confidence in the product.

After saturating each town, the sales force moves on, like an infantry company following an artillery barrage. This is a great way to use direct mail.

Some advertisers use both direct mail *and* display advertising to develop new contacts. Firms who sell through agents use plenty of direct mail because only a few magazines reach a heavy proportion of potential agents.

Novelty and gift-catalog firms often use both display ads and direct mail.

The moral to the story is that you should use *every* medium that will pay you any profit on your money. Only in that way can you maximize your earnings.

In two important ways, direct mail is *easier* to use than display advertising:

1. The time lag between mailing and getting enough returns for accurate predictions is much less than the lag between placing your ad in a magazine and getting predictable returns from it. This means you can make more money *quicker* in direct mail than in display advertising. And you recover your investment quicker.

2. Some direct-mail advertisers will scream to high heaven that I'm wrong about this, but: direct-mail *testing* is much more accurate than display-ad testing (except for split-run copy testing). From any set of results the direct-mail advertiser can get a much better idea than the display advertiser about what will happen when he repeats his original advertising.

Yes, it is true that the results ordinarily will fall off when you go back to a list after a test. But the direct-mail advertiser can take account of that in his calculations. Seasonal effects can also be allowed for.

The display advertiser, however, is at the mercy of changes in the position of his ad in the magazine, more or less competition, better or worse editorial matter, and many other factors. The display advertiser never does as well on the second insertion either (all else being equal), but he has more trouble estimating the dropoff than does the direct-mail advertiser.

The greater predictive power of direct-mail results means that the direct-mail advertiser can proceed more rapidly, with greater confidence, than can the display advertiser.

These two advantages are *not* reasons for choosing to use direct mail. Whether or not you use direct mail *must depend on the product*. There may, however, be reasons for choosing a *product* that can be sold by direct mail.

THE ADVANTAGES AND DISADVANTAGES OF CLASSIFIED ADVERTISING

The *advantage* of advertising in classified columns is that, for almost any product, a dollar spent in classified advertising will bring back more profit than a dollar spent in any other space unit. That is a fact, proved many times. Chapter 13 shows a comparison of the effectiveness of classified against other space units. That is why so many advertisers that use display ads—and even full-page ads—also continue using the humble classified columns. Correspondence schools almost all use both display and classified.

Furthermore, many large firms got their start with their original ads in classified columns. Fuller Brush began with classified.

You can't generate large volume and create a big business in classified columns alone, however. You may not think so at first, but the number of places in which you can run profitable classified is small, and this restricts your business badly. Few classified advertisers can invest even $1,500 per month in classified. Most of them are limited to a much smaller expenditure by the lack of media. I doubt that fifty advertisers in the country spend more than $500 a month on classified even in the best of months.

A small investment means a small possible profit. You'll have to be a very efficient and clever mail-order man to net an honest $750 on a $500 advertising investment.

This limitation also explains why classified advertising is not used by many firms that *should* use it. An advertising agency's 15 percent commission on $500 doesn't look very big compared to the work involved in billing and handling the paper work. So agencies do not recommend classified to their clients. This problem could be solved profitably for everyone concerned if there were a system of increasing the agency's commission on classified (perhaps as high as 30 percent), or paying the agency on a fee basis, or cutting the agency in for a fixed percent of the total volume on the gross profit. Until very recently, this suggestion would have been considered unethical by advertising and media people, but practices are changing now.

Classified is an excellent place for the mail-order novice to begin. He can test products and gain invaluable practical experience with very small amounts of capital. Anybody can afford to risk $10 for a test ad in a million-circulation magazine. The thrills and experience will be worth that much even if the first attempt, or the first five attempts, are total busts.

The novice who advertises in classified does not have to arrange for typography, layout, or art work. In classified he *can* get into the mail-order business with his ad written on scrap paper and sent direct to the magazine.

Most classified advertisements offer free information to develop inquiries. Direct sales are seldom made from the classified ad. The reason is obvious: it is rare that you can tell enough about a product in ten words or twenty words so that the potential customer (1) wants the product, (2) understands what it is, and (3) knows how much it costs and where to order.

However, it is relatively easy in a small number of words to whet a person's desire for further information. And since he risks no money, he does not need to be convinced of your reliability in order to inquire. In your follow-up letter you have plenty of time to describe the product in detail, convince the prospect that you are honest and reliable, and that the product is a good buy. Chapter 17 describes in detail the follow-up letters you send in response to inquiries.

Some products are sold directly from ads, *as well as* through inquiries —often next to each other in the same magazines—by different firms. And neither forces the other out of business. These are usually information manuals (employment information, how to start a credit business, etc.) that sell for $1 directly from the ad, or for $2 or $3 from follow-up letters to inquirers.

Most successful classified ads are of these types:

1. Ads for agents to sell products house to house. This is a more complicated business than other types of mail order.

2. Ads to produce inquiries for books, correspondence courses, and other information. This includes all "homework" schemes.

3. Ads that sell pamphlets directly from the ads.

4. Few classified ads are for repeat products, or for catalog business. Catalogs of hypnotism books are an exception.

SELLING THROUGH AGENTS VERSUS OTHER MAIL-ORDER METHODS

There are two basic ways that you can use agents as part of a mail-order operation:

1. Your agents can go out and find prospects for your goods, and sell them directly. This method is used for those types of mail-order products that almost necessarily require the use of agents: men's shoes

and suits, for example, and cosmetics for women. These products require demonstration before the customer will be willing to buy.

Direct salesmen get up to 60 percent commission on their sales.

2. A second method is to build a sales force to close leads *you develop by mail.* Encyclopaedia Britannica, major insurance firms, and top correspondence schools use this method. So do smaller outfits like Enurtone (a device to prevent bed-wetting).

The salesman can generally double the number of sales you could close by mail alone, and his commission runs from 5 to 15 percent. Usually a product must sell for at least $50 to make this method profitable.

Either method of selling through agents is somewhat more complicated than other types of mail-order methods, and usually involves a larger investment and greater preparation. You not only have to develop the advertising to sell the final customer, but you must also develop the selling campaign to convince prospective agents that they should sell your product for you.

But don't underestimate the potential of selling through agents. Many of the largest mail-order firms work through sales agents. One expert in this field estimates that there are 350,000 agents in the country who make a full-time living selling for mail-order firms, and lots more who work part-time.[1]

7

The Tactical Decisions in
Mail-Order Advertising

*Sell from the Ad or from Follow-Ups? • What Price
Should You Set? • Cash Offers, Credit Terms, and
Guarantees • Installment Credit versus Cash on
the Barrelhead*

These are the important decisions you must make about the selling
proposition:

1. Whether you will try to close the sale

    a. Directly in your ad or letter.
    b. By the inquiry-and-follow-up technique.
    c. Through agents.

2. What price you should set.
3. What kind of trial offer or credit terms you will give.

SELL FROM THE AD OR FROM FOLLOW-UPS?

As a general rule, offers priced at $10 or over cannot be sold directly
from a display ad. For a purchase involving a lot of money, the prospect
needs a longer sales pitch than you can deliver in a space ad. You need
a follow-up or direct mail to do the job.

However, sporting-goods firms succeed in selling kits of shop tools
and fishing equipment for around $15, direct from ads. Perhaps this offer
works because the merchandise is well known to the prospects, and the
basic appeal is the bargain price.

51

The standard technique for merchandise priced over $10 or $20 is either (1) to run display advertising offering further information, and then follow up with direct mail; or (2) to solicit with direct mail only.

If you use the two-step display-plus-follow-up technique, don't show the price in the ad. Like a good encyclopedia salesman, you don't want to scare the prospect away before you have had the opportunity to make him want the product very badly.

Ordinarily your first direct-mail piece to a prospect will aim to make the sale. However, some products require such elaborate and expensive sales presentations that you can afford to send them only to prime prospects. If so, your first letter is just a canvass technique to obtain really hot prospects. Then you send them the full presentation.

The famous Southern Roofing direct-mail campaign first canvassed for inquiries. People who returned the inquiry card then got follow-up letters containing full information.

WHAT PRICE SHOULD YOU SET?

The basic rule is that you should pick the price at which you will make the most money.

The way to find that "best" price is to test many different prices.

Prices are much more flexible in mail order than in retail businesses, because potential customers have no standards of comparison. The merchandise is almost always new to them, so they have no prior knowledge about prevailing prices. And they can't shop from store to store, to check for the best buy.

A manual can sell as a book for $3.95 or $6.95. Or the same information in a slightly different format can go for $24.50, $39.50, or $59.50. Whether you sell for $3.95 versus $6.95 or $24.50 versus $59.50 will be a matter for testing. But whether you sell as a book or as a correspondence course is a more basic strategic question.

The price of a mail-order item depends relatively little on the wholesale cost to you, but it depends heavily on the costs of advertising and selling it.

How to Test for the Best Price

To choose the best price, you must know how to figure the profit you make at that price. Here's how to figure the profit you make on a single ad:

1. Add:

   a. Advertising cost.

   b. Cost of merchandise, including labor, postage, and other incidental costs.

2. Subtract from total dollars received.

3. The difference is your profit on the ad.

An example: Packages of a dozen ball-point pens cost you 40 cents per order to ship, including all merchandise and handling costs except advertising. You run two ads, each costing $100, which are identical except for the price advertised. Ad A asks $1; Ad B asks $1.98.

Ad A

Pulls 300 orders @ $1—Total revenue.................. $300
Cost—300 × 40¢ for merchandise........................... $120
    Advertising cost..................................... 100
                                                         $220

$300 − $220 equals profit of $80

Ad B

Pulls 130 orders @ $1.98—Total revenue................ $257.40
Cost—130 × 40¢ for merchandise........................ $ 52.00
    Advertising cost................................. 100.00
                                                       $152.00

$257.40 − $152 equals profit of $105.40

The $1.98 price in Ad B is clearly the more profitable price.

This simple example shows you that the ad at twice the price does *not* need to pull twice as many inquiries to be more profitable. However, the cheaper price is often more profitable.

If the purpose of your advertisement is to create customers for your other products, as well as to sell the product advertised, then you must figure differently. Very often you will be willing to sell at a lower price, and to take less profit directly from the ad, in order to increase the number of customers added to your list.

The correct way to figure the price in this repeat-business case is to add the future dollar value of the customers to the immediate profit of the ad. Chapter 15 teaches you how to figure the dollar value of customers.

A group of leading mail-order men recently got together for some talks at New York University. One of the published[1] results of those talks was Table 7-1, which shows maximum costs in relation to price. I don't think much of this approach, but you might find it helpful.

Table 7-1

Selling price	Maximum cost as % of price	Maximum cost
$2 item..........	10%	$0.20
$3 item..........	15%	0.45
$4 item..........	20%	0.80
$5 item..........	25%	1.25
$7 item..........	32%	2.24
$10 item..........	38%	3.80
$12 item..........	41%	4.82
$15 item..........	44%	6.60

This is how one mail-order man[2] breaks down his costs for a "typical article," probably a printed manual, that sells for $2.98:

Product and postage..............	$0.45
Overhead—5%..................	0.15
Shipping container................	0.06
Shipping label....................	0.02
Instruction sheet.................	0.02
Order processing.................	0.15
Reserve for refunds—5% of sales...	0.15
Bank charges....................	0.05
	$1.05 = Total merchandise costs

At a selling price of $2.98, any ad that brings in orders at an average advertising cost of less than $1.93 makes a profit for him on this article. In other words, if a $50 ad brings 32 orders (for $95.36), the average advertising cost is $50 divided by 32, or $1.56 each. The profit per order is $1.93 less $1.56, or 37 cents each.

How to Guess the Best Price

In your first test ad, you should try the price that has the best possibilities. These observations should help you pick a price:

1. Victor Schwab[3] says that $2 or $1.98 is the lowest price at which you can make money without follow-up sales. Schwab may be generally right about that, but I myself have made many happy thousands of dollars selling products for a buck a throw. That includes manuals and merchandise, too. Of course the cost of the goods, plus postage, must be under 25 cents.

On the basis of split-run tests, Schwab[4] found:

$2 did 62.2% better than $2.50 (product sold to women).

$1.98 did 87.7% better than $2.75.

$2 did 26.7% better than $4 plus free premium (seven months of a magazine vs. twelve months of the same magazine).

2. Harold Preston[5] found that a $1 or $2 price would outpull a fractional price (like 98¢ or $1.98), probably because it is easy to mail one or two dollar bills. But above $2 he found that fractional prices do better.

Preston certainly is right at the $1 level. But more firms use $1.98 than $2, which makes me think $1.98 may be generally better. Preston made his observation twenty years ago, and more families use checks now than they did then.

Catalog houses even use fractional prices under $1. Their customers usually buy several items at a time, however; hence their situation is different.

Even-dollar prices also have the advantage of getting you more cash and fewer checks. Checks cost 3 to 5 cents each to cash, plus clerical costs, no matter how small the check is, so they are undesirable.

(CAUTION: A few mail-order men think that the hard-to-trace cash dealings in mail order make a perfect setup to beat the income tax. It isn't so. One very famous mail-order man shot himself because he was discovered to have had $40,000 in small change in his safe. You'll live a happier and freer life if you play it straight, with the government and with yourself.)

3. Verneur Pratt observes that "large mail-order houses (like Sears and Montgomery Ward) consistently cut prices on standard goods, the value of which are known, and make up the loss by selling 'blind merchandise at long-profit prices.' "[6]

Competition doesn't always set the price. Two firms have sold hypnotism manuals successfully for years in tiny classified ads. One sells for $1, the other for $2. Some customers must obviously think they will be getting a better product for $2, even though the ads give them no reason to believe that is true. Two other firms have sold hypnotism manuals at $1.98 and $3.98, respectively, in display ads.

It usually holds true that even if your product is printed material, where cost is small relative to the advertising cost, you generally will need returns greater than one and a half times the cost of an ad to make money directly from the ad.

Furthermore, overhead is always higher than you think it is. You'll be lucky to make a profit if your advertising, plus your goods, cost you more than 70 percent of your revenue.

CASH OFFERS, CREDIT TERMS, AND GUARANTEES

The terms of the offer can have a terrific effect on your sales. It is very important that you choose the most *profitable* terms. And the most profitable terms are not necessarily the terms that pull the most orders.

The Refund Offer. It is a practically unbreakable rule in mail order that you must guarantee satisfaction or money back. Even if you don't want to offer a guarantee, many advertising media will accept your advertisement only if you agree to do so.

It is true that some people will return goods. Some people even are cranks about returning goods. Others will find interesting ways to sting you. And none of us likes to part with money that has once been paid over to us.

Nevertheless, you will almost surely wind up with more *profit* overall by making the refund offer. The extra sales will more than counterbalance the refunds you pay out.

Once in a while you may offer a product on which returns are so high that you lose money. If that happens it's usually because the product is rotten, and that should be an indication for you to pull it off the market until you can improve it.

Returns can be quite high and the offer still make money. Booksellers who offer a seven-day free trial without payment of any sort expect 20 percent of the books to be returned, and 20 percent more not to pay. They can still wind up in the black.

Returns can be very small if customers are truly satisfied. I sold thousands upon thousands of a tiny sixteen-page booklet that cost under 3 cents apiece to print—for a dollar a booklet. I offered an unconditional guarantee of satisfaction with no time limit. I received exactly one request for a refund—from an apologetic fellow who said he had bought another copy months before.

There are several types of guarantees you can make. You can offer money back within seven days, within a month, or within a full year. You can offer double-your-money-back, too. The strength of the guarantee will affect the pull of the ad, as well as the number of returned orders. If you have a really strong product, make the strongest possible guarantee.

If the number of returned orders you get on the strongest possible guarantee is significantly large, your final decision will depend upon a *test* of the various refund-offer plans.

If you offer a full-year guarantee, you don't need to wait a whole year to find out how many returned orders you will get. How fast they come back depends upon the product and how long it takes customers to give it a real trial. But in any case, you can almost always count on more than half the returns coming back within a month of receipt.

When you make your guarantee, emphasize in your ad that if your customers want their money back, they'll get their money back. A money-back guarantee always seems a little too good to be true. And readers are suspicious that you will find some excuse not to refund. Write your guarantee as powerfully as you can to put that fear to rest. "Iron-clad." "Unconditional." "Legally binding guarantee." "No questions asked."

No matter how powerful your language is, country shrewdness makes people want to keep a tight hold on their money till they are *sure*. That's where the COD comes in. They are willing to pay extra to be sure that you won't run off with their money without sending the goods. This is especially true for mail order over the radio. People have less faith in the spoken word than in the printed word.

Offering the COD option will increase your returns compared to "Sorry, No COD's," especially if you word it strongly enough. Lately the fashion has been to say "Free 7 day Trial" when you mean that the customer orders by COD and has the right to return within seven days.

Even on installment deals, COD can help. Schwab[3] quotes a test in which a $2 COD first payment did 23 percent better than $1 cash in advance.

COD mailing charges cost money to everyone, of course. It costs the buyer more: 40 cents plus your postage charge for merchandise under $10. And it costs you, too, in clerical costs, plus the COD and postage costs for refusals of orders. Nevertheless, most firms that sell articles for $2 to $10 offer COD, so it obviously pays for most firms.

To help you figure, Baker[7] estimates that for shopping-section items, COD refusals will average 5 to 8 percent of orders shipped. For less expensive merchandise than that Baker talks about, the refusal rate will be less. And like everything else in mail order, the COD refusal rate will vary among customers from different media.

COD's are absolutely essential for radio advertising.

Push the prospects hard to send cash with order. Emphasize the high cost of COD, and that you prepay postage for cash with order. Even offer an extra premium for cash payment.

Many firms that sell articles for $4 and up—and sometimes for $2 articles—ask for $1 deposit on COD shipments. The seller keeps the deposit if the COD is refused. That way the seller can't lose by the shipment even if it is refused. The deposit also cuts the refusal rate. But I've never seen results to prove that the deposit method is more profitable overall.

An *Esquire* newsletter suggests five ways to reduce COD refusals:

1. *State the terms of your offer clearly.* Don't say "$2.95 plus a few cents postage," the customer may think a "few cents" postage means six or eight cents. But 18 cents postage plus 40 cents COD is not just "a few cents." Phrase your offer this way: "Only $1 postpaid, or COD for $1.38." The customer knows definitely how much money to have ready when the package arrives. This not only cuts down refusals but stimulates cash orders by offering a saving for cash payment.

2. *Ship the merchandise the same day the order arrives, if possible.* If you delay for three or four days, the customer may be out of the city, may change his mind, or may have spent the money on something else. It's always a good idea to ship the merchandise while the customer is hot.

3. One advertiser switches COD's into cash in this manner: "Check here if enclosing your remittance. We pay the 58 cents postage and COD fees. Same 7 day return privilege." When the customer knows what saving can be made by sending cash, your cash sales will increase and COD refusals decrease.

4. *Acknowledge COD orders* and let the customer know how much money to have ready for the postman. You can do this with a postcard, filling in the exact amount of money needed.

5. *Ask for a deposit with the original order.* This reduces refusals to a minimum. When the customer has some money invested in the merchandise it is very unlikely that he will refuse the shipment.[8]

Schwab[9] ran a test on a $4.68 encyclopedia of "Send No Money" versus "Send $1" COD. "Send No Money" pulled 10 percent better. That suggests to me that after all the costs and revenues were calculated, "Send No Money" would come out ahead.

People like to keep their money in their hands until they have the goods. They also like to delay their final purchasing decision as long as they possibly can. The trial offer is designed to get around the reluctance that people have to commit themselves. The trial offer gives people the feeling that they have maximum freedom to return the merchandise after they have examined it.

(People also seem to prefer to delay payment, even when the commitment is made. Think how many times you have said "Bill me later" even when you knew the purchase was final.)

Here are some figures that show the power of the trial offer, from Schwab's tests:

> 1. A 5-day examination before payment versus cash on the line. The full-examination offer pulled better by 60%, 98%, 24%, and 34% in four tests.
>
> 2. A 10-day examination before payment versus COD. The approval offer *pulled* 62.6% better (this was a $2.50 article).
>
> 3. A seven-day-approval examination versus COD, on a $1.98 offer. The seven-day approval did 28% better.[10]

Naturally, what you *really* care about is the amount of *profit* you wind up with. Just because a trial offer pulls more requests doesn't mean you make more that way.

According to Paul Grant,[11] firms that ship on approval average 65 percent payment, 20 percent returns, and 15 percent nonpayment. These figures probably apply to merchandise priced higher than that studied by Schwab, and therefore they are probably more conservative.

You can also raise your rate of profit by offering an extra discount, premium, or other throw-in. Grant gives us these observations:

> a) A five percent discount for promptness in ordering usually with a two week limit) usually increases the number of orders from 2% to as high as 9%.
>
> b) An offer to prepay parcel post postage on products weighing from four pounds, up, usually results in bringing orders more quickly (with the same two week limit) and has been known to increase orders as much as 4%.
>
> c) Where a choice of COD or cash is given the purchaser, an offer to pay postage on cash orders results in a higher percentage of cash receipts ranging from 3% to as high as 10%, depending upon the weight of the product and the distance it is to be shipped.
>
> d) A 5% discount instead of prepaid postage as in Par. C. has approximately the same effect on increase in the number of orders.
>
> e) Offering a desirable giveaway in consideration for a prepaid order or for orders received in a limited time has been known to increase the number of orders from 2% to as high as 8%.[12]

Grant says that these figures apply particularly when the offer is fully repeated in the coupon or order blank, even though it may appear elsewhere in the advertisement, or the mailing piece.

INSTALLMENT CREDIT VERSUS CASH ON THE BARRELHEAD

Every top mail-order man agrees that you *must* offer installment-payment terms to sell almost any article priced over $10. (Leslie's high-class catalog operation sells up to $20 without credit, successfully. This proves that there *is* an exception to every rule. But the exception doesn't, in turn, *prove* this or any other rule.)

You will prefer to get cash immediately, of course. So you offer a substantial discount (maybe 10 percent) for immediate payment. Five to ten percent of your customers will take you up on that discount. Later in the series of payments you will again offer discounts for immediate payment of the full *balance*. That will help get the cash, too.

You'll have to sweat for the rest. The minute a due date passes, you must send out the first letter in your collection series. And you must keep on following up with collection letters until it's no longer any use.

You will finally receive perhaps 60 percent of the total billings, if you sell a correspondence course priced at $50 or up. Charles Atlas eventually collected in full from 73 percent of the purchasers of his $20 course. Higher-priced correspondence schools figure they are doing well if 60 percent of the purchasers pay up in full.

The installment contract should be written by a lawyer, then put into simple English by you and checked by the lawyer. The contract usually holds the purchaser liable for the *entire sales price*, even if he stops taking a correspondence course.

Merchandise with a relatively low markup—shop tools, jewelry, home furnishings—and high-markup printed material present different problems. The low-markup merchandise has real value to you if it is returned in default. For high-markup stuff, your problem is to extract as much money as you can from delinquents, and forget about merchandise returns. Your chief weapon will be a series of collection letters. The letters should range from polite to stern. Their actual composition is crucial. Write your letters from samples that other mail-order firms use, or from models in books of collection letters.[13-15]

You will have to tinker around to find the best intervals between letters. Best intervals for various products can range from *one day* to more than three weeks.

Bringing suit for your money seldom pays, unless the sale price is well into the hundreds of dollars.

Collection agencies *may* help you. Since you pay them only if they succeed in collecting, you can't lose anything. But chances are they won't see much prospect of collecting your accounts, and therefore they won't work on them.

8

How to Start a Classified-Advertising Business

*The First Steps to Classified • The Terms of a
Classified Offer • How to Write a Classified Ad •
How Long Should the Classified Ad Be?*

This chapter is about the classified columns of *magazines,* and it does
not deal with newspaper classified advertising. With few exceptions,
newspaper classified columns will not pay off for mail-order advertisers.
Some correspondence courses, books, and book-finding services are
exceptions to the rule, however.

The classified sections of nationally distributed newspapers like the
National Enquirer, Wall Street Journal, the *National Observer,* and the
New York Times are good for some mail-order offers. Many weekly farm
newspapers also are excellent for mail order.

The arena of classified includes far more than a few magazines like
Popular Science, however. There are over 300 magazines that are good
classified media, most of which you have never heard of. They are listed
later in Appendix I, along with complete data on them.

THE FIRST STEPS TO CLASSIFIED

Your first step toward a classified mail-order business is the same first
step we talked about in Chapter 3. *Examine the media and the competition.* Write a postcard to every medium listed in Appendix I as carrying
classified, asking for a sample copy of the magazine and rates for
classified advertising. Rate information on classified is omitted from
some rate cards and from some *Standard Rate & Data* listings.

Then get hold of the back issues of magazines from back-date magazine shops. Or, you can examine the back files of *Popular Science, Workbasket, Popular Gardening, Popular Photography,* and others, at your nearest public library.

In the list of classified media you will note *Publishers Women's Monthlies, Publishers Men's Monthlies,* etc. These are *groups* of many magazines whose classified sections are sold together by Publishers Classified Department, a firm in Chicago. You cannot buy classified space individually from the magazines in those groups. These and other groups are an important part of the classified mail-order industry because of their tremendous size.

Clip the classified pages out of the magazines, and file them alphabetically. At the same time, make up a 3-by 5-inch file card on each magazine, noting on the card the products and firms advertising in it that interest you. Don't spend much time thinking about what you're doing until you have looked at the classified pages of at least 50 different media. Then you can begin to consider what looks good and what doesn't. You are, of course, looking for the ads and products that appear in many media, and over a long period of time. Those are the *successful* products.

Pay most attention to the magazines whose cost is *highest* per word. That's where the gravy is. If you can't use the expensive magazines successfully, your operation will be tiny potatoes at best.

Your product need *not* appeal to everyone; it need *not* be able to run profitably in all media. If you have an offer that will be successful in most of the farm magazines, you are in good shape. On the other hand, if your offer will be profitable only in the automobile-magazine classifieds, the volume will probably be too small to justify your investment of time.

THE TERMS OF A CLASSIFIED OFFER

Judging from the time-tested behavior of classified advertisers, it usually is not wise to charge the inquirers even a postage stamp for further information. Asking for a coin or stamp severely cuts down the number of inquiries. It is undoubtedly true that the people who do send the coin are the best prospects. Nevertheless, you will do better to obtain the poorer prospects and try to sell them, too.

The coins or stamps that you get will usually not be a significant source of revenue, and the extra wordage in the ad necessary to ask for a dime or a quarter may cost you more than the coins you get. But most important, the request for a coin cuts responses greatly.

However, you will find it profitable to ask for a small sum if you offer an expensive catalog that many people would like to have even if they are poor prospects. If your catalog costs you a dollar to two, you can't afford to send a copy to everyone who would like to look at its pretty pictures but who never intends to buy. You ask for the coin *not* because of the value it represents, but because it helps you separate the good prospects from the poor ones. Sears, Roebuck accomplishes this *not* by asking for a coin (many years ago they sold their catalogs for sums up to 50 cents), but by insisting that a person be a *proved customer* before receiving their expensive book.

Prices

As a very general rule, $1 is a better price than either 50 cents or $2— in *classified,* and for printed products whose cost is low. From my own experience I have found that you will not make twice as many sales at 50 cents as at $1 and in that case $1 is more profitable than 50 cents. I have also found that $1 gets considerably *more* than twice as many sales at $2, enough more to make the $1 price best.

CAUTION: My experience should be only a *suggestion* to you. The opposite results will occur for some kinds of products. You must *test* various prices for your own product and offer.

Remember that the more the product costs you to make and mail, the more you must get for it. But the price does *not* go up in proportion to the costs. See Chapter 7 for a full discussion of how to set the best price for your product.

When reckoning your costs and revenues, don't forget the value of the names of your customers or inquirers. Satisfied customers can later be sold other products, and each customer's name then comes to be very valuable. And even if you yourself never try to sell anything to the customer again, or even if the prospect never bought from you, the name has value and should *never, never* be thrown away. You can convert names into money either by renting the list, or (more likely for beginners and small businesses) selling the names. See Chapter 15 for a discussion of lists, list brokers, and how to sell or rent lists.

HOW TO WRITE A CLASSIFIED AD

We shall go into some detail on this topic, because the art of writing classified ads is not covered in the books that discuss display-advertising copy.

What is true of *all* advertising copy is *especially* true for classified writing: the copywriter must be absolutely precise and economical with the words and language he uses. Every fuzzy or useless word takes a chunk out of potential profit. A single word that is not true to its mark and completely clear may turn potential customers away from the ad.

That's why writing classified ads is superb training for creating all types of advertising. The head of a large and important agency once voiced the wish that all his high-priced copywriters had had a six-months apprenticeship in writing classified ads at the start of their careers.

Furthermore, the same elements that make up a successful full-page ad must also go into a good classified ad. In the order in which the elements generally appear in the classified ad:

Element 1: Gaining the Attention of the Reader. This is less of a problem with classified advertising than with display ads. The potential customer actively reads the classified ads, usually in the order in which they appear, and he tends to read or skim almost every ad. Nothing you can say in your classified ad will attract readers who are not already looking through the classified section. Those who do read the classified section are almost a captive audience, and you don't have to use showmanship tricks to attract them to your ad.

Nevertheless, your ad must compete with the other ads for the reader's fullest attention as he skims through. You must try to attract that large portion of the readers who might not read *through* your ad carefully.

Attracting attention is done in display ads by the headline, the layout, and the artwork. Your classified ad has no artwork and no layout other than the standardized block of type. The whole job of leading readers into and through your ad, therefore, must be done by the first word (or words) in the advertisement. The first word or words are set in capitals, and the *best* first words will be those that are most exciting and interesting to the potential purchasers of your product.

The principles of writing the lead words of the classified ad are exactly the same as the principles of writing the headline of a display mail-order ad. The lead words will go right to the heart of the product, and will never tease or be cute. A successful classified ad will never contain a general appeal like "Have Extra Fun with Your Family."

Element 2: The Promise. If the product is a manual or course on self-improvement or making money, the classified ad will contain the "big promise" or "emotional appeal" that is the key element of many mail-order display ads. This promise must have more power to attract the reader than any other words. "$70–$100 Weekly Possible," "Giant Arms," "Second Income from Oil," etc.

Element 3: Telling What the Product Is. If the product is solid, *tangible* merchandise, the classified ad will dive right into an exciting description of the product, or will name the product in the lead words. "Jeep Parts," "Patent Searchers," "Socialist Books," "Accordions," are examples. The heading of the classification also serves the function of naming some products quite precisely: "Cameras and Photo Supplies," "Farms, Acreage and Real Estate," "Music and Musical Instruments."

Element 4: Calling to the Prospect. Many kinds of products use the lead-word technique of calling out to potential prospects: "Inventors,"

"Writers," "Bookhunters." If the classification heading performs this function, calling out to the reader will probably not be successful or necessary in the individual advertisements.

Element 5: Description of the Product. After the lead words, the good classified ad will contain whatever descriptive words are necessary to tell enough about your product to make the prospect want it, *and* to convince him that you are telling the truth and are reliable. All that can sometimes be done in three words. More about that below.

Element 6. Then the *price*, if you are trying to make direct sales.

Element 7. Perhaps a *call to action* like "Write today" or "Send." Some ads can do without the call to action; others benefit from it.

Element 8. Perhaps a *guarantee*, if you are making direct sales. I have found, in every single test I have run, that the guarantee increases my profit. But some other advertisers evidently don't agree, because they don't include a guarantee in their ads.

Element 9. Then the *key* and the address. You will find instructions on keying in Chapter 10. Never use more than a one-word name: "Violinco" will do just as well as "Violin Company" and saves money. Omit "Street" and street numbers if the postmaster will give you his OK. After a while you can omit your address completely if you live in a small town. In a fair-sized city you can use a single block of letters for your post office box and key.

Steps in Writing the Classified Ad

These are the actual steps that I follow in writing a classified ad. I can only recommend them to you as one man's method. Your approach may be different but just as good.

1. Study the ads of your successful competitors.

2. In the order in which they come into your head, scribble down every word or idea or group of words that would help you to sell the product if you had all the space you wanted. In addition to all the words about your product, include all the classic selling words: "News," "New Discovery," "Bargain," "Free," "Save," etc. Include every important word that is in your competitor's ads.

3. Write down your lead word (or words). Your first ads will have the best chance of success if your lead words express the same *idea* as your most successful competitor's ads. (But make your words *different* from his.)

4. Using your list of important words and phrases, write the best ad you can, without trying to make the ad short or concise. Just make sure that you have in the ad everything you think must be in it, in the correct order. Include every "selling idea" that your successful competitors have in their ads.

5. Then hone and polish the ad. Try for the most powerful and

evocative words you can find. It is amazing the difference that a single word can make. I found that the words "Manual" and "Book" brought in *twice as many* orders as did "Instructions" in an ad for a how-to-do-it booklet I was selling. Every experienced mail-order man has at least one story like this.

6. Squeeze out every single *extra* word. Keep in mind that one extra word can cost you $500 in a year's time. Use figures instead of words ("50¢" for "fifty cents"). Leave out "the," "a," "an." But don't abbreviate, because a short word costs you as much as a long word. Long words help because they make the ad look bigger.

Use as much punctuation as possible to make the ad look exciting and big. Use quotation marks ("New Discovery"), dots ("Quick . . . Cheap . . . Powerful"), exclamation points (Now!!!).

Remember that publishers generally count each letter or group of letters as a word. ("Department J" is two words.) Hyphenated words usually count as two words, also. ("Do-It-Yourself" is three words.)

7. After that, you're on your own. You will have to test new words and new ideas, to see if they increase your returns. Test action words, like "Write today." Test extra description words. Test new lead words. Test leaving out various words and ideas. Test everything, and keep testing, till you have really profitable copy. Then test some more. See Chapters 9 and 18 for instructions on how to test.

HOW LONG SHOULD THE CLASSIFIED AD BE?

When asked how long an ad should be, advertising men like to paraphrase A. Lincoln's famous remark: The ad should be long enough to do the job. The advice is sage, but not very helpful except to point out that the best length for an ad must differ from situation to situation.

Properly, the length of an ad is determined by these two factors:

1. *The ad must be long enough to tell the basic story.* If any crucial element is left out, the ad will fail completely. For example, if you do not include enough description of the product so that readers understand what it is you are selling, you make no sales at all. Telling the reader what the product will do *for* him may be a crucial element. Telling him the product is new may also be crucial.

2. *"The more you tell, the more you sell."* Assuming that all the crucial elements are present, further sales talk will increase sales to *some* extent. The problem is to determine *how* much more than the crucial elements it is profitable to pile into the ad.

Not only does each extra sales word increase your sales somewhat, but the sheer size of an ad affects its selling power. In other words, even if you just added neutral dummy words like "the," "and so forth," "Now Now Now Now," etc., you would probably increase sales somewhat. But dummy words seldom or never increase sales *sufficiently* to make them profitable.

You can find the best size of your particular ad only by actual testing. Try an ad 50 percent longer than your basic ad. Try another ad 100 percent longer. Try a third ad that leaves out some of the elements in your basic ad. Then calculate which ad is most profitable. Then and only then will you know the best size.

If you find that the bigger ad is more profitable, then try an even bigger ad. If the smaller ad is more profitable, try an even smaller ad.

This is how you *calculate* which is the most profitable advertisement:

1. Figure how much you net on each *sale*, exclusive of advertising cost. Take everything into account, including labor, *but exclude advertising cost.* If a pamphlet sells for $1, and printing, binding, etc., costs 10 cents, outgoing postage 6 cents, clerical labor (including your own) is 5 cents, reserve for refunds is 3 cents, labels, envelopes, other costs are 8 cents, adding to 32 cents, then $1 less 32 cents equals 68 cents net, exclusive of advertising cost.

2. Determine how many *more* orders the bigger ad brings in than does your basic ad, and multiply by the 32 cents net. (In other words, if the big ad brings in 80 more orders than the little ad, multiply 80 × 32¢ which equals $25.60.)

3. Calculate how much more the bigger ad costs than the basic ad. (In other words, cost of big ad minus cost of small ad.)

4. If the cost in 3 is less than the extra net in 2, then the bigger ad is profitable. Otherwise, run the basic smaller ad.

You should understand very clearly that an ad twice as long (and therefore twice as costly) as your basic ad definitely does *not* have to bring in twice as many orders to be more profitable. Wrong figuring will lead you to lose much profit. The *only* correct way to figure is the way set forth above.

9

How to Test and Run Classified Ads

*Where and How to Test • How Much to Spend
for Tests • How to Interpret Test Results • The
Second Round of Testing • Where to Run Your
Ads • When to Run Your Ad • How Often to Run
Classified Ads • How to "Classify" a Classified
Ad • Extra Gold from the Classified Mine*

WHERE AND HOW TO TEST YOUR CLASSIFIED OFFER AND ADVERTISEMENT

We assume that by now you have chosen your product, and you have decided whether you will offer it in one step or two steps. You have selected the price you will try first. Next you must find out whether your product will make money, and how and where it will make the most money. In other words, you need to place "test" ads.

This section discusses how, where, and when to place test ads, and how to interpret their results. The following sections discuss how to write a classified ad, and how large it should be.

How to Place a Classified Ad

By now you should have rate cards for all the classified media. Chapter 11 tells you how to read the rate card to find out the cost per word, where to send the ad, and when the closing and publication dates are. That section also tells you how to read information from the *Standard Rate & Data* publications.

Chapter 21 tells you how to set up an advertising agency through

ORDER BLANK FOR PUBLICATIONS
(COPYRIGHT OCTOBER 1956)

JULIAN SIMON ASSOCIATES
972 BROAD STREET
NEWARK, N. J.
MITCHELL 2-6766

☐ IF CHECKED HERE THIS IS A SPACE CONTRACT

[X] IF CHECKED HERE, THIS IS AN INSERTION ORDER

TO PUBLISHER OF SATURDAY REVIEW
25 West 45th Street
CITY AND STATE New York 36, New York

NO 1759

DATE November 12, 1962

PLEASE PUBLISH ADVERTISING OF (advertiser) Custombland Company
FOR (product) Coffee

SPACE	TIMES	DATES OF INSERTION
Classified	2	Next two open issues (Dec 3 and 10?)

FREE COFFEE Booklet. "All About Coffee". Sampler: Eight quarter-pounds originating different countries $2.75 (guaranteed!). Custombland, 28-CSR22, Millburn, New Jersey

POSITION
Personal

COPY KEY
Key CSR23 second insertion

CUTS

ADDITIONAL INSTRUCTIONS

RATE
$.55 per word, 19 words

LESS AGENCY COMMISSION 15 PER CENT ON GROSS

LESS CASH DISCOUNT 2 PER CENT ON NET

SAMPLE ONLY

JULIAN SIMON ASSOCIATES PER Julian L. Simon
NEWARK, N. J.

Order Blank for Publications Copyright October, 1956. American Association of Advertising Agencies, Inc. (OVER)

FIG. 9-1

which you can receive credit and place ads at a discount. It also tells you how to choose an advertising agency that will help you with your ads.

But at the beginning it will be sensible to send your ads directly to the media, at full card rates. You can simply type (or write, if necessary) your advertisement and instructions for proper classification, and send it in with your check to the magazine. The magazine will take care of the rest for you.

If you want to get really professional, or if you want to try to establish your own "house" agency, you can have standard (AAAA) forms printed up by offset, for $10 or $11 dollars for a thousand (two sides). See Chapter 21 for more information about how to go about it. Figure 9-1 shows a filled-out copy of the standard form.

The Quick Test

Time is important. You are always in a hurry to find out how good your product is, so that you can quickly increase your volume to profitable levels. Therefore, you want to test your ads in media that will give you quick information about how good your offer is.

Capper's Weekly, Grit, and the *National Enquirer* are favorite testing media for classified advertisers. In *Capper's* you can reliably test any offer for the farm market. *Grit* gives you a test of rural, small-town, family readers. The *National Enquirer* tests the less stable, thrill-seeking, alienated, portions of the lower economic classes who are also the readers of the important Exposure, Romance, Men's Detective, etc., magazines.

The virtue of these test media is that no more than two or three weeks elapse between the time you place the ad and the time the ad appears. And within a week of publication you have sufficient results to predict accurately how your test will turn out (see Chapter 11 for details on how to predict quickly). Compare this with the requirement of some media for copy three months before publication, and from which the returns come in so slowly that another two months may elapse before you have enough data to draw a conclusion.

Many of the farm papers have relatively short closing dates, and some of them—*Rural New Yorker,* for example—are good test media for general products.

HOW MUCH TO SPEND FOR TESTS?

Chapter 18 gives you the full story on testing. Read it before starting your advertising campaign.

You must understand that the information you get from a test is worth money. It is often profitable and necessary to run a test ad even if you have to send back all the money you receive. And it is common practice, though perhaps not strictly ethical, to place ads before you have the merchandise.

Your test must produce enough results so that the conclusions you base on the ad will be fairly accurate. A rule of thumb: you must usually spend at least $10 in advertising for your first classified test of a product, *or* an offer, or a piece of copy. That means two $5 tests, one $10 test, etc., for each offer *or* piece of copy, etc. A smaller test volume than that will not give you enough information about whether even to test further.

HOW TO INTERPRET TEST RESULTS

So you have placed your test ads, and the results are coming in. On the basis of the partial results, you estimate the total orders or inquiries you will receive. Use the tables in Chapter 11 to make that prediction.

Remember that the prediction will not be perfect. First of all, the tables are imperfect. Furthermore, you should modify the tables for classified advertising because classified responses tend to come in faster than display ads (perhaps because it is easier to cut out a display ad and save it for awhile).

Your results may be higher or lower than they "should" be because of sheer chance (see Chapter 18 to figure how accurate your prediction is likely to be). You must also take into account the seasonal variation from month to month when interpreting your test results.

Then you must decide, on the basis of your predicted results, whether the test is a success or a failure. Chapter 11 will help you decide. These are some very rough rules of thumb:

1. If you are selling a manufactured product for $5 to $25, you must take in at least three times the cost of the advertising.

2. For printed products in which the cost of the material is very slight, dollar results more than twice the cost of advertising should be solidly profitable, but under 1½ times the cost of advertising you will probably lose money.

3. Fifteen cents per inquiry is a fair cost for a $2 to $3 item.

4. A dollar per inquiry is a fair cost for a $50 item or for agents.

These rules of thumb assume that you can improve your advertising and your offer after your test ads.

Calculating the success or failure of a repeat-sale product is more complicated. Chapter 15 tells more about this.

You should also make an adjustment to your results to account for the fact that media like *National Enquirer* and *Capper's* will both pull more volume per dollar than most other media you will use. (That's why they carry so much classified advertising.)

THE SECOND ROUND OF TESTING

Many a man has lost his shirt because he went pell-mell ahead with a full campaign on the basis of one or two test ads. Don't let it happen to you.

If your first ad (or ads) makes you think that your offer is profitable, you should then expand your schedule to run perhaps three or four times as much advertising (measured in dollars) as your first test. Go into several different *kinds* of magazines that may be good prospects, rather than sticking to one type. For example, if you tested in *Capper's* don't stick to farm magazines when you retest. If it seems at all sensible to do so, try perhaps *Popular Science, Successful Farming, Grit,* and *Sports Afield,* in addition to several state farm magazines. If your offer looks definitely profitable, follow the instructions in the rest of this chapter.

WHERE TO RUN YOUR ADS

Let's assume you have already tested your offer in one or more of the magazines mentioned in the previous section. The results are promising, and you now want to make some real money by advertising in every medium that will be profitable.

Your next move is to test the various *categories* of magazines that seem promising for your offer. Here are category breakdowns that you can use:

Men's mass-circulation magazines (including Publisher's Men's Monthly, Publisher's Men's Bimonthly, Publishers Exposure, and Quality Men's)
Women's mass-circulation magazines (including Publisher's Women's Monthly, Publisher's Women's Bimonthly, and Quality Women's)
General (including Quality Fraternal)
Better men's magazines (including Mechanics and Fishing and Hunting magazines)
Farm magazines and papers
Specialty and Hobby magazines
Salesman's magazines
Magazines under 50,000 circulation

Try magazines under 50,000 circulation *last.* They give you the least profit for your time and labor. They seem to work for some offers. But wait until you know your offer is thoroughly profitable before trying them.

If you have an item that appeals to men, try the better men's magazines before the "mass" men's magazines, because their closing dates are shorter.

If your offer pays off in the one or two magazines you test in any category, advertise in *all* the magazines in that category immediately. If you are a more cautious person, advertise in the best half of the magazines in that category (those magazines with the biggest classified sections). But never place an ad until you have examined the classified section of that magazine and found that it contains other similar advertisements.

At the same time that you are spreading your offer into all the magazines *within* groups, test out other groups. A profitable offer will make money in some very unlikely places. Some offers to women have done very well in the mechanics and fishing and hunting magazines (under "Of Interest to Women").

At all times keep your eye on the big media, especially Publishers Classified. The few big media are worth ten or twenty times as much attention you pay to other media.

Appendix I lists the various classified media and the relevant data on them.

WHEN TO RUN YOUR AD

Some months of the year are better for mail order than others. Chapter 12 gives you a table that helps predict how good the various months will be, for products that are not themselves seasonal. (Swimming equipment will naturally do better in spring and summer than in fall and winter, and you would not use the table for such a product.)

The most general ranking of the months, from best to worst, is: January, February, March, October, November, September, August, April, May. December is worst for some offers, not quite so bad for others.

Remember that the figures in the table in Chapter 12 refer to *issues of magazines,* and not to the number of replies you will receive in *calendar months.* For example, the May issue may do far worse than the September issue, but you may get more replies from *all* your ads in May than in September. Remember also that the month refers to the time the magazine really *appears,* and not to the "cover date" of the magazine.

Unless your ads are pulling very well indeed, you probably should schedule no ads from May to August, and none in December unless you have a gift item. If you figure you can make money on the ad even if replies are only *half* of what they are in the best month, then it is safe to plan ads for the low months.

The summer is worse for one-shot items than for repeat or two-stage-inquiry propositions, because the media cost is only a small part of the total selling cost for a follow-up business. The other costs—follow-up letters, postage, labor—will remain more or less proportional to replies received, all year round. So, the smaller your media advertising is as a percentage of total selling cost, the safer it is to keep advertising during the summer.

CAUTION: Be especially careful your first summer in the business. Taking losses can be very discouraging, indeed.

HOW OFTEN TO RUN CLASSIFIED ADS

It is generally true that if your offer is good enough to make any profit at all, it will be profitable to run the ad in every consecutive issue of *monthly* magazines, with the exception of the low months.

Don't worry about results dropping off in monthly magazines. If there is any dropoff, it will be slight, and results will soon reach a plateau. New competition is a much greater danger than dropoff, and you must grab your profit while the field is still relatively clear.

The reason why classified ads are so immune to dropoff is that only a small portion of the readership reads the ad in any one issue. Each issue leaves the reservoir of potential customers almost untouched. The slight decline in that reservoir is offset by the changing readership of the magazine.

Here's why it pays to run in every issue even if there is some dropoff. Compare these two plans of action, assuming that dropoff is *much greater* than it will be for most classified ads:

Issue	1	2	3	4	Profit
Plan A cost..........	$20	Not Run	$20	Not Run	
Plan A net revenue*...	$50	...	$50		
Plan A profit.........	$30	Not Run	$30	Not Run	$60 Total
Plan B cost..........	$20	$20	$20	$20	
Plan B net revenue*...	$50	$45	$42.50	$42.50	
Plan B profit.........	$30	$25	$22.50	$22.50	$100 Total

* By "net revenue" I mean the amount of revenue that is left after all costs except advertising have been subtracted.

You can see that Plan B earns $100 profit while Plan A earns $60 profit, even though Plan A's rate of return on the invested capital is higher.

Furthermore, in view of the small amount of dropoff in the monthly magazines, you can run the same ad over and over again *without changing it*. Another reason for not changing the ad is that the attention-getting element is what you usually change in display ads, and this element is a less important part of the classified advertisement.

Dropoff will be least in magazines that are sold mostly on newsstands. If you run a classified ad so large that dropoff might be a factor, the potential trouble spots will be in *all-subscription* magazines like Fraternal publications and Religious magazines.

I have found no sign of appreciable dropoff for a ten-word ad I ran in *American Legion Magazine* for many consecutive months, even though it is 100 percent subscription. (The results were standardized for seasonal variation in this comparison.)

"Till-Forbid" Orders and When to Use Them

Placing an insertion order for an ad takes quite a little clerical time for you, and for the magazine, too. The paper shuffling, typing, and filing consumes enough time so that if you had to make a new insertion each time an ad ran, it would not be economical to run any ads that cost less than perhaps $10 per month, and the profit on all ads would be cut sadly.

The situation is much the same at the magazines.

The "till-forbid" order solves this problem. Once you have tested your offer and your copy enough to feel sure that it is profitable, you then tell the magazine to run the ad *automatically* each month until you tell them to stop ("till-forbid," or "TF"). Each month they push the key number forward in accordance with instructions you give them.

Not only does this procedure save you the cost of labor, but it saves advertising costs as well. Because repeating a TF order saves them money, many magazines pass on the savings to you by giving you a discount on repeated insertions of the same copy.

It is not wise to place TF orders until you are *quite sure* that your offer and copy are as good as you can get them. Not only is it laborious to kill a lot of TF orders and to place new ones, but you increase your risk of making costly mistakes of duplication and omission.

HOW TO "CLASSIFY" A CLASSIFIED AD

The idea behind classified ads is that the classified section is like a department store. People look at the department (classification) which carries the particular product they are interested in. A man who wants to buy a cow looks under "Livestock" and a man who wants to make extra money looks under "Business Opportunities."

That's why it is important to place your ad under the classification that most of your potential customers will look at.

The best classification to try first is the classification that your competitors use. Don't make the mistake of thinking that that classification is "occupied." (Notice that competitors use different classification headings in different magazines.) Once you are well established, you can test other classifications. Your competitors don't have *all* the answers, either. (But they must know how to learn by experience and be right *most* of the time or they would be out of business.)

When there is not enough competition to provide guidance for you, or when you are testing media in which the product is new, you must use your common sense. Look for the *special* interest of the product. You will find that it pays to run a product under a specific relevant heading, rather than under a more general heading of "miscellaneous." For example, a hypnotism manual will do better under "Hypnotism" than under "Books and Education" or "Miscellaneous." The specific heading will do better even though the overall readership is lower. In the table below you can see that the readership in the "Tobacco, Smoker's Supplies" heading is only two-thirds of that in "Miscellaneous." But those who sell tobacco have evidently found that the former category is better for them.

Readership in Some Classified Categories[1]

Readex Survey in Popular Mechanics

"Tobacco, Smokers Supplies".......... 12%
"For Sale—Miscellaneous".............. 16%
"Wanted—Miscellaneous".............. 12%
"Miscellaneous"....................... 18%
"Personal"............................ 12%

These figures also suggest that if your common sense tells you that your offer belongs under *either* "Personal" or "Miscellaneous," you should try "Miscellaneous" first.

If the magazine has no heading that is specific for your product, ask them to put one in. The heading acts like a very powerful lead word. The magazine may ask you to pay extra for the special heading, and often it is worth the extra cost.

If two headings are quite similar—"Money-making Opportunities" and "Business Opportunities," for example—try first one, then the other, to see which does better.

If two classifications seem otherwise alike, the one that comes first in the classified section has an advantage. "Additional Income" comes first in *Spare Time*, and is better for some products than "Business Opportunities."

Because of the position advantage, some publishers—especially Publisher's Classified Department—alternate the order in which the classifications appear from month to month. But some of these publishers will honor a request if you name two alternate classifications and specify "whichever comes first."

You should also see to it that magazines give you a fair shake in putting you before your competitors a good part of the time. But don't expect to rate with the competitor who has run steadily for years, until you have proved you are a steady customer, too.

I offered a product every single week in *Saturday Review*. I alternated between "For the Gourmet" and "Personals." The results continued quite satisfactory. I did not test this alternation against keeping the ad under one heading each week. But since the ad pulls equally well under each heading, we could not *logically* expect any possible improvement from staying under one heading only.

The equality of results under the two headings is curious and interesting. It could be due to one of these factors:

1. The product is not extremely specialized or particularly relevant to gourmets.

2. *Saturday Review* readers could be such avid classified readers that they read *all* classified ads.

3. Sheer scientific coincidence could explain it, too.

EXTRA GOLD FROM THE CLASSIFIED MINE

As we said before, the great disadvantage of classified is the limited number of media available in which a given offer can make a profit. And so, classified advertisers must make maximum use of the most profitable media by running two or more ads under different headings in the same issues.

You can increase your profit by running two or more ads *if, and only if,* these conditions hold for a magazine:

1. The magazine must carry three or more full pages of classified ads. The Mechanics magazines, Fishing and Hunting magazines, and *Workbasket* are some of the few magazines in this category.

2. The magazine must have over 300,000 circulation, preferably much of it in newsstand sales.

3. Previous insertions of the ad must have pulled almost *twice as many* replies as the ad needed to break even. This figure includes a slight margin to allow for imperfect calculation of response.

The second ad will *not* double your response, and the third ad will not *triple* it. Two ads should produce perhaps one and a half times the response to a single ad. The reduced response to the second ad is partly the result of the second ad being placed under the second choice of classification headings.

Until you have considerable experience with your offer, and with classified advertising generally, you will be wise to run a second ad only in magazines where other advertisers run more than one ad.

Some multiple-ad advertisers use the same wording in all the ads, while others use different copy. If different wordings are equally good, they stand an increased chance of attracting more total readers. But you must *test* several times to be sure that the second piece of copy is as good as the first.

Multiple insertions may also be used as a means of testing copy. You run both ads in two successive issues, reversing the classifications under which they appear. For example, the first month Copy A runs under "Business Opportunities," and Copy B runs under "Educational." In the second issue they reverse: Copy B runs under "Business Opportunities" and Copy A under "Educational." Then you can compare to determine which copy is better and which classification is better.

10

How to Key, and How to Keep Advertising Records

How to Key a Magazine Advertisement • How to Key Direct Mail • Record Keeping

Writers on mail order often state flatly that a post office box number produces fewer orders than a street address. But I have never seen any *evidence* on this. It is *probably* true that if you ask for money in the ad, and if the ad is small enough to look insubstantial, a *high* box number in a *big city* might reduce response. But other than that, I'll bet it doesn't matter *what* address you use.

The lower the number of the box or drawer, the better. In general, a low number sounds impressive and old, while a high number sounds anonymous. But more than that, a number in two digits makes some kinds of keying easier than three or four digits (one digit is even easier).

HOW TO KEY A MAGAZINE ADVERTISEMENT

These are the jobs that the key and address in a mail-order ad must do:

1. The key must indicate clearly which ad the customer is answering.

2. *The key must be easy to identify by clerical help.* What *not* to do is illustrated by the advertisers who used to key with the material on the back of the coupons. The editorial or advertising matter was different for each coupon, all right. But the clerk who recorded the key had to remember the back of each coupon, or compare it to a sample. That was a slow, expensive process. And some people send in the coupon pasted to a sheet of paper!

3. *The key must make it easy for magazines to advance the key each month,* in order that you have a separate record for each issue. Some advertisers key by using only a different name in each magazine. This practice is not wise unless you already know the results from the magazines so well that you don't need a monthly record.

4. *The key must make it easy to tabulate returns* in your media records. This means that you need some sort of alphabetical or numerical code in the key.

5. For classified ads only: *the key must use minimum word count.* The zone key (a fictitious number inserted between city and state) requires no word count at all in most magazines. Of course, it can be used only in cities that do not have postal zones. And it often gets too cumbersome. It is possible to use both letters and numbers in the zone key ("Zotzburg DF 22, New Jersey"). But this often gets cumbersome, looks a trifle ridiculous, and will end by the media demanding payment for it.

The Zip Code system will undoubtedly change this, sooner or later.

It may make sense to use the zone key for ads in classified groups. This can make a considerable saving at one fell swoop without much extra bother in tabulating.

The best system for classified ads that include a post office box number will be a single block of numbers using one of the key systems described below.

There are many methods of keying. You can use "Drawer," "Department," "Studio," "Room," or similar words, followed by the actual code. If you sell several products, you can use a different introductory word from the list above. This will ease your keying problems, and will speed the job of sorting the mail.

You can also use different street numbers, if you live in a small town, and if you get the postmaster's permission. Or you can address the mail to different first names. (But if you are asking for money in the ad, you will need to stick to one name so you can deposit checks easily.)

The crucial problem is: What letters and numbers shall make up the key?

This is the solution I have found best: A typical key is "71-F233" as in "Samco, Drawer 71-F223, Hoboken, N.J.," the third ad in a series in *Field and Stream.*

"Drawer 71" is the number of the post office box.

"F22" stands for the magazine, and is established by referring to an alphabetical list of magazines. *Field and Stream* is the twelfth magazine alphabetically among the F's. (If a magazine is alphabetically between 1 and 9, it gets redesignated with a number from 91 to 99.) I use the *Standard Rate & Data* index list, but you can use any list, including the list of magazines found in Appendix I.

If the magazine is not on the list, it is designated 81, 82, etc. Or you can start your list with every other number, and fill in the spaces with unlisted magazines.

The "3" is for the third issue. The fifteenth issue becomes "F2215."

The major virtue of this system is that it permits records to be kept in the order in which keys are listed, and still in nearly alphabetical order. This eases the record keeping and tabulating in a great may ways that you won't appreciate until you have tried other keying systems.

This system also meets the other requirements cited above.

It *is* possible not to key each issue separately. This procedure saves some clerical labor in tabulation. But it loses much information that is extremely valuable unless you already have several years of experience with the media in question.

The crucial things in keying are:

1. *Don't forget to key.*
2. *Key correctly.*

It is usually in the very first ads for a product that you omit the key or you duplicate keys, because you have not yet set up a complete system. And unfortunately, it is those first ads that give you the most valuable information that your records can supply. So *don't forget to key,* and *key correctly.*

HOW TO KEY DIRECT MAIL

Direct-mail keying is easier than periodical keying, because the customer does not need to write down the key. You print or stamp the key on either the return envelope or the coupon that the customer sends back—a different key for each list you test. You can also code the key to show the date sent out.

An alphabetical key is still best, for the reasons mentioned above.

If you use a two-step selling system, you often want to key the follow-ups so you can know how many dollars each medium finally produces. The commonest and easiest system is to type the original incoming key onto the address label for the follow-ups. The address label is then placed on the order coupon, and arranged so that it shows through a window envelope. The date of receipt is also typed onto the address label in most cases.

As you examine samples of direct mail, you will notice examples of other types of keys.

RECORD KEEPING

The record sheets (Figs. 10-1 and 10-2) that follow should be easy to understand.

DAILY RECORD SHEET

Product____________ Date__________ Sheet____________

Key	Inquiries	Conver-sions	Dollars			Key	Inquiries	Conver-sions	Dollars		
						No Key					
						No Key					
						No Key					
						TOTAL					
						Refunds					
						Gross Net					

FIG. 10-1

Advertising Record Sheet

Key__________ Publication______________ Date__________

Cost__________ Space__________ Price__________

	Jan	Feb	Mar	Apr	May	June	July	Aug	Sept	Oct	Nov	Dec	
1													1
2													2
3													3
4													4
5													5
6													6
7													7
8													8
9													9
24													24
25													25
26													26
27													27
28													28
29													29
30													30
31													31

FIG. 10-2

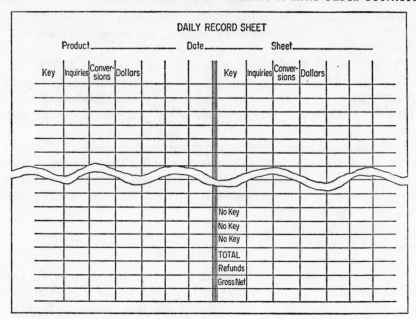

Each day you fill out a Daily Record Sheet for each product that you sell, classifying the letters by the key they show.

Then you prepare an Advertising Record Sheet for each advertisement you run.

Each day you transfer the results for each day from the Daily Record Sheet to the Advertising Record Sheet.

Keep the records clearly and up to date, and never throw them away. The Daily Record Sheet is especially valuable for income tax purposes.

11

Display-Advertising Procedure and Testing

How to Place an Ad • Exploratory Testing of Your Offer • How to Estimate Results Quickly • Have You Got a Winner? Standards for Decision

So you have a product and an offer that you think will do well in magazine display advertising! You think you're ready to get into print and into business. This chapter will guide you in your next steps.

We shall not discuss the arts of writing copy and laying out ads. Constructing display ads calls for competent professional skill. Amateur dabbling just won't get by. One solution is to use the services of an advertising agency. (See Chapter 21 on picking a *mail-order* advertising agency; avoid ordinary advertising men like the plague.) Or else you must make yourself into a copywriter of semiprofessional skill.

No short lesson can teach you to write good mail-order ads. If you want to learn how, get hold of *at least two* of the books listed below, and *study* them thoroughly. ("Study" means much more than "read." It means "read many times with very close attention.") And then you will need practice and more study to learn your trade. But it's worth it.

The following article packs more walloping know-how into seventeen short pages than does any other:

Victor O. Schwab, "Mail-order Copy and Headlines," in *Advertising Handbook,* Roger Barton (ed.)[1]

These books were written by truly great mail-order copywriters:

John Caples, *Tested Advertising Methods*[2]
Victor D. Schwab, *How to Write a Good Advertisement*[3]

These two volumes can help you give yourself a fine general education in writing advertising:

Clyde Bedell, *How to Write Advertising That Sells*[4]
G. B. Hotchkiss, *Advertising Copy*[5]

Even though we won't tackle the subject of stringing words together to sell goods by mail order, this chapter will include all the reported results of mail-order display-ad tests that I could find in writing or in my own records, and that are reasonably sound and valid.

HOW TO PLACE AN AD

If you use an agency, and if your account is sizable, an advertising agency will handle many or all of the technical problems for you. But the beginner—who needs help the most—has only a small account to offer an agency, and hence he gets little service from the agency. Therefore, whether you set up your own house agency, or whether you have an agency, you must know how to produce and place an ad.

Getting to be an agency is simple in principle, and not much harder in practice. All you need is a supply of insertion orders and stationery, plus recognition and credit from the media.

Remember to choose an agency name distinct from your mail-order firm name, in order to maintain the fiction of a separation. The media have no desire to ferret out the connection, because it might cost them business. But everyone concerned must join together in maintaining the phony appearance.

(Actually, there is some question whether media have the legal right to deny the same discount to direct advertisers as to agencies.)

Gaining recognition and credit with media is a bootstrap operation; if one magazine thinks that other media have given you credit, it will, too. So you have to develop a list of references. The newspapers are toughest on credit, perhaps because they have to wait longer for their money.

Start by merely sending off your ads, on regular agency forms, to the media you choose. If the magazine questions you, offer to pay in advance. That will almost surely end their squawks.

Once you have placed ads in several media, either on credit or with cash on the barrelhead, you can use those media as references. Just tell other magazines the names of the media in which you have placed ads. In a relatively short time, you will be able to satisfy all but the toughest credit managers.

I do not suggest that you seek recognition from the various media associations because I assume your assets are too limited to make a good showing. But if you can deposit a chunk of money in a separate checking account, and if you can claim some experience in marketing and advertising, you might try for formal recognition.

Reading a rate card and the Standard Rate & Data listings is confusing at first, but really quite easy. Two rate cards are shown on the following pages.

The *Spare Time* rate card practically duplicates its *Standard Rate & Data* listing.

Your Romance Group is composed of two magazines: *Your Romance* and *Thrilling Confessions.*

QUARTERLY

YOUR ROMANCE GROUP

Your Romance   **Thrilling Confessions**

32 West 22nd Street
New York 10, N. Y.
ORegon 5-3566

Rate Card No. 5
Effective
May-June, 1962 Issue

1—GENERAL ADVERTISING

a. Rate per line .... $ 2.00
b. Time discounts none.
c. One col. (140 lines) 200.00
   Half page (210 lines) ... 300.00

Full page (420 lines) $400.00
2nd cover, 1 color 500.00
3rd cover, 1 color 500.00
4th cover, 2 colors 600.00
Cover positions non-cancellable.

d. Minimum size of advertisements, 14 lines.
e. Orders specifying positions other than those known as preferred positions are not accepted.

2—READING NOTICES   (Not accepted)

3—COMMISSION AND CASH DISCOUNT

a. Agency commission 15%.
b. Cash discount 2%—10 days.

c. The cash discount is allowed for payments on or before due date.

Neither agent's commission nor cash discount allowed after that date.

4—MECHANICAL REQUIREMENTS

Pages are 3 columns wide by 140 lines deep; 420 lines to the page.

1 page ....7″ x 10″
½ page ....7″ x 5″
1 column ....2¼″ x 10″

Insides printed in offset, no cuts necessary.
Original photographs of drawings give best results.
Advertisements containing cuts, black-faced type, borders, etc., are subject to publishers changes and resetting.

Ad copy due the 5th day of 6th month preceding cover date. For example, copy for Feb.-Mar., 1960 is due August 5, 1960.

Covers and inside printed in offset . . . Original copy required in one piece.

5—CIRCULATION

a. Locality of Circulation—National. Guaranteed — 300,000 yearly average.

6—MISCELLANEOUS

a. We reserve the right to refuse any advertisement we deem unsuitable.
b. We assume no responsibilities for errors in key numbers and will allow no deductions on this ground.
c. Rates subject to change without notice.
d. Contract and Copy Regulations: Advertisements containing personal references, names or pictures of living per-

sons are acceptable for publication by the Publishers, but only on the absolute representation that the Agency or Advertiser submitting the same have the written consent of said person involved to publish the same, and the Advertiser and the Agency jointly and severally agree to indemnify the Publisher for any damage and legal expenses sustained by the Publisher arising out of said publication.

New York	Published by	Chicago
Harold Hammond	Crestwood Publishing Co., Inc.	Chas. B. Stearns, Jr.
32 West 22nd St.	32 West 22nd St.	35 East Wacker Dr.
New York 10, N. Y.	New York 10, N. Y.	Chicago 1, Ill.
ORegon 5-3566		ANdover 3-2240

FIG.   11-1

4630 West Burleigh Street
Milwaukee 10, Wisconsin
Telephone Hilltop 5-6350

Rate Card No. 4b
Issued June 1, 1958
Effective Sept., 1958 issue

SPARE TIME
THE MAGAZINE OF
MONEY-MAKING OPPORTUNITIES

Published 4 times a year
FEBRUARY • MARCH
SEPTEMBER • OCTOBER
500,000 copies per issue

MAILING INSTRUCTIONS

Send all production materials (copy, plates, etc.) to 4630 West Burleigh Street, Milwaukee 10, Wisconsin.

1 — PERSONNEL

President & Publisher — Harvey R. Kipen
Vice-President — Michael Ivers
Secretary & Treasurer — Betty Hinz

2 — REPRESENTATIVES

None.

3 — COMMISSION AND CASH DISCOUNT

a. Agency commission, 15% on display and classified.
b. Cash discount, 2% on net.
c. Bills rendered 5 days after mailing of an issue begins. For example: Mailing of the February issue begins January 15; bills rendered January 20. Cash discount date, 10 days from date of invoice.

4 — GENERAL

a. Rates subject to change without notice except on contracts which have been accepted and acknowledged by the publisher.
b. Advertising which is either objectionable or misleading in the opinion of the publisher is not accepted.
c. Orders specifying "editorial support" — not accepted.

5 — GENERAL ADVERTISING RATES

1 page (224 lines)	$1650.00
½ page (112 lines)	868.00
¼ page (56 lines)	454.00
1 inch	119.00
Agate line	8.50
2 page spread	$3135.00

Advertisements other than standard units charged for on the following basis:

56 to 98 lines, per line	$8.10
112 to 196 lines, per line	7.75
Over 224 lines, per line	7.37

No frequency discounts.

6 — DISPLAY CLASSIFICATIONS

None.

7 — COVERS

Back cover (2 colors) $1980.00

8 — COLOR

Red, per page, extra	$120.00
Red, smaller units, extra	100.00
Special color, per page, extra	150.00

9 — INSERTS, GATE-FOLDS

Rates on request.

10 — BLEED OR OVERSIZED PLATES

Cannot handle outside bleed. Mechanical requirements for gutter bleed (2 page spread) on request.

11 — SPECIAL POSITIONS

No extra charge. Requests for special position will be granted when available according to space and date of order. Bigger space users get first priority.

12—CLASSIFIED, READING NOTICES, SPLIT RUNS

a. Classified: per word, $2.00. Minimum space accepted, 15 words — $30.00. First line set in Caps. All copy set solid without display, leaded or blank spaces. Name, address and key numbers must be included at regular rate. Remittance in full must accompany all classified orders unless placed by recognized advertising agency.
b. Reading notices not accepted.
c. Split runs — information on request.

13 — CONTRACT AND COPY REGULATIONS

a. Copy must be received by closing date in order to get proofs for approval.
b. Publisher does not assume responsibility for errors in key number and no allowances or deductions are given for such errors.
c. No accounts opened except with recognized advertising agencies. Cash must accompany orders unless credit has been established.

14 — MINIMUM DEPTH — ROP

1 column, 7 lines; double column, 14 lines.

15 — MECHANICAL REQUIREMENTS

a. Publication trim size: 6⅞ x 9⅞".
b. Standard units in inches:

	Width - Depth
Full page	5½" x 8"
½ page	5½" x 4"
½ page	2⅝" x 8"
¼ page	5½" x 2"
¼ page	2⅝" x 4"
One inch	2⅝" x 1"

c. Width of column: 2⅝"; double column, 5½".
d. Depth of column: 112 lines.
e. Pages are 2 columns, 224 lines to a page.
f. Halftones, 85 screen.
g. Kind of printing: letterpress.
h. To insure best printing, supply original halftones, etched deep and open. Can use mats. Stereos billed at cost.
i. Publisher assumes no responsibility for cuts uncalled for 6 months after date of insertion.

16 — ISSUANCE, CLOSING AND CANCELLATION DATES

a.

Issue	Mailing Begins	Closes
February	Jan. 15	Dec. 10
March	Feb. 15	Jan. 10
September	Aug. 15	July 10
October	Sept. 15	Aug. 10

b. Mailed at rate of approximately 50,000 copies per day. Complete mailing of an issue (500,000 copies) takes about two weeks.
c. Cancellations not accepted after closing date.

17 — CIRCULATION INFORMATION

a. Character of circulation is among men (85%) and women (15%) who are known to be looking for opportunities to make money in spare or full time, either as sales people or as operators of small, independent businesses.
b. Source of circulation: names drawn for each issue from carefully selected lists of new, fresh names known to have answered specific ads.
c. Locality of circulation: national.
d. Rates based upon a guaranteed circulation of 500,000 copies per issue.
e. Publisher supplies photostatic copy of postal receipt when requested by advertiser.
f. Subscriptions: 4 issues for 50¢; single copy, 15¢. Mailed free to selected readers.

18 — MISCELLANEOUS

a. Established 1955.
b. Published by Kipen Publishing Corp., 744 No. Fourth Street, Milwaukee 3, Wisconsin.
c. Member: National Association of Direct Selling Companies.

(Standard Form of Rate Card recommended by the American Association of Advertising Agencies, Inc.)

SPARE TIME
THE MAGAZINE OF
MONEY-MAKING OPPORTUNITIES

• 2 million copies per year
• Most comprehensive coverage of direct selling prospects
• Lowest cost per thousand in the field
• Results are outstanding!

FIG. 11-2

These are the items of special interest to you:

The Cost per Agate Line. There are fourteen agate lines to the inch. Notice the decreasing cost per line as you take larger units of space. Some magazines offer much greater discounts than others do.

The price of space is theoretically the same to all comers. However, "distress covers"—covers that remain unsold at the last minute—are sold at a cut price to major mail-order advertisers. Other special deals are also made from time to time.

There are discounts for repeated insertions in many magazines.

Theoretically, the price of space also remains the same all year round. But the publishers are well aware that mail-order results drop off drastically in the summer, and many of them offer special summer rate reductions. Three insertions for the price of two is a common inducement to advertise in the poorer months.

Size of the Circulation. Usually you will decide about a magazine without considering the circulation, solely on the basis of the other ads it carries. If, however, your product requires merely huge numbers of readers, examine the ratio of cost-per-line/circulation. Fifty cents per line per 100,000 readers is the going price for totally unspecialized, low-class magazines, good for many mail-order products. Specialized magazines may get as much as $3.20 per line per 100,000 (*Popular Photography,* for example).

Type of Circulation—Newsstand or Subscription. Magazines whose circulation is almost entirely by subscription distribute almost the same number of copies every month, whereas newsstand magazines sell fewer in summer. The readers of subscription magazines are the same people, month after month. Different people buy at newsstands from month to month, increasing the relevant circulation for the mail-order advertiser who advertises in consecutive months. Still another difference is that returns come in slower for newsstand magazines.

Method of Printing. *Spare Time* is printed letterpress and requires a plate, or you can send copy. *Your Romance* Group specifies offset, and requires reproduction proofs or material "ready for camera."

Width of Column. The column width determines the layout you must send. But it also affects how much you pay per inch. The wider the column, the fewer the inches of space you require to tell your story.

Editorial Mention. Item 4 on the *Spare Time* card is an interesting item. It suggests how prevalent is the practice of making deals for editorial mention along with the advertising space purchased.

Advertising Representatives. Many mail-order magazines solicit advertising through independent agents known as publisher's representatives. Work through them whenever possible.

Closing Date and Publication Date. The *Your Romance* card teaches you how to calculate the correct dates. The actual publication date is important because it determines whether the month will be good or poor for mail orders. The lag between closing date and publication date is the period you will have to wait for results from the medium.

If you have a small ad, you can sometimes get the ad into a magazine after the listed closing date. Call the representative to find out if the issue is still open, or send the order in specifying the exact issue you want to be in, even if it is past the closing date.

EXPLORATORY TESTING OF YOUR OFFER

Even though you know that a competitor is making money with an offer, you can't be sure that your ad will make money until you try it. Even if you run in the same media that he does, you may not make money, if (1) your ad is inferior to his, or (2) the market is too small to support both of you.

Some sharp mail-order men check on the power of their advertisement compared to the competitor's by running an ad identical to the competitor's—changing only the name and address—and comparing the results to their own ad's results. This practice *might* be considered either unethical or illegal, however.

Ideally you will run your first ad in a medium that (1) is used by your competitor and (2) has a short closing date so that you can get quick results. The time of the year doesn't matter much because you can use the information in Chapter 12 to predict how the ad will do in other months of the year on the basis of any month's results.

How do you find the media in which the competition runs his ads? By intensive study of mail-order media, of course.

The competition may not run in any short-closing medium, however, and you still need a quick test. So you will run a test in a short-closing medium anyway. The results will still give you a good idea of how good your ad is.

The best short-closing media for your product will depend on the offer, of course. If the product is a novelty or style item, the magazine sections of the Sunday papers will be a likely bet. The *New York Times Magazine* is the standard test medium for such outfits as Spencer Gifts, Sunset House, and Walter Drake. See *Standard Rate & Data* and our Appendix I for the names of other Sunday newspaper magazines. The closing date for these magazines is two to four weeks before publication.

Other kinds of offers will do better in the regular mail-order sections of the Sunday papers, *Capper's Weekly* (which has a special low test rate), *Grit,* or the *National Enquirer.*

The *National Enquirer* is the favorite testing place for off-color or "private" offers related to sex, hypnotism, patent medicines, etc.

The Sunday papers are extremely discriminating about the ads they accept. They find many mail-order propositions objectionable and refuse to carry them. However, if *The New York Times* accepts your proposition, most of the others will, too. So sometimes it pays to try the *Times* first and convince them. Then you're in.

Your first ads will probably be bigger than later ads, because you don't want to risk leaving anything out of the ad that will cause a flop. After you have found a successful combination you can sharpen up and compress your copy, find the most economical layout, and generally refine the ad.

Your first ad should be *approximately* the size of the competing ads. In other words, if the competition runs 4-inch, one-column ads, you will probably run 3- to 6-inch ads, rather than a full page or a 1-inch ad.

Your exploratory ads will probably be all type and no artwork, if the product is a book, or a course, or anything that doesn't absolutely require a picture to sell it. All-type ads can almost always do a *satisfactory* job, though artwork may make the ad much more profitable. Your test media usually will set all-type ads for you without extra charge. Artwork, plates, and typographer's type for a fancier ad often cost more than it pays to spend while you are still in the experimental stage.

HOW TO ESTIMATE RESULTS QUICKLY

If you had all the time in the world, mail order could be almost a sure thing for you. At each step along the way you could wait until you were absolutely sure you had enough information before taking the next step. Of course you would always take the risk that just when you were finally about to go ahead full steam, a faster-footed competitor would swing in and pick up all the marbles.

The mail-order professional doesn't wait to proceed until he is sure. He can't afford to. He has to get plenty of ads running in a short time so that he can produce volume and profit. He therefore must take risks by acting on insufficient information.

A man's ability to take risks smartly *and* boldly determines how well he will do in mail order. The fellow with no guts doesn't have to be so shrewd to make money, but he'll only make peanuts. The fellow with guts and bad judgment will lose his shirt. Only the operator with courage *and* judgment can make a pile. In this respect mail order is like all other businesses, but much more so.

This gives an advantage to the beginner who enters the mail-order business in his spare time. He can take much more time between steps than the man who depends on mail order for his bread and butter. The extra information he gains by taking plenty of time offsets his lack of knowledge and experience—at least partly—and gives him a fighting chance to make money (a little bit, anyway), while he serves his apprenticeship.

First you must estimate, when a small part of the returns are in, how well an ad will have pulled when *all* the returns have come in. Then you must estimate how well the ad will do in future insertions in the same medium and in other media, based upon the guess in the first part of the estimate.

Now we shall talk about how to guess the total results on the basis of the early results. Remember that, like any other scientific estimate, the estimate must be only approximate. The accuracy of the guess will depend upon the amount of information you have available, and upon how shrewd you are at considering all the pertinent circumstances.

Table 11-1 summarizes the prediction tables given by several writers on the mail-order business. The elapsed time in each case dates from the day the first inquiry is received, except as noted. The numbers indicate the total percent of responses received by the end of a time period.

Baker says that many of his clients report faster returns than the figures he shows. By my findings he seems very slow, too. Cates' data is old, so don't rely on it very much.

Sumner says that the method of distribution has a particularly large effect on return rates in the women's-service-magazine category. He shows these data:[14]

	10 days	30 days	60 days	90 days	1 year
Subscription.........	32.9	66.5	82.0	88.3	98.4
Newsstand...........	13.3	51.4	81.7	87.0	97.8

In each of the schedules in Table 11-1, the figure given for "First week" means the number of returns in hand on the seventh day that returns came in.

But things are not so simple. The "first day" can mislead you. Frequently, an employee of a publication writes for the offer himself, weeks before the magazine has been distributed. Many mail-order men believe that when this happens, it is an infallible omen of good results. Maybe, but it certainly fouls up your prediction schedules. You can ignore returns that come in prior to magazine distribution. But remember that the distribution date varies from month to month, by as much as ten days. Remember also that some magazines mail their subscription copies over a period of many days. The magazines that go to direct salesmen, *Spare Time*, for example, mail over a fifteen-day period.

Returns vary by *type of product*. John Moran[15] asserts that the higher the unit of sale, the slower the returns, but I've seen no statistical evidence of this.

Table 11-1. Time Rates of Returns

Media	1st wk.	2d wk.	4th wk.	8th wk.	26th wk.	52d wk.
TV						
Baker[6]...........................	82	96	99	100		
Radio						
Baker...........................	80	94	99	100		
Daily newspaper						
Grant[7]...........................	90					
Baker...........................	42	78	95	98	100	
Cates[8]...........................	70	95	99	100		
Sunday news supplement						
Baker...........................	35	65	79	89	99	100
Graham[9]........................	[33% in first 4 days]					
Sumner[10]........................	[50% in first 4 days]					
Sunday predates						
Graham...........................	[50% in first 10 days]					
Weeklies						
Baker...........................	21	41	65	82	96	100
Graham...........................	33					
Simon (H. K.)[11]..................	30					
Cates...........................	41	78	96	100		
Segal (Alexander)[12]................	[20% in first 2 days, 33% in first 3 days, 50% in first 4 days]					
Biweeklies						
Baker...........................	15	30	60	77	93	100
Fraternal monthlies						
Baker...........................	7	28	61	83	99	100
Simon (J. L.).....................		35	67			
Monthly magazine shopping section						
Baker...........................	7	33	65	85	100	
General monthly magazine						
Grant...........................			60	75	96	
Baker...........................	5	18	45	68	91	100
Graham...........................	[50% in 1st month]					
All-newsstand monthlies						
Baker...........................	4	13	26	57	87	100
Segal...........................	25	[50% in 30 days]				
Salesmen's magazines						
Simon (J. L.).....................	60–70%					
All-newsstand bimonthlies						
Baker...........................	1	4	12	36	80	100
3rd-class direct mail						
Segal (Alexander).................	33	66	80	91		100
3rd-class direct mail to business firms						
Stone[13]...........................	49	81	[87%, 3rd week]			

Returns may vary by *size of ad.* I have observed that classified returns come in faster than display ads. A possible explanation: the bigger the ad, the easier it seems to be to clip it out and save it.

I'd suggest placing little faith in a prediction based on other people's schedules until you reach the point that should produce 50 percent of the returns. Once you have run ads for your own product, you will have the most accurate information for your purposes. The second time you run an ad in a magazine you should know within the first week or two how well the ad will pull. Another good trick is to compare the highest-return days of the two insertions. This high day will occur fairly early for non-newsstand media, usually. The comparison is usually not as accurate as a comparison of several weeks' totals, because it is based on relatively few returns. But it avoids the problem of when the "first day" is.

HAVE YOU GOT A WINNER? STANDARDS FOR DECISION

Let's say that you ran an ad in a Sunday newspaper magazine, and by twelve days after publication you have more than enough returns to cover all your investment including the cost of merchandise sold. In other words, returns for a week and a half bring you over the break-even point.

You then know that the ad will make a profit. And if you wait a reasonable length of time until you place your next ad, if the season is just as good, and if everything else is the same, a repeated ad in the same medium should also bring you a profit.

But you don't make much money running your ad in just one magazine. How will your ad do in other places?

There are a few experienced mail-order men who have enough know-how and guts to jump immediately into a wide range of media based on incomplete returns from a few test ads. But if you try this you'll lose your shirt.

The amateur has an advantage because he isn't in such a big rush to cash his chips, and therefore he can play safer.

Some first-test media can yield deceptive results. For example, offers tested in the *National Enquirer* sometimes do *twice as well* as they do anywhere else. In that case, you should proceed with extreme caution in entering other media unless the *National Enquirer* results are *more than twice the break-even point.*

On the other hand, tests in Sunday supplements will often give poorer results than will the shopping sections in the "shelter" magazine (for example, *House Beautiful*). That's why the shelter magazines run so many more mail-order ads than do the Sunday supplements. So even if your test results in the Sunday supplement are only "almost profitable," you *may* have a winner elsewhere—especially if you can improve the ad.

Your next step will be to insert your ad in two or more additional media, probably of different types. How to choose the *categories* is discussed later. As more results come in from your test ad that make you surer that you have a winner, and as the amount of profit seems to be higher than your early estimates, go into more categories and more media.

12

Profitable Display Advertising Operation

Where to Advertise • When to Advertise • How Often to Repeat a Winning Ad • Free Advertising: The Potential of Editorial Mentions • How to Obtain Free Editorial Mentions • Per-Inquiry Deals in Display Advertising

This chapter is about the decisions you must make after you have run a successful test.

WHERE TO ADVERTISE

Are Your Chores Done? Long ago you should have written to every mail-order magazine for a sample and a rate card. You should also have made a card file containing an entry for each magazine. The card should show how much mail-order advertising the magazine carries, and the kinds of products advertised there. Soon you'll be using that file very hard, so check that it is complete.

Which Categories of Magazines Will Make Money for You?

The general answer to picking categories is the same as the answer to everything else in mail order: go where the competition is, because that's where the profit is. Read through your sample copies again, looking for the ads of your competitor.

Here is an illustration of how being a copycat can help you and why you should not fear the presence of competition in media: As I write this, I am developing a correspondence course for the mail-order market. Right now I'm in no rush to market the course. One competitor has come a little way into the market. And I am glad to see him, because he is thoroughly professional and will do much of the job for me. He will test out media and product offers, and find out just how much of a market there is. If he does very well, I'll speed up my project. If he does poorly, and gets completely out of the market, I'll take stock again—perhaps run a few tests—with an eye to dropping the project. If I didn't want to write this course for the fun of it, I would have waited to start it until I saw how the competition did.

The rest of this section discusses the situation when you can't just follow your competition—either because your product is somewhat new, or because your competitor hasn't developed his media schedule fully enough. (Be suspicious, though. He's smart, too, and he likes his profit. If the competitor is not advertising widely, there may be good reason for it.)

Look at the list of mail-order magazines listed in Appendix I. Quite a few, aren't there? Some will produce a profit on your particular offer; some will not. Your problem is to find out which will, and which won't.

Testing the magazines one by one would be difficult and time consuming. What you can do, instead, is to consider the various *categories* of magazines, one by one, using one magazine to test a category.

When we talk about categories, we shall use the *Standard Rate & Data* classification.

First you select the categories in which your offer has the best chance of success, using your judgment. Then you run your ad in the best prospective medium within each category. (That is, within each category you would probably pick the medium with the most mail-order advertising.)

After the results are in, you will know which categories *will* work for you. Then you will place ads in every magazine in the categories which test out profitably. You will probably also place ads in a few of the magazines in more questionable categories, and if they pull well, you can then try the others.

For the time being, place no more ads in those categories that did not show a profit. But don't forget about them entirely. You may later come back to one or more of them successfully, either because you have improved your copy, or because the magazine you tested was not representative of the rest of the group, or because your original test went astray by chance.

Remember that you cannot infallibly choose categories for your product by the names or readership of the categories. Men's products have been sold profitably in women's magazines, and vice versa.

All decisions described above should be considered in the light of seasonal variation, of course.

Most of the time you will stick to media on our list. There may be times when you have a very specialized product (i.e., by definition a product that appeals only to a narrow group of people). In that case you *may* successfully go into magazines that carry little or no mail order. An example: Electroplating kits appeal to the hot-rod set, and are sold successfully from some automobile magazines that carry no other mail-order advertising.

Do All Magazines in the Same Category Pull the Same?

In general you can expect magazines in the same category to be more like one another than like magazines in other categories. But there can still be great differences between magazines that are listed together, and that seem similar.

Here is an unusual (and perhaps unbelievable) example of different results in the same category. These are the results of the same ad in three similar salesman's magazines, as reported by publication Z, of course:

Publication	Ad cost	No. orders	Volume
X	$520.00	106	$1,002.50
Y	487.50	88	511.50
Z	422.00	1,132	7,772.05

When prospecting for new media, or shopping between media for the best magazine for your test, keep an eye on the cost per agate line per 100,000 readers. For many kinds of offers, you want just circulation and more circulation. One dollar per 200,000 circulation is a basic, low line rate.

But don't forget to look at the width of the column. A wide column means you get more advertising space per inch.

For low-class magazines, especially, space is generally bought through publishers' representatives rather than directly from the magazines. It is preferable to work through them in order to gain their goodwill, advice, and assistance.

WHEN TO ADVERTISE

Remember this principle first and always: The best months for *your* product may run entirely contrary to the general findings for most products. Of course you won't be enough of a darn fool to advertise bathing suits in the winter. But other products have less obvious, but just as significant, seasons that have nothing to do with general buying trends. Every month in the year is the best month for *some* types of offers.

Whether or not your product is a gift will affect its seasonality. Gifts hit a peak before Christmas, of course. Much of the merchandise advertised in the "shelter" magazines is gift merchandise. Examine the data in Table 12-1. But it is *not* true that, because there are ten times as many ads in November as in January, *House Beautiful* ads will *pull* more than ten times as well in November as in January. They won't. A *small* drop in expected returns will lead *many* wise advertisers to stay out because the small drop is enough to change a profit into a loss.

Products that do not serve as gifts don't do so well just before Christmas. And money-making offers do wonderfully well in January.

Just as soon as you have seasonal data on your product, use your own data as a guide rather than referring to the general results. Your own data are always *much* more accurate for your purposes than anyone else's data can be.

Table 12-2 compiles data from several reports that rank the months for general display advertising, from best to worst. (Index numbers for relative pull are also given in parentheses.)

I hope you're a little confused at the differences between the various rankings of the months. Your confusion should teach you this: While there are some *general* seasonal principles, eventually your decision must depend upon your own product and your experience with that product.

Over the years, International Correspondence Schools has amassed

Table 12-1. Mail-order Lineage in *House Beautiful*[1]

Month	1951		1952	
	Number of ads	Lineage	Number of ads	Lineage
January...............	90	658	87	5,786
February..............	188	12,982	183	12,032
March.................	175	11,564	209	13,486
April.................	213	15,434	270	18,928
May...................	278	18,922	306	21,114
June..................	249	15,680	256	16,888
July..................	104	6,876	126	8,228
August...............	91	6,412	109	7,776
September.............	221	15,524	260	17,244
October..............	431	30,720	490	36,223
November.............	887	62,338	986	68,871
December.............	531	35,694	530	34,424

Table 12-2

Month	Baker[3] (Mostly novelties, probably)	Moran[4]	Fate Magazines[5] (Book advertisers)	Stone[6] (Direct mail)	Grant[7] (Mostly money-making offers, probably)	O. E. McIntyre, Inc.[8] (From magazine and book publishers)
Jan....	3 (116)	3	1 (127)	1	1 (120)	1 (125)
Feb....	4 (111)	1	9 (96)	3	2½ (118)	3 (106)
Mar....	7 (100)	2	8 (98)	2	4½ (115)	8 (98)
Apr....	8 (95)	7	4 (102)	6	10½ (80)	10 (89)
May...	9 (84)	9	12 (83)	10	12 (70)	11 (88)
June...	12 (73)	10	11 (86)	11	9 (85)	12 (86)
July....	11 (79)	11	5 (100)	12	8 (90)	6½ (100)
Aug....	9 (84)	8	3 (104)	9	6½ (100)	2 (108)
Sept....	4 (111)	5	6 (99)	5	2½ (118)	4½ (101)
Oct....	1 (121)	4	2 (111)	7	4½ (115)	9 (95)
Nov....	1 (121)	6	6 (99)	4	6½ (100)	4½ (101)
Dec....	6 (105)	12	10 (94)	8	10½ (80)	6½ (100)

a wealth of advertising statistics. Their seasonal fluctuation is considerably greater than indicated in any list shown above. International Correspondence Schools' advertising boss has said that "during the best month of the year our inquiry cost is one-half that of the worst month of the year."[2]

Yet International Correspondence Schools advertises the year round. Why? Because they and the other large correspondence schools are not pure mail-order organizations. Their direct-mail literature is not expected to close the sale. The inquiry names are sent on to salesmen in the various localities, and it is they who close the sale.

Salesmen have to eat and to work, summer as well as winter. So even though summer inquiries cost twice as much to obtain, the correspondence schools are willing to pay through the nose anyway, in order to give the salesmen work year round, and hence maintain their organization intact. (But don't weep for the correspondence schools. They make it up in winter.)

The extent of the seasonal fluctuation also depends on the type of circulation a magazine has. The more copies it distributes by subscription, the less we expect the mail-order sales to fluctuate from month to month. Like readers of subscription magazines, readers of newsstand magazines purchase less by mail during the summer. But the *number* of newsstand readers *also* drops during the summer, whereas the number of *subscription* readers stays much the same.

Remember that we are *not* talking about sales in *calendar months*. We are talking about total returns to issues that appear in particular months. It is easier to understand why May is so relatively poor and August so relatively good if you understand that the May issue is in readers' hands in June, July, etc. (the summer doldrums). The August issue has much life left in the lively fall. The fact that direct mail does poorer in June and July than in May supports this reasoning.

However, my own data suggest that the general seasonal patterns shown above indicate something about calendar-month sales as well as about issue months. In other words, May is a poorer calendar month than September, which is just as summery.

Not only the seasons of nature can affect the pattern of sales. Human events can make a dent, too. During the first month of the Lindberg kidnapping, returns were reported to slump 30 to 70 percent. Pearl Harbor also reduced sales volume drastically. There isn't anything you can do in advance about cataclysms. But understanding their effect can help you interpret your test results.

It would make sense for magazines to drop their advertising rates during the summer, and some do. (You will get offers of one-third off for summer issues.) But too few magazines show the good sense to drop their rates, or perhaps they believe it is important to be a one-price store.

HOW OFTEN TO REPEAT A WINNING AD

How often you can repeat your ad in a single medium depends upon these factors:

1. The size of the ad
2. The medium and its readership (especially, how much of the circulation is from newsstands)
3. How many other magazines the ad is running in
4. The number of ads run by your competitors
5. The type of product
6. The profitability of your ad

Running several different ads rather than the same ad, in an attempt to prevent results from dropping off, poses issues that are similar.

We shall consider the above factors one by one. But first let's put one more bullet into an old myth that refuses to die (perhaps because it is to the advantage of some people to keep it alive). The myth is "cumulative advertising effect." It does not exist, most especially in mail order.

There is no doubt that two insertions have a greater total effect than one insertion. But the implicit notion in the cumulative-advertising-effect argument is that two insertions have *more than twice* the effect of one insertion. Not only is there no evidence for this, but every single report by mail-order men shows that the second insertion *never* pulls better than the first, unless the results are confused by seasonal changes.

The first scientific book about advertising, *Analytical Advertising*, by W. A. Shryer, was mostly a factual polemic against the cumulative effect notion. On the basis of a huge amount of data, Shryer flatly concluded: "The first insertion of a tried piece of copy in a new medium will pay better, in every way, than any subsequent insertion of the same copy in the same magazine."[9]

(Mind you, I am not saying that the second insertion has no effect. A person who sees the ad twice *is* more likely to buy than the person who sees it *only* once. But many of the very best prospects purchase from the *first* insertion, skimming the cream of the market.)

The data in Table 12-3 show the results of a popular magazine's campaign to secure subscriptions. The data are from Shryer, and are half a century old, but they are as useful now as when they were first published.

Notice that in every case the cost of inquiries from the second insertion was *substantially* higher than from the first insertion. Average costs per inquiry were $0.85 from the first insertions, $1.91 from second insertions. The third insertion was so unprofitable that it was tried only once. Part of the dropoff from the first to the second insertion might have resulted from the declining mail-order season as the winter and spring went on, but this would not have explained the bulk of the results.

Effect of Size of Ad on Repetition. A small ad can be rerun more frequently than can a big ad. Schwab[11] estimates that a second insertion of a full-page ad within thirty to ninety days of the original insertion will pull 25 to 30 percent less than the original insertion. The third insertion within a short period will drop to 45 to 50 percent of the original insertion. Schwab claims that a wait of six months to a year is required before the repeat insertion will do as well as the first insertion. These estimates apply to *identical* advertisements, and not to different copy.

The same *small* ad can run month after month in *some* media and continue to be profitable. However, even classified ads can suffer a dropoff, too. I ran a classified ad in *Western Farm Life* in two consecutive issues of the little all-subscription twice-monthly. The second insertion pulled just 80 percent of the first insertion. A third insertion a month later pulled less than 50 percent of the first insertion. A fourth insertion two weeks later pulled 37 percent of the first insertion. Until I stopped them, subsequent insertions took a beating, ranging from 32 percent to 4 percent of the original insertion. We were bucking a seasonal trend, but the trend could account for only a small part of the effect.

However, the same ad in the *Saturday Review* ran almost indefinitely,

Table 12-3. Results of a Magazine Subscription Campaign

Date run	Medium	Cost of advertisement	No. of subscriptions	Cost per subscription
March......	*Technical World*	$ 40.00	51	$ 0.79
April.......	*Technical World*	40.00	20	2.00
Feb. 19.....	*Saturday Evening Post*	250.00	338	0.72
Mar. 6......	*Saturday Evening Post*	250.00	181	1.38
March......	*Circle*	30.00	10	3.00
April.......	*Circle*	30.00	3	10.00
Feb. 19.....	*Literary Digest*	45.00	58	0.74
Mar. 19.....	*Literary Digest*	62.50	35	1.80
Feb. 3......	*Chicago Journal*	12.00	17	0.71
Mar. 3......	*Chicago Journal*	27.00	13	2.07
Feb. 6......	*Chicago Examiner*	90.00	258	0.35
Feb. 27.....	*Chicago Examiner*	90.00	94	0.95
Mar. 6......	*Chicago Examiner*	90.00	57	1.60
Mar. 13.....	*Chicago Examiner*	90.00	25	3.60
Feb. 6......	*New York American*	112.50	131	0.85
Mar. 6......	*New York American*	112.50	71	1.38
Feb. 13.....	*Chicago Inter Ocean*	15.00	20	0.75
Mar. 6......	*Chicago Inter Ocean*	33.75	29	1.16
Feb. 15.....	*New York Journal*	49.00	62	0.79
Mar. 8......	*New York Journal*	112.50	53	2.12
Feb. 27.....	*San Francisco Examiner*	30.00	67	0.45
Mar. 20.....	*San Francisco Examiner*	42.50	9	4.71
Feb. 27.....	*Minneapolis Journal*	11.00	21	0.52
Mar. 13.....	*Minneapolis Journal*	24.75	2	12.37
Mar. 27.....	*Minneapolis Journal*	24.75	1	24.75
Feb. 27.....	*Philadelphia Times*	12.00	22	0.55
Mar. 20.....	*Philadelphia Times*	27.00	3	9.00
Feb. 27.....	*Los Angeles Examiner*	10.00	16	0.62
Mar. 13.....	*Los Angeles Examiner*	22.50	11	2.22
Feb. 27.....	*Chicago Tribune*	30.00	72	0.41
Mar. 20.....	*Chicago Tribune*	67.50	9	7.50
Feb. 27.....	*Boston Post*	20.00	32	0.63
Mar. 13.....	*Boston Post*	45.00	7	6.42
Feb. 20.....	*St. Louis Post-Dispatch*	20.00	38	0.52
Mar. 13.....	*St. Louis Post-Dispatch*	45.00	26	1.73
Feb. 20.....	*Cincinnati Enquirer*	18.00	24	0.75
Mar. 20.....	*Cincinnati Enquirer*	40.50	8	5.05

SOURCE: Shryer.[10]

week after week, changing only its classification. After an initial not-too-sharp dropoff that coincided with the seasonal trend (I can't esti-mate the dropoff accurately because there was a copy change), the ad hit a plateau and pulled the same gratifying results week after week.

Neither *Western Farm Life* nor *Saturday Review* is typical of classi-fied sections. *Western Farm Life* is all subscription, twice a month. *Saturday Review* is also almost all subscription, weekly. Therefore, their results are not samples of classified advertising generally. The differences *between* them might be explained by the greater amount of classified carried by *Saturday Review*.

It is easy to understand why big ads should suffer greater dropoff than small ads, if we consider the difference in the number of people who "notice" the ads. About 4 percent of the readership of *Popular Mechanics* will "notice" a 1-inch ad, while anywhere from 20 to 60 percent will "notice" a full-page ad. The second month it runs, the small ad can put itself before the eyes of 96 percent of the prior audience who never saw the ad before, and almost 4 percent will again "notice" it (assuming no change in readership). But the big ad has used up a very substantial chunk of its audience.

Furthermore, except for completely subscription magazines, far more than 4 percent of the readers of any issue will not have *read* the previous issue. (But keep in mind that the people who "notice" an ad are not a random sample of the readership. Rather, they are those people who have the highest perception for a product and the greatest likelihood to buy.)

Subscription versus Newsstand Circulation. It stands to reason that if exactly the same people see every issue of a magazine, the dropoff must be greater than if there is a turnover of readership. The more newsstand copies sold, the greater the turnover, and hence the less the dropoff.

This effect will be greater upon big ads than upon small ones, of course.

Number of Media Used. The pool of magazine readers in the United States is huge. But it is not limitless. If you insert a big enough ad often enough in enough magazines, you can certainly reach the point where the returns will decrease. This is akin to the saturation concept of general advertisers.

It is unlikely that the returns to a *small* ad will be much affected by the number of magazines in which it runs.

Competition. Competitors move in if they sniff the pungent aroma of a golden goose. The competitors can kill your goose if they deluge the media with ads. Their potential customers are your potential customers, too.

It still remains true, however, that more often you are competing against inattention and inertia in your audience than against other advertisers.

Fads and Repeat Items. Some products are of interest once in the lifetime of a customer. A book on karate is an example. Other products are repeat sellers—clothes, for example. Still a third type are products that people are likely to get interested in only at special times in their lives —specialized correspondence courses are one such item.

It is more likely that you can "force" the market for karate books than for clothes or correspondence courses. And once you have forced the market, it takes a couple of years for the market to recover. Products that you can "force" are like fad products. This is the only possible explanation for the waves of saturation ads, for such commodities as karate books, that roll in for a year or two, then disappear for a while. (However, many propositions that disappear drop out because the government muscles them out, and not because the market is temporarily exhausted.)

How Profitable Is the Ad? Just as with classified ads, you should repeat a *very* profitable display ad more often than a borderline ad—despite the continuing drop in returns to the profitable ad. As we proved in the classified discussion, you will almost always make more total profit by running two insertions at less than maximum results, than you will by running one insertion that gets you maximum results.

Not only will your own profit be greater, but you have a better chance of keeping competition out if you run your ad more frequently. The competition may be attracted by apparent success as shown by your frequency of insertions. But when he runs a test ad, *his* results will be lower under the frequent-insertion plan, just as yours are. And so the results appear less attractive to him, and he is not so likely to continue competing.

What about running *different* ads instead of the same ad, in an attempt to foil the dropoff effect? If you run full-page ads, it certainly pays you to follow the example of such experienced advertisers as International Correspondence Schools, who run several different ads each season. But the advertiser who runs small ads or classified ads will find it too costly and too time-consuming to work with several ads. Instead, he will run the same ad at such intervals as he finds profitable.

Customary repetition intervals for small ads are (1) every issue in monthlies that are largely sold on newsstands; (2) not quite so often in all-subscription magazines; and (3) every month or every two months in Sunday supplements.

Shryer gave us the sound rule of thumb that the interval between insertions should be long enough for the earlier ad to pay out its break-even costs. This is on the conservative side.

Before we leave the subject of repetition, here are a couple of inspirational notes:

• The full-page Sherwin Cody ad pulled 225,000 inquiries, 11,000 orders, and $328,500 in a ten-year period. This ad has never really been changed in over thirty years, though many ads have been tested against it.[12]

• La Salle Extension University's basic 1-inch ad occupied $300,000 worth of space and produced $3,000,000 in sales over twenty-five years. (Several years after those figures were collected, the ad is still going strong.)[13]

FREE ADVERTISING: THE POTENTIAL OF EDITORIAL MENTIONS

Many mail-order products appeal to the pipe dreams and unrealized hopes held by many people. Not in so many words, of course, because government agencies will crack down. But the nature of those pipe dreams is such that the imagination seizes on vagueness in the ad to create its *own* belief.

Examples of these pipe dreams include "Reduce Weight Quick," "Be Irresistibly Sexy" (both men and women), and "Increase Personal Efficiency Miraculously." Among the most notoriously powerful of the pipe dreams are "Get Something for Nothing" and "Get Rich Quick Without Risk."

Some mail-order men have used the idea of "free ads" (editorial mentions) to appeal to the get-rich-quick dream of people who want to get into mail order. Seems wonderful, doesn't it? Ads for your products in the best magazines without costing you a cent!

There is some truth in the appeal, of course. New and interesting products are real news, and readers *are* sufficiently interested so that dozens of magazines really do have "shopping sections."

"Editorial mentions" are mostly to consumer products publicized in the shopping sections of consumer magazines. But such editorial mentions are really just one type of the general public relations art of crashing the editorial columns of the media.

It is standard procedure for the manufacturer of new industrial products to obtain free write-ups of his product in business and trade publications. News of new products is one of the most important types of news that a professional magazine can print, and editors are anxious to receive such publicity notices.

Book reviews are another form of "free advertising." Book editors seek out those books which will be of most interest to their readers.

News of products that are being offered for the first time to jobbers or dealers is another important type of "free advertising." You should always consider the possibility of merchandising a new product through dealers as well as by mail order.

We shall concentrate on the problem of obtaining editorial mentions for consumer mail-order products, however.

HOW TO OBTAIN FREE EDITORIAL MENTIONS

You obtain editorial mentions by sending a news release plus a sample and a photograph to the editors of shopping sections of magazines whose readers might be interested in your products.

The news release itself should be in the form of a letter that tells the editor about your product, and asks for publicity. Along with the news release, or within it, you include a product write-up which is suitable for publication in the magazine. The write-up is not the same as an advertisement. Rather, it should resemble editorial material, and especially the editorial material in the shopping section of the particular magazine to which you are writing. Naturally, you will not write a separate release for each magazine, but it may be good policy to create a separate news release and product write-up for each different *type* of magazine. The release should organize the important facts and present them in such a way that the editor of the shopping section can write up your product with a minimum of time and trouble.

The best way to learn what should be in a write-up is to study the editorial mentions in the "shelter" magazines (*House Beautiful*, etc.).

If your product is really very desirable, the magazine will create good copy from the raw material you send them. But you are even better off if you hire a professional public relations man, or an advertising agency with experience in this line, to do the job for you.

You should indicate in the write-up, or in the news release letter, that a money-back guarantee goes with the product. Shopping-section editors want to protect their readers and themselves. The guarantee makes them feel protected, in addition to increasing your sales.

Remember that a news release must contain *news*. The purpose of shopping sections is to tell readers about *new* products. So emphasize *news* in your letter and write-up.

Your write-up should not sell too hard. Some magazines want only the bare objective facts, while others give you more leeway in praising your product.

Key the address in each write-up so that you know from which magazine the orders come. That will be valuable information for you when you are deciding where to purchase advertising.

A sample of the product will help you obtain editorial mentions. But whether or not you send a sample, the photograph you send should do a good job in showing off your product. Eight- by ten-inch glossy photographs are customary, and they are not too expensive when you order them in quantity. Be sure to hire a good photographer.

Perhaps the most important part of the job of obtaining editorial mentions is to send your news release to the right magazines. You are just wasting your time and postage if you send a news release on fishing equipment to a magazine that goes to new mothers. Study the magazines to see if your product will fit the readers.

Read the following words of wisdom from *Esquire*, one of the important shopping-section magazines:

WHY PRODUCT RELEASES GET REJECTED

A lot of product publicity is inept and amateurish, consequently much of this material is filed in editors' wastepaper baskets. It's amazing how many releases are mailed indiscriminately to publications without regard to their editorial compatibility with the magazine.

Some are so poorly written, so badly organized and so lacking in information that they are completely unusable. Many editors will not risk eye strain trying to read releases that come in on fourth, fifth or even sixth carbons! Product photos, too, are of such poor quality or so unimaginative that a self respecting editor cannot possibly publish them. Releases often make ridiculously exaggerated claims. Some sound like technical manuals; the writer obviously doesn't understand what the product can do or how it is applied and cannot explain the same in plain, simple English.

Here are several suggestions that can be helpful in getting you better product publicity:

1. Put your news in the first three lines of your release.
2. Limit your adjectives.
3. Know your publications.
4. Don't ask for tear sheets [copies of the page on which it runs].
5. Don't mention advertising possibilities.
6. Get to know the editors to learn their problems.
7. Don't make an old product sound new.[14]

Appendix I contains a list of consumer magazines in which to seek editorial mentions.

Obtaining editorial mentions is not as easy as it seems. It requires a public relations effort, and the public relations campaign is just as risky as an advertising campaign.

Furthermore, a large proportion of editorial mentions for mail-order products are given to *advertisers*. Much shopping-section space is "sold" just like advertising space—only more cynically. Advertisers and media sometimes make deals which provide for one editorial mention for each four ads, one for two, or even one for one.

If you have a truly new and interesting product, you *may* get a *start* with editorial mentions. Don't let what I say discourage you. A friend of mine with absolutely no experience in mail order recovered most of a $20,000 investment in a product he invented, with editorial mentions. But sooner or later you must start paying for display space, just like anyone else, if your business is to prosper.

PER-INQUIRY DEALS IN DISPLAY ADVERTISING

When you watch the mail-order ads long enough, you will notice that exactly the same ad appears with the name and address of more than one firm, or at more than one address. Very often, one or more of the addresses will be in mid-town New York.

Variation in addresses is usually the sign of a "PI" (per-inquiry) deal, in which the magazine obtains inquiries or orders at its own address, and then "sells" the inquiries or orders to the advertiser at a fixed rate per inquiry or per order. The advertiser pays only for the inquiries or orders turned over to him.

Of course this sounds fine to you—the advertiser does not have to risk a cent. But it is easy to arrange PI deals only when you have a tested and proved advertisement and offer. And very often you can make more money with a tested offer by buying space outright. Furthermore, many magazines want no part of PI deals.

13

The Display Advertisement

*What Almost Every Good Ad Contains • Appeals
and Copy • Layout and Artwork • How Big
Should an Ad Be? • Where Is the Best Place in the
Magazine for Your Ad to Be?*

You must either learn mail-order copywriting from experience plus
one of the top-notch books referred to earlier, or use an agency. There
are no short cuts to the vitally important art of creating ads. That's why
this book makes no attempt to teach you how. But we will provide some
facts and figures to aid your judgment.

WHAT ALMOST EVERY GOOD AD CONTAINS

Here are some *facts* about mail-order ads and their selling power:

1. *The power of a single word can be incredible.* In an eleven-word
classified ad, the offer of a "book" or "manual" pulled nearly twice as
many dollar bills as did "instructions."

2. *Never write a classified ad without a guarantee in it. And never
forget to play up the guarantee in a display ad.* The extra word may up
your cost almost 10 percent in a classified ad, but in my experience it
ups the returns perhaps 20 percent—even when no one uses the guarantee.

Don't be afraid of refund demands even if the product is information
that can be read and then returned—as long as the merchandise is good
and customers don't feel gypped. Charles Atlas offered to return the
first payment after seven days, or to return payment in full plus 6 percent after completion, to dissatisfied customers. Only 1 percent are reported to ask for their money back.

On the other hand, I know of a firm that sold a shoddy money-making manual for $2 and offered a money-back guarantee. The 20 percent who wanted refunds made the operation a losing venture.

3. *Always offer the customer a chance to trade up* to "de luxe" models, and/or an opportunity to purchase accessory merchandise. Schwab[1] quotes these results of comparative split-run tests:

    a. Choice of three types of products did better than one model by 19.7 percent and 30.4 percent in two tests.

    b. Choice of six did 52.6 percent better than choice of four, and 261.8 percent better than one model.

    c. Choice of two did 52.9 percent better in number of orders and 25 percent better in dollars than one model.

Maybe the effectiveness of choices is that they lead people to ask, "Which one?" rather than "Should I?" A classic closer of face-to-face salesmen is "Which model would you like?" or "What size, please?" However, such speculation is unnecessary, even though it is fun. What counts is the oft-demonstrated useful effect of offering the choice.

4. *These are ways to encourage quick action:*

    Time limit
    Limited supply
    Prices about to rise
    Combination offers
    Cut-price leaders
    Copy technique[2]

Incentives to quick action get more total orders. If the potential customer waits awhile, his desire to buy very often cools off.

If you use any of these devices, keep them truthful or the Federal Trade Commission may get you.

5. *Harold Preston[3] gives us this quote on colorful language:*

    Victor O. Schwab, a leading authority on mail selling, advises you to use words in your headline that the public doesn't expect, "words that *stop* the casual reader—startle him—grip his eyes and his interest."

    Mr. Schwab cites such words as "Pushover," "Ain't," "Don't Belly-Ache," "Scatterbrain," "Weasel," "Hog," "Skunk," as eye-arresters that substantially increased the returns from advertising in which they were used. Words like "Bunk," "Bosh," "Gee," "Phooey" are in the same class . . . By changing the conventional salutation of a letter to "Yousah, Yousah," I tripled the returns of a subscription campaign.

6. *Use as many testimonials as you can.* People must believe before they'll buy. Testimonials are a powerful means of inducing belief.

If you wait around for completely unsolicited testimonials, you'll be gray before you have a handful of testimonials, even if you're giving gold nuggets away free. You can obtain "unsolicited" testimonials by writing to your customers some time after the sale, saying that you appreciate their patronage, and asking if you can help them further. This kind of courtesy and conversation stimulates some of them to write you chatty letters in which they will say nice things about your product.

But remember that you can't stretch the truth by using testimonials. Any statement in a quoted testimonial must be as true as if you yourself make the statement. Recheck Chapter 5 on what you can and can't do with testimonials (While I'm talking about testimonials, I'd appreciate hearing from any of you who are willing to write me comments —even criticism. It won't be for quotation, unless you so indicate, but rather to help me when I again write about mail order. You can address me in care of the publisher.)

Here is evidence of the importance of belief and trust from a split-run test: Using an unknown firm name brought in 77 orders to each 100 orders pulled by the identical ad *signed* by a well-known company.[4]

APPEALS AND COPY

"Appeal" is what advertising men call the basic selling idea of an ad. If the ad emphasizes how the product will make money for you, money-making is its appeal. If the ad suggests that the product will make a woman devastatingly beautiful, the appeal is sex. And so on.

The best way to pick an appeal is the same as the best way to pick a product and a media schedule. Use the same appeal as your successful competitor—at least to start with.

Gather all the information you can on the words and ideas other people use to sell the product. Before I sat down to write copy for a book on hypnotism, I not only read the competitor's ads, but also examined hypnotists' listings and displays in the classified phone directory, read book jackets, and pored over hypnotism catalogs and brochures. I jotted down every selling idea I could find in all that reading, and used it for my material.

Following the competition will take you a long way, but to make the most money, you must also be a leader. Like any other kind of a leader, however, you must not leap too far from where the pack is at any one time. Instead, you make changes gradually on the basis of your analysis and your hunches about which appeals can be emphasized.

The only way to determine which appeal is best for a product is to test. Testing methods are described in Chapter 18.

Schwab's split-run tests for his clients produced these results *for the products on which he worked:*

• Reducing did 138 percent better than Relieving Nervous Tension, and 266 percent better than Improving Your English. (However, this was a test of three *different books* as well as different appeals, which makes the test less conclusive.)

• Sex did 211 percent better than Succeed in Business, and 223 percent better than Selection of Vocation.

• Newness improved an ad 75.4 percent and 79 percent in two tests.[5]

This is a good basic list of important mail-order appeals:

> *Better health.* Greater strength, vigor, endurance; the possibility of longer life.
>
> *More money.* For spending, saving, or giving to others.
>
> *Greater popularity.* Through a more attractive personality or through personal accomplishments.
>
> *Improved appearance.* Beauty; style; better physical build; cleanliness.
>
> *Security in old age.* Independence; provision for age or adversity.
>
> *Praise from others.* For one's intelligence, knowledge, appearance, or other evidences of superiority.
>
> *More comfort.* Ease; luxury; self-indulgence; convenience.
>
> *More leisure.* For travel, hobbies, rest, play, self-development, and the like.
>
> *Pride of accomplishment.* Overcoming obstacles and competition; desire to "do things well."
>
> *Business advancement.* Better job; success; "be your own boss"; reward for merit.
>
> *Social advancement.* Moving in better circles; social acceptance; "keeping up with Joneses."
>
> *Increased enjoyment.* From entertainment, food, drink, and other physical contacts.
>
> *People also want to:*

Be good parents	Appreciate beauty
Have influence over others	Be proud of their possessions
Be sociable, hospitable	Be creative
Be gregarious	Acquire or collect things
Express their personalities	Be efficient
Resist domination by others	Win others' affection
Satisfy their curiosity	Be "first" in things
Be up to date	Improve themselves mentally
Emulate the admirable	Be recognized as authorities

> *And they want to save:* Money, time, work, discomfort, worry, doubts, risks, embarrassment, offense to others, boredom, personal self-respect, and prestige.[6]

This list of appeals should help you choose copy themes. It will also help you decide whether or not a particular *product* has mail-order potential.

How to Qualify Prospects

To "qualify" prospects means to weed out poor prospects who cost you money for catalogs and direct mail, but at the same time keep the attention of the good prospects.

Here is a list of ways Moran[7] suggests for qualifying prospects:

1. Make headline selective
2. Reduce emphasis on free offer in headline and copy
3. Charge for booklet
4. Ask for age, sex, occupation, etc.
5. Make it obvious that booklet is a sales piece.
6. Show that product has limited use to a special few
7. Eliminate coupon
8. Insert stipulations, restrictions, etc., in coupon
9. Show the price

LAYOUT AND ARTWORK

Coupons

A coupon is a crucial part of almost every mail-order ad that is big enough to contain one. The only time the coupon is omitted is when the advertiser wants to qualify prospects very strictly, and not make it too easy for them to respond.

Notice that most advertisers who run even a 4-inch ad find it profitable to spend *one-quarter of the advertising cost* just for the coupon area. That's how important the coupon is in increasing response!

The coupon makes it "easy to order." The prospect doesn't have to think what to say, or how to write it. All he does is fill in his name and address, and perhaps check a box or two. That's why 70 to 85 percent of responders will use the coupon.

The coupon suggests *action,* and it also seems to suggest getting something free or at a bargain rate. The coupon itself attracts many readers to the ad. Many years ago general advertisers suffered a fad of testing their copy by couponing ads for free booklets and other giveaways. They soon quit the practice when they found that the rate of response depended as much on the size of the coupon as it did on the excellence of the copy.

Some advertisers use a coupon that is too small for anyone to use. Nevertheless, it has much of the effect of a coupon in increasing response and it saves space. Inquirers write their name and address in the margin of the page next to the coupon.

Some advertisers use a heavy dashed border around the entire ad. "Tear Out and Mail Today" at the bottom of the ad is also used fre-

FIG.   13-1

quently. The whole ad looks like a coupon even though there is no room for name or address. I have found that this device gives a good boost to small ads composed entirely of type.

The list below is Henry Musselman's check list of important items in the coupon for a *direct-mail piece.* The list is just as valid for display ads.

Leave room for complete name and address.
Require only a fill-in for sizes, colors, etc.
State the proposition clearly.
Tell prospect just what to do.
Convenient size and shape.
Keyed to denote source.
Re-state the guarantee.
Stand out from rest of ad.
If premium is offered, the offer is included in coupon.[8]

In full-page ads, put the coupon at the outside bottom of the page. Some advertisers who drive terrifically hard for inquiries—e.g., the Duraclean rug-cleaning franchise ad—seem to have success with making the coupon the dominant element in the ad's layout. (In his recent best seller, David Ogilvy triumphantly trumpets as a discovery this well-known mail-order device.[9])

Points of Interest about Layout and Art

Readers often pay more attention to editorial matter than to advertising, and they have more faith in it. The "reading notice" tries to take advantage of that fact by making the ad look like the adjoining editorial columns. The headline must also look like "news." Figure 13-2 illustrates a reading notice.

Some media charge extra for "readers." Others do not accept them because they regard them as undesirable.

General advertising strives for an esthetic quality in advertising, and perhaps wisely so. The general advertiser aims at a huge audience with whom its reputation is precious. The general advertiser therefore cannot afford to irritate its potential customers with unpleasant ads.

But mail-order firms have different requirements for an ad. Many successful mail-order ads look crowded, vulgar, and garish—called "buckeye" by the trade. The buckeye format creates "excitement," and uses space to the utmost.

Split-run tests comparing a "busy" layout to a balanced and artistically unified layout showed that the "busy" layout did 111 percent better, 68 percent better, and 30 percent better than the artistic layout, in three tests.[10]

Baker[11] points out that the "busy" layout technique uses lots of

y in-
anzi-
rned
ward
spice
rous
oviet
u a l
no
gan-
rican
i s h

been delivered.

FRANKLIN ESTATE PAPERS ARE FILED

Petition for the appointment of an administrator for the estate of Earl L. Franklin, who died Jan. 1, was filed Monday in probate court.

The petition lists $4,000 in personal property and asks that John and Ralph Franklin of Champaign be made administrators.

ther-
y re-
Day
67th
the
Feb.

will
aken
meet-
p.m.
hool.
from
beech
her
illikin
d re-
grees

et to Be Feb. 3

k at Council Event.

ed by The Mothersingers.

Committees for the banquet are:

Arrangements, Mrs. P a u l Bricker and Mrs. Tracy Stevenson; program, Mrs. Walter Chaplin and Mrs. Harold Walker; decorations, Mr. and Mrs. Thomas C. Buschbach; reservations, Mr. and Mrs. Robert Jacob; program books, Mrs. George Anderson, Mrs. Donald Cupp, Mrs. Morris McCarty, Mrs. Richard Schmall, Mrs. Richard Spitz and Mrs. Murray Outlaw, and publicity, Mrs. Roy Michael Jr. and Mrs. Willis Busch.

General chairman for the affair is Mrs. Joseph Grimsey.

ovid-

Shrinks Piles Without Surgery —Relieves Pain

al) —
has
ance
ty to
itch-
hout

after
rove-
veri-
tions.
ptly.
ving
r re-
place.
all —
main-
ctor's
nued
nths!
hor-
able
tate-

ments as "Piles have ceased to be a problem!" And among these sufferers were a very wide variety of hemorrhoid conditions, some of 10 to 20 years' standing.

All this, without the use of narcotics, anesthetics or astringents of any kind. The secret is a new healing substance (Bio-Dyne®) — the discovery of a world-famous research institution. Already, Bio-Dyne is in wide use for healing injured tissue on all parts of the body.

This new healing substance is offered in *suppository* or *ointment form* called *Preparation H*®. Ask for individually sealed convenient Preparation H Suppositories or Preparation H Ointment with special applicator. Preparation H is sold at all drug counters.

school all this week.

It was suggested that those parents interested in seeing the exhibit might go a little early to the PTA meeting scheduled for 7:30 p.m. Thursday, or stop by at their convenience during the week.

Mrs. Fred Omer, dance teacher, will hold a demonstration class at 3:30 p.m. Friday at the school. This will follow the procedure of a regular class. Parents are invited to attend to see what their children are learning to do.

Mrs. Johanna Braunfeld currently is making recordings of the German speech of her pupils. Parents are to be notified later of a time when they can hear those recordings and have an evaluation of their children's progress.

All the classes have met since October under the supervision of a Yankee Ridge PTA committee headed by Mrs. Bruce McCormick.

Could This Be You?

the quality of patient care."

JOHN REGNELL WILL ATTEND RADIO SEMINAR

John Regnell, assistant manager of University of Illinois radio station WILL, will attend the National Educational Radio Seminar Wednesday through Friday at the University of Chicago.

Sponsored by the National Association of Educational Broadcasters, the seminar will discuss such topics as "The Future of Educational Radio" and "Future and New Uses of Educational Radio."

POTLUCK SLATED

Bement — The Stitch and Chat Club will hold a potluck dinner at 12:30 p.m. Feb. 13 in the home of Mrs. Rue Malone and Miss Opal Huffcutt of Bement.

FIG. 13-2

gimmicky "spot art": scissors on top of the coupon, a hand pointing at the guarantee, one-sentence claims thrown all around the page. Figure 13-3 is a good example.

So—don't let any "fine artist" sell you a bill of goods about how your ad is ugly and should be beautified. You're liable to find that as artistic satisfaction increases, profits sink.

FIG. 13-3

Special inserts into magazines cost more than ordinary full-page ads, but some are worth the added freight. According to Stanley Rapp,[12] reply cards increase returns by three to six times for some advertisers, two to three times for others of his clients (probably including record clubs).

About *color* in ads: split runs indicated that color outpulled black and white by 182 percent, 83 percent, 224 percent, and 26 percent for a *home-decoration* product.[13] So for *that* product, color was worth the usual 50 percent surcharge. But a marriage book would undoubtedly not get the same benefits from color as a home-decoration product.

HOW BIG SHOULD AN AD BE?

Mail-order advertisers figure the size of an ad in this way: They increase the size of their ads in each medium until a further size increase would cost more than the revenue it would produce.

There are some types of mail-order products that *demand* large space. For example, a 4-inch ad may pull *more* than four times as much as a 1-inch ad for *some* products. This usually occurs when it is impossible to tell a full advertising story in less than the 4 inches. Four inches may be the "natural" space unit for that product. A half page may be the "natural" unit for other products. The famous Charles Atlas course found that the ad had to be at least one column by 98 lines (7 inches) in order to show Atlas' picture effectively. Small space was no good for that offer.

Generally speaking, however, the published evidence is overwhelming that increasing the size of an ad will *not* increase the returns in proportion. For almost every mail-order advertiser who cares to use them, classified ads are far and away the most productive medium—often three times as productive, dollar for dollar, as the most effective display space. A full-page ad will practically never pull twice as many orders as a half-page ad. La Salle Correspondence University has never found *any* display ad that performs as well as its thirty-year-old 1-inch ad.

Fifty years ago Shryer found, when selling his correspondence course on starting and managing a collection agency, that the cost of inquiries went like this:

Classified 5 lines............	30¢	per inquiry
7-line display..............	53¢	" "
16-line display.............	69.9¢	" "
56-line display.............	76¢	" "
half-page display...........	92¢	" "

In many cases the five-line classified ad made more *total profit* than did the fifty-six-line ad in the same medium.[14]

This effect still holds in our day, and for many kinds of products. An agency man who serves many mail-order clients writes: "Many small space users find their most efficient use of space ranges between 28 and 50 lines."[15]

But it *is* economical and rational to increase the size of the ad as long as the profit from the increased orders is greater than the increased cost of the space. If a quarter page costs $400 and returns *net* a profit of $200 on sales of $800, a half-page ad *may* net a profit of $250 on sales of $1,400. If that is the case, it pays you to run the half-page ad.

The advertisers who run large ads are those who pull very successfully in small space. They are the advertisers who (by definition) face a large potential market. The large ad demands that a large percentage of the medium's audience have an active interest in the product.

John Caples wrote:[16]

> . . . if the reader of a publication does not have a corn, your full-page ad, no matter how attractive, will not sell him a corn remedy. On the other hand, if the reader does have a corn that is bothering him, he will be stopped by the one-word headline, CORNS, in a small ad. Since you cannot predict when the readers' corns will be troublesome, you are better off with a small ad in every issue of a publication than with a big ad once in a while.

And Robert Baker[17] ventures to qualify the relationship, saying: "If the item is of genuine interest to 25 percent or more of a particular medium's readership, you can effectively use as much as a full page. But if your item is of limited interest, probably you should confine yourself to small units."

Mail-order advertisers cannot increase their total profit by running more small ads instead of fewer larger ones. There are always too few media that will pay out a profit, and the trick is to use each of them to the limit. That is why, unlike general advertisers, the mail-order man does not fix a budget and then spread it over the various media. Instead, you will keep spending as long as it is profitable to do so. If medium A will make more with a big ad than a small one, then the big ad will run in that medium. That decision will stand independent of decisions about media B through Z. (This principle also explains why you sometimes will also advertise in months that are half as productive as the best months.)

As a practical matter, then, you will begin with the smallest ad that can do a complete selling job, and gradually increase the size of your ads until your profit begins to diminish.

Some magazines give discounts for larger space units that make it profitable to run larger ads. The discounts are huge in some magazines. You can sometimes purchase a whole page of a three-column magazine for little more than two columns would cost. On the other hand, the discounts in other magazines are not worth bothering about. The smaller the discount, the smaller the ad you will run.

The discounts almost always mean you should use even units of space, however. Use a full column instead of almost a full column. You get more space and actually pay less.

"But then," you say, "why do the biggest and smartest firms in the country run full-page ads in *Life* and *Time*?"

There are several parts to the complicated answer. This is one of the possible reasons: repeated surveys have shown that a half page gets 55 to 60 percent as many *readers* as does a full page. But in a huge study, Rudolph found that a half page produced almost 70 percent as many *coupons* as a full page.[18]

National advertisers want *readers*. Mail-order firms want *coupons* (and money). That's part of the reason why mail-order firms advertise differently than auto and soap manufacturers do.

Furthermore, the biggest advertisers are not always the smartest advertisers. A big firm can often get away with stupidity that would break a small, competitive producer. And a big national advertiser can't measure its successes and failures as accurately as a mail-order firm can.

One Big Ad versus Several Small Ones

Pratt[19] sometimes found it "profitable, where several items are to be sold, to advertise them separately in the same periodical on different pages, rather than combine them in one advertisement." But production problems are greater with several ads, and you may forego important bulk-space discounts.

Thoresen is a large mail-order firm that does both: during a single month it may take a full page to display many products together and it also may run fifteen small ads all over a magazine like *Detective Cases*.

WHERE IS THE BEST PLACE IN THE MAGAZINE FOR YOUR AD TO BE?

The position of an ad on the page (if it is smaller than a full-page ad) and the location within the magazine can affect the ad's pulling power. You need to know which spots are best for two reasons:

1. To make a more accurate judgment of how well the copy is pulling.
2. To request the best space.

If you run a small ad, you have little control over where the ad runs. Mostly it's potluck where the layout man will fit you among the big ads and editorial features. However, when you become a steady customer and develop a good relationship with a magazine or its advertising representative, they may heed your request for a favorable spot.

Observations of people's eye movements suggest that the upper part of the page does better than the lower part, and that the outside of a page is better than an inside column. Dollar results confirm it. My data for a 3½-inch ad show that the outside top corner does 15 to 30 percent better than the inside bottom corner next to the gutter.

Results based mostly on full-page ads indicate that right-hand pages are slightly better than left-hand pages. Inquiry results for La Salle Extension show that the right-hand page pulls 10 percent better than the left.[20] Readership surveys range from no difference to 10 percent difference.[21]

La Salle Extension also finds that the front of a publication averages 40 percent better than the back pages.[22] From readership surveys, Daniel Starch[23] figures the front as 10 percent better than the middle or back. Victor Schwab[24] says it is better to be well forward on a left-hand page than on a right-hand page far in the back of the book. However, small-space advertisers may find it more advantageous to be in a back-of-the-book shopping section than to be in the front of the magazine.

The back cover is almost universally acclaimed as the best position, and it therefore costs more than inside pages. One mail-order writer says it produces three orders to two for the average inside page.[25]

This is Schwab's[26] list of the best locations, in descending order: back cover, page facing second cover, pages 3, 5, 7, page facing inside back cover.

Lucas[27] gives high value to the page opposite the first editorial page, page 1, the center spread, and the page opposite the index to advertisers. But remember that the Lucas data did not come from mail-order results.

It is better to be near editorial matter than near other advertisements, as a general rule. Coupon ads don't do so well on the inside front cover because people don't like to cut the cover.

Segal[28] says that a gutter position cuts results 20 to 40 percent on the average, and sometimes up to 80 percent. He finds narrow-column books are worst for gutter positions. Sumner estimates that gutter position cuts returns by 50 percent.[29] (The "gutter" is the inside of the pages where the magazine is stitched or pasted together.)

14

The Direct-Mail Piece, Postage, and Results

The Mailing Piece • General Principles of What to Send • The Letter • Repeat Letters • The Brochure or Circular • Outer Envelopes • Coupons, Order Cards, and Reply Envelopes • Types of Postage • How to Estimate Results Quickly

By now you have found a product or a line of products that you have chosen to sell. And you have tentatively decided the terms of the offer you will make: price, credit, etc.

As in other media, in direct mail the offer is most important of all in bringing about success or failure. The choice of good lists is next most important. Copy and the "letter package" are the third important factor in success or failure. Despite this order of importance, most mailers spend a disproportionate amount of time preparing and testing copy and the physical characteristics of the mailing, when they would do better trying to improve their offers and the lists they use.

In this chapter we are not specifically discussing the follow-up letters sent to inquirers stimulated by space advertising. Much of this chapter does apply to follow-ups, of course, but Chapter 17 discusses that special problem in detail.

This chapter is about "cold" mailings that offer your product to rented or purchased lists, or to your own list of customers.

THE MAILING PIECE

So you have decided to try direct mail with your offer! This is a quick summary of how you proceed. Each step is spelled out in detail later.

120

First, you must select a list to test (usually with the help of a list broker). The test list will be your guess as to the best possible list available. More about that later. Second, you work up a mailing package —a good, standard type of copy and package—also discussed below. And next you mail your package to a test portion of the list you selected. Read Chapter 18 to determine how big a test you should use.

Then you sit back to await the results. A section in this chapter teaches you how to predict the total results before they are all in. Compare the *predicted* returns against your costs, to establish whether you have a success or a failure. Another section discusses the proper accounting techniques for this comparison.

A success? Go back to the list you tested, and mail either a much larger test, or the entire list. Chapter 18 helps you make that decision. And start testing other lists, in order to widen your scope and increase volume.

GENERAL PRINCIPLES OF WHAT TO SEND

This section will not try to teach you to write direct-mail copy, or to create direct-mail layouts and packages. Those lessons are well taught by

Robert Stone, *Successful Direct Mail Advertising and Selling*[1]
The Robert Collier Letter Book[2]
Yeck and Maguire, *Planning and Creating Better Direct Mail*[3]

Study those books. Even if you hire outside help, you will need as much expertise of your own as you can develop.

The very best short introduction is the article by Robert Stone in the *Advertising Handbook*.[4]

Many of the principles of display copy apply to direct-mail copy, of course. Testimonials improve results. Premiums improve results. Time limits improve results.

This section will try to give you some *facts* about direct-mail packages that apply for mail order. Many of them come from tests run by the National Research Bureau.

The proper use of the graphic arts is crucial in direct-mail mail order. Chapter 19 tackles that subject.

The Elements of the Best Direct-Mail Packages

There are no hard and fast laws about what elements will make up the best direct-mail package. But subject to innumerable variations and exceptions, most direct-mail men agree that the best direct-mail piece will consist of either (1) letter, reply card (or coupon and reply envelope), outer envelope; or (2) letter, brochure or circular, reply card, outer envelope.

The letter is the single most crucial part of the package. No salesman would ever walk into an office, slap down his presentation, and expect the prospect to do the rest of the selling. Sending a brochure or circular without a letter does just that—and it isn't good enough.

Brochures and circulars work best when your product requires illustration.

Other Offers in the Package

Every direct-mail seller eventually gets the idea that he can increase his revenue by adding extra offers in the package. And with that idea comes the dream: "If it costs me no more to mail 10 offers than one. . . ."

Sometimes you can increase revenue in this fashion. In fact, a catalog is just a big bunch of offers. But sadly, your original offer will never pull quite as well when you include other offers in the package.

Whether or not it is profitable to add further offers to your offer is a question you must test for yourself.

You must test everything important, of course. Chapter 18 tells you how to make the tests. But you must also be discriminating about *what* you test. Don't waste your time testing hand-sealed versus machine-sealed envelopes, or Remington versus IBM typewriter face. Save your testing energy for the big and important things: price, extra offers, presence or absence of a brochure, etc.

THE LETTER

Write as much copy as you need to write. Never cut your sales argument short because you think the prospect won't read that much. Successful sales letters have run to four and six pages, out-pulling shorter letters. In general, a two-page letter out-pulls a one-page letter.[5]

But don't be wordy. Say only what you must say, and nothing more.

A good *letterhead* is very important. The best letterhead fits the spirit of the letter. The National Research Bureau finds that a letterhead specially designed to fit the offer usually outpulls a "standard" letterhead. And two-color letterheads out-pull one-color letterheads, they find.[6]

The quality of the paper *may* matter, but sometimes does not. Moran[7] reports a Standard & Poor test in which cheap paper pulled the same number of returns as expensive paper. (This test, unlike so many others, was large enough to be reliable.) Usually 20-pound stock is quite satisfactory, except for letters to professional groups.[8]

Make the letter as interesting to read and look at as possible. Avoid any repetitive regularities in style. Use plenty of subheads, indentations,[9] underlinings, capitalization of paragraphs, handwritten interjections, and even spot art to jazz up the appearance. But never make the letter so jazzy that it cheapens the product. Good taste, experienced taste, suited to the market, the price, and the product, is your only guide.

A two-color letter usually will out-pull a one-color letter.[10] Furthermore, B. M. Mellinger says that the second color almost always proves to be worth the extra cost.[11]

A long time ago a *Forbes* magazine test[12] showed that colored paper would out-pull white-paper letterheads very substantially. The best colors were, in this order: pink (260), gold (210), green (160), corn (140), white (90). (I don't put much stock in the figures. The differences are far too big to be believable.) Several writers say that canary, goldenrod, and pink pull better than blue and green. I have seen no definite figures, though.

But nowadays big mailers find that colored paper is seldom worth the extra cost. Instead, they frequently use colored ink.

The same *Forbes* test showed that two small illustrations on the letters raised the response considerably (400 to 210). (Again the differences are not believable.)

A two-page letter on two separate sheets is better than two sides of the same sheet.[13]

REPEAT LETTERS

Sometimes a list pulls so well the first time around that it pays to mail to the same list again. What should you mail then?

> *Nation's Business* recently tested to find the best method. An original mailing to a list of 20,000 which got excellent results was followed up the next month, but the follow-up was split into four groups of 5,000. Here are the results:
>
> 1. Simulated carbon copy of original letter with memo attached—same offer—77% of the original return.
> 2. A different letter reminding about the first mailing—same offer—52%.
> 3. A different letter containing the same offer, but making no mention of the original mailing—65%.
> 4. A completely different letter with a different offer, no mention of original mailings—50%.
>
> The conclusion: *A good offer is worth repeating.*[14]

THE BROCHURE OR CIRCULAR

Brochures and circulars come in such a remarkable number of sizes and shapes that I know of no valid generalizations about the best-pulling styles. The distinctions between brochures, circulars, and book-

lets are not clear, either. What we call a "circular" is usually short—
one, two, or four pages. If it is longer, we call it a "brochure" or "booklet." "Booklet" usually suggests that it contains other information than
just your sales pitch. And we usually think of a brochure as a very
fancy selling piece.

A two-color circular out-pulls one color regularly.[15] Four-color circulars are sometimes worth the money. And a circular separate from the
letter will usually do better than a letter-circular combination.

A typeset circular costs more than a typewritten circular but is worth
it. And a reply coupon on the circular adds extra returns.[16]

Testimonials are powerful no matter where you use them—in the letter
or in the circular. Some advertisers devote entire brochures to testimonials. Naturally, this technique will work best when the reader
has some doubts about claims made in the letter. Most testimonials
are not spontaneous. Some are solicited outright with questionnaires.
Other "unsolicited" testimonials are obtained by writing customers a
chatty letter that expresses your hope that they are satisfied, and asks
if you can help them further. If they are truly satisfied, a gratifying
number of testimonial letters will follow.

OUTER ENVELOPES

In a recent test of self-mailers versus envelope-enclosed packages,
the extra cost of the envelope was much more than recovered in extra
orders.

The envelope should be used for copy whenever possible. A catalog
house claimed to sell more from the envelope copy than from the best
page in the catalog. Most well-tested magazine circulation efforts use
copy on the envelope. But keep the envelope bare of copy if taste demands it in your particular line of business.

The National Research Bureau claims that illustrated envelopes are
effective when used properly.[17]

Preston[18] recommended the baronial sizes, rather than conventional
envelopes. A 500,000-letter test to women showed the baronials to be
more than worth the extra cost. Preston observed informally that
baronials are worth their cost to men, also.

Odd shapes and oversized envelopes are generally reported to be
effective, subject to cost and post office regulations that make most
odd shapes illegal. They are especially effective in a series of letters to
the same people.

COUPONS, ORDER CARDS, AND REPLY ENVELOPES

The most important fact about coupons and reply envelopes or reply
cards is: *Always* include one or the other in *every* mailing. The theory

is, "Make it easy to order." Evidence is abundant that return envelopes and order cards increase returns substantially, far more than their extra cost. Baker[19] estimates an average 5 to 10 percent increase for the reply envelope. Musselman[20] says a coupon "increased sales 22%."

I have found that 98 percent of those who respond will use business-reply envelopes, and 92 percent will affix stamps and use *ordinary* reply envelopes. The rest will use their *own* envelopes.

Business-reply envelopes versus ordinary reply envelopes is not a clear issue. Innumerable advertisers have tested one against the other, and yet some use each, with the preponderance of mailers using business-reply envelopes. Some mailers don't use the business-reply envelopes because they are (sometimes irrationally) annoyed by nuisance returns of empty envelopes.

Some advertisers may misread their test results because of the greater number of respondents who use plain envelopes *rather* than ordinary reply envelopes. This *could* lead to misevaluation of tests in favor of business replies. When I took account of this factor on a test that I ran, business replies were just about a break-even proposition against ordinary reply envelopes.

The higher the unit cost of your item, the more profitable business-reply envelopes are.

To get a business-reply permit and number, just fill out the free permit application at the post office. You then pay 7 cents for each business-reply envelope you receive.

Mailers should consider the wide variety of trick reply-envelope forms available for various purposes. These include outgoing self-mailers that convert into reply envelopes, and "wallet" replies that are basically order forms.

I'd suggest careful testing before using any expensive trick envelope for long runs.

The reply envelope is an important carrier of sales messages for many firms. Macy's uses its reply envelope with monthly bills to sell shirts. Other firms have worked out deals with subscription agencies who supply reply envelopes with magazine-subscription sales copy on them. The reply envelope is such a powerful medium for this type of selling because it is always "close to the money" and never gets thrown away.

Color and design of the reply envelope can affect the results. Moran quotes data showing that a gaudy reply card out-pulled a plain card 22 to 14, and green out-pulled brown six to four.[21] (No reliability estimate on either figure; suggestive but inconclusive data.)

An illustration on the reply card will usually increase returns. And "guarantee stubs" for the purchaser to rip off and keep as a receipt usually increase response, too.[22]

Repeat the *proposition* on the coupon and order card. Leave plenty of room for name and address, and leave space for "State." You will be surprised by the number of people who expect you to know where they live without their telling you.

Offer an opportunity to trade up on the coupon or reply card. Add a check-box for "Morocco binding $9.98" or "2 sets $14.95." A substantial number of purchasers will usually take advantage of the deluxe offer, quantity offer, or offer of allied merchandise.

Sometimes it pays to throw in extra reply cards, with a note: "Pass them along to your friends." One advertiser found that 10 cards was the best number to include with his particular proposition.

Some outfits who sell merchandise priced under $10 include a safety coin envelope with the mailing. Printed on the safety envelope is a legend that says something like: "SAFETY ENVELOPE. Don't be afraid to send cash. . . . It is entirely safe to send cash by mail. No need to write a check. We will be responsible for safe delivery if you use the enclosed, postage-free envelope."

The purpose of the safety envelope is twofold:

1. To make it easier to order for people who want to send cash. Often people go to great lengths to wrap coins, and to hide bills in paper so they can't be seen through the envelope. The safety envelope saves them that trouble.

2. To increase the number of orders that send cash rather than check.

Each check you receive costs 3 to 5 cents bank charge, plus a cent or so in your own office handling, and if you sell items at $2, say, this is an important bite out of your revenue.

I have no data on how the safety envelope affects returns, but enough firms use them to indicate that they are sometimes worth their cost.

Stock safety envelopes are available in bulk from several envelope companies.

Airmail reply envelopes and cards will increase responses *if* there is a reason for urgency.[23]

TYPES OF POSTAGE

Very few mailers find that first-class postage pays for itself. Many find that third-class even pulls just as many orders, at a lower cost. And airmail postage is seldom worth the extra tariff.

Metered mail generally does just as well or better than stamped mail. Prospects are not as much against business mail as many observers think. A "designed imprint" pulls as well as metered mail.

Here are the results of an interesting test of the effectiveness of different types of postage, as quoted by Paul Bringe:

> Four groups of 75,000 pieces each were mailed. Group A—No. 9 colored window envelope with bold teaser line on face, printed third class indicia. Group B—same but with 2½¢ stamp rather than indicia. Group C same but with 4¢ first class stamp. Group D—No. 9 white window, re-

turn address on flap, "First Class Mail" printed on face, 4¢ commemorative first class stamp.

	Orders pulled	Relative cost per order
Key D (equals 100)	100	100
C	89	112
A	75	101
B	70	110

The first class mailing that *looked* like first class (D) brought the most orders at the lowest cost. But it also brought back 3,962 non-deliverables. The first class mail that *looked* like third class (C) brought only 204 non-deliverables at a 12% higher cost per order.[24]

Replies to *inquiries,* however, are generally sent first class. A prospect's enthusiasm cools off quickly if he doesn't hear from you soon after writing. Grant states that inquiries "lose 1%" for each day not answered.[25]

Appendix B gives you basic facts on classes of postage and mailing procedures.

HOW TO ESTIMATE RESULTS QUICKLY

The art of predicting total results from partial returns is discussed at length in Chapter 11. Here are some rules of thumb for *direct mail*—showing the percent of responses you can expect. The "first day" is the day the first reply comes back, *not* the day of mailing.

ROBERT BAKER[26]

6th day	13th day	27th day	8th week	26th week
35%	72%	89%	96%	100%

KEN ALEXANDER (SEGAL)[27]

5th day	8th day	15th day	23d day	29th day
33%	52%	72%	77%	81%

ROBERT STONE[28]
(To business lists rather than consumers; 1st replies on 5th day after mailing)

1st day	2d day	5th day	6th day	7th day	8th day	9th day
8.06%	16.08%	29.96%	37.20%	48.60%	59.16%	68.48%

12th day	13th day	14th day	15th day	16th day	19th day
74.01%	77.21%	81.26%	83.06%	84.13%	87.21%

American Heritage[29]
Mailed on Friday, one-half of responses on or before 2d Friday following

PAUL GRANT[30]
(*From old customers*)

1st week	2d week	3d week
52%	85%	90%

(*From "cold" prospects*)

1st week	2d week	3d week
46%	80%	89%

ART KEMBLE[31]

1st week	2d week	3d week	4th week	8th week	26th week
30%	58%	75%	84%	95%	100%

15

Direct-Mail Lists

List Brokers • Types of Lists • How to Choose Lists • Duplication of Names on Lists • List Building and Maintenance • How Much Is a Customer Worth? • Extra Revenue by Renting Your List • When to Mail • How Often to Remail to a List • How Long to Keep an Inactive Customer on Your List

This fact bears repetition: The choice of lists is absolutely crucial in direct mail. A winning offer in a winning package will fall flat on its face when sent to the wrong list. If you ever sell mail-order products by direct mail, you'll learn this lesson for yourself sooner or later, and the lesson will be expensive.

LIST BROKERS

List brokers are of vital importance to almost every direct-mail mail-order firm. It is their function to bring together the owners of lists and the firms that want to rent lists. They usually get a flat 20 percent commission on the rental, and it is to their advantage that each test you rent be successful, because you will then use the whole list and boost their fees. The broker is unlikely to make any money on a test that fails.

Brokers have a wide knowledge about choosing lists, which they pass on to you as part of their service. But brokers, like other people, are fallible. Don't be afraid to let your judgment override the broker's judgment on occasion.

Brokers also may *own* compiled lists, which they rent to you outright

Code No.	Quantity	Description	Dollars Per Thousand
Ht 14	17,000	rose bush buyers	15.
Ht 15	95,228	garden supplies, seed and nursery item buyers	15.
Ht 16	40,000	plant food, planters & garden supply buyers	15.
Ht 17	82,000	seed, ornamental shrubs, and fruit plant buyers	15.
Ht 18	2,067,100	buyers of lawn care magazine, supplies	15.
Ht 19	209,000	women buyers of dutch bulbs (home owners)	15.
Ht 20	10,000	buyers of water plants, lily pool supplies	19.
Ht 21	17,000	former subscribers to famous horticulture magazine	17.
Ht 22	150,000	members of horticulture groups and societies	17.
Ht 23	30,000	persons interested in raising orchids	15.
Ht 24	7,725	subscribers to Tropical Homes & Gardens (Florida)	15.
Ht 25	40,000	90% women who sent money for iris bulbs	15.
Ht 26	1,689,290	bought products for lawn care (in central states)	14.
Ht 27	22,500	retail florists	20.
Ht 58	45,000		15.
Ht 59	37,500	buyers of geraniums, violets, ivy plants	15.
Ht 60	11,850	bought tree & shrub seeds	15.
Ht 61	50,000	bought nursery products	15.
Ht 62	23,077	buyers of quality seeds	15.
Ht 63	30,000	seed, bulb, plant buyers	15.
Ht 64	56,000	75% are repeat buyers of fruit trees	15.
Ht 65	15,000	leading female flower growers & gardeners	15.
Ht 66	140,000	buyers of trees, roses, evergreens, shrubs, etc.	13.
Ht 67	125,904	buyers of fruit trees and other nursery items	14.
Ht 68	95,000	buyers of pompon, mums, azaleamums	15.
Ht 69	140,000	above average income home owners who bought fruit trees, berry plants, seed	15.

Page 72

Code No.	Quantity	Description	Dollars Per Thousand
Ht 70	12,000	members of Plant of Month Club, buyers of shrubs	15.
Ht 71	25,000	subscribers to Popular Gardening	15.
Ht 72	24,000	buyers of flower seeds, bulbs, rock gardens	15.
Ht 73	180,000	fine seed buyer list	15.
Ht 74	44,700	buyers of nursery items	15.
Ht 75	39,000	buyers of choice flowers (glads, etc.)	15.
Ht 76	32,000	women buyers of Hawaiian good luck plant	14.
Ht 77	14,200	hobbyists who purchased orchid plants	15.
Ht 78	29,117	orchid fanciers who bought catalog and growing instructions	15.
Ht 79	90,103	U.S. florists and nurserymen	15.
Ht 80	10,930	80% public spirited men, members of American Forestry Association	17.
Ht 81	30,000	buyers of horticulture supplies, violets	15.
Ht 82	13,000	catalog requests (50% women) for seeds, garden supplies	13.
Ht 83	135,000	buyers of perennial plants, lawn seeds, etc.	15.
Ht 84	50,000	buyers of grass seed, shears, garden hose	14.

HOUSEWARES

Code No.	Quantity	Description	Dollars Per Thousand
Hs 1	25,900	buyers of aluminum cake molds	13.
Hs 2	100,000	buyers of electrical appliances	15.
Hs 32	117,000	bought thermal salad bowl	13.
Hs 33	119,000	buyers of personalized door mat	15.
Hs 34	49,000	99% women who buy household cutlery	15.
Hs 35	100,000	buyers of colorful plastic dinnerware	13.
Hs 36	69,900	buyers of many household items	14.
Hs 37	64,000	buyers of top quality home accessories, toys	15.
Hs 38	1,500,000	buyers of kitchen gadgets	15.
Hs 39	50,000	buyers of colored burlap	15.

Page 73

FIG. 15-1

for their own account. There are other firms that specialize in compiled lists, too.

Don't ever consider buying or renting the cheap lists of names offered direct by tiny, unknown firms to anyone who runs a classified ad or small display ad. Even if the lists were satisfactory, they are far too small to do you any good.

Consult a broker about future rentals of *your* list, today. Do this *before* you have a big list, because the broker's advice may affect the way you maintain your list.

Rental Means Rental. You use the names once and that's all. The owner of the list is protected by the criminal law against your stealing the list. He guards against stealing by placing "decoy" names on the list, made-up names which you couldn't know of unless you use his list. Decoy names are evidence in court.

Many list owners forego a considerable extra income by refusing to rent their lists, out of fear of theft. Their caution is understandable, because their lists are the most important assets of their businesses. But their caution is probably not justified, and costs them extra profits each year.

Appendix G contains the names of several list brokers. Figure 15-1 shows sample pages from a list broker's catalog.

To arrange to rent lists, call or write one or more brokers. Tell him what you are selling, and if possible, include a mailing piece. The broker will recommend lists by sending you cards with full information about the lists he recommends.

The mechanics of renting lists vary, but they are always simple. The two most usual arrangements are: (1) You send your envelopes to the renter or to his letter shop, who then returns the addressed envelopes to you. (2) The list owner sends you gummed labels to affix to your envelopes.

TYPES OF LISTS

There are three basic types of mailing lists: (1) compiled lists, (2) lists of mail-order buyers, and (3) the "house list." They are very different, but all have their important uses.

Compiled lists are lists of people who have some characteristic in common. The common characteristic may be as simple as that the addresses are in the same area. (For example, the crisscross telephone directories that list people up and down the street, "occupant" lists, and "rural box holder" lists.) Or the common characteristic may be that the addressees all belong to the Interplanetary Study Society.

Compiled lists are derived from many sources—mostly records of trade organizations, professional organizations, and publicly available records. But even if the original material is available to you, you will usually find it cheaper in the long run to use the services of a list broker.

Mail-order buyer lists are lists of people who have bought from particular mail-order firms. People on mail-order buyer lists have *two* things in common:

1. They have bought or expressed interest in a particular type of merchandise.

2. They are inclined to buy by mail.

The importance of 1 is obvious; 2 has been *proved* crucial, time after time. All else being equal, it is tremendously harder to sell by mail to people who have no record of buying by mail, than to mail-order buyers.

The house list is the list of people who have bought from you in the past. Paul Bringe gives this example of the tremendous power of the house list:

> . . . the Republican Party is having good results with its fund raising by mail effort. First mailings last year brought an average 3% response of $11 each at a cost of 17½ cents per dollar collected. "Renewals" this year from last year's donors brought a 50% response at a cost of 1½ cents per dollar.
>
> This is a good demonstration of the great difference between a qualified list and a non-qualified list. The first year the Republican mailing was probably made, with the aid of census tract information, to upper income groups suspected but not known to be Republican.
>
> The second year's mailing went to known customers who, if they did not contribute, would have to admit to themselves that they made a mistake the first year. Such an admission is difficult for anyone to make. Doesn't this indicate that in many cases an outright loss the first year could prove mighty profitable thereafter? Magazine publishers have known it for years.[1]

HOW TO CHOOSE LISTS

These principles may help you to analyze lists for your offer:

1. Use the same lists, or the same types of lists, as your competition does. This is our old key principle, of course, of following along wherever success has been proven.

2. Use your competitor's lists themselves, if you can get permission. Many competitors exchange lists.

3. Among the likely lists, test the *biggest* lists first. Only a big list can give you the big volume that makes a heavy profit. (On the other hand, there is some tendency for smaller lists to be of better quality.)

4. Use *fresh* lists, or *well-maintained* lists. The Direct Mail Advertising Association estimates that *each year* changes in address or name in-

clude 22 percent of householders, 23 percent of merchants, 39 percent of advertising executives.[2] Stone[3] estimates 20 to 30 percent annual changes on buyer lists. And there was a 25 percent change in a single year in job addresses from a McGraw-Hill list.[4]

The meaning of these statistics is clear: because of the "nixie" undeliverables, a one-year-old list can give you up to 25 percent less revenue than a new list, a difference bigger than your probable profit margin.

5. Compiled lists are seldom good for consumer items. But they are invaluable for commercial and industrial sales.

6. Inquirers versus purchasers: purchaser lists will always do better, because there are no "curiosity seekers" among them. The interest of a purchaser is bound to be higher than that of an inquirer.

7. Price of item bought. The higher the unit sale, the more money the customers obviously had to spend—and the more they are able to spend for your products, too.

8. "Class" of lists. High-class lists do very well for a variety of customers. The Diners' Club list is a favorite. Leslie's gift list is another "high class" example.

9. Moran[5] says that these are the lists rented most often:

a. Business executives
b. Buyers of luxuries
c. Men purchasers
d. Buyers of health specialties
e. Book buyers
f. Woman buyers
g. Psychology book and course buyers
h. Buyers of beauty specialties

These further principles may help you:

1. Ask yourself, "Are these the kind of people who will be interested in this offer?" There is no replacement for sound intuition, experience, and knowledge in answering that question.

2. Rely on your list broker. He is on your side. The very nature of your financial transactions with him means that his interests are your interests.

3. Consider whether you can use only *some of the states* on a list, or consider dropping out the cities. Often you can greatly increase the average results from a list in this way, because you are weeding out the areas that would drag the average down.

4. Mail to businessmen's homes may pull better—but it may annoy some customers who prefer to get business mail at their office.

Direct-mail experts disagree on many points, but on this they are unanimous: *the best list is the list of your old customers.* It will pull two to ten times better than any list you can find. The people on your list know you and patronize you as they would patronize an old friend.

Second best to the house list is a list of people who have purchased similar goods by mail. Third best is a list of people who have purchased *anything* by mail. Next is a compiled list of people with some special characteristic to which your goods will appeal. Poorest of all is just any old list of people, such as the alphabetical telephone directory. Few and far between are the offers so good they will make money on such "cold" lists.

Exceptions to these rules:

1. *Commercial venders.* If you sell steel in 10-ton lots, no list of mail-order buyers will do you any good. What you need is a list of manufacturers that use steel.

2. *Retailers.* The delicatessen around the corner in a big city can *only* use the crisscross phone book (in which the listings run up and down the street, rather than alphabetically). And many a retailer has done well with this kind of direct mail. (Retailers can use other local lists, too, on occasion.)

DUPLICATION OF NAMES ON LISTS

Some names appear on many lists, of course, and it is to your advantage not to send six appeals to the same fellow on the same morning. But generally, the avoidance of duplication is far more costly than are the wasted letters. So you must accept duplication as a necessary evil.

You can reduce the duplication waste by mailing similar lists at different times. That way, your duplicated letter has several chances to sell the customer. The second and third letters are not completely wasted as they are if they arrive on the same day.

My guess is that direct-mail men complain so much about duplication because they themselves are on so many lists for business purposes. Few consumers will get as many direct-mail pieces as people in the direct-mail business do.

LIST BUILDING AND MAINTENANCE

You *must* have as big a house list of active customers as possible. You must build this list in any way you can and maintain it in tiptop shape. Your list is vital for rental income as well as for your own use. Jack Leslie[6] says that list rental accounts for 25 percent of his not inconsiderable annual gross, and list rental has a terrific profit margin.

The post office helps you maintain your list, though their help costs you money. The most important help is informing you of new customer addresses. And you *must* keep up to date with accurate addresses.

To obtain this list-correction service, your third-class mail should

bear an imprint "Return requested." The post office employees will return your third-class mail to you with the forwarding address marked
on it, charging you 8 cents per letter. Another part of keeping your list
clean is to scratch off the first-class nixies that are returned as unknown.

The post office helps in other ways, too, depending on what you
request on the envelope. Check with your postmaster, and your *Postal
Manual,* because procedures change from time to time. (By the way,
a *Postal Manual* should be your first investment in your mail-order
business.)

It is sometimes helpful in building a list to ask your customers for
the names of their friends who may be interested in your products.
Satisfied customers are glad to cooperate, especially if you offer them
a small free gift.

HOW MUCH IS A CUSTOMER WORTH?

Perhaps the crucial question in list maintenance is how long to
keep a customer on the list after his last order. Mailing "dead" customers
is very costly indeed. But to drop a potentially live customer can be
even more costly.

Before you can decide how long to keep a customer on your list,
you must know how much a customer is worth to you. We shall now
tackle that problem.

The procedure I shall describe here should not cost you more than
$200 including clerical time, no matter how big your list is. I practically
guarantee that the information will increase your profit by many
thousands of dollars in the future, if your business is any size at all.

There are good customers and poor customers, and obviously the
good customers are worth more than the poor customers. But we're
talking now of *average* customers. When you first get a *new* customer,
you can't tell whether he will be a good customer or not.

And when you are deciding whether to keep an old customer on
your list, or drop him, you have no way of telling whether he will
again be a good customer—except on the basis of how other *old*
customers behave.

The value of a customer is the total *profit* he will bring you. Not
the *volume,* mind you, but the profit. You certainly would not pay
me $2 to bring you a customer who will give you $10 in volume but
only $1 in profit. But if you had a high-margin business and $10 volume
gave you $4 profit, you *would* pay me $2 to bring you in a customer
who would spend $10. In fact, you'd be willing to pay me almost $4 for
him.

The circulation director of *Life* supplied excellent data[7] on *Life*'s
circulation advertising results, summarized in Table 15-1. Like every

TABLE   15-1

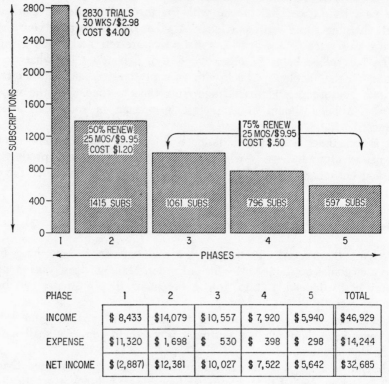

PHASE	1	2	3	4	5	TOTAL
INCOME	$ 8,433	$14,079	$ 10,557	$ 7,920	$5,940	$46,929
EXPENSE	$11,320	$ 1,698	$ 530	$ 398	$ 298	$14,244
NET INCOME	$ (2,887)	$12,381	$ 10,027	$ 7,522	$5,642	$32,685

other magazine, and like other repeat-business mail-order firms, *Life* would go broke if it depended on the revenue from the first orders. For the sample shown, the first year the net *loss* is $2,877. But by the end of five years the profit is $32,685.

Assume for the moment that "fulfillment" costs of producing and distributing the magazine equal the revenue from advertising—a pretty good assumption for mass consumer magazines. Then *Life* should figure how much it can afford to spend for a new customer in this way:

1. Subscription revenue from an *average* customer during the "life" of the customer equals

$$\$46,269 \div 2,830 = \$16.60$$

2. The total cost of soliciting *renewals* for a group of customers divided by the number of original customers in the group equals

$$\frac{\$1,698 + \$530 + \$398 + \$298}{2,830} = \$1.03$$

3. The most that *Life* should spend to get a customer, then, is

$$\$16.60 - \$1.03 = \$15.57$$

Note how, after the trial-period renewal, customers fall away at about 25 percent *each year*. It will be true for practically every mail-order business that a constant *percentage* of a group of customers will drop out each year. Once you have estimated the customer fall-off rate for one year for your business, you have a terrifically valuable tool for future planning.*

Knowing the value of a customer is crucial. You must know that value so you can know how much of a loss you can afford to take on a first ad in order to get repeat business.

To calculate the value of a customer to you, you should first find the *volume* your average customer will spend with you in the future. To make things simple, we shall assume that the future ends after three years. Anything you take in after that is gravy, a margin for error. For several economic reasons this won't distort our calculations very much.

If you have been in business over three years, the figuring is a breeze. All you have to do is take a sample of people who bought from you over three years ago, and see how much they purchased in the first three years after you first heard from them.

IMPORTANT: You *must* sample *both* the customers who are still active *and* those who are now in your inactive of "dead" file. If by some unfortunate accident you have thrown away the records of inactive customers, you will need a procedure slightly more complicated than we have space to describe here. Any statistical consultant should be able to set up a satisfactory procedure for you in a few hours.

I can't tell you the *exact* size of the proper sample for your business. But 300 customers should be more than large enough in most cases, and a sample a little too big won't cost you much extra.

---

* Even if you cannot trace sales from individual ads to individual customers, as is the case for general advertisers, you can use a similar formula to find the optimum advertising appropriation. The paradigm is to compare the profit levels of the various proposed levels of advertising, using this formula:

$$\text{Profit} = \frac{1}{1 - d\rho} \left(\sum_{T=1}^{t} R_{T,t} - d \sum_{T=1}^{t-1} R_{T,t-1} \right) - A_t$$

d = amount of sales retained from period to period in absence of further advertising; ρ = discount rate of money ($1 -$ interest rate); T = revenue period; t = advertising period; R = net revenue; and A = advertising.

This Is All You Have to Do to Take a Sample

1. Take a *fair* (random) sample of the names of 300 customers—active and inactive—who first bought over three years ago.

2. Add up the total amount they have purchased in the three years from the date of first purchase.

3. Divide by 300.

4. Multiply by your average profit margin (in percent).

The figure you come out with is the amount it is worth to you to *get a customer onto your books*. Never lose an opportunity to get a customer for anything less than that cost.

This is the best way to take a fair random sample: Use a ruler to make a mark at equal intervals in your customer files so that there are *300 equal intervals*. This saves you the trouble of counting off the cards. Take the first customer *over three years old* that comes after each mark.

If you have been in business only a short time, you can *estimate* the same data by first figuring out how the average customer's purchase frequency drops as time goes on. Then you project the effect for a three-year period. Better get some help from a statistician on this. Actually, this procedure is especially vital for new businesses. It is only this way that you can accurately decide whether you are making or losing money.

EXTRA REVENUE BY RENTING YOUR LIST

Not only is your house list worth a great deal to you in repeat sales, but you can boost your income greatly by renting your list to other mailers.

You can rent your list yourself by offering it to other mailers. Or you can use the services of a list broker to help you rent your list. The list broker usually takes a 20 percent commission, and he is almost always worth it.

An advertisement for the Leslie Creations

FIG.   15-2

list provides interesting information about list rental. This is a list of "blue-chip" firms that have rented the Leslie lists:

Added Touch Gifts
Ambassador Leather
American Federation for Blind
American Heritage
Amsterdam Company
Art in America
Atlantic Monthly
Atlas Magazine
Bachman Pretzels
Battle Creek Equipment
Better Magazine Club
Better Reading Program
Biltmore Securities
Book-of-the-Month Club
Boy's Athletic League
Capitol Record Club
Chalmar Gifts
Changing Times
Children's Village
Cobbs Fruit
Columbia Record Club
Columbia University
Connoisseur's Choice
Consumer Reports
Cue Magazine
Disneyland Records
Doubleday & Co.
Doyle Stationery
Drumcliff Company
Dun & Bradstreet
Encyclopaedia Britannica
Epicure's Club
Esquire
Federal Association for Epilepsy
Foster Gallagher
Gulf Park Estates
Haband Company
C. S. Hammond
Harper's Bazaar
Heath Company
Hi-Fi & Stereo Review
High Fidelity
Holiday Magazine
Horticulture
House Beautiful
House & Garden
Insider's Newsletter
Jackson & Perkins
Kaskel Jewelers

Kozak Auto Dry Wash
Lakeland Nurseries
Lane Book Company
Larchmont Investors
Les Echalottes
Macmillan Company
Markus-Campbell
McGraw-Hill, Inc.
Meredith's
Merrin Jewelers
Miles Kimball
Mission Pak
Mummert Farms
National Geographic
National Observer
National Society for the Prevention of Blindness
National Wildlife Federation
Newsweek
New Yorker
New York Times
Old American Insurance
Pecan Joe
Pinnacle Orchards
Priester's Pecans
Process Corporation
Radio Shack
Random House
Reader's Digest
Réalités in America
Reporter
Rose Mill O'Milford
Rosicrucian Order
Russ Photo Service
Saturday Review
Save the Children Federation
Shopping International
Show Magazine
Simon and Schuster
Stanford Institute
Street & Smith
Swiss Colony
Thomas Young Gifts
Time
Travel Magazine
Vermont Crossroads
Walter Weintz Co.
Webster's Unified
Wisconsin Cheeseman
Wm. H. Wise & Co.
Yield House

At an estimated rental price of 2 cents per name per rental, you can guess for yourself how much revenue the estimated 100,000-name Leslie list has brought in. Figure 15-2 is an example of a list owner's advertisement.

WHEN TO MAIL

If you mail first class, it may be wise to spot your mailing on a specific day. But you third-class mailers can't depend upon any correlation between when you *mail* third-class material and when it gets there. Tests show variation from 6 to 15 days in getting across the country.

In a recent test,[8] one batch of catalogs were mailed in New York on March 26. They arrived in New York on March 27, in a suburb of New York on April 3, in Chicago on April 2, and in Los Angeles on April 3. Another batch of catalogs were mailed in Chicago on March 26. They arrived in New York on April 6, a New York suburb on April 9, in Chicago on April 2, and in Los Angeles on April 4.

The only possible conclusion is that the speed of third-class mail is practically unpredictable.

American Heritage always mails on Friday. National Research Bureau mails on Saturday. But every day of the week has been best in somebody's test.

The effect of the *month* on mail-order returns is discussed in Chapter 12. Stone[9] says about direct mail: "Most mass mailers who test in the summer months get a 25 to 30 per cent higher return during their mailing season" than during the summer test. This dropoff in the summer is *less* than in display ads, especially from newsstand magazines. Periodicals have a lower *readership* in summer, *and* the actual readers purchase less. But direct mail suffers from only the latter of those two effects.

Grant[10] lists direct-mail mail-order months in this order: October, November, January, February, September, April, March, May, December, August, July, June.

Seasonal gift mail must go out early. September, or even August, is not too soon for Christmas mailings.

HOW OFTEN TO REMAIL TO A LIST

You will mail to your own house list of customers just as often as you can develop new products to sell them. You can never mail *too often* to your own customers. They will never tire of hearing from you.

But you can also mail more than once to cold lists. If you mail an offer to a rented list and the results are *far* above your break-even point, wait a while, then rent the same list again and mail the *same offer*.

Samuel Hall[11] said that "if a large mailing of an entire list pulls as much as twice your break-even point, then you can safely remail to the entire list 45 days after you deposit your first re-mailing, without retesting."

HOW LONG TO KEEP AN INACTIVE CUSTOMER ON YOUR LIST

Emanuel Haldeman-Julius[12] said that when the great depression of the '30s hit in earnest the expense of mailing to his huge list of 2 million buyers of "Little Blue Books" was killing him. So he resolved to take heroic measures to pare the list of all except the really live customers. He then sent out a *half-price* offer. Every single person who didn't accept the half-price offer was dropped from the list.

Heroic and necessary as Haldeman-Julius's method may have been, there were almost surely better methods for the long and short run. But few mail-order men are willing and able to tackle this problem statistically, even though it is quite easy to calculate the best answer.

You already know how much a live customer is worth to you. You also know that it is expensive to keep shooting mail at a customer who hasn't bought for so long that he is almost surely dead. The trick is to know the proper time to give up on a customer.

First, figure out how much *profit* you make on an average-sized order. Start by estimating the size of the average order. Go back to the 300 customers you randomly sampled when you wanted to find the value of the average *customer*. Take the average of their last orders. Then multiply by your *average profit margin*. The result is your profit *on an average sale*.

Then estimate how many mailings you can make for a cost *equal* to your profit on an average sale. For example, if you sell yard goods, your monthly swatched mailing piece may cost you 25 cents each. If your profit on an average order is $4, you can mail sixteen pieces for that cost ($4 divided by 25 cents equals 16).

And so—keep a customer on your books for a period of time long enough to mail pieces equal in cost to your average profit on a sale. The yard-goods man should keep customers on his books for 16 monthly mailings from the date of the last order.

(This procedure depends on an assumption that customers will tend to buy at a constant rate over time. This assumption could be wrong in either direction. Customers may tend to buy more often, or less often, the longer they are on your books. Nevertheless, the procedure described above should not take you far astray.)

16

Using Other Mail-Order Media

Television • Radio • Match Books • Package Stuffers • Bill Stuffers • Transit Advertising • Daily Newspapers • Other Media

Mail-order men have always been ingenious and resourceful. At one time or another they have tested almost every medium except skywriting and fluorescent raincoats to see if they would pull profitably.

Most products, most of the time, do best in the standard print media we have discussed so far. But in this lesson we shall talk briefly about the special media that can be of great importance under the right circumstances.

TELEVISION

Television has terrific power to sell many general products. But it is little used by mail-order firms. Why? The reasons are too complex to go into here. And besides, you're interested in when it *will* work, and not when it won't work.

TV can be successful for special products that can tie the entertainment to the sales pitch. For example, a record company offers "Fifty Great Moments in Music." The program itself plays the musical excerpts as the camera focuses on "appropriate" paintings. The entire program is a sales demonstration which only needs to be completed by the price, time element, and premium offer.

This particular offer, like others on TV, is almost surely a PI (perinquiry) deal between the record company and the television stations. The mail-order firm tapes the program, except for the station identification, and distributes the tape to the stations. The commercials ask

142

for money to be sent to the station. The station sends the letters on to the company, which then reimburses the station a fixed amount for each offer.

A commercial also will pull better if the address is a local station, because of the confidence that people feel in doing business with a local station as compared to a faraway, unknown firm.

Full information on stations' addresses, rates, and other necessary data is found in *Standard Rate & Data*.

RADIO

Radio carries more mail-order advertising than does television because it costs much less per thousand listeners. The offers which do best on radio are also those that tie in the program with the commercial. One example is Sidney Walton's "Profit Research." Walton gives a talk on some money-saving or money-making topic, and then makes a pitch for his books in the same field of interest.

Another famous example was the White House Company's "18 Top Hits" records.

Lately I have heard the Standard & Poor Company pitching their investment information services on Texas stations. Maybe the Texas millionaires make a good market for Standard & Poor.

Per-inquiry deals constitute a good deal of radio mail-order advertising. If you have a product with radio possibilities, you must work up a sales letter to send to stations, pointing out how they can earn extra money with air time that would otherwise be without profit to them. Whether or not a station accepts your offer will depend on how persuasive you are in convincing them that the deal will be profitable, and it will also depend on station policy and the amount of air time they currently have available.

Advantages of radio are that you get results quickly, and you don't tie up your money for long. Timeliness and short closing dates are other advantages. A disadvantage of purchased radio time is that it requires extremely close watching and tight control. If your ads stop pulling, and you don't notice for a while, you can lose your shirt.

Clear-channel stations—those that broadcast over a wide area of the country at night without interference from other stations—may be your best bets for a PI deal.

Mail-order offers have made money from radio, many of them on a straight time-purchase basis. A firm that sold "three maps for a dollar" did fabulously well on radio, if my memory serves me right.

One major disadvantage of both radio and television is the absence of a coupon that makes it "easy to order."

Descriptive data are in *Standard Rate & Data*.

MATCH BOOKS

A large proportion of match books that are distributed nationally carry mail-order advertising. Match books are an excellent medium for offers that appeal to a mass audience rather than a specialized audience. Correspondence schools, especially those that offer high-school-completion courses, use match books a great deal. Address labels, Arizona and Florida land sales, insurance, and auto-accessory firms use match books. Surprising to me, at least one stamp firm appears to find match books profitable.

The biggest problem with match books is that the cheapest test purchase runs to several thousand dollars. However, if your offer is well proved in other media, you can safely bet that even if the test is not a roaring success, you aren't likely to lose much, either.

A major advantage of match books is that the entire inside cover makes a natural coupon. A frequent technique is to use a reverse block at the left of the inside cover as an arrow pointing to the fill-in lines.

Results come back slowly from match book advertising: 20 percent in the first six months, 75 percent in the first year, according to an industry source.

For further information, contact Match Industry Information Bureau, 1 East 43rd Street, New York, N.Y., or the following firms:

Diamond Match Division, Diamond National Corporation, 723 Third Avenue, New York, New York
Match Corporation of America, 3421 48th Place, Chicago 32, Illinois
Universal Match Corporation, 3305 Wilshire, Los Angeles, California
Atlas Matchbook Advertising, 605 South Serrano, Los Angeles, California

PACKAGE STUFFERS

Never send a package to customers without including an order blank for re-orders and sales literature on other products. Package stuffers are the cheapest yet most productive medium for many mail-order firms.

Sometimes it is profitable to insert sales literature for drop-ship merchandise (i.e., merchandise that the wholesaler or manufacturer stocks for you). The manufacturer will often supply the sales literature to you. For example, White River Industries of Muskegon, Michigan, supplies complete sales literature for their branding iron, telling how it can be used to personalize items. Or you might even include an entire drop-ship catalog.

BILL STUFFERS

If you have a proved mail-order offer that will offend no one's taste, you may be able to make a deal with department stores to include your sales literature, with their name and address on it, in the monthly bills they send to their customers. This is a per-inquiry, drop-ship arrangement. You pay them a fixed commission for every order they obtain, and you then ship the goods under their name.

A wide variety of mail-order merchandise has been sold in this way, especially the staples of mail order. Personal stationery and address labels use this medium regularly. And there are several firms that specialize in selling magazine subscriptions through this medium. (The magazine-subscription firms go even further in making special arrangements. They print return envelopes for customers to return their monthly payments, which include the advertisement for the magazine inside the envelope flap.)

Some big-ticket (i.e., high-unit-sale) merchandise, including cameras and optical equipment, has been sold through this technique.

TRANSIT ADVERTISING

This medium is known as "Take One" advertising, because the bus poster for a mail-order firm always includes coupons on a hook, with the caption, "Take One."

A typical coupon is shown in Figure 16-1. Home-study courses for high school completion use a great deal of transit advertising, and it evidently is profitable for them. Transit advertising reaches a very wide mass market, which is good only for unspecialized mail-order products that interest all kinds of people.

Why be held back by a lack of a High School Education? Mail this card today!

BE SURE TO PUT YOUR NAME AND ADDRESS ON OTHER SIDE

Post Card

PLACE
4¢
STAMP
HERE

ACADEMY FOR HOME STUDY

C/o Transportation Advertising Co.
3500 Prudential Plaza
CHICAGO 1, ILLINOIS

FIG. 16-1 (front)

TAKE ONE

FREE!

INFORMATION ON HOW TO

Get Your
High School
Diploma

at home in spare time

No matter what your age or how long it has been since you attended school, we can help you get your high school diploma through our special approved home study lessons. Full credit given for previous schooling. No classes to attend. Begin whenever you like — study whenever you like. Many students finish in half the normal time.

MAIL THIS CARD TODAY

·YOUR NAME

(Please Print)

ADDRESS _____ APT. ____

CITY _____ ZONE ____ STATE ____

OCCUPATION _____ AGE ____

FIG. 16-1 (back)

Standard Rate & Data, Transportation Advertising Section, contains names and addresses of the media. The media will give you full details on what you need to know.

The fact that the bus company address is given on the coupon in Figure 16-1 leads me to think that it is a per-inquiry deal. You might check on this if you have an offer that would go well in transit advertising.

DAILY NEWSPAPERS

Daily newspapers are not generally a successful mail-order medium. It is only the rare offer that can use them successfully. Almost always, it is a product that does not appeal to a specialized audience, but rather a product whose purchasers must be drawn from the population as a whole.

Correspondence courses in conversation improvement and English correction, antismoking remedies, seeds and nursery products, and special "health" clinics are examples of the successful users of daily newspapers.

Most of the examples given above use the "reading notice" form of ad. The ad looks like editorial matter and reads like a news story, offering further information at the bottom, without a coupon.

Big-city and small-city dailies are used by these offers at irregular intervals.

Some offers run ROP ("run of paper," i.e., wherever the newspaper finds it convenient to place the ad). Other offers specify sports page, garden page, etc.

OTHER MEDIA

Cooperative Mailings

Several offers can be mailed for the same bulk-rate postal charge. This naturally leads to the idea of splitting the cost among several different advertisers.

There are several firms that are in the business of organizing such mailings. For example, today I received a mailing to "occupant" containing offers from *Life*, Colgate, United Film Club, and Ajax.

An outfit called *Mailbag* that mails to teenagers has produced fine returns for several advertisers.

Shoppers Information Service, Inc., in New York, has mailed huge quantities of a unique cooperative deal. For 10 cents the inquirer can get further information about any five offers that include correspondence courses, hearing aids, home-movie outfits, trips to Europe, insurance, franchises, and other offers that differ from mailing to mailing. The mail-order firms pay Shoppers Information Service a specified amount for each inquiry.

Under the name Pat Roy, at 216 West Jackson Boulevard, Chicago 6, Illinois, another firm sends out cooperative mailings for firms that seek women agents for their products, or for women who want to work at home. Offers include Tandy Leather, H. B. Davis Catalog Sales, "Miracle Baskets," candy-and-cake correspondence course, Christmas cards, etc.

Mass Consumer Magazines

For most mail-order firms, *Life, Look, Saturday Evening Post, TV Guide,* and other similar magazines are not likely to be profitable media. But there are some firms that use them profitably on scattered occasions. These are offers that have a very wide market, involve considerable

NOW! a genuine
CULTURED PEARL
on a 15-inch goldtone chain
in a polished or Florentine-finish goldtone metal case

YOURS
FOR ONLY **1.00** with proof of purchase of any Rexall Brand Product

PEARL SHOWN
ACTUAL SIZE

Handsome, goldtone metal cases are reusable as pill boxes for your purse.

CLIP THIS COUPON

MAIL TO: CULTURED PEARLS
P.O. Box 3554, Beverly Hills, California

I enclose $_____ for _____ Cultured Pearl Necklace(s), plus proof of purchase of one Rexall Brand product for each Necklace ordered. Check choice of case: ☐ Round or ☐ Square.

NAME _____

ADDRESS _____

CITY _____ ZONE _____ STATE _____

Enclose cash, check or money order. No stamps, please. Allow 3 weeks for delivery. This offer is not effective in any jurisdiction prohibiting, licensing, taxing or regulating such offers. Offer expires June 30, '63.

FIG. 16-2

sums of money over the long haul, and have almost saturated their other mail-order markets.

Examples of such firms are the record and book clubs, La Salle Extension University's law courses, and film developing.

Analysis of profitable media and seasons in mass consumer magazines must be different from other mail-order media, because there are no competitive ads to check. Therefore, you must analyze readership, rates, and seasonal patterns just the way non-mail-order advertisers do. However, the second time you advertise, you will be able to use your own figures as a basis for your reckoning.

Assorted Minor Media

Mail-order men are ingenious, and they have successfully used many odd types of media from time to time. For example, Figure 16-2 shows an offer on a shopping bag handed out in drugstores.

Though we call these media "minor," any one of them can be major to you, if your product fits the medium.

17

Follow-Up Letters to Inquirers

*What to Send • How Many Follow-Ups Should
You Send? • When to Send the Follow-Ups*

In this chapter we assume that you have chosen to sell a high-priced product—perhaps a printing press or a correspondence course. The price is far above $10, so you can't sell the product directly from the ad. Instead, your advertisements call for people to write for further information.

This chapter is about the information you send—in a series of letters —to people who inquire.

The purpose of follow-ups is quite different from the direct mail that you send to people on your *mailing list* when you sell stationery or food delicacies or other repeat items. Each letter in a follow-up series is designed to sell the *same item,* whereas you advertise a whole line of items in a repeat-business operation.

Furthermore, if you sell a line of repeat-purchase goods, all the people on your mailing list get the same direct mail from you at the *same time.* Follow-ups, on the other hand, go out on a schedule that starts the day the inquiry is received.

These are the questions about follow-ups that this chapter will help you answer:

1. *What* should you send?
2. How *many* follow-ups should you send?
3. How should you *space* the follow-ups?

The best way—and the only way—to understand follow-ups thoroughly is to study what successful operators do. Write to every correspondence school whose ads you can find in single issues of *Popular Sci-*

ence and *Workbasket*, both the ads in display and those in classified. (A few salesmen will telephone you from the handful of biggest correspondence schools, but they won't bother you if you tell them you are not interested at present. Besides, hearing their pitches will be instructive to you.)

Many of the correspondence schools send beautiful brochures for their first follow-up mail-out. But you are mainly interested in the series of letters after the first follow-up.

The first follow-up piece will almost always come under first-class postage—even if it costs 32 cents—so that the inquirer's curiosity will not have time to cool. But the pieces that follow will come third class, so write the date on the envelope when each one arrives. Save everything that comes, of course, for your files.

Remember that follow-ups are not just an unnecessary frill to the business. If correspondence courses were limited to one mailing piece —or even to two follow-ups—many firms would have to go out of business. The first mailing for an experienced operator will only get about *half* the orders he will eventually develop with his entire series of follow-ups.

WHAT TO SEND

Follow-ups are direct mail, and *good* follow-ups will obey the rules for good direct mail. Reread the preceding two chapters to refresh your memory on the subject.

The first follow-up provides no special problems about what to send. It will be a complete, hard-working mailing piece—exactly the same kind of mailing piece you would send even if there were no more follow-ups to come. But obviously, the second, third, fourth, and succeeding follow-ups must be related to the first piece and to each other, and that's what we discuss in this section.

The first follow-up will generally be longer and more complete than any subsequent follow-up. It will usually contain every major reason that will help persuade the prospect to buy.

Some mailers—particularly those who sell industrial goods and use automatically typed letters—find that a *carbon copy* of the first letter is very successful.

Each subsequent follow-up usually hammers away at a *single* major reason for buying.

> The first letter of the series may bring out the value of the article from a dollars-and-cents standpoint. The second may advance the theory that the article will pay for itself within a short time. The third may stress pride of ownership. The fourth may emphasize the enjoyment feature, and so on through the scale of selling appeals.[1]

Or, different follow-ups can offer different sales terms. If the first follow-up offers $10 down and $10 per month, the second follow-up may offer $5 down and $7 per month. Or a follow-up may push the "Free Trial."

It is generally *not* wise to reduce the overall price of the merchandise, and few major firms do so. Customers may lose faith in firms that offer to cut their own price. And record keeping becomes more complicated and troublesome if you cut your price.

Some outfits reduce the price but "justify" the reduction to the consumer by giving an excuse for the reduction. One way to justify a price reduction is to offer the merchandise without some fringe benefit, i.e., without the consultation advice, or the customizing feature, or the fancy binding.

Another way to justify the reduction is by offering "a few slightly soiled pieces at half price."

Still another practice is to set up another company name in another town and offer the same merchandise cheaper.

Though almost everyone else is against this practice, Charles Atlas starts by offering his course at $25, and by the eighth follow-up he is down to $5. And Atlas has been a very successful operation.

In any case, never reduce the price until the customer must otherwise be considered dead.

In your last letter to otherwise-dead customers you should throw in every gimmick and premium you had offered at any time. If that collection of appeals won't get him, nothing will.

Each follow-up should give the prospect a good reason why you are writing again. ("Perhaps my letter went astray" . . . "Perhaps you were too busy" . . . "I received this letter from a satisfied customer yesterday and I thought you would be interested" . . . or "My boss authorized me to offer special terms at this time of the year" . . . .)

But, never forget that each letter must repeat the basic story line of what you are selling, why the prospect should want it, and how he can buy it immediately.

Each follow-up should *look* different from the others. Vary the color of the paper or the ink, or change the letterhead. Use a different shape of envelope. But retain the *basic identity* of the letters. Keep the trademark and the typography uniform. The letters should seem as if they are *different members of the same family.*

Some advertisers use a different signature, from a different "officer" of the firm, for each letter. I have never understood the logic of that practice, but it evidently is successful for some firms.

Change the testimonials in each follow-up. One of your follow-ups might consist almost *entirely* of new testimonials.

HOW MANY FOLLOW-UPS SHOULD YOU SEND?

If the first letter doesn't sell, then maybe the second letter will, or the sixth. Make up your mind that once you have a prospect who is at least interested in your product, you won't stop soliciting him until a series of letters brings back less money than it actually costs—and that could be the tenth letter or later, depending on the product.

La Salle Extension University sends about ten follow-ups in its first series, at one- or two-week intervals. Then it sends two or three mailings each year for several years. It has made money on mailings to prospects who inquired as long as five years before![2]

Here are a few case histories for which we have the data:

• Charles Atlas closed one-third of his sales with his first letter and booklet. The other two-thirds were scattered over the next nine letters, each letter doing only slightly worse than the one before it.

• Musselman[3] mentions a correspondence course selling between $50 and $100. (The average inquiry cost 45 cents—very cheap, indeed!) The mailings pulled this way:

1st follow-up	½%	
2d follow-up	½%	
3d follow-up	½%	
4th follow-up	¾%	(easier terms)
5th follow-up	1%	(reduced price)
6th follow-up	½%	(reduced price)
7th follow-up	¼%	(reduced price)

• At one time the New York Institute of Photography obtained inquiries for 56 to 70 cents each. A series of six letters went out over a six-month period—the early letters at shorter intervals than the later letters. They closed 6 to 7 percent at a sales price of $88. More than half probably paid in full.

I'd guess that the total of six mailings cost perhaps $1, so the total cost of a prospect was about $1.65. The revenue per inquiry was above $2.75—a very nice profit, indeed.

• More than fifty years ago W. A. Shryer[4] obtained these results in selling his credit-collection course:

1st follow-up	0.012%	8th follow-up	0.0046%	15th follow-up	0.0052%
2d follow-up	0.015%	9th follow-up	0.0033%	16th follow-up	0.0052%
3d follow-up	0.011%	10th follow-up	0.0038%	17th follow-up	0.0032%
4th follow-up	0.0106%	11th follow-up	0.0062%	18th follow-up	0.0025%
5th follow-up	0.0106%	12th follow-up	0.0074%	18th follow-up	0.0039%
6th follow-up	0.018%	13th follow-up	0.0031%	20th follow-up	0.0009%
7th follow-up	0.013%	14th follow-up	0.0071%		

Shryer's results are an interesting demonstration that the basic principles of the mail-order business have not changed in a long, long time.

Shryer's follow-up series consisted of five regular letters at short intervals, and then a special letter every three months.

In general, each letter will pull slightly less than the preceding letter. If a later letter does better, it probably means that the copy and appeal are stronger than the preceding letter. You should then consider putting the stronger copy in the earlier letters.

Stop sending follow-ups when the cost of the follow-up is greater than the dollar returns it brings back. For example, if printing, postage, handling, and other costs add to $80 per thousand for a follow-up, and if you keep $75 after fulfillment costs for each $100 of revenue you receive, then each follow-up must bring back more than $106.67.

$$\frac{100}{75} \times \$80 = \$106.67$$

Stop the follow-up series when the results fall below $106.67.

The more expensive the item, the more follow-ups you will find it profitable to send.

WHEN TO SEND THE FOLLOW-UPS

In general, the early letters go out at short intervals while the prospect is "hot." Grant[5] writes of a successful series in which the second follow-up went out just *one day* after the first (though probably the second went out by third-class mail and therefore arrived several days later).

The first letter, especially, must go out *immediately*—and by first-class mail. Time is absolutely of the essence. On one offer I first obtained better than a 10 percent response, sending letters out promptly and first-class. This dropped to just above 8 percent when the printer made us several weeks late in getting them out and when we sent them third-class. (These are reliable data: over 200 replies in one case and over 380 in the other.)

Grant recommends the second follow-up a week after the first, and the other follow-ups two weeks apart—except for a price reduction, which should follow a considerable delay. He also states, "Never mail a follow-up in December or June."[6]

Another plan schedules first a one-week delay, then a two-week delay, then a three-week delay, then a space of one month between letters.

The *best* policy will be to test various intervals for your own proposition, however.

18

The Vital Brain of Mail
Order: Testing

*What Is Testing All about? • The Science of Mail
Order • "Buying Information" • What to
Test • Testing in Periodical Advertising •
Direct-Mail Testing Techniques • Will This New
Offer Make a Profit? • How to Test a List • How
to Test One Piece of Copy against Another • How
to Select a Test Sample*

WHAT IS TESTING ALL ABOUT?

Mail order is something like poker. In poker you try to maneuver into
a position where you have a really good hand, and then you play it to
the hilt. In mail order, you try like the dickens to find a big-winning
proposition, and then you try to milk it for all it's worth. (But don't
get me wrong. Mail order is much less of a gamble than most other
types of business.)

Testing tells you whether or not you have a big winner, and how much
you can try to milk it for. Important? Testing couldn't be more important. If you don't understand testing, you'll never make a good buck
in mail order.

(But you *don't* have to understand some of the more complicated
stuff I discuss in this chapter. Lots of successful mail-order men won't
know what I'm talking about. I'm convinced, though, that they would
be far *more* successful if they did understand and use all these ideas.)

Sometimes you will try a loser. Either it is a brand-new product and people don't want it, or it's an established product whose market is not big enough for you *and* the competition.

You would obviously prefer not to wind up with any costly stock on your hands in a situation where you can't sell it. The fear of this keeps many people from testing good products.

But there is a partial answer. Large industrial manufacturing companies test a product—perhaps a new type of steel—by asking their customers in advance whether they can use it. Their customers are likely to give accurate answers.

Major concerns that sell direct to household consumers find that they cannot rely on their customers' answers. Consumers just cannot predict their own behavior in advance well enough to give you accurate information. So these concerns resort to many other stratagems, including motivation research.

The mail-order advertiser is less interested in the way that people react to the goods and more interested in the way they react to the advertising. What you *can* do, then, is to advertise before you have any merchandise, to find out how great the response will be.

This practice never really feels very good ethically. But on the other hand, it is not really bad, either. The worst that happens is that a customer wastes time and a 5-cent stamp in writing to you. If you do put the product on the market, he merely has to wait awhile until you are ready. Whether or not the practice feels right to you, you should know that Bennet Cerf of Random House (one of America's largest publishers) asserted that this practice was a necessary and common trade practice, when he was in a discussion of the ethical relationships of publishers to booksellers.[1]

The Science of Mail Order

Mail-order selling is the *most* scientific business in the world. By that I mean that *figuring* and *calculating* can control a firm's decisions more than in any other line of trade. Aside from the selection of the offer and the creation of copy, the "human factor" and other imponderables have a smaller effect in mail order than in any other business, no matter how large the business is.

For example, the split-run test (more about that later) is the most perfect experiment ever devised in the social sciences. Its accuracy and validity are fantastically greater than any psychologist, sociologist, or economist ever hopes to achieve in his work.

It would seem, then, that mail-order men would respond readily to improvements in methods of figuring. But alas, no, they're just not very interested. Like everyone else, mail-order men are satisfied to get along. They're convinced that their knowledge is basically pretty complete.

"Buying Information"

When you spend a dime to call the Weather Bureau for the latest report, you are buying information. When you lay out $300 for an encyclopedia you are also buying information—not books, mind you, but *information*.

Testing is also a way of buying information. You spend a little extra time and energy to obtain some factual data that you can then use to increase your profit. A test is good only if it costs less than the information is worth.

Here is an example. You have a proposition that has proved to be a winner in four out of the five magazines in which you have run. Now you are in a hurry to find the greatest number of magazines that will pull a profit for you.

In that situation, you should not be too cautious in your testing. You should take a chance on every magazine that has even a *reasonable* chance of paying out. Here's why. If you think you have a one-in-three chance of making a profit on a magazine, you should test in it. Based on your test of the five magazines above, you know that you won't lose your shirt. The most you can lose is some small part of the cost of the ad and merchandise. If you *make* money, you can rerun the ad far more than three times. And more than two insertions in a paying magazine will more than cover the losses in two nonpaying magazines.

So it pays to think of testing as buying information that will allow you to build a profit in the future. Don't think of the test as an investment all by itself. If you understand this principle, you will test more freely and you can pyramid your profits remarkably fast.

What to Test

All through this manual I've been saying, "Test this" and "Test that" or "You'll have to test this for yourself."

But test *only* the important things. Don't test petty things. Mail-order men have spent huge amounts of time and energy testing such picayune items as exact shades of color, one type face versus another type face, etc., *ad nauseam*. Such tests spend more to buy information than the information is worth. The results don't make enough difference to matter much.

To paraphrase Victor Schwab:[2] Test for differences that *scream*. Don't test for differences that whisper . . . Test for differences in headlines that could double your profit. Test for a price that could increase your take by 40 percent. Test a brochure that could increase sales 15 percent.

When you first put an offer on the market, your testing will be very different from the testing that you will do later on in the product history. Your first advertisement tests the offer, but it *also* tests the medium and the copy. If any one of those elements is bad, the whole test fails. That's when you have to exert judgment to decide whether to drop the whole thing, or to repair what you think is the faulty element.

Later on, after you *know* what your offer and copy will do, you can compare one magazine against another, and your test results will give you information purely about the magazines.

Or, you can change the copy but keep the same offer, and run in a medium where you ran the old ad. In that case, the results give you a straight answer about the copy.

Testing has different meanings at the various stages of your mail-order campaign.

Does Scientific Testing Work?

People who don't understand testing don't trust its results. As an eye opener to direct-mail people, William Doppler and the Book-of-the-Month Club tested random sampling on over *a million* letters. The results were just exactly as predicted by sampling theory.[3]

(Of course, any statistician would have known that any such test was totally unnecessary. He would know that the results *had* to be the way they turned out.)

TESTING IN PERIODICAL ADVERTISING

A true split run is a perfect test for two pieces of copy. In a split run two different ads are set up for a single issue of a publication. The test is arranged so that each ad is in exactly half the copies, appearing in every other copy in each pile of magazines or newspapers that leaves the printing plant.

The split-run ads are keyed differently, and the number of returns is a perfect test of whichever copy or price is better.

Several magazines and newspapers have true split-run facilities, for which there is an extra charge. *Standard Rate & Data* lists these publications.

There are also some publications that offer *regional* "split runs." In this setup all the copies going to the West, perhaps, have one ad while all the copies going to the East have another ad. The results are not perfectly reliable because readers in different parts of the country may have different tastes and needs. This is not a true split-run test. Nevertheless, it can sometimes be useful.

Split runs test only copy and various offers against each other. And split run is only available to the large advertiser. The small advertiser must use other testing techniques.

Problems in Testing

You need plenty of good judgment to interpret display-ad tests. As a matter of fact, how good your judgment of tests is may decide how successful a display advertiser you are. And I think that the trickiest job in mail order is to estimate, on the basis of one or more ads, how other ads or other media will pull.

These are some of the problems in judging test results:

1. If you test two different ads in two consecutive issues of a magazine, you must take account of the difference in pulling power in different months.

2. Two ads may appear in different positions in different issues. Good position can pull twice as well as poor position.

3. A given issue of a magazine may be especially attractive and sell extra copies on the newsstand, giving an extra boost to ads in that issue.

4. National events, such as a war scare, can affect results.

5. One issue may carry more competitive advertising than another issue.

These are some of the reasons why you must evaluate the results of a particular test very closely. Chapters 11 and 12 on display advertising give you information that should help improve your judgment of test results.

General Methods of Testing Ads and Media

1. If you have a piece of copy that you have used in many media before, you can use that copy to test new media. La Salle Extension University has used one piece of copy to test new publications for over 35 years.

2. You can get a fair comparison of two ads in the "crisscross" method. In this method you run Ad A in Medium X and Ad B in Medium Y the first issue. The next issue, Ad A goes into Medium Y, and Ad B goes into Medium X. The ad which pulls more total responses should be better.

However, different conditions can still distort the picture, even though the crisscross reduces the likelihood of that happening.

3. If you have plenty of time you can alternate ads from month to month. After four or six months your results should be satisfactorily reliable.

4. Mail-order men are fond of saying that you can test only one thing at a time. That saying is not always true. Let's say that you have run your first test ad, and the results are highly satisfactory. Now you are in a great hurry to test out perhaps eight new media and perhaps eight forms of offer, price, and copy.

I am convinced that your best bet is to put a different ad into each different medium. The insertions that pull the very best suggest to you that *both* the ad and the medium are strong. The insertions that pull worst suggest the opposite.

On the next time around, place the ads from the better-result insertions into many media, including the media whose insertions pulled only middling well on the first test. But place no ads in the media where the first insertions did poorly. After this second round, by a simple and obvious deduction, you can say with much greater accuracy which media are best, and which ads are best.

The advantage of this approach is that you get a lot of information rapidly. The rationale depends on the fact that your offer is generally quite profitable, and for that reason it is possible and profitable to *buy* the further information.

One of the disadvantages of display advertising is that it takes a long time to get results. *Some* media give you a quick test, though. Chapter 11 also discusses the problem of guessing from one medium's results what the results in another medium will be.

Readership Reports

In mail order it is *orders* that count, not the number of people who read your ads.

Nevertheless, readership surveys can sometimes give you interesting data about the effectiveness of various *parts* of a magazine. They also can give you a faint clue to the effectiveness of competitors' ads.

Readership reports are available on request to many of the larger magazines.

DIRECT-MAIL TESTING TECHNIQUES

Every self-respecting direct-mail tester should ask himself these two questions each and every time he runs a test:

1. How do I design the best test for this particular direct-mail problem? Usually—but not always—this question boils down to: How big a test sample should I use?

2. How do I evaluate the results of the test after the returns are in? This question *always* breaks into two subquestions:

    a. What is my *best guess* about what the test shows?
    b. How *accurate* is that best guess likely to be, given the test-sample size?

The answers to these questions will be different from test to test. There is no cheap and easy set of rules you can follow blindly. There is no two-dollar board into which you can plug your jack for an automatic answer.

But even *before* those questions, the direct-mail tester must consider:
1. What he is trying to find out from the test.

2. What decisions will be influenced by the test results.

3. How the test results can guide him in the decisions he has to make.

4. How much money is involved.

Depending on these considerations, the testing situation will fall into one of three major categories:

I. Will this new offer make a profit?

II. How should I test a *list?*

III. How do I test one piece of copy against another?

WARNING: At this point I want to warn you that there is a *better* method of looking at these problems than the one I shall describe. That method is the method of "decision theory," which takes into account not only the probabilities of various events taking place, but also the size of the monetary gains or losses that may take place, and the best guesses of the manager about what will happen.

That better method is described for the example of a direct-mail book-club publisher, in Robert Schlaifer's book *Introduction to Statistics for Business Decisions.*[4] However, few mail-order men are likely to be willing to follow through on Schlaifer's method. They will boggle, especially, at estimating the monetary gains or losses that will follow as a result of various possible test outcomes.

Estimating how much risk you are willing to take obviously depends upon how much money is at stake. Nevertheless, many people are probably willing to state how much of a risk they want to take, even if they will not estimate the dollar amounts directly. And in that circumstance, the methods that I describe are the best that I know of.

We shall consider these major categories, listed above, one by one.

Will This New Offer Make a Profit?

You want to know whether your product or offer is attractive enough for further investment. Commonly you tackle this problem by selecting a potentially excellent list, writing the best possible copy, and mailing at a good time of the year. (You might mail in an off season if you know how much to upgrade the results you get.) You figure that if you have a winner, further experimentation will improve the techniques and unearth even better lists.

How big a test? How many tests? There is no stock answer. Are you selling a $5.95 product or one that goes for $5,950? Is it a one-shot solicitation, or is it a repeat-business operation?

Let's try an example. You want to sell an auto accessory priced at $15. For simplicity we'll say that it is a one-shot offer, though a sound analysis should include the future value of having the customers on your list for future solicitations. You figure that a 1.125 percent return will return your investment and leave something for overhead and profit. In other words, 1.125 percent is the break-even point you choose.

If your offer pulls that well or better over the long haul, you'll consider the offer a success rather than a failure.

How big a test sample should you mail? Let's say that you want to be 85 percent sure that chance will make your test results no more than 25 percent higher than repeated mailings. You obviously don't care at all if follow-ups would be *higher* than the test results. You merely want protection against test results that are too high, leading you into unwise further investment.

(NOTE: When we say "85 percent sure," we mean that the right betting odds in a horse race would be 17 to 3. Note also that at this point we are discussing the variation in results due only to chance factors. We shall discuss the falloff effect later.)

You estimate that the offer will pull 1.5 percent. The difference between your estimate of 1.5 percent and your break-even point of 1.125 percent is 0.375 percent, which is 25 percent of 1.5 percent.

To find the correct sample size to satisfy your specifications, refer to Table 18-1. Go along the horizontal top line until you find 25 percent, the dropoff percentage you want to guard against. Then proceed down the 25 percent vertical column until you reach the 85 percent degree of surety you demand. The number in the box will be the number of returns you must set up your test sample to obtain. To find the correct sample size, divide the number of returns in the box (14 in this example) by the percent return you expect (1.5 percent in this case): 14/0.015 equals 933. So try a test of 933, or around 1,000.

Perhaps you are selling a higher-priced product like kitchenware. Your experience leads you to expect a return of 0.5 percent. As in the

Table 18-1

*Percent of Dropoff**

(*The percentage difference between the estimated return and the break-even point; or the dropoff percentage you wish to guard against*)

The Degree of surety. (How sure you wish to be that the result will be over the break-even point.)		50%	25%	12½%	6¼%
	75%	1.8	7.3	29.2	116.8
	85%	3.5	14.0	56.0	
	90%	6.6	26.2	104.8	
	95%	11.0	42.8		
	99%	21.7	86.9		

* The numbers in the boxes represent the number of returns the test must be arranged to obtain in order to meet the dropoff requirement and the degree of certainty required. Note that this table, like the other tables in this chapter, is approximate. Note also that it holds only for return percentages under 10%.

revious example, you desire to guard against a dropoff of 25 percent rom test results to continuation results, and you demand a surety of 5 percent. You therefore would need to get the same number of returns as in the previous example (14), and your sample size therefore s 14 divided by 0.5 percent, or 2,799. You would probably test-mail 2,500 or 3,000.

But if you expect 0.5 percent return and are willing to settle for 75 percent surety against a later dropoff of 25 percent or more, you need a test sample of 7.3 divided by 0.5 percent, or roughly 1,500.

Let us return to the auto-accessory example.

So you run a test, expecting 1.5 percent on a test sample of 1,000, and you get results of 1.3 percent. Your *best guess* is that future mailings will pull 1.3 percent, provided the copy, list, seasonal conditions, etc., stay the same. (Don't sneer at this apparently simple-minded statement. The "best guess" is not always so obvious, and many a mailer has run into difficulty because he made a wrong "best guess.")

But how sure are you that future results will be above your break-even mark of 1,125 percent? Certainly you are not sure as you hoped to be after the test. But such are the vagaries of testing.

The difference between what you obtained (1.3 percent) and your break-even point (1.125 percent) is 0.175 percent, which is roughly 13.5 percent of 1.3 percent by my dollar slide rule. Use the figure of 13.5 percent to enter Table 18-2. Go across the horizontal top row to the column headed 15%, closest to 13.5 percent. Then run down the column to 12.4, which is closest to the 13 returns you obtained. In the vertical column to the left you can read that you are roughly 70 percent sure that repeated tests will bring home an average return of better than your break-even point. (Actually, since the 13.5 percent figure you were working with is less than the 15%, you are even less sure than 70 percent.)

Given that information, you are probably *not* satisfied that your test results will support further heavy investment without further testing. Run another test, then, perhaps the same size as the first, or somewhat larger. Then *combine* the results of the *two* tests as if they were just one large test, and go back to Table 18-2, following the previous instructions. By this time you should have sufficiently unambiguous answers to either push forward with confidence or drop the project. This combination technique is probably not logically waterproof, but it is simple, easy to communicate, and free of serious error.)

For the situation where your test results fall *below* the break-even point and you wish to know the chances that repeated mailings would be *above* the break-even point, you can still use Table 18-2. Substitute break-even and test results for each other, and subtract the degree of surety in the table from 100 to find the desired figure.

Table 18-2*

$$\frac{\text{Observed return \% } - \text{ break-even return \%}}{\text{Observed return \%}} \times 100 = \%$$

		10%	15%	20%	30%	50%
Degree of surety that future return percentage will be above break-even percentage.	60%	6.5				
	70%	27.6	12.4	6.6	3.1	
	80%	67.2	30.0	16.8	7.5	
	90%	163.8	73.0	40.9	18.2	6.6
	95%	.....	121.2	63.1	30.3	11.0

The number in any box is the number of returns a test produced—irrespective of the sample size.

* Note that Tables 18-1 and 18-2 contain the same type of statistical material. We include Table 18-2 only for the convenience of the different headings.

How to Test a List

Assume that your product offer is already fixed, as is your copy. You are committed to selling the product, and you have been successful with other lists. What you want, then, is to mail to every list that gives you even a dollar of profit.

Note that in this situation you will compute overhead in a manner different than for the problems in the section above. When you are just *considering* a product, you must take *all* costs into overhead—including setup and organization costs—and apply them to each unit you mail. But when the question is, rather, "Do I or don't I mail *this* list?" you should only load your overhead calculations with the cost of the overrun of stock, postage, addressing, and direct handling costs. This is important, because you may otherwise pass up mailing chances that would increase your total year-end profit.

How large is the entire list you want to test? The size of the list *should* affect the size of your test sample. But contrary to popular notion, the size of the list does not affect the *accuracy* of your test, but only the *economics* of the test. On a test of 2,000, it matters little for accuracy whether the entire list is 10,000 or a million. As long as your test sample is less than one-fifth of the total list—as it always will be—the accuracy will be almost the same no matter what the list size.

But—the larger the total list, the more *valuable* your test information will be, and therefore the more you should be willing to lay out for the test, i.e., the higher the degree of surety you should demand. If the entire list is 10,000 and you expect a profit of 5 cents per piece mailed, the most you can make from the list after your 2,000 test is 5 cents times 8,000 or $400. But if the list is a million, your potential profit is 5 cents times 998,000. So errors are much more expensive if the list is very large. *That's* why a larger test may be warranted for a larger list.

Next you must decide the break-even point with which you are going to work. Then estimate the percent return you expect, and how sure you want to be of your results. Example: You estimate the return will be 2 percent, and your break-even point is 1.5 percent. (The break-even estimate should be accurate, but the estimated return estimate can be off considerably without harming the calculation.) You state that if you *do* get a return of 2 percent on the test, you'd like to be 75 percent sure that subsequent mailings will be above 1.5 percent.

To find the proper sample size, read Table 18-1 down to 75 percent (because that is the surety you have chosen to demand), read across to 25 percent [because $(2.0 - 1.5)/2.0$ equals 25 percent], and the number in the block (7.3) tells you how many returns you need to get. Then divide the number in the block by the percent return you expect. The result—365—is the sample size you need.

If you expect a 1 percent return, and you still don't want to fall below 25 percent of your expected return (i.e. your break-even point is 0.75 percent), you will work with the same block in the chart. You will still set your test up to get 7.3 returns, but the sample size will be twice as large—730.

But we all know very well that much more must go into this than straight statistics. With most lists you face the problem that when you go back to the list after the test, the returns will fall below the test mailing. We usually assume that this phenomenon results from tests that are not random samples of the whole list. Lewis Kleid's report "Importance of Stipulating Test Samples"[5] gives excellent directions for obtaining random test samples. If you follow those directions, you can prevent falloff from this cause. However, Orlan Gaeddert[6] suggests that when many lists are mailed in large blocks, the probability of duplication increases, and this may cause dropoff in results when you go back to lists.

If you expect that follow-ups will fall below the test results, there are two possible solutions:

1. You can go back to the list in several successive mailings. Each mailing should do worse than the last, and you keep mailing till you fall below your break-even point. The first remailing will be close to the test results, and you may use the technique above to predict what you will obtain. Or,

2. If it is inconvenient for you to mail to the list in several sections, and if you can't bludgeon the list owner into giving you a random sample, your only recourse is to guess how much the entire list, on the average, will drop below the test. If you figure that the list will average

80 percent of a fair test, then reduce the test returns by 20 percent and go on from there in your calculations.

(A seller of professional books turned the falloff effect to good advantage. He mailed test samples of 5,000 each to 50 different lists—with no intention of ever going back to any of the lists—and his overall results were pleasantly high. The same firm estimates that a mailing indirectly sells three times as many books in bookstores as through direct replies.)

To evaluate the test results *after* they are in, go back and use Table 18-2 in just the same way you did when testing a product offer. Find the blocks that contain numbers close to the total returns you received. Each block gives you a combination of a degree of surety and a boundary to your guess. If you received seven returns, you can be 60 percent sure that follow-up mailings will not fall more than 10 percent below the test average; *or*, you can be 80 percent sure that the follow-ups will not fall more than 30 percent below your test average. (Pay no attention to the coincidental sequencing of numbers. The two figures cannot be added or subtracted.)

How to Test One Piece of Copy against Another

In the simple copy-testing situation the *cost* of both letter units being tested is the same. All you care about, then, is which letter unit pulls "better." And you need no calculations to tell you that you should go with whichever package shows up better on the test, no matter how small the margin between the two. Post-test calculating will only help you to decide whether your first test was conclusive, or whether you need to test further.

When the cost of the two letter units is different, the situation is more complex. Then you must balance the margin between them against the extra cost, using test results as your guide. The solution to that problem is beyond the scope of this discussion.

For the simple case, begin by asking yourself: How *big* a difference am I interested in? You obviously don't care if one letter unit is 1/10,000 better than the other, no matter how large your mailings will be. But you certainly do care if one mailing piece will bring in twice as many returns as the other, no matter how small your mailing will be. You must ask yourself at what point you cease caring, given the particular requirements of your situation.

As an example for discussion here, let's say that you wouldn't bother to test if you thought that the difference between the two proposed letter units would be less than 10 percent (of the average return).

Next you must ask yourself: *if* the difference is as big, or bigger, than I care about, how *sure* do I want to be that the test will indicate which is the better letter unit? In other words, how sure do you want to be that the test will not mislead you? For example, here, let's say that you want to be 85 percent sure that the test indicates the better letter unit.

With those two values in mind, refer to Table 18-3. Read across to 10%, then down to 85%, and you find that you would require 424 returns to satisfy your requirements. You immediately decide that that would be too expensive and you decide to scale down your demand for surety to 75 percent, and concern yourself only with differences of 20 percent or more of the average return. You then find that you need to get 45.5 returns. If you expect an *average* return of 2 percent for the two test samples, *each* test sample must then be 45.5 divided by 2 percent, or 2,275. In total, you need to mail 4,550 to satisfy your requirements in this case.

If the *real* difference between the letter units is even greater than you are testing for, you stand an even better chance of the test being right. If the real difference between them is less than you care about, you stand a greater chance of the test being wrong. But you have said that if the latter is the case, you are not concerned.

After the test is over, and the results are in hand, you will probably *not* want to determine *how sure* you are that the test is right. If the difference between the mailing-piece returns is great, you need no further test. If the difference is slight, there isn't much point in further testing. Shoot the works with the letter that does better—no matter by how little it does better.

The fallacy has somehow gone abroad that you can test only one variable in a mailing. Not so. You can, in the same mailing, test headline, and colors, and copy, and other variables. Testing more than one variable at a time does require extreme caution and attention lest you go astray. But it also can give you a great deal of information at a relatively low testing cost.

Table 18-3*

The difference you care about:

			Percent return, letter 1 minus % return, letter 2				
			(Average percent return, letters 1 and 2)				
			4%	10%	20%	35%	50%
Degree of surety (How sure you want to be that the test results indicate the better letter.)		75%	1,237.5	182	45.5	14.3	7
		85%	. . . .	424	106	34.7	17
		90%	. . . .	656	164	53.0	26
		95%	. . . .	. . .	272	86.7	43.5

* The number in the box shows the number of *returns* you must expect from the *average* of the two test samples. To obtain the sample size for *each* test sample, divide number of returns by estimated average return.

Let's say that you want to test two headlines against each other, and you also want to test a pink versus a blue reply envelope. You will mail four equal-sized random test samples: headline 1, pink; headline 2, pink; headline 1, blue; headline 2, blue.

How big a test should you make? My recommendation is that you should use test samples just as large as if you were only testing headline 1 versus headline 2, pink versus blue. (See preceding pages for guidance on that problem.) So you are getting two tests (almost) for the price of one.

To analyze the test, look at the *total* numbers of pink versus blue, and headline 1 versus headline 2. See the example in Table 18-4 below.

Blue is the color that pulled the greatest total number of returns, and it is probably better. Similarly for headline 2 that pulled the greatest total number. But which *combination* is best is a difficult question. Apparently the combination of headline 2 and pink did better than any other combination. However, that could be a fluke of the sample. Unless you think that there is likely to be some *interaction* between the color and the headline, then you would disregard the highest-score combination. I do not think such interaction is likely, and hence I would bet that the combination of the best headline taken by itself and the best color taken by itself—headline 2 and blue—would be the best combination.

Proceed with great caution in multiple testing. You *cannot* use the tables shown here to help you with tests of three or more letter units that vary on the same dimension, i.e., when there are three or more different headlines, or colors, or what have you. It is crucial to understand that the more variations you test on the same dimension—eight different headlines, for example—the more the variability you must expect in your results, and the larger the tests must therefore be. An analogy may help to make this clear. The more evenings you play poker, the more likely you are to come up with a royal flush—even though the chance of drawing it in any individual evening will remain the same. To test eight different headlines, *each* of the eight test samples will have to be *much* larger than *either* of the test samples when only testing two headlines are being tested.

Furthermore, if you test eight headlines, the percentage of returns

Table 18-4

(Hypothetical data)

	Headline 1	Headline 2	Color totals
Pink...................	40	60	100
Blue...................	50	58	108
Headline totals..........	90	118	208 Overall total

for the *best* test sample is not—repeat, *not*—your best guess about what that headline will pull in the future. In Table 18-5 below, headline 4 is your best bet, but chances are that subsequent retests of the headline will not pull as high as 2.9 percent. I can't prove that statement here, and the body of theory is weak on this issue, but take my word for

Table 18-5

Headline	Return (in percent)
1	2.3
2	1.8
3	2.7
4	2.9
5	1.9
6	1.9
7	2.0
8	2.2

it anyway. (See technical note 6 in Appendix F for more discussion of this point.)

Conclusions about Direct-Mail Testing

1. The more willing and able you are to make follow-up tests, the smaller your original samples can be.

2. The higher the unit sale price (the smaller the percent return needed to break even), the bigger the test sample you need to obtain the accuracy you choose to get.

3. Ever-larger test samples are not the necessary answer to your search for reliable information. Careful thought, together with *proper* test-sample sizes, is the answer. Very small samples can yield a great deal of information. An expert can often come to very important—and sound —conclusions on a test large enough to produce only 10 or 25 responses.

4. Extremely precise statistical methods are not necessary in direct-mail testing. This is true partly because test samples are often badly unrepresentative, and partly because a mailer wants the *big* indications that make a big difference in the pocketbook. (Listen to differences that scream, not the differences that whisper.) Nevertheless, the *theory* of statistics plus crude rule-of-thumb approximations can be tremendously helpful in making and saving you money.

5. If you are testing many different variations of headline, or color, etc., you must look for differences much bigger than if you were testing just one variation against another. (Just *how* much bigger is a tricky question.)

6. We have said nothing about the mechanics of splitting test samples "randomly." Most direct-mail people are aware of how easy it is to foul up a test by sending all one sample to one state, the other sample

to a second state; or by splitting so that the first half of the alphabet gets one letter unit, the last half of the alphabet the other letter unit. The surest guarantee of a fair test, of course, is to send one letter to every other name on the list—no matter what the original order or disorder of the list. In any case, don't forget that if your lists are not reasonably randomly selected, all other technique is for nought.

The purpose of this section has been to give *some* of the benefits of statistical theory to direct-mail testers who don't wish to study statistics or the philosophy of science. But the wise will recognize the risks in this short cut, and will not look upon it as a substitute for expert advice when tricky problems arise.

HOW TO SELECT A TEST SAMPLE

There are two methods of choosing test samples that will give you satisfactory tests. (When I say "satisfactory," I mean that you will not obtain false information that can lead you into a costly or disastrously bad decision.)

One satisfactory method is to select a scientifically "random" sample of the names on the list. William Doppler made these interesting interview comments on random sampling in a Lewis Kleid report:[7]

QUESTION: Many mailers consider that a list arranged alphabetically automatically gives you a representative sample. What are some of the factors that might influence response on an alphabetical list?

ANSWER: It is *not* correct to test an alphabetical list by taking the names in sequence. You must space the names in a random pattern. Alphabetical sequences give you unbelievable distortions. I would look upon results from such sampling with suspicion.

QUESTION: Bill, could you give me an example of "random" selection in testing a list arranged alphabetically?

ANSWER: Random means a situation where each name has an equal chance to be selected. Most random sampling is based on tables of random numbers. Under ideal circumstances, give each name a number and pull those which match with the random numbers in the book. Random samples are expensive. Random sampling takes a lot of time and labor.

QUESTION: It seems to me that scientific sampling is a very involved affair which requires a lot of clerical labor and tabulations. What does it cost to pull a scientific sample?

ANSWER: Let me give you a case history. We had a list filed alphabetically. The total number of names was 400,000. We figured the size of the sample based on expectation, error, and confidence and came up with 2,000 names. The next question was how are we going to select the 2,000 names. We had made some studies on alphabetical sequences and had learned that any group of names in alphabetical order gave us a distorted and, therefore, unpredictable sample.

We also had some experience with sampling in lots or batches. For example we could have divided the 2,000 names into 20 lots of 100 names, each lot in alphabetical sequence. Sampling by lots gave us a better sample than the alphabetical sequence, but still not a sample reliable enough to make predictions. So we decided to sample by individual cards. We decided to stand up every card at intervals of 200. We did not have to count the cards—we measured the distance between 200 cards, made a couple of wire gauges and went through the file drawers. When we got finished with the sampling job we had a sample which was a reasonably true cross section of the list. The cost of the sample was about $50 per 1,000 names. We used this sample over and over again for different kinds of tests. So the actual cost of the sample per test was not too bad. The results we obtained from the sample were confirmed by the mass mailings with an astounding degree of accuracy. Obviously, a mailer cannot expect to buy a true scientific sample at the standard rental addressing price of $15 per M.

However, it is seldom possible to obtain a true random sample from a rented list. The second test-sample method is usually the best alternative. This method tries to obtain a reasonably *representative* sample.

There are several methods of obtaining a representative sample. Lewis Kleid describes them this way:[8]

1. *Alphabetically Arranged Lists*
   List owners should address an equal number of names from each of 5 sections of the list:

   A–E
   F–J
   K–O
   P–T
   U–Z

2. *Unarranged Lists*
   List owner should address test names from at least three different parts of the list.
3. *Chronologically Arranged Lists*
   List owner should address a proportionate quantity of names for each year or period covered by the list. He should be further cautioned *not* to address only the latest names.
4. *Geographically Arranged Lists*
   Test cross sections should be worked out using the major eleven geographical sections of the country.

A good list broker should be able to help you work out the details of a satisfactory geographical sample or the other types of representative samples.

It is very important that you should not be satisfied simply to *ask* for "a fair sample." A fair sample is exactly what you won't get unless you *make sure* that you get a good test sample by specifying exactly what you want.

19

How to Produce and Print Mail-Order Advertising

*The Many Ways of Putting Ink on Paper • Type
and Typographers • How to Prepare an Ad for
Letterpress • How to Prepare an Ad for Offset*

Printing is a world in itself—a fascinating, technical world. The more you know about printing and the graphic arts, the more that printing will interest you and give you pleasure. Knowledge of printing processes will also profit you in the mail-order business.

Our purpose in this chapter is to tell you only the bare facts about printing that you need to run a mail-order business. If your business grows big enough so that you have very long runs of catalogs or direct-mail pieces, you will need to hire a production specialist.

Here's a tip you are sure to forget, and sure to regret forgetting: take out the *very first piece* of any printing you buy and place it in your file of samples. Then take out another five pieces and throw them into a junk file. Never remove a piece from your sample file. Time after time you will need these old samples, and you'll curse and scream when you can't find the ones you need.

THE MANY WAYS OF PUTTING INK ON PAPER

Letterpress

The letterpress process with movable type is what Gutenberg invented. The letterpress printer places metal type and/or engravings into a "chase," and then places the chase on the press. The printing press rolls ink across the raised type and then brings the type in contact with the paper.

Large sizes of type for headlines and special effects are set by hand from "fonts" that the typographer or printer has available. Small type for body copy is cast by automatic linotype machines that the printer operates like a typewriter.

Illustrations are printed in one of several ways, depending upon the type of artwork. Toned illustrations (illustrations with varying shades from white to black, rather than just light and dark) are most difficult. In general, illustrations are transformed into engraving by photographic means. Engravers are specialists who operate separately from printers.

Printing presses of the letterpress type come in all shapes and sizes. Most newspaper and some magazines use the letterpress process. But more and more publications are shifting to offset printing, especially for the inside pages.

When you send a small ad to a letterpress publication, you can ask the publication to set the type for you. Chapter 11 discusses how to work with the magazine to get them to do what you want. Or you can send the publication a complete "cut" (engraving) of your ad which you have made up by an engraver from typographer's type.

You yourself will probably not use the letterpress process very frequently in your daily work, except for envelopes and odd work like labels and some four-color brochures. Offset may be better, however, for very long runs of envelopes and other pieces.

Letterpress has always been noted for its faithful reproduction and therefore is chosen for four-color printing. But recent improvements in offset printing have narrowed that difference.

Offset Lithography

"Offset," "lithography," and "planographing" all refer to the same process. "Multilith" is the trade name for one brand of offset printing press.

In the offset process, the platemaker (or the offset printer, if he makes his own plates) *photographs* the "dummy" (the material that you want printed). Artwork is photographed separately, through a "screen." The image is then transferred from the photographic negative to a metal plate. The plate is treated with a chemical solution that reacts to light. Wherever light does not shine on the plate, ink will not stick to the plate because of subsequent treatment, in the same way that water or ink will not stick to greased areas of a piece of metal or glass.

Then an ink blanket rolls across the plate, and the ink remains on the plate only in the pattern of the original material to be printed. A rubber blanket rolls over the plate and picks up the picture in ink from the plate. The rubber blanket then rolls across the paper and prints the material. (The process is called "offset" because the picture is offset from the plate to the paper by means of a rubber blanket.)

The most complex lithographs are illustrations in full color ("four color"). If you understand the following description written by the lithographers' union[1] for an ad in *The New York Times*, you will understand all about one-color illustrations and "line" jobs, too.

HOW A LITHOGRAPH IS MADE

1. Using special high-precision camera equipment, the original color artwork is photographed four times—through four different color filters— to produce four color separation negatives, one for each of the primary colors, yellow, red and blue, plus one for the black.

2. These color separations are made on black and white film. Each negative now contains, in relative degrees of gray from white to black, the values of intensity of one of the four colors in the original.

3. Each color separation negative is now retouched by expert craftsmen before being inserted into a camera which operates on the principle of a photographic enlarger—projecting light through the negative onto unexposed film. In this second photographic process, however, a fine "screen" is inserted between the color separation negative and the unexposed film.

4. This screen is made of two large discs of optical glass on which have been scribed microscopically fine lines. Set at right angles to each other, these lines form a grid of minute squares. The number of these squares will range from 14,400 to 90,000 per square inch, depending upon the fineness of the screen.

5. In exposing each color separation negative through the screen to produce a "screen positive," diffusion of light by each square of the grid breaks the image into minute dots or squares. The sizes of these dots on the developed film positive vary according to the amount of light passing through each square. Thus, on the yellow film positive, each dot on the filmed image represents the intensity of light projected from the yellow negative through its corresponding square of the screen: the greater the intensity, the larger the dot!

Note: Eventually these dots will be transferred onto metal plates— one plate for each color—to become ink-bearing surfaces. Because of this, the size of each dot will determine the volume of ink it will hold, and hence the intensity of the color it will print.

6. The dot sizes on each screened positive must therefore be exactly right. To make certain of this before the plates are made, the four screened positives now undergo a highly skilled process known as dot etching. Over a light table, each positive film is examined minutely. Using fine brushes and acid, master craftsmen work over the dots, adjusting them where necessary to the precise sizes that are correct for the color values required. To make a particular shade of brown, for instance, the dot etcher must know the precise dot sizes required on the yellow, the blue and the red positives—and adjust those dot sizes so that the correct volume of each color will be printed—dot by dot—to produce the color pattern that creates the original brown in the artwork.

7. Each of the four screened and color-corrected positives is now stripped into a master form sheet of "flat" composed of all the elements of art and typography that will appear on the four color plates. With the aid of master register marks—attached to the original copy and reproduced on each separation negative and positive—skilled craftsmen work to precisions measured in thousandths of an inch. A separate "flat" is made for each color.

8. We're now ready for platemaking. Light-weight, flexible metal plates are first coated with a light-sensitive emulsion in a centrifugal whirler, converting the surface into a "photographic" plate. (Plates also can be bought pre-sensitized.)

9. Each of the four master flats—one for each color—is placed against a light-sensitive plate under pressure and exposed to light.

10. It is this photo-process which makes possible one of the important economic advantages of lithography. For multiple exposures can be made on each plate, repeating the image as many times as the plate size permits. In this operation known as "Step & Repeat" or "Photo-Composing," these multiple exposures are made with all the precise registering between the different items and the different plates for each color automated in the platemaking stage to eliminate costly time on the press.

11. The exposed plate is now developed, and a grease-receptive lacquer is applied which adheres only to the image-bearing areas, making them water-repellent. For the principle of lithography is based upon the chemical fact that water and oil repel each other.

12. The four plates—one for each color—are now curved around the press cylinders, fastened, and adjusted for hairline register. Each minute dot on each plate is now an ink bearing surface which will hold a precise volume of colored ink, in volume according to its size.

13. On press, each of the four plates comes in contact with three sets of rollers: the water roller which moistens all non-inkbearing surfaces— the ink roller which imparts the plate's particular color to the ink-bearing surfaces—and the rubber "offset" cylinder onto which the inked impression is transferred, 14. and which in turn transfers that impression onto the paper as it passes through the press. (Hence the term offset.)

Offset Prices on Job Printing. For the standard 8½ by 11 inch, 16-pound sheet of white paper, you should pay no *more* (1964) than $5.50 for the first 1,000, and much less for succeeding thousands. If no printer near you will approach those prices, you can do business by mail with New York or Chicago printers. The "Business Services" column of the classified ads in *The New York Times* Sunday Business Section always carries several listings of printers who will handle your job for you.

Rotogravure

"Roto" is a photographic process in which the picture is actually etched *into* a metal plate. It provides very fine reproduction, and it is good for very long runs. That's why much rotogravure is used in Sears, Roebuck catalogs and in some Sunday newspaper sections.

You will have little contact with rotogravure at first. If you send copy to a rotogravure magazine, send the material you would send for offset reproduction.

Mimeograph

In this process you type holes in a clothlike stencil. The stencil is then wrapped around an inky drum, and when the drum is rolled over paper, the ink feeds out through the impressions you made with your typewriter.

Mimeograph is a good reproduction process for short runs (under 5,000) of some kinds of sales literature. It has the advantage of being quick. A girl can type a mimeograph stencil and run it off immediately. There is no costly type to set, and no platemaker to wait for. Mimeo is usually cheaper than offset for runs under 500.

A *good* mimeographing job of typewritten copy will look very nearly as good as an offset job. And now, new electronic scanning devices will transfer an illustration or a letterhead to the mimeograph stencil. (But the reproduction of illustrations by mimeograph is nowhere near as sharp as an offset job, and it is *not* cheap.)

It's handy to have a mimeograph machine around your office. But chances are there is a professional letter shop near you who will do the job better, and at lower true cost.

Spirit Reproduction

This is a process in which you type on a sheet that deposits a layer of carbonlike substance on a master. The master is then wet with alcohol or other "spirit" substance. When the wet master is brought into contact with the blank paper, it leaves part of the carbon on the blank sheet, thereby reproducing what you typed.

Spirit reproduction is used for a small number of copies—10 to 200— when the appearance does not matter very much. It is not good for any sales piece.

Spirit duplicators are sometimes called "fluid duplicators" or "liquid duplicators," or by various trade names including "Hectograph" or "Ditto."

Automatic Typewriting

This process is used when it is essential that each letter look hand-typed. (There are very few times in mail order when this is necessary, however.)

The operator cuts a roll that looks like the roll in a player piano, and the rolls are then inserted into one or more automatic typewriters. The letter is typed out exactly like the original. You can leave blank spaces to type in later the name and address or any other special message you desire.

The Hooven system is the only automatic typewriter system I know about.

Cost of automatically typed letters is not low, but it is less than the cost of having them typed by hand.

TYPE AND TYPOGRAPHERS

Every advertisement and direct-mail piece uses type—lots of type. You must learn to choose the type face you want, and the arrangement of type; or, at least you must learn to be a good critic of whoever "specifies the type" for your ads.

A letterpress printer does set type. But for almost all your jobs you need more skill in typography and a wider variety of type faces than a job printer possesses. That's where the typographer comes in.

A typographer is a specialist who sets type for you according to your instructions, and then prints only a few "reproduction proofs," which you then photograph and convert into either an offset plate or a "cut" for letterpress.

All that you need to learn from this paragraph is *not* to expect a printer to do the job of a typographer, or you will be disappointed. The letterpress printer is seldom equipped to set type for the kind of printed pieces that you need to sell your product effectively.

Type for headlines can be of very many different type faces. You will want a type that has a "personality" in keeping with the product you are advertising. You don't want the thickest, blackest, strongest type if you are advertising lingerie. The typographer's judgment may be

THE SIX FACES OF TYPE

1. 𝕿𝖊𝖝𝖙

2. Roman

2a. Oldstyle

2b. Modern

2c. Mixed

3. *Italic*

4. **Gothic**

4a. Sans Serif

4b. Sq. Serif

5. *Script,* Cursives

6. NOVELTY

FIG.   19-1

SOME REPRESENTATIVE TYPES

𝕮loister 𝕭lack, h   𝔊oudy 𝔗ext, h

Garamond, Te   Caslon, TeA

Goudy Bold, Ei   Cloister Oldstyle, T

Bodoni Book, Tt   **Ultra Bodoni**

Cheltenham BC AGg   Bulmer, T

Caslon Italic   ***Bodoni Bold Italic***

R RR GOTHIC

Sans Serif BC   Sans Serif Light

Spartan Ex B   Sans Serif Bold

Stymie Light   **Stymie Bold**

Brush Script   *Coronet Cursive*

Hobo, ygpq   LOMBARDIC

P. T. Barnum   Typewriter Type

FIG.   19-2

good as to which type you should use, but an artist's judgment is likely to be much better.

Beware of typographers and artists who want to give you a "good-looking ad." Mail-order ads are seldom good to look at.

If you want to specify the type yourself, get hold of a book of type faces and look through it till you find what you want. If the typographer doesn't have that exact style, he can come pretty close in matching it.

The four basic kinds of type are:

Old Style Roman

Modern Roman

Sans-serif (Gothic)

Special-purpose types

Caslon and Garamond are classic examples of Old Style Roman. Bodoni is a good example of Modern Roman. There are dozens more types of both. The various strokes in Modern Roman differ more from each other in width than in Old Style, and the "serifs"—the tiny strokes at right angles to the main stroke—are flat. Old Style serifs are round.

Sans-serif Gothic is just what it says: without serifs. Gothic headlines give you the most punch for your money. Most of your headlines will be in one or another of the Gothic families. Franklin Gothic is an example of this family.

Not only are there various families of type, but there are also variations within a family. For example, a family may be condensed, extended, bold, light, etc.

There are also *italic* faces in many families of type. Italics can sometimes be good for headlines, especially when you want the ad to look like editorial matter for a reading notice.

Don't use several different faces of type in your various headlines and subheads. Many different faces are confusing, and are even uglier than a mail-order ad should be. (However, I have no data to *prove* that this dictum holds true in mail order.)

Use type as big as you can squeeze into the width of the space you have available. This is especially true for the overall heading. Reverse type (white on black) gives your headline even more punch.

For the type in the *body* of your ad, follow your typographer's recommendation. Never use Gothic or italic, because they are hard to read. Generally, you will use a very small body type—sometimes smaller, in fact, than your printer has available. In that case, you can reduce the size of the type with a photostat.

But don't try to be *too* greedy and set your type *too* small. Five-point or six-point type is probably best for most situations you will run into. Follow the examples of good mail-order ads whose purpose is similar to what you are trying to do.

ABCDEFGHIJ SMALL CAPITALS abcdefghijklmnopqrstuvwx*abcdefghijklmnopqrstuv* 12 pt.

HERE ARE TEN POINT CAPITALS ABCD SMALL CAPITALS ABCDEFGHIJKLMNOPQRSTUVWXYZ ABCD
lower case abcdefghijklmnopqrstuvwxyz abcdefghij *ITALIC abcdefghijklmnopqrstuvwxyz abcdefghijklmno* 10 pt.

CASLON OLD FACE:

HERE YOU SEE TEN POINT CAPS ABCD SMALL CAPS ABCDEFGHIJKLMNOPQRSTUVWXYP AB 10 pt.
lower case abcdefghijklmnopqrstuvwxyzabcdef *ITALIC CAPS Italic lower case abcdefghijklmnop*

HERE YOU SEE EIGHT POINT CAPS ABCDEFJ SMALL CAPS ABCDEFGHIJKLMNOPQRSTUVWXYP ABCDEFGHI 8 pt.
lower case abcdefghijklmnopqrstuvwxyzabcdefghijklm *ITALIC CAPS Italic lower case abcdefghijklmnopqrstuvwx*

GARAMOND

24 pt. T. S. ELIOT speaks with an *authority a*

18 pt. REX WARNER spins a sonnet or a *thoughtful ode and*

BODONI

ABCDEFGHIJKLMNOPQRS
TUVWXYZ& abcdefghijklm
Franklin Gothic

FIG. 19-3

Typography service is expensive, because of the large investment a typographer must make in type and equipment. It will pay you to get everything as clear as possible before he starts work, and then to make as few changes as possible.

In the last couple of years photographic typesetting has come onto the market. In this process, the typesetter only has *one* size of each type face. You get the exact size you want by photographic enlargement. Photo-setting is as sharp as ordinary typography, and may be considerably cheaper for your needs. It's worth checking on.

Paste-up type is a quick and cheap substitute for typography. Sometimes it is very satisfactory. You buy an entire sheet of letters for about $1.50 in the type face and size that you need. You lay the letters you want over a lined-off piece of paper, and rub the letters off the sheet and onto your paper. Repeat the process until you have your headline.

An even cruder method is to cut letters out of magazines. In a pinch it can work fine.

You should memorize these measurements: 14 agate lines = 1 inch; 6 picas = 1 inch; 72 points = 1 inch. You measure the width of an ad in picas or columns, the height in agate lines or points.

HOW TO PREPARE AN AD FOR LETTERPRESS

Let's first talk about *magazine ads* in letterpress publications. (The rate card tells you which magazines use letterpress.)

A letterpress magazine *will* set type for your ad, if you desire. This can be an advantage. When you run the first test of an ad, you may not wish to shell out typographer's charges when you know you will be changing the ad.

On the other hand, the typesetting the magazine produces for you will be far inferior to that of a typographer. You are *not* likely to obtain exactly the effect you want. Your choice of type faces will be limited, and the arrangement of the type will *not* be just as you wish.

Furthermore, most magazines will not make cuts of illustrations for you. (A few shopping-section magazines such as *House Beautiful* and the *New York Times Magazine* will do the whole job—because they get a lot of business from amateurs in the mail-order business.)

When your ad has been tested and you are reasonably sure that you will be inserting it repeatedly, you should perfect the ad in the way you want it, then have an original cut and duplicate cuts made. At this time you should call in an artist or use an advertising agency. You need professional help to specify how each of the elements in the ad should look, and then to fit the entire ad together.

The first element in the ad will be the type. You will get a "reproduction proof" from the typographer with your exact requirements in

Proofreaders' Marks

⊙	.	Period	lc	lower case Word
⌄	,	Comma	cap	Capital letter
⌄	'	Apostrophe	sc	SMALL CAPITAL LETTER
⌄⌄	" "	Quotation marks	bf	Boldface type
;/	;	Semicolon	ital	Italic type
⊙	:	Colon	rom	Roman (type)
?/	?	Question mark	wf	Wrong font
!/	!	Exclamation mark	#	Insert space
=/	-	Hyphen	⊂	Close up
⅟ⁿ	–	En dash	⊙	Turn letter
⅟ₘ	—	Em dash		
2/m	——	Two-em dash		
(/)/	( )	Parentheses		
[/]/	[ ]	Brackets		

ℒ	Delete
ℒ	Delete and close up
□	Quad (one em) space
⊔	Move down
⊓	Move up
⊏	Move to left
⊐	Move to right
eq #	Equalize spacing between words
X	Broken letter
¶	Begin a new paragraph
no ¶	No new paragraph
stet	Let type stand as set
⑦	Verify or (supply) information
tr	Transpose letters or marked words
SP	Spell out (abbrev) or 7)
∪	Push space down
=	Straighten type
‖	Align type
run in	Run in material on same line
bu	Change (x/y) to built-up fraction
sh	Change x/y to shilling fraction
⩗	Set as subscript
⩘	Set as exponent

FIG. 19-4

choice of type face, size of type, width of typesetting, and heading. If you don't get exactly what you want, get a second proof.

The second element in the ad will be the artwork—either a photograph or a dummy.

Then you paste up the artwork and the type into a "dummy" or "mechanical," which you send to the engraver. The engraver first makes an original plate of the ad, and then makes duplicate plates. In most cases you will retain the original plate in case you want to make additional copies. You send the duplicate plates off to the various magazines in which you want to run.

Take your engraver's advice on the type of duplicate plates to use. There are many different kinds: electrotype, stereotype, plastic plates, and molded rubber plates.

Different types of media have different column widths. Newspapers are narrower, generally. Each different column width requires a different size of plate. Of course you can "float" a small plate in a wider column, but that is not an economical use of space.

Width of columns is specified for each medium on its rate card and in *Standard Rate & Data*.

Multicolor letterpress jobs are too technical to discuss here.

As we said before, you probably won't use letterpress much except for letterpress magazines and for special jobs.

HOW TO PREPARE AN AD FOR OFFSET

Offset is remarkably flexible. Anything you can put on a piece of paper can be printed easily and quickly in offset, without extra costs for engraving or special preparation. Preparation for the "camera" is the same for direct-mail pieces and for publication ads.

The simplest ads to prepare for offset are all-type ads, of course. You paste the headline down where you want it (using rubber cement). You paste the body copy where you want it. And that's all there is to it. You don't need to worry about minor imperfections because the camera won't pick them up.

The camera won't pick up the full strength of any color except black unless you make special arrangements. And it won't pick up light blue at all, so you can use a light blue pencil to mark up the copy.

Rubber cement is invaluable. With rubber cement it is easy to position or remove elements in the ad. Stray drops rub off smoothly with a ball of dried cement, or with your fingernail.

"Line drawings"—drawings that have no darks and lights, but only straight ink lines—can also go onto any ordinary piece of offset copy. The camera picks up the lines in the drawing just the way it picks up type or pen lines.

"Tone" artwork must be "screened." The section on offset early in this chapter tells you about screening. After the artwork is screened, it is "stripped" into the negative along with the unscreened type elements.

One of the advantages of offset's flexibility is that you can easily experiment with your ad. You can paste in new headlines, paste on a border, increase the size of the headline, paste in a new price, etc.

An X-acto knife, a single-edged razor, a draftsman's T square, and a wooden drawing board are necessary and inexpensive tools of the trade. You can do much of this work very well after you have had a little practice, even if you are totally without art skills.

You will generally get body type for publication ads from a typographer. But in your direct-mail pieces, you will use typewriter type most of the time. This is one of the very great advantages of offset. You can type out a letter, get it to the offset shop, and often have them complete the job within an hour. At least one large offset shop in New York City does a great deal of its work on a "While-U-Wait" basis.

To type a page for offset, use the whitest, flattest paper you can find. The best bond paper is *not* good, because it is not flat. Paper from typewriter pads sold in stationery stores is best.

Make sure your typewriter keys are very clean and make a sharp impression. Use a new ribbon. An electric typewriter gives you the best-looking job, but it is not essential.

There are two typewriterlike machines that you can use for your body copy for publication ads. They are the Varityper and the Justowriter. With both of them you can insert many different type faces. Also, they justify your copy. (That is, they space out the letters—on the second typing—so that all lines end at the right-hand margin.)

The IBM executive typewriter also justifies your lines.

But for a direct-mail letter, you will do better with a raggedy right-hand margin because it looks more informal and more like a letter. Never justify a letter.

If you find you have more to say than you can fit onto the page even with an elite (small-type) typewriter, have the printer *reduce* your ad photographically. Don't forget that when you plan on reduction you should run wider on the width as well as deeper on the length. A 10 percent reduction—which means 10 percent reduction for both width *and* length—reduces the total area by 19 percent. This means you can increase the amount of copy by more than 23 percent with a 10 percent reduction.

You can "blow up" an ad, too. You will do that mostly for the artistic effect.

When you reproduce a letter by offset, you reproduce both the letterhead *and* the rest of the letter, simply by pasting them up together.

This is one of the great economies of the offset process for the mail-order man.

MISCELLANEOUS PRINTING MATTERS

Envelopes

Buy your envelopes from an envelope maker, and *not* from a printer. The envelope house will print your envelopes and charge you a fraction of the price a printer will charge.

Look for envelope suppliers in *The New York Times* Sunday Business Section in classified, under "Business Services."

There are dozens of types of trick envelopes that combine various elements of the direct-mail package. These cost more, but may be worth it in special situations.

For very long runs, and special copy printed on them, it will pay to have your envelopes run offset, and made up afterwards. Check printers and prices on this.

Paper

There are many different kinds of paper available at many different prices. But nine times out of ten you will use the cheapest 16-pound or 20-pound paper. For two-side printing, 20-pound paper is a necessity.

Colored paper may be good for short runs to liven up your mailing. But for runs of more than a couple of thousand, use colored ink instead. It is cheaper.

For anything except long runs, buy paper through your printer. He purchases in large quantities and gets a much better price than you can get.

Miscellaneous Operations

Direct mail must be folded, inserted into the envelope, sealed, stamped, and perhaps sorted and tied into bundles. All these operations should be done mechanically, except in the smallest runs.

Printers can fold your letters for 50 cents to $1.50 per thousand (8½ by 11). Unless you have inserting equipment yourself, you will do better to use a letter shop, preferably a letter shop that has a Phillipsburg or other model of automatic inserter. The inserter places all the pieces in the envelopes and seals them. If you use a letter shop, let them do the folding too.

For comparison purposes—assume you have a two-page letter and a business-reply envelope to go inside a No. 10 envelope. A good letter shop (in 1964) will do 5,000 pieces for a maximum of about $7 per thousand—folded, inserted, and sealed.

Most automatic postage meters will seal envelopes as well as apply postage. If you send follow-ups that must be keyed inside the envelope, you will need an automatic meter to seal the envelopes just before you send them out.

There are also plain envelope sealers available for under $200 new, and around $100 secondhand.

If you send out a great deal of direct mail, it is economical to take advantage of the bulk rate. But then you must sort the mail by destination. Many rented lists are already separated by geography. In that case, your letter shop will use an automatic tying machine to make bundles and deliver the mail directly to the post office. You should get a receipt from the post office—a receipt that records the number of pieces mailed and the amount paid.

How to Deal with Printers

When you want more than one sheet printed at a time, keep in mind that printing presses are of a few standard sizes, and the price will be cheapest if you can utilize all of that printing area. This is the principle of "gang runs."

For example, if you want to print a sheet 5½ by 8½, you would probably make two identical pieces of copy, paste them on an 8½ by 11 sheet, have the printer run them on his small press, then cut them apart. In this way the price to you is for 1,000 pieces rather than 2,000.

You can also gang-up two or more different pieces of copy at the same time.

Purchasing printing so as to get quality *and* service *and* price is a real art. To begin with, let me give you some yardsticks of *minimum* prices (1964) for some basic units of printing:

1,000......	8½ × 11	One side	16 lb	$ 5.00
5,000......	8½ × 11	One side	16 lb	17.00
5,000......	5½ × 8½	16-page booklet		135.00
1,000......	No. 10 envelopes			3.50
1,000......	No. 6 business-reply envelopes			3.00

Here is one firm's price schedule for printing on 16-pound bond paper:

ONE SIDE

Size	Quantity						
	250	500	1,000	2,000	3,000	4,000	5,000
8½ × 11.......	$ 5.65	$ 5.90	$ 6.50	$10.50	$14.50	$18.50	$22.50
8½ × 14.......	8.00	8.75	10.50	17.00	23.50	30.00	36.50
11 × 17........	11.30	11.80	13.00	21.00	29.00	37.00	45.00
17 × 22........	22.60	23.60	26.00	42.00	58.00	74.00	90.00

TWO SIDES

	250	500	1,000	2,000	3,000	4,000	5,000
8½ × 11.......	$11.00	$11.25	$11.80	$18.60	$ 25.40	$ 32.20	$ 39.00
8½ × 14.......	14.50	15.50	17.00	26.00	35.00	44.00	53.00
11 × 17........	22.00	22.50	23.60	37.20	50.80	64.40	78.00
17 × 22........	44.00	45.00	47.20	74.40	101.60	128.80	156.00

It is interesting to note that this same firm, under another name, offers to do the above jobs for about 25 percent less for orders which it receives by mail with check enclosed.

This is a schedule of the same firm's extra charges for special services:

Additional Charges, if Applicable

General:

$1.00 per thousand for 20-lb. white bond per 8½ × 11 unit
$1.00 per thousand for 16-lb. colored bond per 8½ × 11 unit
$2.00 per thousand for 20-lb. colored bond per 8½ × 11 unit
$2.00 overall charge for colored ink (8½ × 11 or 8½ × 14)
$5.00 overall charge for colored ink (11 × 17 or 17 × 22)
$1.00 for opaquing excessively dirty or pasted-up copy per 8½ × 11 unit
$0.50 for cutting each 1,000 sheets of paper (per cut)
$0.25 for shipping carton

Folding:

Operation	First 1,000	Additional millions
8½ × 11 or 11 × 17, once in half..........	$2.50	$1.50
8½ × 11 to fit No. 10 envelope............	2.50	1.50
8½ × 11 to 4¼ × 5½ inches.............	3.50	2.50
8½ × 11 to fit 6¾ envelope..............	3.50	2.50
11 × 17 to fit No. 10 envelope............	3.50	2.50
11 × 17 to 5½ × 8½ inches..............	3.50	2.50

Punching:

Two or three regular holes—$1.50 per 1,000 sheets

Padding:

10¢ per individual pad 8½ × 11 up to 100 sheets—minimum charge $1.00

The prices shown are low because they are standard units and require no special adjustment to presses. They use standard-size paper fully.

Many printers will charge you twice as much as those prices and not be robbing you. If you can't find a local printer who will give you those prices, look on the back page of the *New York Times* Business Section and write to the firms advertising there.

Dealing with printers so as to get the work you want by the date you want it is particularly difficult. Printers face great problems in scheduling their work. One day they have nothing to do; next day they're loaded with customers screaming for rush jobs. Unfortunately, few printers have the courage to turn down the customers whose work they can't complete by the date the customers request. So they lie and stall, and you, the customer, find yourself way behind.

There are several ways to *try* to handle this problem with printers:

1. Be willing to pay extra for service. No one likes to do this, but sometimes you have to.

2. Be very smart in your scheduling and never need anything quickly. Then lie to the printer and tell him you need it a week earlier than you really need it. Few of us are smart enough to do the former. The latter is against my taste because I don't think it is fair to the printer.

3. Find a printer with whom you can form a relationship of trust, and then give him all your business and treasure him like gold. Beware, though, of the honeymoon. Printers are irrationally willing to break their necks to satisfy a *new* customer. Then, once they have him, they often neglect him, raise prices to him, and finally drive him away. Why? I don't know.

I found a printer who studied industrial engineering in college and who runs his small shop like General Motors. I know he thinks straight, plans well, and doesn't *permit* situations that require alibis. (Well, practically never.) I'm so satisfied I don't even squawk when bills are too high.

This is a short check list of instructions to cover when you tell your printer what you want to have done:

Name and type of piece to be printed	Placement of copy on page
Size of piece	Color(s) of ink
Color of stock	Printing process
Paper texture	Exact copy
Type faces and sizes	

20

Filling Orders and Keeping Records

*How to Find a Supplier • Drop Shipping versus
Consignment versus Cash Purchase • Buy It, or
Make It Yourself? • How to Handle Mail and
Orders • Addressing Systems • Order Records
and Customer Records • Handling Complaints •
Shipping Orders*

This lesson is about almost everything in the mail-order business except
getting the order. The fact that we need only one lesson for filling orders, in contrast to so many lessons for getting orders, should emphasize
the importance of the advertising in mail order.

HOW TO FIND A SUPPLIER

There are no special sources of mail-order products. If you sell a
drug, you will obtain it either from a firm that already manufactures it
and will put it up for you under your own brand, or from a manufacturing chemist who will make it up for you specially. If you sell auto parts,
you will buy them from distributors or manufacturers. And so on.

Ingenuity and diligence will locate suppliers for you. The best place
to start is by examining the competitors' products for a manufacturer's
name printed on the product. Once you have the name of the maker,
the rest is easy.

There are several firms that sell directories of distributors who will
drop-ship, or sell outright, items that may work in mail-order catalogs.
I have no direct knowledge of how satisfactory these directories are,
but I am a little skeptical. Certainly you cannot make a profit in selling
any one of those items alone.

The Manhattan classified phone directory is invaluable. Your local library will have one, or purchase a copy from the New York Telephone Company. Look under many different headings until you find what you want. If the product is foreign-made, look under "Importers." Then get firms on the phone or write to them, and if they can't supply what you want, be sure to ask them for their advice as to where you *can* get it. Such good-natured referrals will lead you to the right place more often than any other method.

Thomas' Directory and *Macrae's Blue Book* are other valuable sources. They list firms all over the United States. Again, if you don't find what you are looking for under the likeliest heading, look under three or four other headings.

Other useful source books: *Premium Suppliers' Directory* (*Blue Book Issue*), *Playthings Directory, Gift & Art Buyers Guide, Toys and Novelty Buyers Guide*.

Trade associations can often help you. Almost every industry from steel to art materials has a trade association, and the staff can often guide you to the likeliest source of just what you want. For the names and addresses of associations, check the *Encyclopedia of Associations*[1] at your local library.

The purpose of the consulates of the various foreign countries is to inform you where you can buy products made in their countries. They will direct you to importers in this country, or manufacturers abroad, whichever is appropriate. Use your common sense in choosing the likeliest consulates: Japan and not Ghana will probably sell you telescopes cheaply. The consulates will also advise you on tariffs in many cases. Or better yet, call the U.S. Customs Office for tariff information.

If you plan to sell books, manuals, information of any kind, or other printed products, you have a double supply problem: the written copy and the printing of the copy.

You yourself may write what you plan to sell. Or you can hire a ghost writer to write for you. You can contact ghost writers through ads in the literary sections of Sunday papers, and in the *Saturday Review* and writers' magazines.

Printing the material is not a problem, but finding a cheap, reliable printer is a real art. Prices of printing can vary 100 percent and affect your profit margin greatly.

One outstanding advantage of selling information is that you have perfect control over your product. You are not at the mercy of any supplier. Furthermore, the copyright on your material (don't forget to get a copyright!) will present a barrier to competitors if the content is at all complex and difficult to reproduce.

Full-scale books and correspondence courses can also be ghostwritten. Frequently you can find a book that is out of copyright that will serve as is, or can be brought up to date. Or you may find a book presently on the market whose publisher will give you an exclusive and guarantee supply for some period of time.

Note that the seller of printed material pays less for the physical paper-and-ink product he sells—as a percent of the sales price—than sellers of almost any other product. He is really selling *information*, not paper and ink. The cost of the *information* is laid out only once, when the information is gathered and written down.

DROP SHIPPING VERSUS CONSIGNMENT VERSUS CASH PURCHASE

Many suppliers will do business with you only if you buy outright, cash on the barrelhead.

If you can buy on consignment, it is always preferable to buying outright. Consignment buying has all the advantages of the outright purchase plus the privilege of return if you can't sell the merchandise.

Drop shipping *may* be better than purchasing outright or on consignment. When you sell with this method, your capital is not tied up in stock, you take no inventory risk, and you need no storage space.

Drop-ship arrangements are seldom available on anything but expensive merchandise. And drop-ship has disadvantages, too:

1. You usually pay more per unit when you buy on a drop-ship arrangement. The supplier is no dope. He knows that tying up *his* capital and warehouse space costs money, and he makes you bear the burden in the price you pay him.

2. Drop shipping is never as dependable as having the merchandise in your office. You *know* what *you* are going to do. You never know when the supplier's stock boy will take a day off.

3. Drop shipping introduces an extra step, and extra delay, between the customer's order and his receipt of the package. This extra delay makes the customer unhappy and that costs you money in the long run in lost customers.

Drop shipping is most useful:

1. When you are first testing merchandise and you have no idea how well it will go over, and

2. If you sell a very wide assortment of expensive units of merchandise.

But drop-ship operation is seldom a short cut to riches in mail order for people who have no investment capital.

BUY IT, OR MAKE IT YOURSELF?

One of the common business fallacies is to set too low a cost price on an item or service you render to yourself—usually because you don't include the cost of your own labor and overhead in the total cost. Let's say, for example, that you can either send material out to be mimeographed nearby, for 60 to 80 cents per hundred copies, or you can buy a mimeograph machine and run things off in your own shop. If an employee of yours does the work on a mimeograph machine of your own, the cost may be only 30 cents for paper plus 15 cents for labor—a total of 45 cents, and apparently a saving of 15 or 25 cents per hundred sheets.

But when you figure the cost of supervision of the job, the cost of space to house the mimeograph, the amortized cost of the machine itself, and miscellaneous other overhead expenses, you will often find it much cheaper to send the work out.

The same argument will hold true for folding, sealing, addressing, and most small manufacturing operations.

The primary advantage of doing the work in your own shop is that you have greater control over time of execution, and better quality control.

The biggest corporations in the country, from General Motors on down, send out much work that they could do for themselves—but at a higher cost. Learn your lesson from them.

HOW TO HANDLE MAIL AND ORDERS

These are the usual steps in a day's work. I will describe them very generally so that they will fit many types of businesses:

1. Sort incoming mail by key numbers.
2. Record returns—both inquiries and orders—for each day. (See record forms in Chapter 10.)
3. Open mail.
4. Sort mail into piles of similar inquiries and similar orders.
5. Type address labels for each pile, making as many carbons as necessary for your particular needs. Key the labels in a way that reveals what the person ordered or inquired about. A crayon line that touches each label on a sheet of labels is often all you need.
6. Place labels on orders and inquiry follow-ups.
7. Put postage on orders and outgoing letters.
8. Place extra carbon labels on index cards, and file them.
9. Handle complaints, questions, and other nonroutine mail.

Remember that the routine varies greatly among businesses. Some kinds of businesses omit many of the steps above. Other firms include many more steps.

Sorting Incoming Mail by Key Numbers. If you have large volumes of several different products, it will pay you to rent more than one post-office box and put different addresses in your ads, in order to reduce sorting costs.

Sorting for key analysis can be a very time-consuming, laborious, and expensive chore when you receive upwards of 500 letters per day. You can slice this clerical expense to a fraction by *sampling* the returns to key numbers. For example, if you receive 500 to 1,500 inquiries for a given product each day, go through the pile and count off each third (or second, or fifth) inquiry, and send the other two-thirds on to the next step in the procedure. Then sort the one-in-three sample by keys, and record the results (multiplying to get the correct estimated number, of course).

You should decide what fraction of the letters you should analyze on the basis of the number of returns the average ad will receive. My rough recommendation: choose a fraction that will allow most of your *ads* to get 50 or more *recorded* returns over the time it pulls. In other words, the average ad will receive 50 times as many letters as the fraction you choose.

For example, if your average ad pulls 200 returns, analyze one in each four returns.

The fraction can be changed without trouble. At one point I used a fraction of one in five. A fall in results caused us to shift to analyzing one in every three returns.

This sampling process is extremely accurate and very economical. But mail-order firms are so blind to the value of statistical methods that few firms, if any, use this procedure.

Opening the Mail. Open the mail, probably after, but possibly before, sorting for key numbers. Your common sense will tell you which is better for your operation.

By all means get an *electric* letter-opener. You can buy a secondhand model for $90 to $120. I have found the Bircher Lightning a fine machine. An electric opener will justify its cost if you receive as few as 50 letters a day. Besides, it is fun for you or your employees to operate.

It is usually best to staple together the letter, the order, and the envelope. That saves all important information, including the crucial address. Often you will need the postmark to address the label correctly.

If you have thousands of cheap inquiries (costing under 25 cents a piece, for example), it may be economical to keep only whichever piece —letter or envelope—has a complete address. You will still need to save both envelope and letter in many cases, however.

Typing Labels. Type labels for new customers or inquirers with as many carbons as are needed. Use the sets of two, three, or four sheets of labels that come with carbons. Or make address plates or other addressing-system cards.

If you receive large numbers of inquiries, you might consider using home typists. They need no office supervision and you pay for no fringe benefits (though you must pay taxes for them just as for other employees). And home typists supply their own typewriters. They work for less, for the privilege of earning money where they can tend children and choose their own hours.

Insist on reliable workers. Home typists are so plentiful (an ad in the newspaper brings in dozens) that you can hold out for the best.

A good average typist types 150 addresses an hour on labels.

Have your typists save time by omitting periods after abbreviations like "Mrs," "NJ," "St". This is a substantial saving in typing time.

Copy the address just the way the addressee writes it. Check all doubtful towns or states in the Directory of United States Post Offices. (Get at least one copy from the Superintendent of Documents, Washington 25, D.C., for $3. This is almost the first thing you need in the mail-order business.)

Abbreviations. Never abbreviate the name of any city. Don't abbreviate such words as "Center," "Junction," "Spring," etc., or "North," "South," "East," and "West."

If you want to do business with the customer again in the future, don't abbreviate any part of his name. Write his name exactly as he writes it and *never* misspell it.

Use the following state abbreviations:

Alabama	Ala	Kentucky	Ky
Alaska	Alaska	Louisiana	La
Arizona	Ariz	Maine	Maine
Arkansas	Ark	Maryland	Md
California	Calif	Massachusetts	Mass
Colorado	Colo	Michigan	Mich
Connecticut	Conn	Minnesota	Minn
Delaware	Del	Mississippi	Miss
District of Columbia	DC	Missouri	Mo
Florida	Fla	Montana	Mont
Georgia	Ga	Nebraska	Nebr
Hawaii	Hawaii	New Hampshire	NH
Idaho	Idaho	New Jersey	NJ
Illinois	Ill	New Mexico	N Mex
Indiana	Ind	New York	NY
Iowa	Iowa	North Carolina	N Car
Kansas	Kans	North Dakota	N Dak
Ohio	Ohio	Texas	Tex
Oklahoma	Okla	Utah	Utah
Oregon	Ore	Vermont	Vt
Pennsylvania	Penna	Virginia	Va
Rhode Island	RI	Washington	Wash
South Carolina	S Car	West Virginia	W Va
South Dakota	S Dak	Wisconsin	Wis
Tennessee	Tenn	Wyoming	Wyo

ADDRESSING SYSTEMS

If you will be doing a repeat business with your inquiries and customers, or if you expect to rent your list, you will want to use some type of automatic addressing equipment. Before investing in any expensive machinery, you will surely find it sensible to investigate thoroughly and talk to all salesmen about equipment of all kinds. Also, before purchasing *any* addressing system, I would recommend that you read Jerome B. Osherow's article "Mechanizing the List," in the July, 1963, edition of *The Reporter of Direct Mail Advertising*.

Brief descriptions of the major addressing systems follow.

Addressograph. This system uses metal plates that require special machinery for cutting. The plates cost about 10 cents apiece. The addressing machine itself is also expensive, no matter which model you choose, except for a slow hand model that is suitable only for very small lists.

The plates can be notched in one of several ways for ease in sorting. This allows you considerable flexibility in picking out only certain portions of your list.

The advantage of the Addressograph system is that the plates can be used almost forever without wearing out.

The disadvantage of the system is its high cost. However, you can have a service bureau handle your list for you on Addressograph plates without any investment.

The Elliott System. This system uses tiny mimeograph stencils within a cardboard frame. These stencils cost only a couple of cents each and can be cut on a regular typewriter. They may also be notched in several ways for easy sorting.

The Elliott plates will not last forever, as the Addressograph plates will, but they are good for *many* hundreds or even thousands of impressions—more than enough for any ordinary business.

Addressing machines for Elliott plates come in a variety of sizes and speeds, down to hand machines that sell for under $100. The Elliott is certainly one of the less expensive systems for small operators.

Speedaumat. The Speedaumat system is roughly similar to the Addressograph system. The plates cost about half as much as Addressograph plates, but the system is practical only for large mailers.

Pollard. Pollard Alling is another metal-plate system that is useful only for the very large mailers who do not need to select special portions of their list.

Dashew and Scriptomatic Spirit Systems. These systems place a coating of special carbon onto a card, and then each time the card is used, a little bit of the carbon is applied to the envelope with an alcohol-like solvent. These addressing systems use exactly the same principle as the spirit "Ditto" duplicators found in thousands of offices throughout the country. (That's the one that gives you the purple copies. It is probably the cheapest office duplicator available.)

A single card wears out in somewhat less than 200 impressions, though it is possible to make a second card from the first. The cards are made on an ordinary typewriter, with a special carbon, at a cost of about 1½ cents each.

A variety of addressing machines is available, at a variety of speeds and with various optional equipment.

The spirit addressing systems have several advantages for the mail-order firm:

1. Low cost of both cards and machines. Dashew offers much cheaper basic systems than Scriptomatic.

2. The same card can serve as the address card and as a record card for customer's orders and other such information. Having all the information in one place saves enormous amounts of clerical work. It is also the only perfect and easy way to maintain your address system in complete agreement with your customer records.

3. It is possible to use IBM cards as the basic card. This gives you a remarkable degree of flexibility that is available with no other system. You can sort out all those customers who have not ordered in six months, or all those who bought a given product, or all those who live in a given state—all in a matter of minutes. It was undoubtedly this feature that induced Du Pont to *throw away* its old system of *over a million* metal plates (that cost a dime apiece or so) in order to replace them with a spirit system.

It is also possible to use special three-by five-inch index cards or four-by six-inch cards that have holes punched in the margins for selecting various groups of cards. You can then sort these cards with a needle, and punch them with a hand gadget that costs only a couple of dollars. This will do well for up to 5,000 names, I would guess.

Even though the spirit systems have not yet gained general acceptance, they are very much worth your consideration.

IBM Machine Addressing. IBM machine addressing systems are not likely to be useful for the smaller operator at first. Larger operators use them more and more, though my guess is that a spirit system with IBM cards is cheaper and better.

COD Label Systems

Preparing COD labels is another addressing choice. If you send out any significant number of COD's, have special labels made up. They will save lots of writing. Before you arrange for these sets of custom-printed labels, obtain the approval of your postmaster.

This is a description of the COD labels one company formerly sold:

The first, or top form, is the gummed shipping label which sticks on the outgoing package. Preprinted (in red) company name, address and COD number following series given by postmaster. The rest of the label is black. The second form is pasted to the COD tag. The third form replaces the manifold book of the post office clerk.

One thousand sets of labels printed up for you should cost around $16 to $20 per thousand, in lots of 5,000, after the type is set for the first label.

ORDER RECORDS AND CUSTOMER RECORDS

Your files should be your slaves, not your master. Keep all the files and records that your particular type of business needs, and none other. The types of files you need will depend upon the type of business you run.

Customer files are the most crucial files in mail-order businesses. These are some kinds of customer systems you might use:

One-shot Business. If your business is strictly a one-shot proposition, you probably would not want any customer file at all. You merely make an extra carbon of labels which will be the basis for a rental list, or you sell the original letters outright to a firm like William Stroh, Jr., West New York, New Jersey, in which case you need no record of customers at all.

You will hear from customers again only in case of complaints. Later in this chapter I shall tell you how to deal with complaints. In a one-shot deal for under $5, it is cheaper in almost every case to send out a duplicate shipment, rather than to check a file to determine the cause of complaint.

Repeat-sales Business. If your business depends on repeat sales to the same customers, you need a record of each purchase a customer makes. Four- by six-inch index cards usually do the trick. This is a standard form for the cards:

| Name _____ Date of 1st inquiry or order _____ |
| Street Address _____ Key _____ |
| City, State _____ Other Customer Data ____ |

Date	Item	Price	Date	Item	Price

File these cards in alphabetical order until your list reaches fairly large size. Then split them into "alpha-geo" order, filing by states and then alphabetically within each state.

Your customer list is the principal asset of your business. It is very wise to keep a duplicate set in a fireproof location somewhere else than at your business. Don't bother to keep that duplicate set "clean" or orderly, however.

If you use Elliott, Addressograph, or similar addressing systems, your addressing-plate file should be identical with your card file. Whenever you add or drop a name from the card file, you must bring the plate file up to date.

The alpha-geo system speeds name-searching. It also places outgoing mail in the proper sequence for sorting to take advantage of third-class bulk rates.

Spirit addressing systems make it possible to address directly from the back of the customer card. This saves you the extra clerical chore of keeping the address-plate file up to date. It also removes a dangerous source of error.

Inquiry and Follow-Ups. If you sell by repeated follow-ups to inquirers, you will need a tickler-file system to tell you when to send out inquiries. One way to maintain a tickler file is to make up one sheet of carbon labels for each follow-up in your series. Set up a separate file for each follow-up letter, and file each sheet by the date it is to go out.

When an order comes in, you must remember to go through each follow-up file to cross off the name of the customer who has already bought. No point in sending him further expensive solicitations!

Spirit-system addressing can also simplify this procedure. Each day's inquirer cards are punched, all together, with the dates of the follow-ups. Each day you sort for the follow-up to go out. And when a customer purchases, you can stop his follow-up series by removing just that one card from your files.

HANDLING COMPLAINTS

General rules for handling complaints:

1. Be as courteous as you possibly can. Expressing your irritation at a customer will cost you money in the long run.

2. But don't be a patsy for customers who want to cheat you. Let them know where you stand.

3. Honor requests for refunds *instantly* and *pleasantly*, expressing your regret. You can then convert a dissatisfied customer into a valuable, satisfied customer. But if the customer has no leg to stand on, and if the sum is large or if it is a one-shot deal, don't be afraid to stand on your rights.

4. Write as few individual letters or notes as possible. Set up form letters or postcards to handle all matters that come up often. After you send out the same message ten times, you will be ready to create a form postcard, and you'll know what to say.

Always include on a form postcard "Please return this card (or letter) if your package does not arrive within a week," etc. That way you can deal with subsequent correspondence much more quickly.

Sawyer had this to say:

> This is one of the unpleasant features of a mail-order enterprise. No mail business can be carried on without a reasonable number of complaints. These are the most common reasons that people kick up a fuss:
>
> Delay in filling order
> Sending goods not ordered, by error
> Omitting part of order
> Damage to goods in transit
> Delay or loss of goods in transit
> Loss or miscarriage of letter
> Miscarriage of goods
> Dissatisfaction as to goods received.[2]

Sometimes you get a complaint about money that was supposedly sent to you, but never reached your office or never was recorded in your records. *Esquire's Mail Order Newsletter* gives sage advice about this problem:

> Every mail order advertiser faces the problem of having cash remittances lost in the mail. A small percentage of chiselers attempt to make envelopes appear as though *cash remittances* were actually enclosed (pressure is put on envelopes to raise impressions and then coins are removed, the envelopes torn or slit to simulate tampering.)
>
> But the great majority of lost remittances are actually lost or stolen and they are difficult to trace. The Post Office provides form 1510 for the filing of claims for lost remittances.
>
> To shift the headaches and responsibility from the advertiser to the prospect and also to curb chiseling, here's what one large mail order firm does:
>
> 1. It immediately answers orders without remittances with its own form stating that the customer's letter was opened and there was no remittance, the letter apparently having been tampered with in the mails. It goes on to state that the customer's letter and envelope is being returned to him *exactly* as received.
> 2. The Post Office form 1510 is also enclosed and the customer is asked to fill out and take it to the Post Master to file his claim. If the "customer" is a chiseler he will hesitate to file; if he is honest he will, of course, cooperate.[3]

As long as we're quoting Sawyer in this chapter, read this delightful account of one mail-order nuisance:

> In the mail-order business, letters come without signature or insufficient address. Parcels sent to people in accordance with the address they give in their letters will sometimes fail to reach them and ultimately come back to the sender. People sometimes return goods for exchange and fail to put their name on the wrapper of the package and also forget to write any letter to accompany same. Once in awhile, a dollar bill or a quantity of stamps will come in an envelope without the scratch of a pen to show who sent them.
>
> Sometimes a son writes a note of endearment to his mother, enclosing a photograph, and sends it to a mail-order house, the letter being signed, "Your loving son, John"; while a formal order, such as, "Please send twelve white bow ties, for which find twenty-five two cent stamps" may go to the loving mother. The mail-order house does not think it quite fair to throw away the letter containing the photograph, neither is it advisable to tear up that inquiry without the name or address, nor should that returned package be cast aside without consideration. Therefore, a rendezvous for this kind of pieces is naturally created and generally resolves into a convenient box or drawer, where after awhile the envelope that contained the dollar bill matches a communication from the lady who forgot to enclose her letter; the box which came back enclosing the pair of opera glasses finds companionship with a complaint from the fellow who ordered them for a gift to his best girl, but who left for another town before they reached him, and John's letter with the photograph ultimately finds its owner, through the course of John's mother writing John and John straightening things out.[4]

SHIPPING ORDERS

It is crucial to ship orders immediately upon receipt of the order. Every day that the order is delayed in your shop, the more complaints, cancellations, and COD refusals you will have.

It is often a good practice to send out a postcard on the day the order is received, stating that the order follows by parcel post, Railway Express, etc. The postcard keeps customers from worrying about their money and merchandise.

If the order is unavoidably delayed, send off a card explaining the delay and telling the customer how soon you will be able to ship.

If your article is heavy, you may find it cheaper to ship by means other than parcel post. And if the article is very heavy, or bulky, you *must* find some other means of transportation because the post office won't accept the package!

If you plan to sell a great many of a standard item, shipped alone, you should make careful packing plans. Always make up a model package in advance. And when you make up your model package, watch the weight so that you don't go one-eighth of an ounce into the next pound. On a thousand or five thousand packages that slight difference can add up to a lot of money.

Good Relations with the Post Office

It pays to have an amicable relationship with the post office. You can best keep the goodwill that you need by saving trouble and avoiding extra work for post-office help. This includes:

1. Deliver mail to the post office rather than dumping it in street boxes.

2. Keep outgoing letters faced in the same direction.

3. Use precanceled stamps. (You can obtain a free permit to do this.)

One of the extra services the post office can render for you is to deliver your mail to you even if it is insufficiently addressed. When using a new address for the first time, try the post office out by sending yourself a few postcards using the new address and the possible variations on it.

MISCELLANEOUS OPERATIONS

Checking Advertisements. Either you or your agency must check that each ad you pay for *actually runs*. I have found the easiest checking method for a mail-order firm is to create a reply record sheet for each ad you pay for, indicating "Paid" and the amount on the sheet. Keep a separate file of pages containing your ads, in alphabetical order, as they come in. Start a new alphabetical file every once in a while. If replies come in to that key, you automatically know that the ad ran. If no replies arrive, you verify with your alphabetical file of advertising pages and demand your refund.

Applying Postage. Putting stamps on envelopes is tedious work. The easiest way is to rip the stamps into horizontal strips (rolls of stamps are hard to tear), stand a pile of envelopes upright against a box, wet five or ten stamps at a time, and turn each envelope down as you press a stamp on and rip it off with your thumb.

You can also buy or rent a small machine that applies stamps automatically. But by that time you're probably ready for a postage meter.

Postage meters are wonderful things. They speed stamping (and usually sealing, too), and they protect you from stamp theft. When you are ready for a meter, check prices and models with the local representative of *all* these firms:

Commercial Controls Corp., Division of Friden, Inc., Rochester, N.Y.
International Postal Supply Co., Division of Friden, Inc., Lewistown, Pa.
National Cash Register Co., Dayton, Ohio

Postal Division, Tele-Norn Corp., New York, N.Y.
Pitney-Bowes, Inc., Stamford, Conn.

Metered mail pulls replies just as well or better than stamped mail. No problems from that source.

Labeling. Labeling is greatly speeded by the use of the "label board," a device which moistens your label as you draw it off the board. One or more of these are an absolute must for *any* mail-order business, no matter how small. They cost under $10. Write to Paramount Duplicator Products, 401 Broadway, New York, New York.

Gummed-tape Machines. Gummed-tape machines are another necessity. Get one that takes tape up to 3 inches wide. You just pull a handle to get a length of tape. Secondhand shops very often have a serviceable machine for $15.

Envelope Sealer. An envelope sealer may be handy. But you will probably prefer a postage meter that has an envelope-sealing attachment.

21

General Management of a Mail-Order Business

Various Ways to Have Ads Written • How to
Choose An Advertising Agency • How to Set Up a
House Agency • Merchandising Your Products •
Credit: To Customers and From Suppliers • Don't
Spread Yourself Too Thin • Banks • Why It's
Easier to Get Rich in Mail Order

HOW AND WHEN TO OBTAIN AN ADVERTISING AGENCY AND/OR FREE-LANCE TALENT

When you go looking for an advertising agency, or an advertising consultant, or other people or organizations to help you in your mail-order business, don't expect to find a witch doctor or a miracle man. I can assure you that from New York to Los Angeles you won't find a single mail-order "expert" who will—for a small fee—take you in hand, give you a product, figure out a selling plan for you, make up the ads, and make money for you. The only men who will promise you that are fakers, whose help is about as desirable as the plague.

The truth is that every profitable mail-order scheme and campaign has to be hammered out from scratch. Every new scheme requires full attention and work. Nobody has a "machine" that will make mail-order profits.

It stands to reason, then, that the most talented and most experienced mail-order men will put their skill to work for the biggest of mail-order firms—the record and book clubs, the correspondence schools, or the vitamin companies, because those outfits can pay the most for the expert's knowledge.

Furthermore, those big outfits have no guarantee of being profitable either. Sometimes they make a pile, sometimes they lose their shirt. They have to work and scrounge just as you do in order to make money.

Various Ways to Have Ads Written

Creating advertisements is not a job for an amateur. You yourself may become qualified to create ads if you study and work hard at it. But without some practice, you are unlikely to do a good job. And only good ads make money!

If you will be spending upwards of $10,000 per year for advertising, or if you plan to run large ads, you can develop a relationship with a small advertising agency on a regular basis. They will be glad to have you and will provide full service to you.

Or if you have a product line or a plan that looks as if it has a good potential, you can probably persuade an agency to invest its time and effort in your early ads, even though the early ads won't be profitable to the agency.

The advantage of working through an agency is that their service is "free" to you. The standard system is for the agency to keep 15 percent of the charge made by magazines and other media. And unless you set up a "house agency," you will have to pay the full charges to the media whether or not you use an agency.

The disadvantage of using an agency is that unless your account is really large, you won't get enough attention, or you will receive a second-rate job of creating advertisements and selecting media. After all, an agency is going to devote to you only the amount of service that your billing deserves.

Another way to obtain advertisements is by hiring free-lance copywriters and layout artists. Free-lancers charge by the piece of work, and their fees are not chicken feed. I deal with a copywriter who also creates layouts. Her minimum fee is $125 and even a fairly small ad costs me $200. But she is very talented—i.e., she knows how to make mail-order ads that sell—and she is worth what I pay her.

The classified telephone book in any large city will list free-lancers under "Writers" and "Artists." Most of those persons and firms listed know nothing about mail order, however, despite what they may say. Other free-lancers advertise in *Direct Mail*, the *New York Times* Sunday Business Section, and *Advertising Age*.

Choosing a good free-lance is not easy, of course. Use the same standards as for choosing an advertising agency, which we shall describe below.

How to Choose an Advertising Agency

If you intend to depend upon an agency for the preparation of your advertising, then the choice of an agency will be crucial. A fine agency that knows its business and is honest will bring plenty of returns for your advertising dollars. A poor agency will certainly create nonproductive ads and may even lead you to over-advertise unprofitably so as to increase their commissions.

Keep these points in mind when choosing an agency:

1. Get an agency that specializes in mail-order work. There is a tremendous difference between mail-order and non-mail-order ads, and to use a non-mail-order agency is like using a heart surgeon to fill your teeth.

2. Get an agency that is small enough to take your business seriously. If the agency doesn't need the potential revenue you represent, you will never get first-class work from them.

The classic method of choosing a mail-order agency is to look for very good mail-order ads. Then find out who the agency was that did them. You can find the agency either by looking up the client in *Standard Advertising Register*, or by writing the advertiser direct.

The trouble with this method is that it depends upon your ability to spot good ads. I have severe doubts about *anyone's* ability to do this accurately, let alone a novice.

Appendix H contains a list of several mail-order agencies, large and small.

How to Set Up a House Agency

If you intend to use free-lance talent or create ads yourself, you might as well have the 15 percent commission instead of donating it to the media. Setting up a house agency can save the 15 percent that can represent a good chunk of your profit.

Up until 1954, the magazines and newspapers were very strict about "recognizing" an agency as qualified to collect the commission. But the Federal Trade Commission moved in on the associations of publishers and "persuaded" them to abandon their old practices. Nowadays, the publishers cannot act together to prevent you from earning the commission.

This means that all you have to do is convince most magazines that you are a good credit risk, and they will "recognize" you as an advertising agency.

In fact, if you represent any sizable amount of revenue, you can place it direct with many magazines and save the 15 percent commission, without even pretending to be an independent agency.

Order Blank for Publications
(Copyright October 1956)

Nobody Advertising Agency
180 Nowhere Avenue
Vanished, Nebraska

ANglehorn 4-000

☐ IF CHECKED HERE, THIS IS A SPACE CONTRACT　　　　　☐ IF CHECKED HERE, THIS IS AN INSERTION ORDER

TO PUBLISHER OF　　　　　　　　　　　　　　　　NO

CITY AND STATE　　　　　　　　　　　　　　　　DATE

PLEASE PUBLISH ADVERTISING OF (advertiser)

FOR (product)

─────SPACE─────　　─────TIMES─────　　─────DATES OF INSERTION─────

POSITION

COPY　　　　　　　　　　KEY　　　　　　　CUTS

ADDITIONAL INSTRUCTIONS

RATE

LESS AGENCY COMMISSION　　PER CENT ON GROSS　　LESS CASH DISCOUNT　　PER CENT ON NET

Nobody Advertising Agency _____
Vanished, Nebraska

Order Blank for Publications　　　Copyright October, 1956.　　American Association of Advertising Agencies, Inc.　　(OVER)

FIG. 21-1a

Setting up a house agency is not "shady." Some of the very biggest corporations in the country have done so, including drug companies who spend up to 60 percent of their total revenue on advertising.

Setting up a house agency is easy. About all you need is $10 worth of insertion orders, plus some stationery. Give your agency a name different from your mail-order firm's name, and then print up some forms like those on the following pages—except that you insert your own name in the two marked places, of course.

ORDER BLANK FOR PUBLICATIONS
(COPYRIGHT OCTOBER 1956)

Nobody Advertising Agency
180 Nowhere Avenue
Vanished, Nebraska

ANglehorn 4-000

☐ IF CHECKED HERE THIS
IS A SPACE CONTRACT

**DUPLICATE FOR PUBLISHER'S ACCEPTANCE
PLEASE SIGN AND RETURN TO AGENCY**

☐ IF CHECKED HERE, THIS
IS AN INSERTION ORDER

TO PUBLISHER OF   NO

CITY AND STATE   DATE

PLEASE PUBLISH ADVERTISING OF (advertiser)

FOR (product)

┌──────SPACE──────┐   ┌──────TIMES──────┐   ┌──────────DATES OF INSERTION──────────┐

POSITION

COPY   KEY   CUTS

ADDITIONAL INSTRUCTIONS

RATE

LESS AGENCY COMMISSION   PER CENT ON GROSS   │   LESS CASH DISCOUNT   PER CENT ON NET

Subject to conditions stated below and on back hereof:

Nobody Advertising Agency
Vanished, Nebraska

ACCEPTED FOR PUBLISHER_____BY_____

Order Blank for Publications   Copyright October, 1956.   American Association of Advertising Agencies, Inc.   *(OVER)*

FIG. 21-1b

When you send in your first orders, some of the magazines will accept your orders on credit, if the order is small, without doing any checking at all. No trouble there!

But some magazines and almost all newspapers will ask you for references of other magazines with whom you have placed advertisements. They may also ask you for a full financial statement.

One way to handle this—and a rather good way—is to offer to pay cash, less the commission, of course. After you have paid cash for a while, you will find it easy to get credit. And in the meantime, you can tell *other* magazines that you have placed ads with the magazines who accept your first insertions.

Another way to handle the credit problem is to deposit a good-sized sum in an agency bank account, admit that your agency is brand-new,

CONDITIONS

The advertising agency placing advertising covered by this contract (hereinafter called "Agency") and the publisher accepting this contract (hereinafter called "Publisher") hereby agree that this contract shall be governed by the following conditions:

1. TERMS OF PAYMENT

[a]. Agency agrees to pay for all advertising published by Publisher in accordance with this contract. Agency shall make such payment at the office of Publisher or Publisher's authorized representative on or before the last day of the month following that in which the advertising is published, unless otherwise stipulated on Publisher's rate card. When cash discount is deducted, such payment shall be made on or before the cash discount date specified on said rate card, or if the cash discount date is not specified thereon, on or before the 15th of the month following.

Publisher agrees to hold Agency solely liable for payment, and to render bills to Agency not less often than monthly. Failure to bill at least monthly shall not constitute breach of contract.

[b]. If Publisher at request of Agency furnishes drawings, compositions, cuts or mats, Agency agrees to pay for same, in accordance with Publisher's rate card and in the manner specified in paragraph [a] above.

[c]. Agency agrees to prepay transportation and import charges on all cuts and mats sent to Publisher. If such charges are not prepaid, Publisher may either reject the cuts and mats, or accept them and pay the charges. In the latter case Agency shall promptly reimburse Publisher.

[d]. If, at the end of the advertising period named in this contract or upon prior termination of this contract for any cause, Agency has not used the full amount of advertising contracted for, Agency agrees to pay to Publisher an additional sum on all advertising published, such sum to equal the difference, if any, between the amount due at the rate named in this contract and the amount due at the rate applicable to the quantity of space used as stated in Publisher's rate card. Such additional sum shall not be due unless Publisher renders a bill therefor within 60 days after such expiration or termination. Upon rendition of such a bill, such additional sum shall become immediately due and payable.

Subject to the payment of such additional sum for advertising published, Agency may cancel this contract at any time or may use less space than the amount contracted for.

[e]. Unless Agency makes written objection within 60 days from the rendering of any bill for advertising published under this contract, such bill shall be conclusive as to the correctness of the items therein set forth and shall constitute an account stated.

[f]. Publisher reserves the right to cancel this contract at any time upon default by Agency in the payment of bills or in the event of any other substantial breach of this contract by Agency. Upon such cancellation charges for all advertising published and all other charges payable under this contract, including the short rates defined in paragraph [d], shall become immediately due and payable by Agency upon rendition of bills therefor.

If Agency defaults in the payment of bills, or if in the judgment of Publisher its credit becomes impaired, Publisher shall have the right to require payment for further advertising under this contract upon such terms as he may see fit.

[g]. The post mark date on the envelope properly addressed to Publisher or to Publisher's representative shall be considered the date when payment is made.

2. RATES

[a]. Publisher represents that all of his rates are published. Publisher shall furnish his rates to Agency if requested.

[b]. "Publisher's rate card" shall be understood to mean the schedule of advertising rates of Publisher upon which this contract is based.

[c]. Publisher represents that the rate stated in the contract is the minimum rate at which an equal or less amount of space, for the same class of advertising, to be published in a like position, under the same conditions, within the same period of time, can be secured at the time this contract is entered into.

[d]. If additional space is used within the period covered by the contract, where Publisher has a schedule of graduated rates, any lower rate shall be given if earned, according to Publisher's rate card on which this contract is based.

3. ADVERTISING MATERIAL

[a]. The subject matter, form, size, wording, illustration and typography of the advertising shall be subject to the approval of Publisher but unless otherwise authorized in advance no change shall be made without the consent of Agency.

[b]. If Publisher is unable to set any advertisement in the type or style requested, he may set such advertisement in such other type or style as in his opinion most nearly corresponds thereto, and the advertisement may be inserted without submission of proof unless proof before insertion is requested on the face of the order.

[c]. Where cuts, electrotypes, or material furnished by Agency occupy more space than specified in the contract or insertion order, Publisher should immediately communicate with Agency for definite instructions. If Publisher is unable to secure definite instructions from Agency, the advertising shall be omitted.

[d]. If Agency has contracted for a series of insertions in a publication, and before closing date insertion order and copy for next issue have not been received by Publisher, Publisher shall notify Agency and follow Agency's instructions.

[e]. Advertisements ordered set in "space as required" shall be measured from office ad. rule.

4. PROOF OF INSERTION

[a]. The page containing the advertising or, at the request of Agency, a copy of each issue in which the advertising appears, shall be mailed or otherwise supplied to Agency, which shall be deemed to have received such copy or page unless Publisher is notified in writing of the nonreceipt thereof within thirty days after the date of publication. Publisher may mail or otherwise supply any affidavit of publication in lieu of a second copy or page containing the advertisement. Failure to forward or furnish such copy, page or affidavit shall not constitute a breach of the contract.

5. CIRCULATION

[a]. Unless Publisher is a member of the Audit Bureau of Circulations, Agency shall be entitled, upon request, to a statement of net paid circulation verified by a certified public accountant, or in lieu thereof to the right to examine Publisher's circulation books, except that in the case of a business publication which is not a member of the Audit Bureau of Circulations or Business Publications Audit, Agency shall be entitled, upon request, to a statement of circulation verified by a certified public accountant, or in lieu thereof to the right to examine Publisher's circulation books.

6. OMISSION OF ADVERTISING

[a]. Failure to insert in any particular issue or issues invalidates the order for insertion in the missed issue but shall not constitute a breach of contract.

In newspapers the advertising must appear in all regular editions issued on the date for which the advertising is ordered. Advertisements omitted from any particular edition or editions must be reported to Agency and if received in time and omitted through fault of Publisher must be made up or adjusted unless otherwise instructed.

Unless otherwise stipulated, Publisher shall have the right to omit any advertisement when the space allotted to advertising in the issue for which such advertisement is ordered has all been taken, and also to limit the amount of space an advertiser may use in any one issue.

7. GENERAL

[a]. In dealing with agencies, Publisher shall follow a uniform policy to avoid discrimination.

[b]. Unless later date is specified in Publisher's rate card, advertising in newspapers shall begin within thirty days from the date of this contract, or contract becomes null and void.

[c]. A waiver by either party hereto of any default or breach by the other party shall not be considered as a waiver of any subsequent default or breach of the same or any other provisions hereof.

COPYRIGHT NOTICE

Any advertising agency is authorized to use this copyrighted form on colored paper. Such authorization is a privilege, however, which may be withdrawn in any individual case if it should be reported that the form is being used to deceive or mislead media, or to help perpetrate a fraud on the public, or for other illegal purpose, or to the detriment of advertising. ¶Any medium also is authorized to use this copyrighted form in dealing with advertising agencies. ¶Any changes in the copyrighted Conditions must be clearly and conspicuously noted on the face of the form.
Copyright October 1966, American Association of Advertising Agencies, Inc.

FIG. 21-1c

and fill out the credit forms. Many media will give you credit on that basis.

Credit is so very important in placing ads because of the long time lag between closing dates and publication dates. Without credit you must pay months in advance, and that ties up a lot of your working capital.

It should be unnecessary to add that a touch of bluffing may aid you immeasurably in obtaining credit. If you can make any medium think you credit is good everywhere else, you have the problem licked.

If your advertising budget is too small to justify the exertion of setting up a house agency, you can often get an established agency to "clear" your account for you. They keep perhaps five percent for the trouble of billing you and other clerical work, and you keep the other 10 percent.

MERCHANDISING YOUR PRODUCTS

If you develop a good mail-order product that is not patented or copyrighted, you will have only a limited time to reap the profits before competition swarms in. If you merchandise the product to other firms, you can profit by the swarm of competition instead of being hurt by it. That way you will make a small profit on the large number of pieces your competitors will sell. And on their side, the competitors will prefer to deal with you because you already have developed the item, and can make it available to them immediately, without the development costs they would otherwise incur.

These are various ways to merchandise the product:

1. If the product is a small novelty selling under $5, try the large novelty catalog firms. If you can show them good mail-order results, they will be glad to put it into their catalogs for a trial. Begin your campaign of merchandising to catalog mail-order dealers by going through an entire issue of *House Beautiful* and *House & Garden,* and writing for catalogs from every advertiser in the shopping section. Those advertisers will be your prospects.

You must expect to sell the product at about 30 percent of the retail price on a $1 or $2 item, slightly more for more expensive items.

Don't rush to the catalog houses just as soon as you hit a winner. Wait until you have wiped up most of the gravy, and until competition has had almost time enough to come in.

2. Contact the firms that sell mail-order catalogs to other firms. Some stock the merchandise, including Giftime, 919 Walnut Street, Philadelphia 7, Pennsylvania. Others will want you to operate on a dropship basis, including Gaylords, North Summer Street, Adams, Massachusetts.

3. Other large mail-order firms will take your product and sell it through display advertising. Several firms, such as Thoresen and Scott-Mitchell, get a low rate on newspaper and other space because they buy a lot of space. That cost advantage, plus their know-how, can make it profitable for them to move a lot more merchandise than you are able to do.

4. Atlantic Advertising, at the same address as Gaylords in 2 above, has a service they call "Bullets" which merchandises products to mail-order dealers. For a fee, a write-up of your product goes out to several thousand interested firms. Write to Atlantic for more information. I have no evidence on how effective "Bullets" is.

5. Chains of cigar stores such as Whelan's often sell the mail-order type of merchandise. Try to sell to them.

CREDIT: TO CUSTOMERS AND FROM SUPPLIERS

Let's start with *your* credit. As we said earlier, when we talked about setting up your own agency, credit with advertising media is probably more important then any other line of credit. If you use an advertising agency, credit with them is equally important.

Other suppliers will grant credit if you *sound* reliable and if you can furnish a few solid-sounding references, including a bank. The more business you give a single firm, the better the credit reference he will give for you to other people. This is an argument for using a few reliable suppliers rather than distributing your business widely among many firms.

If you can't get credit, you will have to develop it by paying cash at first.

If your character is good, and if you have a persuasive story to tell, you have a fighting chance to obtain credit anywhere!

Selling on credit is always a difficult problem. If you sell to consumers, and if the price of your product is over $10 or $20, you must expect to sell on the installment plan; otherwise you will lose too many sales. Naturally, selling on credit requires working capital and extra bookkeeping, and you will inevitably have some credit losses. But these difficulties are a necessary part of doing business. Don't eat your heart out about unavoidable credit losses.

Mail-order firms doing business with consumers rarely check credit. The merchandise is often a fairly small cost relative to the selling price, and this makes it sensible to take a chance on anyone. Furthermore, the cost of checking credit is exorbitant.

If you sell to industrial or commercial accounts, you will follow normal credit-checking practices, however.

A good series of collection letters, sent out on a correctly timed schedule, is a mail-order man's best friend. Model your letters after those of other mail-order firms.

DON'T SPREAD YOURSELF TOO THIN

You *cannot* successfully manage *a great many* mail-order products, or several product lines. Everything that makes money for you requires attention, a lot more attention than you think. You must concentrate on the most profitable aspects of your business, and push them hard. That's the only way to operate successfully.

You must keep a watchful eye on each ad's performance, and that takes energy and time. This is the only reason that big companies don't use the classified ads that they know will be a very profitable investment per dollar invested. They don't want to spend the necessary time and energy in management control. This is also why good ads don't spread everywhere immediately.

And you can't spread your ads too thin, either. Though it is true that you can put many different items into a *catalog*, Stone says this about direct mail: "Paradoxically, few mailers are successful at advertising more than one product at a time. The simple fact seems to be that it is difficult to sell more than one idea at a time."[1]

He tested offering collection stickers versus collection stickers plus collection envelopes. The former alone pulled 1.19 percent, and $74 per thousand. The latter pulled 1.24 percent, but the primary offer dropped to 0.85 percent, and the overall revenue was $73.78—at a higher cost per thousand in mailing costs. Interestingly enough, however, the reorder factor made the combination offer worth continuing.

BANKS

Mail-order businesses are not particularly desirable customers for a bank because of the large volume of small checks. Maintaining a large and constant balance in your account will go a long way to sweetening their humor, however.

Even in a single town, banks do not have the same rates for the important matter of the charge on check deposits. In one town in which I do business, charges range from 5 cents per check to 3 cents per check after the first 100.

A tip! Save a nickel per money order by cashing them at the post office rather than at the bank.

Get checks that look businesslike. Use the form that has an invoice box at the left. And *never* mingle business funds with your personal account.

WHY IT'S EASIER TO GET RICH IN MAIL ORDER

It's not just the money you *make;* it's the money you *keep.* And there is a unique characteristic of the mail-order business that permits you to keep more—for quite a while—than in most other businesses.

The tax law says you must pay taxes on earnings that you *invest,* but not on expenses. Therefore, every businessman seeks to justify making an outlay into an expense rather than an investment.

The advertising you do to obtain repeat-business customers is customarily treated as an expense of doing business. But a considerable portion of that outlay is an investment that will pay off in future years! And you pay much lower taxes in the current period than if the outlay were treated as an investment. This is a terrific help in accumulating capital.

Magazines invest in a list of subscribers in this fashion, also, though I believe the advertising cost is always treated as an expense.

Sooner or later, you must pay taxes on your extra profits. But the further into the future the tax occurs, the better for you.

22

How to Buy or Sell
a Mail-Order Business

*How to Find Mail-Order Businesses That Are for
Sale • How to Put a Price on a Business • How to
Sell a Business*

Three major topics make up this chapter. In the order in which we shall
discuss them, these topics are (1) how to find mail-order businesses
that are for sale; (2) how to put a price on a mail-order business,
whether buying or selling it; and (3) how to find customers for a business that you wish to sell.

HOW TO FIND MAIL-ORDER BUSINESSES THAT ARE FOR SALE

Finding a mail-order business for sale is much like finding any other
kind of business that is for sale. One difference is that there are fewer
mail-order businesses than there are drugstores, say, and the fewer
there are of anything, the harder it is to find them. Another difference
is that mail-order businesses are really many different kinds of businesses, and you cannot reach them through the channels of any one particular trade, as you can reach all office supplies firms through their
trade magazine, for example.

The first step in seeking out a mail-order business is by reading the
"Business Opportunities" section of the newspaper classified columns.
The business opportunities section of the Sunday *New York Times* is
one of the best places to look for a mail-order business, no matter
where in the United States you live.

A second step is to contact business brokers. You can try those in your area, or you can write to business brokers in New York. However, any given business broker is not very likely to have a listing for a mail-order business at any given time. (When you talk or write to business brokers, try to make them understand what you mean when you say "mail-order business." Very often they will have listings of businesses that do most of their business by mail, and really are mail-order businesses, but the business broker may have them classified under "Office supplies" or "Stamps" or "Printing" or what have you.)

A third method is to advertise in the business opportunities section of the Sunday paper, especially the *New York Times*. A three-line $12 ad that I ran once brought me over fifty replies from people who wanted to sell businesses. Most of them were not real possibilities, but there were at least six good prospects in the lot. If I were again in the market for a business, I would immediately make this small investment, once a month or so, until I had found a business.

You might also advertise in the classified columns of *Direct Mail*. Many mail-order firms read that magazine.

A fourth method of finding a mail-order business is to write to many mail-order businesses, asking if they wish to sell. You can develop a list of prospects by watching mail-order ads and direct mail. Write to those firms that are in the line of business that interests you, and that seem to be of a size that you wish to purchase. (But don't pay *too* much attention to size. It is very hard to guess the size of a mail-order business by its advertising. Once I was interested in a firm that sells printing by mail. I estimated its yearly gross at $100,000, but a Dun & Bradstreet report indicated yearly sales of $750,000. More often, however, firms are *smaller* than you would guess.)

Use business stationery when you write to firms, and write a letter that indicates that you mean business and that you are a good prospect to sell to. Give them plenty of details about you that will impress them with your reliability and financial capability. I won't give you a sample letter here. You should be able to write your own letter for a task like this.

HOW TO PUT A PRICE ON A BUSINESS

The basic determinant of the value of a business is the amount that the business earns and/or the amount that it can earn under your management.

But the relationship of price to earnings varies with the size of a firm and with the type of business that it does. Very large firms (multimillions of dollars of sales per year) may be worth upwards of seven times earnings, perhaps as high as twenty times earnings. But if you are in the market for a firm of that size, you will go elsewhere for additional advice, I trust.

A mail-order business that grosses perhaps $300,000 a year might be worth five times its yearly earnings. Note that "earnings" does not include the salary of the owner or owners. But how much to count as salary is a very difficult question that we shall not consider here.

A mail-order business that provides perhaps $12,000 to its owner yearly (in salary plus earnings, taken all together) might be worth a price approximately equal to that sum. However, you might pay half a year's earnings or twice a year's earnings, depending upon other desirable or undesirable characteristics of the firm, including its future potential, the pleasantness of the business, and the market at that time for mail-order businesses. The final price will reflect a lot of bargaining, and how badly you want to buy and how badly he wants to sell.

So far, so good. But there is a catch! It is very difficult to determine just how much a business earns, or how much it provides to its owner. Tax returns are always adjusted to show the minimum possible net to the owner, so that he will have to pay the minimum of taxes. And sometimes items that he includes as expenses have value to him just as the earnings have value to him—a company car, for example.

Watch out for the fellow who shows you the records of a business that pays no taxes, or small taxes, and who tells you that the business is really earning a lot of money. First of all, if he is cheating the Internal Revenue Service, he may cheat you, too. Second, many of the expenses that he lists as expenses really must be expenses, even if he tells you that they are not necessary. Third, if he has rigged the books so that they will pass the scrutiny of government investigators, how can *you* ever tell just how much the business is earning?

Watch out also for illegal businesses that are for sale. Unfortunately, there are many mail-order businesses that the government will close up sooner or later because they violate the law. Not only do you prefer to avoid being mixed up in such a business, but you should not take the chance of wasting your money in buying a business that won't be a business for very long.

The tax returns of a business are the best set of books for you to examine, because if they are wrong, the owner is liable to the United States government. Never believe any other records until you have seen the tax returns.

In any case, this is an absolute rule: Always get your own accountant to examine the records of a firm that you are considering buying.

Beyond the Tax Returns

Often the tax returns do not supply all the information you need, however. There are several possible reasons for needing to study other records, including the following:

An owner may wish to sell only part of a business. The tax returns may apply only to the entire business. You must then figure out how much of the entire firm's earnings come from the part of the business he wishes to sell.

You may have reason to believe that the business is being badly run, and that it would throw off much greater net profit under your management. (But don't be taken in by owners who tell you what a great future the business has, even though it is doing poorly at the moment. They invent a million reasons for this, including absentee ownership, disinterest in the business, arguments between partners, etc. The truth of the matter is that if the owner is having a hard time getting money out of the business, it is an excellent indication that it will not be easy for you to make a big profit, either.)

The business may be changing rapidly, or it may have been in existence too short a time for the tax returns to provide a clear indication.

You may not be satisfied that the tax records provide a satisfactory picture of the firm's operations and earnings.

Now I shall give you the outline of a method to estimate the future earnings of a business. These are the steps in the method:

1. Estimate the average volume of sales made to the average customer before he ceases purchasing, including all the sales made to him in future years. Then estimate the *gross* profit on that average volume of sales per customer, by subtracting the cost of the goods and direct expenses of labor, etc., to you. This is the method described in Chapter 15, page 135, for finding the average value of putting a customer onto your books.

2. Determine the cost of creating the average new customer. You calculate this value by dividing the total cost of the advertising (or that part that creates new customers) in the past year by the number of new customers created in the past year. Subtract this value from the value of putting a customer onto your books, as found in 1 above.

3. Multiply by the number of new customers added in the past year. This value will be the expected profit per year, when the firm's business levels off, before substracting for overhead.

4. Subtract whatever you think appropriate for rent, telephone, insurance, and other overhead expenses. What is left is your expected salary plus profit.

5. If you believe that you can increase the size of the business by increasing the advertising, you might be right to include that potential in your figuring. But be sure not to forget that it will get more expensive to create new customers as you expand your advertising.

Despite the fact that you must pay for intangible organization and knowledge when you buy a business, it is often cheaper to purchase than to start fresh. It is surprisingly expensive to begin a business when you consider the amount of time that it takes you to get into action, and there are many hidden expenses that you can't figure in advance. Very often the owner sells you the intangibles for less than they cost him. And when you buy a going business, you avoid the very costly risk that the business you start from scratch may not succeed!

The advice of a person experienced in the mail-order business can be invaluable to you when you are considering buying a business. It is the same as when you ask a skilled mechanic to look over a car that you think you might buy, in order to check for hidden defects and to tell you if the price is fair.

Call a mail-order man in your area and offer to pay him a consultation fee for his time. If you pick a knowledgeable and successful fellow, he will be worth far more than anything that you pay him. He can give you advice and knowledge that no accountant, lawyer, or general businessman can give you.

Of course you should *also* consult an accountant and a lawyer before you buy a business! That should go without saying.

I recommend that you read Chapter 6, "Appraising a Going Concern," in *How to Organize and Operate a Small Business,* by Pearce C. Kelley and Kenneth Lawyer.[1] The authors give you many helpful warnings and pointers. And while you're at it, look through the rest of the book, too. It contains lots of useful information for the person who intends to go into business for himself.

Check on the *real* reason the present owner wants to sell. Don't accept at face value his statement that he has had a heart attack, or is about to retire because he has made his fortune. The *real* reason may be that he has lost his lease, or competition has just entered the field, or he is engaged in something shady. *Find out the truth.*

And before purchasing always obtain a sworn statement from the owner that he will not enter a competitive line of business for two or three years. Remind your lawyer of this before you sign any final papers.

HOW TO SELL A BUSINESS

To find a customer for your business, just reverse the steps you should take to find a business that is for sale.

The biggest problem you face in selling a business, apart from convincing your prospective customers to buy, is the danger of giving out enough information about your business so that the prospective customer could use the information to start his own business. Your customer list is the most secret, of course. But your advertising methods are also an important secret of your business.

William J. Papp[2] tells the story of an enterprising pharmacist who developed a neat little mail-order business peddling an educational device, and then decided to sell out. In an effort to convince purchasers of the soundness of his business, he gave them so much information that very soon several competitors began to advertise exactly the same offer in his best-pulling magazines.

Papp suggests these ways to avoid the worst dangers:

1. Do business through a third person—lawyer, broker, or banker. He can conceal the name of your firm, and can endose its soundness.

2. Indicate whether you are willing to continue as a consultant to the owner.

3. Describe the potential of your firm.

4. After you supply preliminary information, ask that the potential advertiser deposit a substantial sum of money in escrow with a bank of his choice. If he enters competition with you, his money is forfeited. If he does not buy, and refrains from competing, he gets the deposit back after a period of time. Or if your figures and claims prove incorrect, he gets the deposit back.

In Appendix C is a letter that I worked out for a business that a client of mine wished to sell rather abruptly because of another opportunity that was offered. The short period of operation made the selling problem more difficult, but the rapid growth of the business was an aid in selling. The letter might serve as a model when you consider selling.

This is the end of what I have to say. I wish you success and happiness in your mail-order adventures, and I hope that I have been of some help to you. Good luck!

APPENDIX A

How to Lose Money with Mail-Order Franchises and "Deals"

I'm sure you have seen those fascinating ads for "mail-order franchises," for "catalog mailing," and for "cooperative" deals of all kinds. Those ads make powerful promises indeed. What about them?

Catalog-Mailing Deals

Arrangements to mail other firms' *catalogs* probably have no chance at all to make money for you, unless you already have a customer list and are in the mail-order business. This goes for the best as well as the worst of them. *No* firm has yet presented any *facts* to show that the average individual comes anywhere near breaking even, or that *any* of their "dealers" make a significant profit—unless the dealer started out with a list of customers from prior mail-order or retail operations.

The basic reason for the failure of catalog-mailing plans is this: if there really was money to be made in mailing the catalogs to "cold" lists, the supplier would do the mailing himself. You might have some advantage in mailing to your friends (like an insurance man who contacts all his relatives first). But the number of such friends and acquaintances that you can mail to is very limited. After that, you are just pouring money into the supplier's pocket.

Or at the very best, it may be possible to make money in the long run by mailing to *some* rented lists. But you can be sure that the supplier will mail to the best lists under his own name, and only the "dogs" will be left for you.

Don't get the idea that the "catalog-mailing" scheme is new. It isn't. It has been kicking around almost since the mail-order business began.

This is what the author of a 1906 "Encyclopedia of the Mail-order Business"[1] wrote more than 50 years ago:

THE EVILS OF THE STOCK CATALOG

Lest the term "Stock Catalog" be misunderstood, let us explain that this phrase is used when speaking of a catalog that is issued in immense quantities by certain supply houses who carry or pretend to carry all the goods in stock that is listed in this catalog. These catalogs are offered to beginners with their own name and address printed on them, so that the recipient of the catalog would be led to believe that the beginner was really the publisher of this catalog. The argument of the promoter is that the beginner could not publish a catalog of this description unless he spend a great deal more money for this individual printing. Again they argue that the beginner need not carry goods in stock, but can forward the orders to the supply house, who in turn, would fill the order and ship the goods direct to the customer, in the beginner's own firm name. This all sounds very nice, but in all these years during which time countless thousands have been "started" in this way, the writer cannot find more than three or four who actually built up a little business by the use of this catalog, and these injected some originality of their own, to come out ahead of the game. Another inducement some of these promoters offer, is the furnishing of "a list of names" to whom to mail the catalog, or to place some "advertising" for them in "pulling" mediums. But all these schemes are failures. The writer has personally interviewed mail-order customers, he has travelled through the rural districts, stopped over in farm houses, and saw with his own eyes, no less than seven identical "stock catalogs" in one house. The difference was the imprint on the different catalogs. As these promoters advertise everywhere for victims, the people in the rural district know all about the stock catalog, and do no more than bestow pitying glances on this literature—and either throw it into the fire, or give it to the baby to play with, as was the case in the farm house where I was stopping.

In debating with yourself the arguments for and against the use of the common and moss-backed stock catalog, just for a minute consider what sort of a reception it is likely to meet with at the hands of the people to whom it is mailed; particularly when as is often the case, the catalogs are sent to the list of names and addresses of "buyers" furnished by the same firm who sell you the catalogs. The result is that at some remote farmhouse day after day there will be copies of the same cheaply gotten up catalog coming by mail, the imprints of the senders being something like this: One day, The Royal Novelty Co., Squedunk Corners, Me., next day, Imperial Crescent Supply Co., Box 9, Frogs' Hole, Wis., the day following, The Associated Mail Order Manufacturers and Merchants, of Lock Box 12, Hoboes Landing, Perry Township, Fayette County, Mo., and so on and so forth in ridiculous repetition.

To sum up, your aim should be to get out of the beaten track and strike out a path to success for yourself. And of all beaten tracks the stock catalog is the one that stinks loudest in the nostrils of honest men and real Mail Order dealers. It is a track strewn with the bones and rotten carcasses of business hopes and mail order ideals that have been killed and strangled by the nefarious stock catalog and it is heavy with the smoke of money that has been burned in the vain hope of achieving success under the direction of the fakirs who operate under the guise of promoters who will point out the way to success to you. Keep away from that veritable Death Valley and don't let your hopes and your money be destroyed together in the burnt offerings of the misguided fools who in spite of countless warnings continue to keep the misplaced confidence game alive.

The stock catalog *can* be useful and profitable to you if you already have a list of people who buy other goods from you by mail. Gimbel's is said to purchase and mail millions of a stock catalog each year, evidently at a solid profit. The reason why stock catalogs can work if you have an existing list is this: between two and ten times as many people will buy from you if they have done business with you before, as will buy if they have never heard of you. This is the difference between success and abysmal failure. So, if you are already in the mail-order business and if you have a mailing list of satisfied customers, you might well make money by sending them a stock catalog imprinted with your name.

Here are the names of three organizations that supply catalogs and who either drop-ship for you or give you the names of individual drop-ship suppliers. So far as I can tell, these three outfits extort no "franchise" fees and do not try hard to rook unwitting beginners:

Giftime Inc., 919 Walnut Street, Philadelphia 7, Pennsylvania
Gaylords, Adams, Massachusetts
Mail Order Methods, 3902 Flag Drive, Lafayette Hill, Pennsylvania

There are many other reputable firms that supply catalogs that you can use to sell *in person*, but that will not work at all by mail.

I have also noticed advertisements of Franklin M. Katz, Inc., 200 Lexington Avenue, New York 16, New York, offering imprinted mailers for drop-ship merchandise. I would guess that it is a reputable connection for firms that have lists of their own to solicit.

It is very, *very* unlikely that you can mail imprinted catalogs to any "cold" list of people who have never done business with you, and make money at it. Many "suckers" have reported substantial losses, and *Direct Mail*—a leading trade magazine—has run article after article on the dangers of this practice.

Mail-Order "Setup" Plans

A sure-profit business is a very valuable commodity. A business that will earn $10,000 a year for your full-time effort is probably worth $15,000. So why should anyone sell you the "setup" for $5 or even $500?

Furthermore, it is certain that no one can crank out "setups" on a mass-production basis, as must be the case if those who advertise them for a small sum are to make money.

Geniuses like to be rich and famous, too. I can guarantee you that there is no genius with an almost magical inside knowledge of mail order, in Salt Lake City, or Fandango, Maine, or anywhere else, who will "put you into" a profitable mail-order business for a small price. If there ever was such a genius, he is now selling his schemes to large companies for perhaps $25,000 per proposition.

"Cooperative Setup" Deals

Recently, what seems to be a really new scheme has hit the market. In this plan you put up the capital for an already developed ad, then purchase the products from the firm that developed the ad.

In other words, you "rent" the ad from the firm, and run it in a magazine at your expense. Any profit over and above your "rent" would belong to you.

In theory this plan sounds okay. If the ad pulls enough returns, you *could* make money. But the nature of the one-shot mail-order business forces your chances to be small because your "rent" is too high.

The firm that offers the deal takes the first part of its rent in its advertising-agency commission. They argue that you would pay this commission even on your own advertising, but that is not necessarily true. When the firm runs the ad for its own account, it pays no commission, and that commission is an important part of its revenue.

The second part of the rent is the amount, much greater than cost, which you pay them for the merchandise.

But there is an even greater danger. It stands to reason that the firm will run the ad for its own account whenever it is relatively sure the ad will pull enough to be profitable. (And if it would be profitable for you, it will be even more profitable for them!) But they can rent you the ad to run in magazines that will *not* be profitable for them, and that way they take their profit out of your hide.

I come down hard on this plan not only because it is theoretically so bad, but also because the firm in question has shown no proof that there are people who have profited by their deal. If they had such proof, they would certainly show it. (And I would not believe any proof except *consistent and repeated* successes. They could manufacture "proof" by letting a couple of their customers make money on choice media.)

Then there a couple of promoters who offer ready-made mail-order "plans." They promise to furnish you with a product (almost always a booklet) and advertising copy for display and/or direct-mail advertising.

If the "plan" really could make money for you, it could make much more for the promoter. He could make more with it than any inexperienced person, and he would save his own fees. Furthermore, he usually sells you the product itself at a steep price, and this makes it even less likely that you can make any money with the scheme. This should persuade you that you will only lose more hard-earned money in that kind of deal.

A Summing Up

It all adds up to this. There is no pie-in-the-sky scheme that will get you started profitably in mail order. You will just have to study and learn the business, follow the methods and instructions I give you in my book—which should give you a better chance in mail order than anyone ever had before—and take your chances like the rest of us. If you win, you will have a glorious and valuable prize. If you lose, most of what you lose will be your time, because mail-order money investments are characteristically small. And you'll have a great experience in any case. Good luck again!

Basic Postage and Mailing Facts

by Lawrence Miller

First-class mail is 5 cents per ounce. *Airmail* is 8 cents per ounce. Anything within certain size limits on packages may be sent first class or airmail. If undeliverable, first-class mail is returned to you at no extra cost. If it's forwarded, there is no extra charge.

Third-class mail includes circulars, catalogs, and printed material (not actual correspondence); typed and handwritten reproductions (no less than twenty per mailing); proof sheets with or without manuscripts or handwritten corrections; drawings, photographs, and raised matter for the blind; merchandise, including farm and factory products (no second-class newspapers or periodicals); and bills and statements of account (no less than twenty identical copies at one mailing). The limit per mailing piece is 16 ounces.

At the *regular* third-class rate you pay 4 cents per piece for the first 2 ounces, and two cents for each additional ounce or fraction, up to the 16-ounce limit. For one-time mailings of separately addressed identical pieces of 200 or more, totaling no less than 50 pounds, the *bulk* third-class rate is best. At present, in bulk mailings, pieces go for 2⅝ cents for each piece under two ounces. Catalogs go for 2⅝ cents each or 12 cents per pound. This rate is scheduled to rise to 3 cents in the next few years.

The required minimum size of third-class envelopes, cards, and self-mailers is 3½ inches (width) by 4¼ inches (height). This ratio (1:1.4) applies to all larger sizes, also, and envelope shapes must be *rectangular*.

If sealed, third-class mail must have "Third-class Mail" printed somewhere on the envelope. This mark can be on the front or back of the envelope, but it must be legible. If you don't seal your third-class mail (not good mail-order practice), the third-class identification is not necessary. You can buy a government-approved "spot of gum" envelope ("penny saver") that looks sealed but really isn't. It's available from most printers and falls into the unsealed category.

You must apply for a permit in order to enjoy third-class bulk-mailing privileges. For $30, you obtain (Form 3621) a calendar-year permit which expires December 31. Or, you can apply for a permit to mail without postage stamps (Form 3601) for $15. This is canceled if not used within twelve months. You can also pay permit postage with each mailing at the post office. And, you can deposit a stated amount of money at the post office at least twenty-four hours before each mailing, to cover costs. Postage is then deducted from this fund, and you receive a receipt of mailing.

Your postmaster is your best source of information. He can fill you in on the special bundling and labeling procedures for your bulk mailings as well as other important details. A Postal Manual is invaluable, too.

The third-class *return* privilege is a basic way for you to keep your mailing list clean and up to date. Print the words "Return Requested" under your return address, and undeliverable mail will be returned to you with the reasons for nondelivery. Each return costs you the full third-class rate or 8 cents, whichever is higher.

For pieces that weigh *more* than 16 ounces each, the post office has fourth-class mail, commonly known as parcel post. If your material is not limited by first-, second-, or third-class regulations, and weighs 16 ounces or more per piece (in some cases up to 70 pounds), it qualifies as *regular* fourth-class mail. Prices vary accordingly to parcel weight, size, and zone of destination.

Special rates are available for printed catalogs and printed advertising material: 24 pages minimum, 22 or more printed pages, more than 16 ounces and less than 10 pounds, and marked "Catalog."

Merchandise sent at regular or special fourth-class rates must meet certain length and girth requirements. Certain zones require a minimum combined length and girth of 72 inches (20 pounds), others a maximum of 100 inches (70 pounds). Measure the long side of your package for length and the distance around the thickest part for girth. Add both and that's your combined measurement.

As in third class, the post office can open your fourth-class package even if it's sealed. Always be sure to enclose an invoice or bill and stamp "Invoice Enclosed" on the outside of the package.

If your have delicate or live merchandise, you can pay a small fee for "special handling." Additional fourth-class services such as special delivery, insurance (government or private), and return receipts are available at extra cost.

Books that consist of reading matter with *no* advertising qualify for a special rate: 10 cents for the first pound, 5 cents for each succeeding pound. There are no zone restrictions, and parcels can contain 16-mm films and catalogs, printed music, sound recordings, manuscripts for books, periodicals and articles, and printed educational reference charts (processed for preservation). Parcels must be stamped "Educational Materials."

When you send goods by domestic third- and fourth-class mail, or at book rate, the postman can collect the price of the article, carrying charges, and postage from the addressee. This is the familiar cash-on-delivery (COD) service. Goods are automatically insured up to a total of $200. The COD fee runs upward from 40 cents.

If necessary, you can send expensive goods such as jewelry via registered *first*-class mail, COD, at maximum protection. Although $200 is the maximum collectible by the postman, you can insure the parcel up to $10,000 indemnity.

Whenever you average more than three COD mailings at any one time, pick up a free COD account book from the post office. You will be assigned a series of numbers to mark on your parcels. Place a few extra sheets of paper and carbon behind the book's duplicate pages, and you can type an address label, COD tag label, copy for your records, and a copy for the post office simultaneously. Your copy record is postmarked when you mail the goods.

Model Letter to Inquirers
for Sale of Mail-Order Business

XXXXX SECURITIES CORPORATION
— Wall Street
New York City

Re: NEW YORK TIMES Advertisement:
"Mail-order Business. Pleasant, simple. Correspondence study course. Year-round. March net $700. Can be
expanded. $10,000. X2568 Times."

The business described in the advertisement is owned and
operated by a client of ours. The business is quite new —
after months of groundwork it began operation in late December, 19— But it is already completely established and
has proved extremely successful.

The product is a low-priced how-to-do-it manual, sold
through magazine and newspaper advertising by a "two-stage"
process: the advertisements call for inquiries, which are
answered by a sales letter. The manual is then sent out to
purchasers. The entire process is straightforward and simple. All operations — except for the placement of advertising — are clerical (though some supervision is required,
of course). Half the owner's time is more than sufficient.

The business can be conducted in a small space, anywhere.
All that is required is storage room for advertising literature and manuals, plus clerical work space. However, much
or all of the clerical work can be done by arrangement with
typists who work in their own homes. This reduces the space
requirements even further.

The business is neither fad nor novelty, and can be expected to continue indefinitely, making the same rate of
profit or better. There is one successful competitor who has
run identical advertisements for more than four years.

Most of the advertisements, once placed, run "Till Forbid,"
i.e., indefinitely and all year round. It is, however, necessary to keep fairly close watch on the borderline media to
ensure that they remain profitable, or run only in the most
profitable months of the year.

The financial data that follow are working figures, but
they are accurate. The consummation of a sale would be subject to an audit by a CPA of your choosing. No tax figures
are available yet because of the newness of the business.
And since the business is part of a larger business, it is
difficult to allocate minor overhead expenses to the penny.

Since the commencement of business in late December, 19—,
until April 6, 19—:

Direct revenue from manual sales. . $3,288

Revenue realized April 8 to April
16 deriving from pre–April 6 advertising and sales effort. . . .   456

From sale of names to March 6 . . .   141

Unrealized sale of names, to April 6 115

  Gross revenue $4,001

Advertising expenditures. $882.56

Cost of sales literature, including
postage, printing, stuffing,
sealing, etc. 846.30

Addressing of sales literature. . .   141.04

Cost of manuals sold. 101.93

Postage for manuals sold. 43.32

Additional clerical costs (rough) .   50.00

Bank charges (rough). 40.00

Reserve for future refunds. 50.00

Miscellaneous 100.00

  Total expenses. $2,254

  Net profit. $1,747

Note that the first months were necessarily very slow.
Revenue from March 7 to April 6 totaled $1,715. Prorated
expenses would be slightly more than half of the revenue.
Profit for that period, then, would be approximately $750.

Advertising expenditures shown above include the full
costs of all advertisements that produced inquiries on or
before March 6, 19—, plus prorata costs of all advertisements that produced their first inquiries between March 7
and April 6. The prorating of magazines was done on a six-
week basis. This is very conservative (to the purchaser),
as any mail–order consultant will attest. Newspaper advertising costs were written off in their entirety. The advertising cost is net of advertising agency commission, since
the present owner has an interest in an agency. The owner
will aid any purchaser in making arrangements to place advertising at net.

No overhead for rent or owner's salary is included because the business is part of a larger business. However,
space costs should not exceed $30 per month in any but
expensive urban space.

The estimated <u>rate</u> of profit relative to invested funds,
as shown in the display above, deserves a downward adjustment
because the summer will show the inevitable mail—order slump.
On the other hand, the rate of profit <u>as well as</u> the <u>total</u>
profit deserves an upward adjustment and should exceed the
figures displayed above, over the long haul, for these
reasons:

1. The total revenue is considerably understated owing
to the fact that many sales deriving from pre—April 6 sales
efforts will not be realized until after April 16. Only
half the returns may be expected in the first ten days after
mailing the sales letters. The other half trickle in slowly.

2. The advertising expenditures have been estimated in a
conservative manner.

3. At present, no other offers go out in the sales letter.
Experimentation has shown that it is easily possible to offer
a related item (which the owner will give rights to) and
increase total sales perhaps 20 percent at no extra selling
cost. This would be almost all profit.

4. The business may be expanded considerably into another
class of advertising that has not yet been tapped, but
which the main competitor uses extensively, and which could
double volume and net.

5. Up to the present, inquiry names have been sold out—
right in raw form, for the bulk price of 1.5 cents per name.
These names could be developed into a very profitable list.

6. The expenses shown above include the very expensive
experimentation and setup costs necessary to begin any
business.

The selling price for the business is $10,000 or best
offer, with terms possible. No down payment of less than
$5,000 will be considered. The price does not include adver-
tising already placed and paid for but not yet appeared.
The purchaser would have the option of purchasing that advertising at cost as of the purchase date (for something under
$1,000), or he could take possession of the business without
the rights to business from ads already paid for. The latter
option would be severely to his disadvantage, because his
income stream would not begin for almost two months, instead
of on the date of purchase.

The problem with selling a business of this kind is that
much of the value of the business lies in knowledge of its
records, its advertising materials, and its advertising
schedule. The seller cannot disclose valuable trade information in advance of the sale, in order to protect both the
prospective purchaser and himself from the merely curious
prospective purchaser. Therefore, we can reveal neither the
name of the company, nor its product, nor its advertising
materials, until the prospective purchaser has made an escrow
deposit of $1,000 in a bank of his choice, with a written
guarantee that the money will either be applied to the purchase price or left for a year as guarantee that the deposi-
tor will not start a similar business or give information to

another person that would help him enter a competing business. The escrow sum would also be subject to immediate return if a CPA audit showed figures substantially at variance with the claims above.

The present owner would be willing to place a substantial portion of the purchase price in escrow for a period of time as guarantee that all representations made in this letter are honest and accurate.

After the escrow deposit, the prospective purchaser may examine any and all records of the business. However, the names of newspapers and magazines advertised in will not be disclosed until final sale.

The difficulty of this kind of transaction is reflected in a selling price which is very low in relation to earnings— an obvious benefit to the prospective purchaser. This is his consolation for the necessarily uncomfortable feeling of putting money in escrow for something he doesn't know all about.

The present owner of the business is a young businessman who has become involved, in the last two months, with a venture that is much larger and more profitable than this one. The new venture requires both his capital and his full attention. This is not a "hardship" sale — no phony heart attacks, retirements, etc. The owner has developed an extremely profitable property, and now wishes to take his profits at once to go on to exploit his larger venture.

The present owner's personal and business references are impeccable. He would devote one full week to turning over the business, and would remain available indefinitely for consultation. However, he would limit his consultation time to a few hours each week, gradually tapering off as the new owner gained a complete feel of the business.

If you are seriously interested in the business — and are ready to make an escrow deposit — you may communicate with the owner by letter at Box 2568, care of XXXXX Securities. Give such detail about your qualifications, background, and financial capacity as will indicate your capability to handle a business of this type. Please do not call XXXXX, however. We have no further information to supply, and will only ask you to write to the owner.

Sincerely,
J. T. M——, President
XXXXX Securities Corporation

P.S. My personal opinion on the basis of my knowledge of the owner is that whoever purchases his business at the price he asks is going to be getting a fine buy for his money.

Enclosed with the above letter was a cumulative record of inquiries and sales during the recent history of the business.

APPENDIX D

Federal Trade Commission Summary
of Types of Unfair Methods and Practices

The use of false or misleading advertising concerning, and the misbanding of, commodities, respecting the materials or ingredients of which they are composed, their quality, purity, origin, source, attributes, or properties, or nature of manufacture, and selling them under such name and circumstances as to deceive the public. An important part of these include misrepresentation of the therapeutic and corrective properties of medicinal preparations and devices, and cosmetics, and the false representation expressly or by failure to disclose their potential harmfulness, that such preparations may be safely used.

Describing various symptoms and falsely representing that they indicate the presence of diseases and abnormal conditions which the product advertised will cure or alleviate.

Representing products to have been made in the United States when the mechanism or movements, in whole or in important part, are of foreign origin.

Making false and disparaging statements respecting competitors' products and business, in some cases under the guise of ostensibly disinterested and specially informed sources or through purported scientific, but in fact misleading, demonstrations or tests.

Passing off goods for products of competitors through appropriation or simulation of such competitors' trade names, labels, dress of goods, or counter-display catalogs.

Making use of false and misleading representations, schemes, and practices to obtain representatives and make contracts such as pretended puzzle-prize contests purportedly offering opportunities to win handsome prizes, but which are in fact mere "come-on" schemes and devices in which the "seller's true identity and interest are initially concealed. . . .

Using merchandising schemes based on lot or chance, or on a pretended contest of skill.

Aiding, assisting, or abetting unfair practice, misrepresentation, and deception, and furnishing means or instrumentalities therefor; and combining and conspiring to offer or sell products by chance or by deceptive methods, through such practices as supplying dealers with lottery devices, or selling to dealers and assisting them in conducting content schemes as a part of which pretended credit slips or certificates are issued to contestants, when in fact the price of the goods has been marked up to absorb the face value of the credit slip; and the supplying of emblems or devices to conceal marks of country of origin of goods, or otherwise to misbrand goods as to country of origin. . . .

Sales plans in which the seller's usual price is falsely represented as a special reduced price for a limited time or to a limited class, or false claim of special terms, equipment, or other privileges or advantages.

False or misleading use of the word "Free" in advertising.

Use of misleading trade names calculated to create the impression that a dealer is a producer or importer selling directly to the consumer, with resultant savings.

Offering of false "bargains" by pretended cutting of a fictitious "regular" price.

Use of false representations that an article offered has been rejected as nonstandard and is offered at an exceptionally favorable price, or that the number thereof that may be purchased is limited.

Falsely representing that goods are not being offered as sales in ordinary course, but are specially priced and offered as a part of a special advertising campaign to obtain customers, or for some purpose other than the customary profit.

Misrepresenting seller's alleged advantages of location or size, or the branches, domestic or foreign, or the dealer outlets he has. . . .

Alleged connection of a concern, organization, association, or institute with, or endorsement of it or its product or service by, the Government or nationally known organization, or representation that the use of such product or services is required by the Government, or that failure to comply with such requirement is subject to penalty.

False claim by a vendor of being an importer, or a technician, or a diagnostician, or a manufacturer, grower, or nurseryman, or a distiller, or of being a wholesaler, selling to the consumer at wholesale prices; or by a manufacturer of being also the manufacturer of the raw material entering into the product, or by an assembler of being a manufacturer.

Falsely claiming to be a manufacturer's representative and outlet for surplus stock sold at a sacrifice.

Falsely representing that the seller owns a laboratory in which the product offered is analyzed and tested.

Representing that an ordinary private commercial seller and business is an association, or national association, or connected therewith, or sponsored thereby, or is otherwise connected with noncommercial or professional organizations or associations or constitutes an institute, or, in effect, that it is altruistic in purpose, giving work to the unemployed.

Falsely claiming that a business is bonded, or misrepresenting its age or history, or the demand established for its products, or the selection afforded, or the quality or comparative value of its goods, or the personnel or staff of personages presently or theretofore associated with such business or the products thereof.

Claiming falsely or misleadingly by patent, trade-mark, or other special and exclusive rights.

Granting seals of approval by a magazine to products advertised therein and misrepresenting thereby that such products have been adequately tested, and misrepresenting by other means the quality, performance, and characteristics of such products. . . .

Misrepresenting that seller fills order promptly, ships kind of merchandise described, and assigns exclusive territorial rights within definite trade areas to purchasers or prospective purchasers.

Obtaining orders on the basis of samples displayed for customer's selection and failing or refusing to respect such selection thereafter in the filling of orders, or promising results impossible of fulfillment, or falsely making promises or holding out guaranties, or the right of return, or results, or refunds, replacements, or reimbursements, or special or additional advantages to the prospective purchasers such as extra credit or furnishing of supplies or advisory assistance; or falsely assuring the purchaser or prospective purchaser that certain special or exclusively personal favors or advantages are being granted him.

Concealing from prospective purchaser unusual features involved in purchaser's commitment, the result of which will be to require of purchaser further expenditure in order to obtain benefit of commitment and expenditure already made, such as failure to reveal peculiar or nonstandard shape of portrait or photographic enlargement, so as to make securing of frame therefor from sources other than seller difficult and impracticable, if not impossible.

Advertising a price for a product as illustrated or described and not including in such price all charges for equipment or accessories illustrated or described or necessary for use of the product or customarily included as standard equipment, and failing to include all charges not specified as extra.

Giving products misleading names so as to give them a value to the purchasing public which they would not otherwise possess, such as names implying falsely that:

The products were made for the government or in accordance with its specifications and of corresponding quality, or that the advertiser is connected with the Government in some way, or in some way the products have been passed upon, inspected, underwritten, or endorsed by it; or

They are composed in whole or in part of ingredients or materials which in fact are present only to an extent or not at all, or that they have qualities or properties which they do not have; or

They were made in or came from some locality famous for the quality or such products, or are of national reputation; or

They were made by some well and favorably known process; or

They have been inspected, passed, or approved after meeting the tests of some official organization charged with the duty of making such tests expertly and disinterestedly, or giving such approval; or

They were made under conditions or circumstances considered of importance by a substantial part of the general purchasing public; or . . .

They are of greater value, durability, and desirability than is the fact, as labeling rabbit fur as "Beaver"; or . . .

They are designed, sponsored, produced, or approved by the medical profession, health and welfare associations, hospitals, celebrities, educational institutions and authorities, such as the use of the letters "M.D." and the words "Red Cross" and its insignia and the words "Boy Scout". . . .

Misrepresenting, through salesmen or otherwise, products' composition, nature, qualities, results accomplished, safety, value, and earnings or profits to be had therefrom.

Falsely claiming unique status or advantages, or special merit therefor, on the basis of misleading and ill-founded demonstrations or scientific tests, or of pretended widespread tests, or of pretended widespread and critical professional acceptance and use.

Misrepresenting the history or circumstances involved in the making and offer of the products or the source of origin thereof (foreign or domestic), or of the ingredients entering therein, or parts thereof, or the opportunities brought to the buyer through purchase of the offering, or otherwise misrepresenting scientific or other facts bearing on the value thereof to the purchaser.

Falsely representing products as legitimate, or prepared in accordance with Government or official standards of specifications.

Falsely claiming Government or official or other acceptance, use, and endorsement of product, and misrepresenting success and standing thereof through use of false and misleading endorsements or false and misleading claims with respect thereto, or otherwise.

Making use of a misleading trade name and representing by other means that the nature of a business is different than is the fact. . . .

Misrepresenting fabrics or garments as to fiber content; and, in the case of wool products, failing to attach tags thereto indicating the wool, re-used wool, reprocessed wool, or other fibers contained therein, and the identity of the manufacturer or qualified reseller, as required by the Wool Products Labeling Act, or removing or mutilating tags required to be affixed to the products when they are offered for sale to the public.

APPENDIX E

Copyrights

Mail-order firms often need to know the law of copyright. You need to know about copyright in order to protect printed material that you write or have written for you, either sales literature or information that you sell. You may also need to know the law of copyright so that you can determine whether a piece of published material is in the public domain so that you can legitimately use it or sell it.

You should know that *any* material published by the Federal government may be reproduced and sold by anyone. One firm reproduces government-written tax guides intact, and sells them commercially. Another firm apparently has done well recently by reprinting the official English government report of the Christine Keeler case. More commonly, you may wish to include government-written material as part of a book or pamphlet. In the next page of this appendix, I am going to do just that.

The most important thing you must know is exactly how to protect yourself from having work pirated from you. The next pages tell you how. Don't forget to follow the instructions *exactly*. The notice of copyright *must be correct*. If you make a mistake on it at the beginning, all is lost forever. So get it right!

Write to the Copyright Office, Library of Congress, Washington 25, D.C., and ask for *Regulations of the Copyright Office* and *General Information on Copyright*. In the meantime, here are short extracts of the very most basic copyright facts, taken from Copyright Office fact sheets.[1]

HOW TO DETERMINE WHETHER A WORK IS COPYRIGHTED

1. *Notice of Copyright.* A notice of copyright (e.g., © John Doe 1959 or Copyright John Doe 1959) on a published work indicates that copy-

right is claimed in that particular work. (See Sections 3, 10, 19, and 20 of the copyright law printed on the back of this circular.) One function of this notice is to warn potential users not to copy the work without proper authorization. If a published work does not bear the required Statutory copyright notice it is probably not protected by copyright. (For exceptions, see Sections 10 and 21 of the copyright law printed on the back of this circular.)

The absence of a copyright notice on a work which *has never been published* should not be construed to mean that the work is not protected by law. Protection may be available either on the basis of common law literary property rights or by reason of registration in the Copyright Office.

2. *Duration of Copyright.* United States copyright endures for 28 years and may be renewed for an additional period of 28 years, making a total of 56 years' possible protection. If the copyright is not renewed during the 28th year, or if 56 years have passed since the first publication of that particular work, it becomes "public domain" and is no longer subject to the protection of the United States copyright law.

3. *New Versions.* The law provides that copyright can be secured in arrangements, adaptations, translations, dramatizations, and other versions of previous works. If the previous work is in the public domain, copyright in the new version covers only the additions of revisions, and gives no new rights in the public domain material. If the previous work is still protected by copyright, it is necessary to obtain permission from the copyright owner before making a new version or quoting substantially from it.

4. *Copyright Office Records.* The Copyright Office maintains records of copyright registrations and recorded documents. It also publishes the *Catalog of Copyright Entries* which lists all registrations. The *Catalog* is issued in several parts for different kinds of works and each part covers a 6-month period. However, the *Catalog* does not include entries for assignments or other recorded documents.

5. *Copyright Office Searches.* The Copyright Office can make a search of its records upon receipt of the necessary fee (see item 9) and will furnish a report of its search. It is not possible, however, for the Copyright Office to express an opinion on the legal significance of the facts reported, or to search or compare works to determine questions of originality or similarity.

If you are near a library that maintains a file of the *Catalog of Copyright Entries* you may be able to avoid the cost of a search by consulting the printed *Catalog* yourself.

NOTE: The fact that a search of Copyright Office records discloses no information about a particular work does not necessarily mean that the work is unprotected. For example, registration for unpublished works is not required. Some claimants for published works do not file their applications as promptly as they should, and delay in registration generally has no effect on the validity of a copyright. Also, some foreign works are protected in this country under conventions to which the U.S. may be a party without the necessity of registration.

6. *Information Needed for a Search.* When requesting a search, please furnish as much of the following information as possible: title, name of author or authors, copyright claimant, year date of publication or deposit, class of work (book, music, photograph, etc.).

7. *Transfers of Copyright Ownership.* Special searches are required to provide information concerning assignments and other recorded documents relating to changes in the ownership of a copyright. This information is not included in search reports unless specifically requested.

8. *Titles and Names.* If your concern is about using a particular title or name, a search of the Copyright Office records would be of little value. Copyright does not give exclusive rights to titles, and titles as such are not registered at the Copyright Office. Searches are, accordingly, not undertaken to determine whether stated titles or names are original. The records reveal many different works identified by the same or similar titles. In some circumstances titles may be protected under the law of unfair competition, but this is a matter of State law, not copyright. Trademarks are registered in the Patent Office.

9. *Search Fees.* Following receipt of the necessary facts on which to base a search, a fee will be estimated at the statutory rate of $3 per hour.

SECTIONS FROM TITLE 17—UNITED STATES CODE (COPYRIGHTS)

SEC. 10. *Publication of Work with Notice.* — Any person entitled thereto by this title may secure copyright for his work by publication thereof with the notice of copyright required by this title; and such notices shall be affixed to each copy thereof published or offered for sale in the United States by authority of the copyright proprietor, except in the case of books seeking ad interim protection under section 22 of this title.

SEC. 19. *Notice; Form.* — The notice of copyright required by section 10 of this title shall consist either of the word "Copyright," the abbreviation "Copr.," or the symbol ©, accompanied by the name of the copyright proprietor, and if the work be a printed literary, musical, or dramatic work, the notice shall include also the year in which the copyright was secured by publication. In the case, however, of copies of works specified in subsections (f) to (k), inclusive, of section 5 of this title, the notice may consist of the letter C enclosed with a circle, thus ©, accompanied by the initials, monogram, mark, or symbol of the copyright proprietor: *Provided,* That on some accessible portion of such copies or of the margin, back permanent base, or pedestal, or of the substance on which such copies shall be mounted, his name shall appear. But in the case of works in which copyright was subsisting on July 1, 1909, the notice of copyright may be either in one of the forms prescribed herein or may consist of the following words: "Entered according to Act of Congress, in the year   , by A. B., in the office of the Librarian of Congress, at Washington, D.C.," or, at his option, the word "Copyright," together with the year the copyright was entered and the name of the party by whom it was taken out; thus, "Copyright, 19—, by A. B."

SEC. 20. *Same; Place of Application of; One Notice in Each Volume or Number of Newspaper or Periodical.* — The notice of copyright shall be applied, in the case of a book or other printed publication, upon its title page or the page immediately following, or if a periodical either upon the title page or upon the first page of text of each separate number or under the title heading, or if a musical work either upon its title page or the first page of music. One notice of copyright in each volume or in each number of a newspaper or periodical published shall suffice.

SEC. 21. *Same; Effect of Accidental Omission from Copy or Copies.* — Where the copyright proprietor has sought to comply with the provisions of this title with respect to notice, the omission by accident or mistake of the prescribed notice from a particular copy or copies shall not invalidate the copyright or prevent recovery for infringement against any person who, after actual notice of the copyright, begins an undertaking to infringe it, but shall prevent the recovery of damages against an innocent infringer who has been misled by the omission of the notice; and in a suit for infringement no permaent injunction shall be had unless the copyright proprietor shall reimburse to the innocent infringer his reasonable outlay innocently incurred if the court, in its discretion, shall so direct.

INSTRUCTIONS FOR SECURING COPYRIGHT FOR BOOKS

UNPUBLISHED WORKS. The law does not provide for registration of "book" material in unpublished form. Thus, unpublished manuscripts of novels, articles, stories, poems, words of songs without music, and other similar material should not be sent to the Copyright Office. Unpublished books are protected by common law against unauthorized copying, publication, or use without any action being required in this Office.

PROCEDURE FOR SECURING STATUTORY COPYRIGHT. Three steps must be taken to comply with the law concerning copyright in books.

1. *Produce copies with copyright notice.* First, produce the work in copies by printing or other means of reproduction. To secure copyright, it is essential that the copies bear a copyright notice in the required form and position.

A. *Elements of the Notice.* The notice must contain these three elements:

(1) *The word "Copyright," or the abbreviation "Copr.," or the symbol "©."* The use of the symbol © may result in securing copyright in some countries outside the United States under the provisions of the Universal Copyright Convention, which protection might not be secured by use of either of the alternative forms of notice.

(2) *The name of the copyright owner.*

(3) *The year date of publication.* This is year in which copies of the work were first placed on sale, sold, or publicly distributed by the copyright proprietor or under his authority.

B. *Form of the Notice.* The three elements must appear together; for example:

© John Doe 1961

c. *Position of Notice.* The notice must appear on the title page or the page immediately following. The "page immediately following" usually means the reverse of the title page since a "page" is regarded as one side of a leaf.

2. *Publish the work.* Second, publish the work bearing the copyright notice. "Publication," for copyright purposes, is generally regarded as the placing on sale, sale, or public distribution of copies. The copyright law defines the "date of publication" as ". . . the earliest date when copies of the first authorized edition were placed on sale, sold, or publicly distributed by the proprietor of the copyright or under his authority. . . ."

NOTE: *It is the act of publication with notice that actually secures copyright protection. If copies are published without the required notice, the right to secure copyright is lost and cannot be restored.*

3. *Register your copyright claim.* Third, promptly after publication, mail to the Register of Copyrights, The Library of Congress, Washington 25, D.C.: two copies of the work as published with notice, an application on Form A properly completed and notarized and a fee of $4.00. Registration may be more prompt if the application, copies, and fee are all mailed at the same time.

APPENDIX F

Technical Notes on Direct-Mail Testing

1. This discussion of direct-mail testing uses only one-tail tests. I don't believe that the direct-mail tester needs or cares about protection against test results being too low—except in the case where the test results fall below the break-even point. Even then it would be a one-tail test, but in the other direction.

2. Rule-of-thumb Tables 18-1 to 18-3 all depend on the proposition that when the proportion of returns is very low (under 5 percent, say) and the sample size is large, the standard deviation will (approximately) depend only on the ratio of proportion of returns to sample size. This means that the standard deviation can be considered a function of the *number* of returns only.

3. Tables 18-1 and 18-2 are derived from $\sigma = \sqrt{pq/n}$ (where n is large and q is 1) and the cumulative normal distribution.

4. Table 18-3 flows from the following proposition, which, I believe, is novel: The probability that sample means from two populations with different means will be in a reverse order from the populations means (i.e., that the lower sample mean will come from the population with the higher real mean) is the percentage of *one* of the populations that lies beyond the mean of the two population means. Robert J. Wolfson of C-E-I-R, Inc.,[1] supplied a proof that this proposition holds when the sample sizes and standard deviations for the two samples are equal. In direct-mail testing the sample sizes are made equal almost as a matter of course. And with the return proportion that direct-mail testers deal with, we may, without any grave loss of accuracy, treat the standard deviations as being equal.

5. The 2×2 paradigm discussion of testing more than one variable at a time holds only where the variables are effectively independent. But such independence is the rule in direct-mail testing: price, headlines,

colors, first- versus third-class mail, etc., are not likely to interact very much.

6. Multiple-variable tests are hard to evaluate. There are statistical methods of determining whether or not the variability is due to chance —i.e., whether the variables are really different from each other. But that isn't much help to the direct-mail tester who is concerned with *magnitudes* of differences. I think about the multivariate situations in this way: the greater the number of variables tested, the less the information the tester puts into the situation, and therefore the less he can get out of it with a given sample size. In terms of subjectivistic statistics, his prior hypotheses are much less sharp, and therefore when they are combined with the test results, they are of less help in arriving at a final decision.

APPENDIX G

Mailing-list Brokers and Dealers

This is a list of mailing-list brokers taken from the advertising listings in a recent issue of *Direct-Mail*.

Accredited Mailing Lists, Inc., 15 E. 40 St., New York 16, N.Y.
George Bryant & Staff, 71 Grand Ave., Englewood, N.J.
Richard Buehrer Associates, Inc. (D. L. Natwick), 136 W. 52 St., New York 19, N.Y.
The Coolidge Company, Inc., 11 W. 42 St., New York 16, N.Y.
Dependable Mailing Lists, Inc., 381 Park Ave. So., New York 16, N.Y.
Direct Mail Markets Co., Inc., 515 Madison Ave., New York 22, N.Y.
Alan Drey Company, Inc., 333 N. Michigan Ave., Chicago 1, Ill.
Walter Drey, Inc., 257 Park Ave. So., New York 16, N.Y.
Sanford Evans Service, Ltd., Ste 4, 501 Yonge St., Toronto 5, Ontario
Guild Company, 160 Engle St., Englewood, N.J.
Walter Karl, Inc., Armonk, New York
Lewis Kleid, Inc., 25 W. 45 St., New York 36, N.Y.
Eli Kogos, P. O. Box 414, Webster, Mass.
Ceil Levine Screened Mailing Lists, Inc., 250 W. 57 St., New York 19, N.Y.
Willa Maddern, Inc., 215 Park Ave. So., New York 3, N.Y.
Mail Dynamics, Inc., 11 W. 42 St., New York 36, N.Y.
Mosely Mail Order List Service, Inc., 38 Newbury St., Boston 16, Mass.
Names in the News, 45 W. 18 St., New York 11, N.Y.
Names Unlimited, Inc., 352 Park Ave. So., New York 10, N.Y.
People in Places, Inc., 41 Fifth Ave., New York 3, N.Y.
Planned Circulation, 19 W. 44 St., New York 36, N.Y.
The Roskam Company, P. O. Box 855, Kansas City 41, Mo.
C. H. "Hank" Ruby & Co., 339 W. 51 St., New York 19, N.Y.
Wm. Stroh, Inc., 568 54 St., West New York, N.J.
James E. True Associates, 419 Park Avenue So., New York, N.Y.
Felix Tyroller, 55 W. 42 St., New York 26, N.Y.

These firms advertise themselves as owners and compilers of mailing lists. Some of the lists they own are lists of mail-order buyers.

Active Mail Order List Co., Inc., 241 Lafayette St., New York 12, N.Y.
Allison Manufacturing Lists Corp., 329 Park Ave. So., New York 10, N.Y.
Bookbuyers Lists, Inc., 363 Broadway, New York 13, N.Y.
Buckley-Dement, 555 W. Jackson Blvd., Chicago 6, Ill.
Ed. Burnett, Inc., 156 Fifth Ave., New York 10, N.Y.
Catholic Directory, The Official, 12 Barclay St., New York 8, N.Y.
Creative Manufacturing Service, 460 N. Mall St., Freeport, L.I., N.Y.
Alan Drey Company, Inc., 333 N. Michigan Ave., Chicago 1, Ill.
Walter Drey, Inc., 257 Fourth Ave., New York 10, N.Y.
Dunhill International List Co., Inc., Park Ave. So. & 30th St., New York 16, N.Y.
E-Z Addressing Service, 83 Washington St., New York 6, N.Y.
Fisher-Stevens, Inc., 120 Brighton Road, Clifton, N.J.
Fritz S. Hofheimer, 29 E. 22 St., New York 10, N.Y.
Industrial List Bureau, P. O. Box 414, Webster, Mass.
Mailing List Compilation Bureau, 2570 E. 18 St., Brooklyn 35, N.Y.
R. L. Polk & Co., 421 Howard St., Detroit 31, Mich.
Raymond-Loew Associates, Inc., 52 Boardway, New York 4, N.Y.
Research Projects, Inc., 404 Park Ave. So., New York 16, N.Y.
The Speed-Address Kraus Co., 4801-42 St., Long Island City 4, N.Y.
William Stroh, Jr., 568–570 54 St., West New York, N.J.
Zeitler & Letica, Inc., 15 E. 26 St., New York 10, N.Y.

Educational:

Educational Mailing List, 22 W. Putnam Ave., Greenwich, Conn.

Farmers:

Directory Service Company, Inc., 112 N. Thorington, Algona, Iowa

Medical:

Clark-O'Neill, Inc., 1 Broad Ave., Fairview, N.J.
Fisher-Stevens, Inc., 120 Brighton Road, Clifton, N.J.

Occupant lists:

Advertising Distributors of America, Inc., 4444 Cass Ave., Detroit 1, Mich.
Advertising Distributors of America, Inc., 400 Madison Ave., New York 17, N.Y.
Occupant Mailing Lists of America, 239 N. 4 St., Columbus, Ohio

APPENDIX H

Some Agencies That Handle Considerable Mail-Order Advertising

Adams Advertising Agency, ackson-Wacker Building, Chicago 6, Ill.
N. W. Ayer & Son, Inc., W. Washington Square, Philadelphia 6, Pa.
Arthur Bandman Advertising, 1 Main St., Roslyn, N.Y.
Bozell & Jacobs, Inc., Kiewit Plaza, Omaha 31, Nebr.
Diener & Dorskind, Inc., 1501 Broadway, New York 36, N.Y.
Al Fried Associates Inc., 20 W. 43 St., New York 36, N.Y.
Grant, Schwenck & Baker, Inc., 520 N. Michigan Ave., Chicago, Ill.
McNaughton-Laub-Forestal, Inc., 5909 W. Third, Los Angeles 36, Calif.
Roberts & Reimers, Inc., 551 Fifth Ave., New York 17, N.Y.
Harry Schneiderman, Inc., 141 W. Jackson Blvd., Chicago 4, Ill.
Schwab, Beatty & Porter, Inc., 660 Madison Ave., New York 21, N.Y.
A. Serkez & Co., 1133 Broadway, New York 10, N.Y.
Victor & Richards, Inc., 7 E. 48 St., New York 17, N.Y.
Wunderman, Ricotta & Kline, Inc., 575 Madison Ave., New York 22, N.Y.

Data on Mail-Order Media

This appendix has a double purpose. Its first purpose is simply to list the most important mail-order magazines and newspapers. The second purpose is to provide brief data on these media in one place.

Before actually using a medium, you will have to consult *Standard Rate & Data* and/or the medium's rate card. Write the media for their rate cards. *Standard Rate & Data* is probably available at your local library. Or you may be able to beg an old copy from a local advertising agency. When your business gets started, you can get a subscription from the publisher. (If you cancel after a month or so, you will get most of your money back. This may be the cheapest way for you to obtain a copy that will last you for many months.)

The data in this appendix are up to date as of the beginning of 1964. But magazines go into business and out of business fairly often, especially the types of magazines catering to mail-order ads. So don't be puzzled if this listing seems to have errors in it. Consider it only as a general guide while you are learning the business.

Columns for name and address are straightforward.

Circulation is an average for a group of issues. The coded abbreviation indicates the frequency of issues.

Classified cost is listed for those media that carry mail-order classified. You can use that column as a listing of classified media.

The "Magazines in Group" column shows the member magazines of multimagazine groups.

The list of free editorial shopping sections in which to seek editorial mentions does not include the trade and business magazines. But if you have a product which will appeal to some trade or business group, by all means send your release to the appropriate trade magazines.

(*Continued on page 284*)

245

Name	Address	Circulation	If classified, cost per word	Display cost per line (L) or inch (N)	Free editorial shopping section?	Paid shopping section	Magazines in group	Source of basic data
AAA Motor Club Publications	State Street Bldg. 3d & State Sts. Harrisburg, Pa.	Mo 3,407,020		$387.50/N (omits 8 of 47 publications)				C
Ace & Carnival..........	480 Lexington Ave. New York 17, N.Y.	Bi 350,000		2.50/L				O
Adam..........	480 Lexington Ave. New York 17, N.Y.	Mo 400,000		3./L				O
Adventure Men's Group......	205 E. 42d St. New York 17, N.Y.	Bi 335,038		2.10/L/14	Yes	Shopping	Adventure True Adventures Railroad	C
Air Force Times..........	2020 M St., N.W. Washington 6, D.C.	Wk 114,685	$ .50	1.50/L/14				B
Alabama Farm Bureau News..	Box 5218 Montgomery, Ala.	Mo 77,552	.10	.36/L/14				C
Alabama Farmer..........	319 W. Markham Little Rock, Ark.	Mo 87,826	.14/12	.90/L/14				C
Alabama Rural Electric News.	3642 S. Perry St. Montgomery, Ala.	Mo 121,696	*	.64/L/14				C
Alaska Sportsman..........	2131 2nd Ave. Seattle, Wash.	Mo —	.30/10	1.43/L/14				C
All Florida Magazine & TV Week	P. O. Box 5736 Jacksonville 7, Fla.	Wk 672,077		2.28/L		Shoppers Mart		C
American Agriculturist......	Box 514 Ithaca, N.Y.	Mo 195,155	.30/10	2.50/L/7				C
American Armed Forces Features	405 Lexington Ave. New York 17, N.Y.	Mo 838,110						B
American Armed Forces Newspapers	405 Lexington Ave. New York 17, N.Y.	Wk 838,110						B
American Baby..........	180 Riverside Drive New York 24, N.Y.	Mo 311,500		6.20/L/14	Yes			C

Name	Address	Freq.	Circulation			Yes	Shopper	Class	Publications
American Bowler..........	6257 Leland Way, Hollywood 28, Calif.	Mo	—		20./N			C	
American Comics Group......	331 Madison Ave., New York 17, N.Y.	8/year	401,016					C	Forbidden Worlds, Unknown Worlds, Adventures into the Unknown
American Fruit Grower......	37841 Euclid Ave., Willoughby, Ohio	Mo	101,808	.30/10	2.50/L/7			C	
American Girl.............	830 3d Ave., New York 22, N.Y.	Mo	800,000		7.10/L	Yes		C	
The American Home........	300 Park Ave., New York 22, N.Y.	Mo	3,250,000		23.40/L	Yes	Market Place	C	
American Legion.............	720 Fifth Ave., New York 19, N.Y.	Mo	2,714,762	2.95/10	15.50/L/14	Yes	Legion Shopper	C	
American Livestock Journal..	120 E. Collin Ave., Corsicana, Tex.	Mo	192,268					C	
American Poultry & Egg Journal	180 N. Wabash Ave., Chicago 1, Ill.	Mo	177,393	.70/10	5./L/7			C	
American Rifleman...........	1600 Rhode Island Ave., N.W., Washington, D.C.	Mo	603,969	.45/15	5.20/L/7	Yes		C	
American Vegetable Grower...	37841 Euclid Ave., Willoughby, Ohio	Mo	48,047	.30	1.50/L/14			C	
American Weekend...........	2020 M St., N.W., Washington 6, D.C.	Wk	—	Write	Write			B	
Amusement Business.........	188 W. Randolph St., Chicago 1, Ill.	Wk	18,103	.20/20	45./¼ page	Yes		C	
Antiques...................	601 Fifth Ave., New York 17, N.Y.	Mo	41,792	.40/20	87./⅛ page	Yes		B	
Architectural Forum.........	Rockefeller Center, New York 20, N.Y.	Mo	62,170		405./¼ page			C	
Arena Sports Group.........	730 3d Ave., New York 17, N.Y.	Bi	500,000		3.50/L			C	Boxing & Wrestling, Complete Sports, Wrestling World, Basketball, Wilt Chamberlain Basketball, Maurice Richard Hockey

Name	Address	Circulation	If classified, cost per word	Display cost per line (L) or inch (N)	Free editorial shopping section?	Paid shopping section	Magazines in group	Source of basic data
Argosy	205 East 42nd St. New York 17, N.Y.	Mo 1,243,371		$ 15.50/L/14	Yes	Stop to Shop		C
Arkansas Farmer	319 W. Markham Little Rock, Ark.	Mo 50,429	$ .90/L	.90/L/7				C
Army Times	2020 M St., N.W. Washington 6, D.C.	Wk 97,589	.50	1.50/L/14				B
Atlanta-Journal-Constitution Magazine	10 Forsyth St. N.W. Atlanta, Ga.	Wk 504,755		2.30/L				N
Baby Care Manual	52 Vanderbilt Ave. New York 17, N.Y.	Qt 745,082		29.45/L	Yes			C
Baby Post	30 E. 60th St. New York 22, N.Y.	Mo 196,600		9.25/L	Yes			C
Baby Talk	145 Madison Ave. New York 16, N.Y.	Mo 662,725		13./L	Yes			C
Bargains	Tower Press, Inc. Box 591 Lynn, Mass.							C
Beauty Fair	1841 Broadway New York 23, N.Y.	Bi 600,000		3./L	Yes			A
Best Man's Group	1457 Broadway New York 36, N.Y.						Man's Best Man's Adventure Men in Conflict	
Better Homes & Gardens	1716 Locust St. Des Moines 3, Iowa	Mo 6,000,000		640.50/N 45.75/L 100./¼ col.	Yes	Shopping by Mail		C
Better Listening	25 W. 45 St. New York 36, N.Y.	Qt —						C
Better Ranches & Farms	Corpus Christi, Tex.	Mo 95,605		.34/L				C
Bluebook for Men	730 3d Ave. New York 17, N.Y.	Mo 210,000		1./L/L/14				C

Publication	Address	Freq./Circ.			Mail	Departments	Features	Grade
Blum's Almanac	218 N. Main, Winston-Salem, N.C.	An 208,472	.45/10					C
Bold	11 E. 17th St., New York 3, N.Y.	Mo —		2./L/14				A
Boys' Life	New Brunswick, N.J.	Mo 2,150,000		140./N/14	Yes	Schools, Camps & Colleges; Gifts & Gimmicks; Stamps & Coins		C
Bride & Home	572 Madison Ave., New York 22, N.Y.	Qt 159,357		350./⅛ page	Yes			C
Brookside Detective Group	140 W. 42d St., New York 36, N.Y.	Mo & Bi 500,000		2.50/L/14			Detective Cases; Police Dragnet; Police Files; Amazing Detective	C
Buckeye Farm News	245 N. High St., Columbus, Ohio	Mo 59,795	.10/10	.70/L	Yes			C
Business Week	330 W. 42nd St., New York 18, N.Y.	Wk 412,174		14.20/L/14				C
California Farm Bureau Monthly	2223 Fulton St., Berkeley 4, Calif.	Mo 65,065	.90	.85/L				O
California Farmer	83 Stevenson St., San Francisco 5, Calif.	SemiMo 93,391	.25/12	2.05/L/7				O
California Grange News	2101 Stockton Blvd., Sacramento 17, Calif.	SemiMo —	.13	.47/L/14				O
California—Magazine of Commerce, Agriculture and Industry	350 Bush St., San Francisco 4, Calif.	Mo 7,670		1.06/L	Yes			B
Camera 35	9 E. 40th St., New York 16, N.Y.	Bi 64,121	.50/10		Yes			C
Camping	1114 S. Ave., Plainfield, N.J.				Yes			A
Canadian media	See SR & D for data							
Capper's Weekly	8th & Jackson, Topeka, Kans.	Wk 470,873	1.75/L]	2.10/L/14	Yes	Arm Chair Shopping Center		C
Car & Driver	1 Park Ave., New York, N.Y.	Mo 237,160	.50/10	85./N		Mail Order		C
Car Life	834 Production Pl., Newport Beach, Calif.	Mo 115,000	.40/25	35./N		Mail Order Rental		C
Carolina Farmer	Box 1699, Raleigh, N.C.	Mo 165,159		1.27/L/14				C

Name	Address	Circulation	If classified, cost per word	Display cost per line (L) or inch (N)	Free editorial shopping section?	Paid shopping section	Magazines in group	Source of basic data
Cars	26 W. 47th St. New York 36, N.Y.	Mo 181,788	$ .25/10	$ 1.40/L				C
The Catholic Boy	Notre Dame South Bend, Ind.	Mo 73,054	.30/50	12.60/N .90/L				C
Catholic Digest	2059 N. Hamline Ave. St. Paul 13, Minn.	Mo 700,000		190./21⁄8 N	Yes			C
The Catholic Miss	Notre Dame South Bend, Ind.	Mo 92,601	.30/50	12.60/N .90/L				C
Cavalier	67 W. 44th St. New York 36, N.Y.	Mo 400,000		3.40/L/14		Retail Shopping Section School & Book Publishers		C
Challenge for Men	444 Madison Ave. New York 22, N.Y.	Bi 300,000			Yes			A
Charlton Confession Group	Charlton Bldg. Derby, Conn.			1.50/L/14			Actual Confessions True Life Secrets True Nurse Confessions Top Secret Hush Hush	C
Charlton Expose Group	Charlton Bldg. Derby, Conn.	Qt 229,996		.60/L/14				C
Chicago News' Chicago Life	Chicago 11, Ill.	Wk 506,185		1.70/L/14	Yes			P
Chicago's American Leisure & TV Roundup	445 N. Michigan Ave. Chicago 11, Ill.	Wk 547,538		2./L/14		Mail Mart		P
Chicago Tribune Magazine	435 N. Michigan Ave. Chicago 11, Ill.	Wk 1,157,232		3.60/L/14	Yes	Please Send Me		P
Christian Herald	27 E. 39th St. New York 16, N.Y.	Mo 465,996		69.72/N 4.98/L		Books, Records, Schools, Colleges		C
Christian Heritage	14 E. Carolina Ave. Clinton, S.C.	Mo 29,375		.50/L/14				C

Publication	Address	Circulation		Rate	Notes	Titles	
The Christian Science Monitor	Boston 15, Mass.	Daily (esp. Sat.) 194,917		1.20/L/14			C
Christianity Today	1014 Washington Bldg. 15th & N.Y. Ave. N.W. Washington 5, D.C.	BiWk 209,000		31.50/N 4.98/L/7			C
Church Herald	3818 Chestnut St. Philadelphia 4, Pa.	Wk 69,410		11.48/N			C
Church Observer	3818 Chestnut St. Philadelphia 4, Pa.	Mo 7,623		.82/L/14 .30/L/14			C
Circus Review	P. O. Box 112 Portland, Tenn.	Qt 2,850					A
Climax	205 E. 42d St. New York 17, N.Y.	Mo 143,302		1.16/L/7			C
CO/AD	396 Park Ave. New York 17, N.Y.	700,400	1.59/10	119.14/2N			O
Colorado Rancher & Farmer	Box 1349 Denver, Colo.	SemiMo 38,702	.10/10	.75/L/7			C
Colorado-Wyoming Rural Electric News	802 Farmers Union Bldg. Denver, Colo.	Mo 15,750	*	.24/L/14			C
Columbia	17 Meadow St. New York 17, N.Y.	Mo 1,081,230		73.50/N 5.25/L/14	Yes		C
Combination Men's Group	1457 Broadway New York 36, N.Y.	Qt 750,000		2.50/L	Shopping with Laura School Directory	Men in Adventure / Police Detective / A.O.K. for Men / Real Detective / Detective Annual / Action for Men / Man's World / True Action / Sportsman / Adventure Life / For Men Only / Stag / Male / Men	O
Complete Adventure Group	667 Madison Ave. New York 21, N.Y.	Qt —		2.75/L			C
Complete Men's Group	655 Madison Ave. New York 21, N.Y.	Mo 1,108,516		7.50/L/14			C

Name	Address	Circulation	If classified, cost per word	Display cost per line (L) or inch (N)	Free editorial shopping section?	Paid shopping section	Magazines in group	Source of basic data
Complete Women's Group....	655 Madison Ave. New York 21, N.Y.	Bi 1,100,000		$ 5./L/14			Screen Stars Movie World True Secrets My Romance My Confessions TV World Life Story Confessions	C
Confidential..............	ByLine Publ. Inc. 730 3d Ave. New York 17, N.Y.	Mo —		.55/L/10				C
Confidential Flash.........	John Blunt Publ. 230 Adelaide S.W. Toronto 1, Ont.	Wk 43,264		.55/L/10				C
Connecticut Life...........	20 Isham Road West Hartford, Conn.	Wk 145,000		128./⅙ page				C
Cooperative Farmer........	Box 1656 Richmond 13, Va.	Mo 169,965	$ .10	1.95/L/14				C
Cosmopolitan..............	57th & 8th Ave. New York 19, N.Y.	Mo 890,057		11.70/L/7		Cosmoparcels		C
Country Song Roundup......	Charlton Bldg. Derby, Conn.	Qt 104,087		.60/L/14				C
Craft Horizons.............	44 W. 53rd St. New York, N.Y.	Bi 26,400	.30/15	22./N	Yes	Mail Order		C
Custom Rodder.............	26 W. 47th St. New York 36, N.Y.	Bi 155,137	.25/10	19.60/N 1.40/L/14				C
Dakota Farmer.............	1216 S. Main Aberdeen, S.Dak.	SemiMo 96,845	.25/10	1.50/L/7				
Datebook..................	71 Washington Pl. New York 11, N.Y.	Bi —		20./N				C

			Comb. rate	Rate	Mail order	Section	
The Defender	2502 E. Douglas Ave. Wichita 1, Kans.	Mo —					C
Dell Modern Group	750 3d Ave. New York 17, N.Y.	Mo 1,832,046	13.95/10 (comb. rate)	1.13/L/14	Yes	Modern Romances Modern Screen Screen Stories	C
Dell Screen Unit	750 3d Ave. New York 17, N.Y.	Mo 1,000,000	13.95/10 (comb. rate)	6.80/L/7		Modern Screen Screen Stories	C
Dell Sports Magazine	750 3d Ave. New York 17, N.Y.	Bi 140,623		3./L/14			C
Desert Magazine	Palm Desert, Calif.	Mo 22,000		30./2N		Desert Trading Post	C
Des Moines Register & Picture Magazine & TV Section	Des Moines, Iowa			1.30/L		Order by Mail Today	P
The Diners' Club Magazine	10 Columbus Ave. New York 19, N.Y.	Mo 811,279		150./N		Diners' Club Shopping Tour Mail Order Space	C
Dog World	469 E. Ohio St. Chicago 11, Ill.	Mo 45,071	.30/15	22./N			C
Dun's Review & Modern Industry	99 Church St. New York 8, N.Y.	Mo 121,334		5.20/L/14			C
Eagle Magazine	2401 W. Wisconsin Ave. Milwaukee 3, Wis.	Mo 614,167		4./L/14	Yes	Eagle Easy Shopper	C
Ebony	1820 S. Michigan Ave. Chicago 16, Ill.	Mo 708,497		6.80/L/14	Yes		C
Electronics Illustrated	67 W. 44th St. New York 36, N.Y.	Bi 220,688	.50/10	255./¼ page			C
Electronics World	1 Park Ave. New York 16, N.Y.	Mo 203,188	.60/10	56./N			C
Elks Magazine	386 Park Ave. S. New York 16, N.Y.	Mo 1,325,878		7.75/L/14	Yes	Elks Family Shopper	C
Empire State Mason	71 W. 23rd St. New York 10, N.Y.	6/year 300,000		50./N			C
Escapade	Division St. Derby, Conn.	Bi 207,768		2.50/L/14			C
Escape	21 W. 26th St. New York 10, N.Y.	Bi 177,842		1./L/14			C
Esquire	488 Madison Ave. New York, N.Y.	Mo 892,838		980./⅛ page	Yes	Talking Shop with Esquire	C

Name	Address	Circulation	If classified, cost per word	Display cost per line (L) or inch (N)	Free editorial shopping section?	Paid shopping section	Magazines in group	Source of basic data
Everybody's Poultry	Exchange P Hanover 4, Pa.	Mo 31,268	$ .20	$ 1./L/7				C
Exciting Men's Group	505 8th Ave. New York 18, N.Y.	Bi —		3.50/L/14			Real See	C
Exploring the Unknown	119 Fifth Ave. New York 3, N.Y.	Bi —	.25	6./½N				A
Extension Magazine	1307 S. Wabash Ave. Chicago 5, Ill.	Mo 368,818		2.25/L/14	Yes	Window Shopping with Maggie Making Things with Maggie & Mike Baby Patter Teendom Cooking Department Pattern (Sewing) Department Children's Department		C
Family Circle	25 W. 45th St. New York 36, N.Y.	Mo 7,106,099		59.60/L/14	Yes	Every Women's Shopping Circle		C
The Family Handyman	800 2nd Ave. New York 17, N.Y.	Bi 213,034		3./L/14	Yes	Mail Order		C
Family News	P. O. Box 87 Winnsboro, Tex.	Mo 25,525	.09/20	1.33/N/3				O
Family Weekly	153 N. Michigan Ave. Chicago 1, Ill.	Wk 4,455,750		17.85/L/14				C
Farm Bureau Mirror	3609 Derry St. Harrisburg, Pa.	Mo 59,005	.13/15	.60/L/14				O

	Publication	Address	Circulation	Rate	Rate			Publications
o	Farm Bureau Press	7th & High St. Little Rock, Ark.	Mo 50,077	.13/10	.29/L/14			
o	Farm Journal	Washington Square Philadelphia 5, Pa.	Mo 3,037,621	2.90/14	32.50/L/5	Yes	Mailbox Shopping	
o	Farm & Ranch	318 Murfreesboro Rd. Nashville 10, Tenn.	Mo 1,025,778	.90/10	11.15/L/7			
o	The Farmer	55 E. 10th St. St. Paul, Minn.	SemiMo 245,300	.30/10	3.20/L/3			
o	Farmer-Stockman	500 N. Broadway Oklahoma City, Okla.	Mo 431,659	.30/10	4./L/7			
o	Farmers Union Herald	1667 N. Snelling Ave. St. Paul 1, Minn.	SemiMo 200,000	.30	1.20/L/14			
o	Fate	845 Chicago Ave. Evanston, Ill.	Mo 70,419	.25	10./½N			
C	Fawcett Baseball Group	67 W. 44th St. New York 36, N.Y.	An —		3.95/L			True's Baseball Yearbook / Major League Baseball / Baseball 1964 / Official Baseball Annual
C	Fawcett Christmas Group	67 W. 44th St. New York 36, N.Y.	An —		785./⅙ page		Shopping Section	Woman's Day Best Ideas for Christmas / Today's Woman Christmas Idea Book / The How-to Christmas Book / New Ideas for Christmas / Things to Make for Christmas
C	Fawcett Detective Unit	Mason St. Greenwich, Conn.	Bi 297,542		1.30/L/14			Startling Detective / True Police Cases
C	Fawcett Football Group	67 W. 44th St. New York 36, N.Y.	An —		3.95/L			True's Football Yearbook / Pro Football Stars / Pro Football 1964 / Football Forecast

Name	Address	Circulation	If classified, cost per word	Display cost per line (L) or inch (N)	Free editorial shopping section?	Paid shopping section	Magazines in group	Source of basic data
Field & Stream	383 Madison Ave. New York, N.Y.	Mo 1,261,430		$ 12.70/L/14	Yes	Mail Order Shopping Section		O
Fishing Annual	156 E. 42nd St., New York 22, N.Y.	An —		2.85/L				C
Fishing World	50 W. 57th St., New York 19, N.Y.	Wk 48,997	$ .30/15	1.75/L/14	Yes			C
Flower & Garden	543 Westport Rd. Kansas City 11, Mo.	Mo 594,829	1.10/20	7.80/L/14		Market by Mail		O
Flower Grower	1 Park Ave. New York 16, N.Y.	Mo 377,713	5.70/L	6.75/L/14	Yes	General Store		O
Flying	1 Park Ave. New York 16, N.Y.	221,641 SemiMo	.60/L/10	97./N				O
Forbes	70 5th Ave. New York 11, N.Y.	353,449 Mo	2.60	10.14/L/14	Yes			C
Fraternal Classified Group	100 E. Ohio St. Chicago 11, Ill.	2,061,348					Moose Magazine Eagle Magazine Extension Magazine Royal Neighbor Magazine Woodmen of the World	O
Fraternal Magazine Advertising Unit	c/o Peacock Freed & Co. 159 E. Ontario St. Chicago 11, Ill.	Mo 685,388	1.20/10	4.50/L/5				C
Frontier Times	Box 5008 Austin, Tex.	Bi 156,532	.20/10	1.08/L				C
Fur-Fish-Game	2878 E. Main Columbus 9, Ohio	Mo 82,376	.15/10	1./L/14				C
Fury	480 Lexington Ave. New York 17, N.Y.	Bi 200,000		1./L				O
Future	Boulder Park Box 7, Tulsa, Okla.	Mo 219,796		135./¼ page				C

Name	Address	Circulation	Rate	Rate		Section	Special	Class
Gasoline Retailer	17 Union Square W. New York 3, N.Y.	SemiMo 163,510	.20/10	18.08/N				B
Gentlemen's Quarterly	488 Madison Ave. New York 22, N.Y.	8/year 47,242		790./⅟₁₂ page		Gentlemen's Showcase		C
Georgia Farmer	1447 Peachtree St. N.E. Atlanta, Ga.	Mo 53,871	.12/12	.80/L/7				C
Glamour Incorporating Charm	420 Lexington Ave. New York 17, N.Y.	Mo 1,116,231		335./⅟₁₂ page	Yes	Glamour Aisle		C
Golf Digest	1236 Sherman Ave. Evanston, Ill.	Mo 183,222	.75/10	4.20/L	Yes			C
Good Housekeeping	57th St. at 8th Ave. New York 19, N.Y.	Mo 5,244,962		46.50/L/7	Yes	School & Camp		C
Good Negro Group	480 Lexington Ave. New York 17, N.Y.	Mo 250,000		25./N			Jive Hep Bronze Thrills	O
Gourmet	Penthouse Hotel Plaza New York 19, N.Y.	Mo 186,333		5.25/L/14		Garden of Eating Hotels & Restaurants		C
Grade Teacher	420 Lexington Ave. New York, N.Y.	Mo 152,478		2.40/L/7	Yes			C
Grier's Almanac	Box 1435 Atlanta 1, Ga.	An 2,320,209	2.75/12	22./L/7				C
Grit	208 W. 3rd St. Williamsport, Pa.	Wk 897,144	.60	4.10/L	Yes			C
J. Gruber's Almanack	c/o John Cockrell Inc. 116 S. Michigan Ave. Chicago 3, Ill.	An 231,734		2.25/L/14				C
Gun Sport	26 E. 37th St. New York 36, N.Y.	Bi 63,696	.20/10	1./L				C
Guns & Ammo	5959 Hollywood Blvd. Los Angeles 28, Calif.	Mo 117,868	.20/20	1.79/L/14				C
Guns & Hunting	551 Fifth Ave. New York 22, N.Y.	6/year 109,402	.20/15	2./L/14				C
Guns Magazine	8150 N. Central Park Ave. Skokie, Ill.	Mo 121,096	.20/10	27.35/L/3 times				C
Harper's Bazaar	572 Madison Ave. New York 22, N.Y.	Mo 479,601		540./⅟₈ page	Yes	Schools & Camps Retail Ads Shopping Bazaar		C

Name	Address	Circulation	If classified, cost per word	Display cost per line (L) or inch (N)	Free editorial shopping section?	Paid shopping section	Magazines in group	Source of basic data
Herald of Health.........	709 Mission St. San Francisco 3, Calif.	Mo 7,423	.30/10	6./N				C
HiFi/Stereo Review......	1 Park Ave. New York 16, N.Y.	Mo —	.40/10	395./⅙ page				C
High Fidelity............	Great Barrington, Mass.	Mo 115,972	2.75/½N/6 times	185./1/12 page (3 times)		Hi Fi Market Place		C
Hit Parade Teen Group......	Charlton Bldg. Derby, Conn.	Ev. 6 wks 250,000		1.85/L			Teen Hit Parader Teen Age	C
Holiday.............	Independence Square Philadelphia 5, Pa.	Mo 924,554		11.55/L/14	Yes	Schools & Camps Places to Stay Tours, Cruises, Travel		C
Home Business Digest........	G.P.O. Box 972 New York 1, N.Y.				Yes	Holiday Shopper		A
Home Craftsman...........	Davenport, Iowa	Mo 191,315	.50/15	3./L/14	Yes			C
Home Maintenance and Improvement	59 E. Monroe St. Chicago 3, Ill.	Qt 146,774		625./¼ page	Yes	What's Right for Your Home		C
Home Missions	3818 Chestnut St. Philadelphia 4, Pa.	Mo 131,968		1.25/L/28				O
Home Modernizing Guide.....	530 5th Ave. New York 36, N.Y.	SemiAn		600./¼ page	Yes			C
Home State Farm Publications	Cleveland 14, Ohio	Mo & SemiMo 811,410	.20/15 in any one 1, /15 all six	1.40/L/14 1.70/L/14 1.70/L/14 1.80/L/14 1.60/L/14 1.70/L/14	Yes	Shop at Home	Indiana Farmer Kansas Farmer Michigan Farmer Missouri Ruralist Ohio Farmer Pennsylvania Farmer	C

Publication	Freq./Circ.			Yes	Special Section	Related Publications	
Hoosier Farmer............ 130 E. Washington St. Indianapolis, Ind.	Mo 126,973	.18/10	.75/L/7				C
Horticulture............. 300 Massachusetts Ave. Boston 15, Mass.	Mo 81,130	.30/20	2./L/14	Yes	Shop the Easy Way		C
Hot Rod.................. 5959 Hollywood Blvd. Los Angeles 28, Calif.	Mo 637,865		9./L/14	Yes			C
House & Garden........... 420 Lexington Ave. New York 17, N.Y.	Mo 1,251,268		11./L/14	Yes	Shopping Around		C
House Beautiful.......... 572 Madison Ave. New York 22, N.Y.	Mo 1,087,485		11./L/14	Yes	Window Shopping		C
The House Covers Magazine... P. O. Box 67 Paulina, Iowa	Bi 103,620	.30/10	20./N				C
Idaho Farm Journal....... 3204 Overland Rd. Boise, Idaho	Wk 2,088	1./20	1.12/N				C
Ideal Fan Group......... 295 Madison Ave. New York 17, N.Y.	Mo 633,595	13.95/10	3.25/L/14		Ideal Shopping Section	Movie Life TV Star Parade Movie Stars	C
Ideal Movie Group........ 295 Madison Ave. New York 17, N.Y.	Mo 433,164	13.95/10	2.10/L/14			Movie Life Movie Stars Intimate Story Personal Romances	C
Ideal Romance Group...... 295 Madison Ave. New York 17, N.Y.	Mo 482,367	13.95/10	2.50/L/14		Ideal Shopping Section	TV Star Parade Movie Stars Movie Life	C
Ideal Women's Group...... 295 Madison Ave. New York 17, N.Y.	Mo 1,115,962	13.95/10	5.45/L/14	Yes	Ideal Shopping Section	Intimate Story Personal Romances	C
Illinois Rural Electric News.. 416 S. 6th St. Springfield, Ill. Box 178	Mo 121,696	*	1.03/L/14				O
Illinois Union Farmer......... Gillespie, Ill.		.10 or 7./col. N					C
The Improvement Era........ Mutual Funds Inc. 1355 State Salt Lake City 11, Utah	Mo 192,653		2.90/L/14		The Direct Shopper		C
Indiana Rural News........... 20 W. 9th St. Indianapolis 4, Ind.	Mo 143,895	*	.78/L/14				C
The Informer Group of Newspapers	SemiWk 23,000	.09	.22/L			Houston Informer Dallas Express	O
P. O. Box 3086 2418 Leland Houston 3, Tex.							

Name	Address	Circulation	If classified, cost per word	Display cost per line (L) or inch (N)	Free editorial shopping section?	Paid shopping section	Magazines in group	Source of basic data
The Instructor.........	Dansville, N.Y.	Mo 203,049		2.50/L	Yes			C
Iowa Farm & Home Register..	715 Locust St. Des Moines, Iowa	Mo 522,784		1.45/L/14				C
Iowa Rural Electric News......	1114 Reg. & Trib. Bldg. Des Moines 9, Iowa	Mo 118,927	*	1.02/L/14				C
Jacobs Religious List.........	14 E. Carolina Ave. Clinton, S.C.	Write for details 1,993,291						C
Jet.........	1820 S. Michigan Ave. Chicago 16, Ill.	Wk 326,971		800./1 page	Yes			C
Journal of Commerce.........	80 Varick St. New York 13, N.Y.	Daily 29,530	.75/L/4	.75/L/4	Yes			B
Junior League Magazine......	301 Park Ave. New York 22, N.Y.	Bi 86,704		31.50/N	Yes			C
Kansas Electric Farmer......	420 W. 9th St. Topeka, Kans.	Mo 68,292	*	.80/L/14				C
Kansas Farm Bureau News...	2321 Anderson Ave. Manhattan, Kans.	Mo 82,641	.10/15	.55/L				C
Kansas Farmer............	125 W. 8th St. Topeka, Kans.	SemiMo 109,487	.20/15	1.60/L/7	Yes			C
Kellogg Group of Railroad Employee Publications	240 State St. New London, Conn.	Bi & Mo 168,918		2.43/L/28			Six Employee Magazines Railroad Corps	C
Kentucky Farm Bureau News.	120 S. Hubbard Lane Louisville 7, Ky.	Mo 76,190	.12/13	.65/L/14				C
Kentucky Farmer...........	Box 210 Middletown, Ky.	Mo 102,381	.20/15	1.20/L/7				C
Keystone Motorist.........	2205 Broad St. Philadelphia 2, Pa.	Mo 148,892		.83/L/14				C

Publication	Address	Freq. / Circ.	Rate	Rate		The Merchandise Mart	
Kiwanis Magazine	101 E. Erie St. Chicago 11, Ill.	Mo 267,055		3.10/L/14			C
KMR Romance Group	21 West 26th St. New York 10, N.Y.	Bi 865,159		4.85/L/14		My Love Secret Confession Real Romances My Real Life Story Real Story Uncensored Confessions Real Nurse Stories	C
Law & Order	72 W. 45th St. New York 36, N.Y.	Mo 18,950	12.50/N	60./⅙ page			
Leisure	15605 Madison Ave. Cleveland 7, Ohio	Bi 73,456		100./N		Mail Order Advertising	
Let's Live	1133 N. Vermont Ave. Los Angeles 29, Calif.	Mo 19,961	5./20 or less	12./N	Yes		C
Life & Health	6856 Eastern Ave. Washington 12, D.C.	Mo 97,004		2.40/L/14			C
The Lion	209 N. Michigan Ave. Chicago 1, Ill.	Mo 534,294		3.25/L/14	Yes		C
Living for Young Homemakers	575 Madison Ave. New York 22, N.Y.				Yes		C
Living Today	414 Pierce St. Tampa 2, Fla.				Yes		C
London Daily Telegraph	410 Park Ave. New York 22, N.Y.	Wk 693,773		2.30/L/14			O
Los Angeles Herald Examiner Pictorial Living & TV Weekly	Times Mirror Square Los Angeles 53, Calif.	Wk 1,073,422		3.30/L	Yes	Mail Mart	P
Los Angeles Times Home Magazine	1 East Wacker Dr. Chicago 1, Ill.	Wk 319,463		25./1/40 page		Shop by Mail	P
Louisville Courier Journal Sunday Magazine	1457 Broadway New York 36, N.Y.	Bi —	2.95/10/PCD	7./N			P
Lowdown							C
The Lutheran	2900 Queen Lane Philadelphia 29, Pa.	BiWk 407,819	1./20	5.26/L/14			C
Lutheran Layman	3818 Chestnut St. Philadelphia 4, Pa.	Mo 132,416		.50/L/14			C
McCall's	230 Park Ave. New York 17, N.Y.	Mo 8,213,829		60.86/L/7			C

Name	Address	Circulation	If classified, cost per word	Display cost per line (L) or inch (N)	Free editorial shopping section?	Paid shopping section	Magazines in group	Source of basic data
McCall's Needlework and Crafts	230 Park Ave. New York 17, N.Y.	2/year 1,237,596		225./$\frac{1}{16}$ page		Gifts & Things		C
MacFadden's Women's Group	205 E. 42d St. New York 17, N.Y.	Mo 5,675,479	13.95/10/PCD	39.01/L/7			True Story True Romance True Experience True Love Photoplay TV Radio Mirror	C
Mademoiselle.............	420 Lexington Ave. New York 17, N.Y.	Mo 619,034		595./$\frac{1}{2}$ col.	Yes	Shop Here Dept.		C
Man to Man..............	21 W. 26th St. New York 10, N.Y.	Bi 203,291		1./L/14				C
Man's Action Group........	1457 Broadway New York 36, N.Y.	Bi 700,000		3.50/L/14			Man's Daring Adventure Man's Wildcat Man's Action Man's True Danger	C
Man's Life...............	32 W. 22d St. New York 10, N.Y.	Bi 200,275		2./L/14				C
Man's Magazine...........	730 3d Ave. New York 17, N.Y.	Mo 195,749		1.15/L	Yes			C
Master Detective..........	205 E. 42d St. New York 17, N.Y.	Mo 183,794		.96/L/7				C
Mecanica Popular..........	666 N.W. 20th St. Miami 37, Fla.	Mo 213,625		270./$\frac{1}{6}$ page				C
Mechanix Illustrated.......	67 W. 44th St. New York 36, N.Y.	Mo 1,212,032	1.10/10	16.50/L/14	Yes	Mail Order		C
Men's Real Adventure Group..	1457 Broadway New York 36, N.Y.	Bi —		3./L/14			Real Men All Man Battle Cry	C

	Address	Circ.					
Messenger of the Sacred Heart	515 E. Fordham Rd. New York 58, N.Y.	Mo 161,324	.15/10	.48/L/7			A
Michigan Farm News	Box 960 Lansing 4, Mich.	Mo 70,316	.20/15	23.80/N	Yes		C
Michigan Farmer	322 Abbott Rd. E. Lansing, Mich.	SemiMo 120,041		.85/L			C
Midland Cooperator	739 John St., N.E. Minneapolis 13, Minn.	Wk 114,286	.13/9/3 times	1.75/L			C
Midwest–Chicago Sun Times	401 N. Wabash Ave. Chicago 11, Ill.	Wk 632,600				Easy Shopper	O
Mississippi Farm Bureau News	Box 1570 Jackson 5, Miss.	Mo 90,700	.10/10	.35/L			C
Mississippi Farmer	308 Dixie Bldg. Jackson, Miss.	Mo 49,291	.12/10	.70/L/7			C
Mississippi Rural Electric News	The Stoneham Bldg. 15th St. Washington 5, D.C.	Mo 94,321	*				C
Missouri Farm Bureau News	Box 658 Jefferson City, Mo.	Mo 34,308	.11/9	.36/L/14			C
Missouri Farmer	201 S. 7th St. Columbia 3, Mo.	Mo 156,692	.20/15	1.50/L/14			C
Missouri Ruralist	125 W. 8th St. Topeka, Kans.	SemiMo 152,211	.20/15	23.80/N	Yes		C
Mobile Home Journal	505 Park Ave. New York 22, N.Y.	Mo 45,597	.55/10	27./N			C
Model Railroader	1027 N. 7th St. Milwaukee 3, Wis.	Mo 85,800	.25	35.50/N	Yes	Commercial Classified Marketplace	C
Modern Bride	1 Park Ave. New York 16, N.Y.	Bi 190,121		505./⅓ page			C
Modern Franchising	549 W. Washington St. Chicago 6, Ill.	Bi —	.90/12	3.80/L/7			B
Modern Man	8150 N. Central Park Blvd. Skokie, Ill.	Mo 181,996	.20/10	1.50/L			C
Modern Photography	33 W. 60th St. New York 23, N.Y.	Mo 228,877	.75/10	95./N	Yes		C
Modern Romances	750 3rd Ave. New York 17, N.Y.	Mo 751,603	13.95/10/PCD	5.50/L/7			C

Name	Address	Circulation	If classified, cost per word	Display cost per line (L) or inch (N)	Free editorial shopping section?	Paid shopping section	Magazines in group	Source of basic data
Modern Screen............	750 3rd Ave., New York 17, N.Y.	Mo 828,246	13.95/10/PCD	5.50/L/7				C
Money Making Opportunities.	299 Madison Ave., New York 17, N.Y.	Irregularly 250,000	.90/12	3.80/L/14				O
Montana Farmer-Stockman...	Box 1529 Great Falls, Mont.	SemiMo 30,008	.09	7.70/N				C
Montana Rural Electric News.	1950 Curtis St. Denver 2, Colo.	Mo 25,214	*	.27/L/14				C
Moody Monthly............	820 N. LaSalle St. Chicago 10, Ill.	100,725		1.90/L/14				C
Moose Magazine...........	100 E. Ohio St. Chicago 11, Ill.	Mo 818,189	2.60	4.95/L/10		Moose Home Shopper		C
Mother's Home Life.	170 E. Second St. Winona, Minn.	Mo —	.20/10	.50/L/3				C
Mother's Manual...........	230 Park Ave. New York, N.Y.	Qt 120,046		4.25/L				C
Motion Picture............	205 E. 42nd St. New York 17, N.Y.	Mo 985,458	8.75	3.95/L/7		Retail Shopping Section		C
Motor Trend Magazine.......	5959 Hollywood Blvd. Los Angeles 28, Calif.	546,105		7./L/14	Yes	Mail Order Section		C
Movie Land & TV Time.	21 W. 26th St. New York 10, N.Y.	Mo 214,628		1.50/L/14				C
Mr............	21 W. 26th St. New York 10, N.Y.	6/year 187,000		1./L/14				C
My Baby Magazine..........	175 Rock Rd. Glen Rock, N.J.	Mo 551,748		10.50/L/35	Yes			C
My Romance Group.........	667 Madison Ave. New York 21, N.Y.	Bi 479,378		3./L/14			True Secrets My Confessions My Romance Life Story Confessions	C

Publication	Address	Freq./Circ.	Rate	Rate	Notes	Code
N.A.R.D. Almanac	1 E. Wacker Dr. Chicago 1, Ill.	An 1,684,325		4.80/L		C
Nation	333 6th Ave. New York 14, N.Y.	Wk 28,231	.74/L	.84/L		C
Nation's Agriculture	2300 Merchandise Mart Chicago 54, Ill.	Mo 61,457	.15	1./L/14		B
National Boating Magazine	James Bldg. Chattanooga 2, Tenn.	50,000	3./L			O
National Enquirer	8117 3rd Ave. Brooklyn 9, N.Y.	Wk 839,782	.45	1./L/14		O
The National Informer	3811 W. North Ave. Chicago 47, Ill.	—	.20	.55/L		O
National Insider	3755 West Armitage Chicago 47, Ill.	200,000	.20/10	.50/L/14		O
The National Jewish Monthly	55 W. 42d St. New York 36, N.Y.	Mo 188,798		1.90/L/14	Publishers Resorts Hotels Schools Camps	C
National Livestock Producer	155 N. Wacker Dr. Chicago 2, Ill.	Mo 288,636	.55/8	3.25/L/7		C
National News	c/o American Legion 777 N. Meridian Indianapolis 7, Ind.	Mo 851,062	1.25	7.40/L/14	Auxiliary Family Shopper	C
National Observer	44 Broad St. New York 4, N.Y.	Wk 165,224	Request	2./L/28		C
National Star Chronicle	17 E. 48th St. New York 17, N.Y.	Biwk 300,000		14./N		O
Nature's Path	343 Lexington Ave. New York 16, N.Y.	Mo —		.84/L/14		O
Navy Times	2020 M St., N.W. Washington 6, D.C.	Wk —				C
Nebraska Electric Farmer	216 N. 11th St. Lincoln, Nebr.	Mo 54,939	*	.61/L/14		C
Nebraska Farmer	1420 P Street Lincoln 1, Nebr.	SemiMo 106,565	.16	1.70/L/7		C
New England Homestead	29 Worthington St. Springfield, Mass.	Mo 82,444	.18	1.50/L/7		C

Name	Address	Circulation	If classified, cost per word	Display cost per line (L) or inch (N)	Free editorial shopping section?	Paid shopping section	Magazines in group	Source of basic data
New Man	299 Madison Ave. New York 17, N.Y.	Bi 150,000		.75/L				O
New Mexico Electric News	208 Petroleum Bldg. Sante Fe, N. Mex.	Mo 40,000	*	1.09/L/14				C
New Republic	1244 19th St. N.W. Washington 6, D.C.	Wk 72,607	.12	1.05/L				C
New York Amsterdam News	2340 8th Ave. New York, N.Y.			.75/L				O
New York Herald Tribune Sunday Magazine	230 W. 41st St. New York 36, N.Y.	Wk 428,011		2.37/L/14		Shop Window		P
New York Journal-American Pictorial Magazine	New York 15, N.Y.	Wk 773,579		2.25/L/14		Shop by Mail		P
New York Sunday News Magazine	220 E. 42d St. New York 17, N.Y.	Wk 3,147,219		550./1/20 page		Newspaper Mail Order		P
New York Times Garden Section	229 W. 43d St. New York, N.Y.	Wk		2./L/10				P
New York Times Magazine	229 W. 43d St. New York, N.Y.	Wk 1,304,447		4.10/L/14	Yes			P
News Front	21 W. 45th St. New York 36, N.Y.	Mo 79,336		355./1/6 page	Yes			C
Newsweek	152 W. 42nd St. New York 36, N.Y.	Wk 1,600,948		25.50/L/14	Yes			C
North Dakota Rural Electric Magazine	Box 1077 Bismarck, N. Dak.	Mo 41,361	*	.70/L/14				C
North West Ruralite	Box 1731 Portland 7, Ore.	Mo 59,628	*	.77/L/14				C
Nugget	545 5th Ave. New York 17, N.Y	Bi 301,986		67.50/N				C
Official Detective Stories	320 Park Ave. New York 22, N.Y.	Mo 292,168		1.50/L/14				C

Publication	Address	Freq./Circ.				Section	Other titles	Code
Ohio State Grange Monthly	1030 E. Broad St., Columbus 5, Ohio	Mo 86,917	.12/22	11.76/N		Trading Post		C
Oklahoma Farm Bureau Farmer	Box 3332, Oklahoma City 5, Okla.	Mo 39,100		.36/L/7				C
Oklahoma Ranch & Farm World	315 S. Boulder, Tulsa 2, Okla.	Wk 153,360	7.56/N	7.56/N				P
Oklahoma Rural News	2726 N. Oklahoma, Oklahoma City 5, Okla.	Mo 110,877	*	.53/L/14				C
Old Farmer's Almanac	Dublin, N.H.	An 959,457	3./20	18./L/14				C
On the QT	21 W. 26th St., New York 10, N.Y.	Bi 175,000		1./N				O
Organic Gardening & Farming	Rodale Press, Inc. Organic Park, Emmaus 2, Pa.	Mo 297,271	17.50/25 or less	83./N	Yes	Mail Order Market Place		C
Our Sunday Visitor—Register Unit	30 N. Dearborn St., Chicago 2, Ill.	Wk 1,307,363	1.40/12	5.80/L/14				P
Outdoor Life	355 Lexington Ave., New York 17, N.Y.	Mo 1,191,792	Request	12./L/14	Yes	Mail Order Shopping Section		C
Overseas Family	380 Lexington Ave., New York 17, N.Y.	Wk 21,224	.15	.65/L/28, 2 col.				C
Pacific Northwest Farm Quad.	401 Review Bldg., Spokane 8, Wash.	SemiMo 172,772	.35/L/7	2.50/L/7			Idaho Farmer, Oregon Farmer, Utah Farmer, Washington Farmer	C
Pack-O-Fun	14 Main St., Park Ridge, Ill.	Mo 188,148	.70/L/10	4.50/L/14				C
Pageant	205 E. 42d St., New York 17, N.Y.	Mo 514,991		795./½ page				C
Parents Magazine & Better Homemaking	52 Vanderbilt Ave., New York 17, N.Y.	Mo 1,889,408		29.50	Yes	Shopping Scout		C
Pennsylvania Angler	1339 E. Philadelphia St., York, Pa.	Mo			Yes			A
Pennsylvania Grange News	1604 N. 2nd St., Harrisburg, Pa.	Mo 41,320	6./N/1	6./N				C
Peril	480 Lexington Ave., New York 17, N.Y.	Bi 150,000		.75/L				O
Personal Romances	295 Madison Ave., New York 17, N.Y.	Mo 268,780	13.95/10/PCD	1.55/L/14				C

Name	Address	Circulation	If classified, cost per word	Display cost per line (L) or inch (N)	Free editorial shopping section?	Paid shopping section	Magazines in group	Source of basic data
Pet Life Magazine...........	245 Cornelison Ave. Jersey City 2, N.J.	QT 241,500		48.50/N		Shopping News		C
Philadelphia Enquirer Today Magazine	400 N. Broad St. Philadelphia 1, Pa.	Wk 1,000,980	2./L/14	175./⅟₂₀ page				P
Photoplay..................	205 E. 42d St. New York 17, N.Y.	Mo 1,616,608	13.95/10	11.96/L/7				C
Pictorial Living...........	701 Hearst Bldg. San Francisco 3, Calif.	Wk 1,180,560		2.30/L (L.A.) 2./L (S.F.)		Mail Man		P
Pictorial Sunday Magazine Group	410 Park Ave. New York 10, N.Y.	Wk 450,503		1.24/L/14			Boston Sunday Advertiser Pictorial Revue & T-Vue Magazine	P
Pimienta...................	155 W. 72d St. New York 23, N.Y.	Mo —		7./N				C
Pines Screen Group.......	355 Lexington Ave. New York 17, N.Y.	Bi 273,300		1.88/L			Screenland Silver Screen	C
Pittsburgh Inquirer "Today"..	400 N. Broad St. Philadelphia 1, Pa.	Wk 1,000,980	2.60/L/14	175./⅟₂₀ page				P
Playboy....................	232 E. Ohio St. Chicago 11, Ill.	Mo —	300./N	300./N	Yes	Mail Order		C
Poise......................	525 Lexington Ave. New York 17, N.Y.	10 yearly 5,124,913		25.50/L/14				C
Police Gazette.............	250 W. 57th St. New York 19, N.Y.	Mo 206,000		1.75/L/14				C
Popular Boating...........	1 Park Ave. New York 16, N.Y.	Mo 187,709	.35/10 (used boats & equip. only)	120./N				C

Magazine	Address	Freq./Circ.	Rate	Rate		Section	
Popular Bowling	215 Park Ave. S., New York 3, N.Y.	Bi 210,652		100./N			C
Popular Dogs	2009 Ramstead St., Philadelphia 3, Pa.	Mo 20,939		12./N			C
Popular Electronics	1 Park Ave., New York 16, N.Y.	Bi 421,489	.60/10	171./N		Bargain Basement Shopping Section	C
Popular Gardening	383 Madison Ave. New York, N.Y.	Mo 325,272	5.10/L/14 (M.O.) .70/20	6.45/L/14	Yes	Mail Order Shopping	C
Popular Mechanics	200 E. Ontario St. Chicago 11, Ill.	Mo 1,325,393	15.50/L (M.O.)	18.75/L/14	Yes	Mail Order	C
Popular Medicine	66 Leonard St., New York 13, N.Y.	Bi 48,575	1.35/10 .50/12	1.25/L			C
Popular Photography	1 Park Ave. New York 16, N.Y.	Mo 397,836	1./10	174./N	Yes	Photographic Market Place	C
Popular Science	355 Lexington Ave. New York 17, N.Y.	Mo 1,254,598	190./N (M.O.) 1.20/10	17.86/L/14	Yes	Mail Order	C
Poultry Tribune	Mt. Morris, Ill.	Mo 163,598	.50/10	5./L/7			C
The Poultryman	N. Delsea Drive Vineland 5, N.J.	Wk 47,935	.20	1.40/L/14			C
Practical Knowledge	210 S. Clinton St. Chicago 6, Ill.	Bi 110,000					
Prairie Farmer	1230 Washington Blvd. Chicago 7, Ill.	SemiMo 359,228	.39/15	3.80/L/7			C
Presbyterian Life	Witherspoon Bldg. Philadelphia 7, Pa.	SemiMo 1,131,532	?	10.35/L/14			C
Presbyterian Survey	341 Ponce De Leon Ave. Atlanta 8, Ga.	Mo 253,102		1.90/L/14			C
Prevention	Emmaus 2, Pa.	Mo 308,621	20./25 or less	120./N			C
Progressive Farmer	821 N. 19th St. Birmingham 2, Ala.	Mo 1,405,316	.94	163.80/N	Yes		C
Psychic Observer	Drawer 90 Southern Pines, N.C.		.30/L/6	6./N			O

Name	Address	Circulation	If classified, cost per word	Display cost per line (L) or inch (N)	Free editorial shopping section?	Paid shopping section	Magazines in group	Source of basic data
Publisher's Men's Bimonthlies	Publishers Classified Department 549 W. Washington St. Chicago 6, Ill.	Bi 7,636,228	7.15/10				Adventures Amazing Detective Best True Fact Detective Crime Confessions Fifteen Detective Stories Fifteen Western Tales Headquarters Detective Man-to-Man Men-in-Action Men's Pictorial Mr. Police Detective Railroad Real Detective Real Police Stories Sir Special Detective Startling Detective True Adventure True Cases True Crime True Mystery Magazine True Police Cases Women in Crime	C

Publisher	Address		Rate	C	Titles
Publisher's Men's Monthlies	549 W. Washington St. Chicago 6, Ill.	Mo 2,929,993	3.85/10	C	Western Story Roundup; Cavalier; For Men Only; Male; Master Detective; Men; Saga; Sport; Stag; True Detective
Publisher's Women's Bimonthlies	Publishers Classified Department 549 W. Washington St. Chicago 6, Ill.	Bi 5,031,429	4.75/10	C	Actual Romance; All Story Love; Confessions; Fifteen Love Stories; Filmland; Hit Parader; Hollywood Stars; Intimate Love Stories; Life Confessions; Life Romance; Love Short Stories; My Confessions; My Romance; Rangeland Romances; Romance Confessions; Screen Life; Screen Star; Secret Confessions; Song Hits; True Secrets; TV Fan; TV People; TV World

Name	Address	Circulation	If classified, cost per word	Display cost per line (L) or inch (N)	Free editorial shopping section?	Paid shopping section	Magazines in group	Source of basic data
Publisher's Women's Monthlies	549 W. Washington St. Chicago 6, Ill.	Mo 11,117,840	13.95/10				Daring Romances, Intimate Romances, Modern Romances, Modern Screen, Motion Picture & TV Magazine, Movielife, Movie Star Parade, Photoplay, Radio-TV Mirror, True Confessions, Revealing Romances, Screen Stories, Secrets, True Experience, True Love Stories, True Romance, True Story, TV Star Parade	C
Puck The Comic Weekly......	410 Park Ave. New York 22, N.Y.	Wk 11,107,115		11,500./½ page				P
Radio Electronics...........	154 W. 14th St. New York 11, N.Y.	Mo 164,356	.50/10	36.40/N				B
Radio-TV Experimenter......	505 Park Ave. New York 22, N.Y.	Qt 110,695	.55/10	40./½ page				C
Rage......................	480 Lexington Ave. New York 17, N.Y.	Bi 150,000		.75/L				O
Railroad Magazine...........	205 E. 42d St. New York 17, N.Y.	Bi 23,851		1.50/L/14				C

Publication	Address	Frequency / Circulation	Rate	Rate	Merchandise Depot		Publications	
Railroad Model Craftsman....	P.O. Box C, Ramsey, N.J.	Mo 36,351		1.41/L/14				C
Real Life Guide.............	150 Lafayette St., New York 13, N.Y.	Mo		35./¼ page				O
Redbook Magazine...........	230 Park Ave., New York 17, N.Y.	Mo 3,708,504 Bi		34.83/L/7	Tops in the Shops	Yes		C
Reese Medical Group..........	1457 Broadway, New York 10036, N.Y.	450,000		1.50/L			Medical Confession, Medical Story, Nurse's & Doctor's Stories	O
Reese Men's Group............	1457 Broadway, New York 10036, N.Y.	Every 6 wks 400,000		1.50/L			Man's Story, Men Today	O
The Reporter.................	660 Madison Ave., New York 21, N.Y.	BiWk 172,160	2.75/L	4.80/L/35				C
Retirement Life..............	1625 Connecticut Ave. N.W., Washington 9, D.C.	Mo 102,000	.25/10	1.25/L/14				C
Rhythm & Blues Group.........	Charlton Bldg., Derby, Conn.	Qt 123,615		.60/L/14			Rhythm & Blues, Rock & Roll Songs	C
The Ring....................	307 W. 49th St., Madison Square Garden, New York 19, N.Y.	Mo —		1.25/L/14				C
Road and Track..............	834 Production Pl., Newport Beach, Calif.	Mo 190,581	5./25 or less	85./N	Mail Order			C
Rogue......................	1236 Sherman Ave., Evanston, Ill.	Mo 291,750	3./L/14	50./N				C
The Rotarian................	1600 Ridge Ave., Evanston, Ill.	Mo 390,811		4.25/L/14	Sale by Mail	Yes		C
The Royal Neighbor..........	230 16th, Rock Island, Ill.	Mo 348,558	.75/10	2.50/L/5				C
Rural Arkansas..............	Box 3446, N. Little Rock, Ark.	Mo 110,709	*	.61/L/14				C
Rural Electric Missourian.....	The Shoreham Bldg., 15th & H Sts. N.W., Washington 5, D.C.	Mo 179,115	*	.90/L/14				C
Rural Georgia...............	Box 929, Millen, Ga.	Mo 93,349	*	.47/L/14				C
Rural Granure...............	201 N. Wells, Chicago 6, Ill.	Mo 650,075		7./L				O

Name	Address	Circulation	If classified, cost per word	Display cost per line (L) or inch (N)	Free editorial shopping section?	Paid shopping section	Magazines in group	Source of basic data
Rural Kentuckian................	4515 Bishop Lane Louisville 18, Ky.	Mo 186,056	*	1.34/L/14				C
Rural Louisiana.................	Box 749 Opelousas, La.	Mo 85,966	*	.46/L/14				C
Rural Minnesota.................	Box 250 Alexandria, Minn.	Mo 107,551	.12	.65/L/14				C
Rural New Yorker...............	311 W. 43rd St. New York 36, N.Y.	Mo 152,124	.28	2.50/L/7				C
Rural Virginia..................	205 W. Franklin St. Richmond 20, Va.	Mo 88,430	*	.89/L/14				C
Rx Health......................	1447 Northern Blvd. Manhasset, N.Y.	Mo 83,387		360./¼ page				C
Sacred Heart Messenger.......	515 E. Fordham Rd. New York 58, N.Y.	Mo 157,690		1.50/L/7				C
Saga...........................	205 E. 42d St. New York 17, N.Y.	Mo 262,700		2.98/L/7	Yes	Shop in the Shops		C
St. Anthony Messenger........	1615 Republic St. Cincinnati 10, Ohio	Mo 336,438		2./L/28	Yes			C
St. Jude.......................	3818 Chestnut St. Philadelphia 4, Pa.	Mo 113,116		1./L/14				P
St. Louis Globe Democrat Sunday Magazine	St. Louis 1, Mo.	Wk 358,523		63./½0 page				P
St. Louis Post Dispatch Sunday Roto Magazine	St. Louis 1, Mo.	Wk 564,337		2./L/42				P
Salesman's Opportunity......	850 N. Dearborn St. Chicago 10, Ill.	Mo —	1./12	4.20/L/14	Yes			B
Salt Water Sportsman.........	157 Federal St. Boston 10, Mass.	Mo 51,498		17.50/N				C
Sample Case...................	632 N. Park St. Columbus 8, Ohio	Mo 233,851	.60/21	1.30/L/14				C

						Mail Mart		P
San Francisco Examiner Pictorial Living in Tabloid "Highlight"	Market & 3d Sts., San Francisco 19, Calif.	Wk 442,350	1.35/L	2./L/14				C
Saturday Review	25 W. 45th St., New York 36, N.Y.	Wk 306,031	.60	8.25/L/14		Retail Display		C
Scene	N. Katz, 480 Lexington Ave., New York 17, N.Y.	Bi 150,000		300./pg.				O
Scholastic Magazines Group	50 W. 44th St., New York 36, N.Y.	Wk 3,900,000		40./L/9			Scholastic Magazines, Co-ed, Science World	C
Science & Mechanics	505 Park Ave., New York, N.Y.	Mo 367,258	.75/10	70./N	Yes			C
Science Newsletter	1719 N St., N.W., Washington 6, D.C.	Wk 75,364	.25/20	1.35/L/14				C
Scouting Magazine	New Brunswick, N.J.	Mo 1,269,779		5.60/L/7				C
Screenland	4355 Lexington Ave., New York 17, N.Y.	Bi 273,300		1.88/L/14	Yes			C
Screen Stars Group	667 Madison Ave., New York 21, N.Y.	Bi 351,329		1.35/L/14			Movie World, Screen Stars	C
Screen Stories	750 3d Ave., New York 17, N.Y.	Mo 252,198	13.95/10/PCD	1.80/L/7				C
Secrets Romance Group	17 W. 44th St., New York 36, N.Y.	Mo 970,014	13.95/10/PCD	5.40/L/14			Secrets, Revealing Romances, Daring Romances, Confidential Confessions	C
Sepia	1220 Harding St., Fort Worth, Tex.	Mo 58,856		1.25/L/14				C
Seventeen	320 Park Ave., New York 22, N.Y.	Mo 1,117,143		8.30/L/28	Yes	Shopwise Section		C
Sexology	25 W. Broadway, New York 7, N.Y.	Mo 180,000		135./½ page				O
Shooting Times	P. O. Box 1500, War Memorial Dr., Peoria, Ill.	Mo 83,241	.10/20	1.39/L				C

Name	Address	Circulation	If classified, cost per word	Display cost per line (L) or inch (N)	Free editorial shopping section?	Paid shopping section	Magazines in group	Source of basic data
Show..................	140 E. 57th St. New York 22, N.Y.	Mo 150,105		180/2N				C
Silver Screen..........	355 Lexington Ave. New York 17, N.Y.	Bi 271,539		1.88/L/14	Yes			C
Sir!..................	21 W. 26th St. New York 10, N.Y	Mo 297,260		1.50/L/14				C
Sir Knight............	N. Katz 480 Lexington Ave. New York 17, N.Y.	Bi 400,000		3./L				O
Ski..................	800 2nd Ave. New York 17, N.Y.	Mo 119,784		5./L/14	Yes	Ski Shopping Guide		C
Skiing...............	7190 W. 14th Ave. Denver, Colo.	6/year 75,104		46./N		Shopping with Skiing		C
Skye Men's Group......	505 8th Ave. New York, N.Y.	Bi 810,000		1./L			Lineup Detective Cavalcade Expose for Men Men in Adventure True Crime	C
Small Stock Magazine...	118 S. Linden St. Lamoni, Iowa	Mo 10,000						A
Song Hits.............	Charlton Bldg. Derby, Conn.	Mo 131,610		1./L/14				C
South Carolina Electric Co-op News	808 Knox Abbott Dr. Cayce, S.C.	Mo 116,090	*	1.03/L/14				C
South Dakota High-Liner...	218 S. Egan Madison, S. Dak.	Mo 64,844	*	.38/L/14				C
Southern Planter.......	223 Governor St. Richmond 9, Va.	Mo 296,177	.32	42./N				C
Spare Time...........	744 N. 4th St. Milwaukee 3, Wis.	Irregularly 503,275	2./15	119./N				B

Publisher	Address	Circulation	Rate (line/issues)	Rate (space)	Guaranteed	Department	Publications	Class
Specialty Salesman	307 N. Michigan Ave. Chicago 1, Ill.	Mo —	1./12	545./1 col.				B
Speed & Custom	26 W. 47th St. New York 36, N.Y.	Mo 170,580	.25/10	19.60/N		Mail Order		C
Speed Mechanics	17 W. 44th St. New York 36, N.Y.	Bi 90,676			Yes			A
Sport	205 E. 42d St. New York 17, N.Y.	Mo 618,032	3.85/10/PCD	5.71/L/7	Yes	Sport in the Shops		C
Sports Afield	959 8th Ave. New York 19, N.Y.	Mo 1,182,776	.70/14	11.75/L/14	Yes	Shopping Afield		C
Sports Car Graphic	5959 Hollywood Blvd. Los Angeles 28, Calif.	Mo 115,753		2.85/L/14		Mail Order		C
Sports Review	502 National Bldg. Minneapolis, Minn.	Qt —						A
Spree	480 Lexington Ave. New York 17, N.Y.	Bi 200,000		1.50/L				O
Standard Magazine Group	355 Lexington Ave. New York 17, N.Y.	Mo —	.30/20	1.10/L/14			Ranch Romances / Popular Crossword / Astrology / New Crossword	C
Star Time	1457 Broadway New York 36, N.Y.	Bi 235,000		1./L				O
Sterling Detective Group	730 3d Ave. New York 17, N.Y.	Bi 197,502		1./L/7			Confidential Detective Cases / Crime Detective	C
Sterling Men's Group	730 3d Ave. New York 17, N.Y.	Bi 204,590		1.30/L/7			Man's Conquest / Man's Illustrated	C
Sterling Movie Group	730 3d Ave. New York 17, N.Y.	Mo 474,588		200./1 col.			Movie Mirror / TV & Movie Screen	C
Sterling Women's Group	730 3d Ave. New York 17, N.Y.	Mo 825,682		3.40/L/7 (4 times)			Movie Mirror / TV & Movie Screen / TV Picture Life / Real Confessions / My Secret Story	C
Street & Smith Group	420 Lexington Ave. New York 17, N.Y.	An 782,856		150./¼ col. 140./½ col. 135./½ col.		Mail Order	Football Yearbook / Baseball Yearbook / Pro Football Yearbook	C
Suburbia Today	575 Lexington Ave. New York 22, N.Y.	Mo 1,598,050		9.25/L/14				P

Name	Address	Circulation	If classified, cost per word	Display cost per line (L) or inch (N)	Free editorial shopping section?	Paid shopping section	Magazines in group	Source of basic data
Successful Farming	1716 Locust St. Des Moines 3, Iowa	Mo 1,322,627	1.35/14	14.56/L/5	Yes	Mail Order		C
Successful Selling	31 W. 47th St. New York 36, N.Y.	Irregularly	.90/12	3.95/L/7				B
Sunbelt Dairyman	318 Murfreesboro Rd. Nashville 10, Tenn. Box 10670	Mo 52,101	.22/10	23.52/N				C
Sunrise	St. Petersburg, Fla.		2.50/L/4	2.50/L/14				O
Sunset Magazine	Menlo Park, Calif.	Mo 716,375		9.85/L/7		Shopping Center		C
Surplus & Salvage Projects	505 Park Ave. New York, N.Y.	An —	.50/10	38./N				C
Sword of the Lord	214 W. Wesley St. Wheaton, Ill.	Wk 71,646	.20/25	.85/L/14				C
Syndicare Health Magazine	25 W. 45th St. New York 36, N.Y.	Mo 111,033		1./¼ col.				C
Tab Men's Unit	509 5th Ave. New York 17, N.Y.	Bi —		2.40/L/14			Tab Vue	C
Teen	5959 Hollywood Blvd. Los Angeles 28, Calif.	Mo 565,253		7./L/14		Mail Order Section		C
Teen Screen	6257 Leland Way Hollywood 28, Calif.	Mo 304,215		3.25/L/14		Mail Order		C
Tennessee Farm Bureau News	Box 313 Columbia, Tenn.	Mo 65,733	.15	5.60/L				C
Tennessee Farmer & Homemaker	Box 210 Middletown, Ky.	Mo 103,289	.20/15	1.10/L/7				C
Tennessee Magazine	1717 West End Bldg. Nashville 3, Tenn.	Mo 148,577	*	1.13/L/14				C
Texas Agriculture	Box 489 Waco, Tex.	Mo 83,569	.20/15	8./N				C

Publication	Address	Frequency / Circulation		Rate	Accepts ads	Special sections	Class
Texas Co-op Power.........	Box 9248 Allandale Station Austin 17, Tex.	Mo 210,035	*	.96/L/14			C
Texas Farm & Ranch......	400 W. 7th St. Fort Worth 1, Tex.	Mo —	.60/L/3	.63/L			O
This Day............	35585 Jefferson St. Louis 18, Mo.	Mo —		1.15/L/14			C
This Week Magazine.	485 Lexington Ave. New York 17, N.Y.	Wk 14,128,727		55.23/L/14	Yes		C
Timely Men's Group.........	509 5th Ave. New York 17, N.Y.	Qt 350,000		2.25/L		Scamp Bachelor Romance Time Screen Parade	O
Timely Women's Group.....	509 5th Ave. New York 17, N.Y.	Bi —		2./L/14			C
Today's Health........	535 N. Dearborn St. Chicago 10, Ill.	Mo 820,389		8.65/L/14	Yes		C
Today's Secretary.........	330 W. 42d St. New York 36, N.Y.	Mo 136,163		95.25/⅛ page	Yes	Today's Secretary Goes Shopping	C
Together............	P. O. Box 423 1661 N.N.W. Highway Park Ridge, Ill.	Mo 757,031		7.85/L/14	Yes	Shopping Together	C
Top Men's Group.........	299 Madison Ave. New York 17, N.Y.	Bi 250,000		1.20/L		Man's Book World of Men	O
Topper............	480 Lexington Ave. New York 17, N.Y.	Mo 175,000		1./L			O
Toros............	P. O. Box 987 Chola Vista, Calif.	Mo 10,000	.15				O
Town and Country.........	572 Madison Ave. New York 22, N.Y.	Mo 91,208		250./⅛ page	Yes		C
Toys & Novelties.........	111 4th Ave. Chicago 11, Ill.	Mo 8,796	.12/50	65./⅙ page	Yes		B
Trail Blazer's Almanac........	206 W. 4th St. Kowanee, Ill.	An 1,000,000	1./14	7./L/10			O
Trailer Topics.........	28 E. Jackson Blvd. Chicago 4, Ill.	Mo 50,908	.25	25./N			O
Travel............	Travel Bldg. Floral Park, N.Y.	Mo 203,113	.75/20	215./⅛ page			O
Tropical Living.........	3671 N.W. 52nd St. Miami 42, Fla.	Bi 6,200	.30/10	1.05/L/14	Yes	Tropical Market-place	C

Name	Address	Circulation	If classified, cost per word	Display cost per line (L) or inch (N)	Free editorial shopping section?	Paid shopping section	Magazines in group	Source of basic data
True.............	67 W. 44th St. New York 36, N.Y.	Mo 2,425,075		27./L/14		Retail Shopping Section		C
True Confessions......	67 W. 44th St. New York 36, N.Y.	Mo 1,143,948		8.65/L/14	Yes	Retail Shopping Section		C
True Detective........	205 E. 42d St. New York 17, N.Y.	Mo 300,222		1.58/L/7				C
True Divorce.........	1457 Broadway	Bi 200,000		.60/L				O
True Experience........	205 E. 42d St. New York 36, N.Y.	Mo 356,529	13.95/10/PCD	2.30/L/7				C
True Love...........	205 E. 42d St. New York 17, N.Y.	Mo 316,946	13.95/10/PCD	2.30/L/7				C
True Medic Group......	32 W. 22d St. New York 10, N.Y.	Bi 163,303		2./L/14			True Medic Stories Real Medic Stories	C
True Men Stories.......	32 W. 22d St. New York 10, N.Y.	Bi 143,910		1.75/L/14				C
True Romance.........	205 E. 42d St. New York 17, N.Y.	Mo 519,735	13.95/10/PCD	2.84/L/7				C
True Story...........	205 E. 42d St. New York 17, N.Y.	Mo 2,116,700	13.95/10/PCD	19.31/L/7				C
True West...........	Box 5008 Austin, Tex.	Bi 167,925	.20/10	1.08/L				O
Turf & Sport Digest......	511–513 Oakland Ave. Baltimore 12, Md.	Mo 41,499		1./L/14				C
Turkey World.........	Mount Morris 2, Ill.	Mo 14,311	.20/10	30.80/2N				B
Uncensored...........	480 Lexington Ave. New York 17, N.Y.	Bi —		2./L/14				C
United Church Herald......	1720 Chouteau Ave. St. Louis 3, Mo.	BiWk 140,267		1.30/L/14				O

Publication	Address	Circulation	Rate	Rate		Market Place	Titles	A
United States Amateur Hockey Magazine						Market Place		
U.S. Camera...............	9 E. 40th St., New York 16, N.Y.	Mo 211,167	.65/10	84./N	Yes	Shopping Guide		C
Variety Store Merchandiser...	419 Park Ave. S., New York 16, N.Y.	Mo 29,115		180,/⅛ page	Yes			B
VFW Magazine..............	406 W. 34th St., Kansas City 11, Mo.	Mo 1,123,327		6.10/L/14 (12 times)		Mail Order Shopper		C
Vice Squad.................	730 3d Ave.	Bi		.75/L				O
Vogue.....................	420 Lexington Ave., New York 17, N.Y.	SemiMo 499,840		545./⅛ page	Yes	Shop Hound		C
Vogue Pattern Book........	161 6th Ave., New York 13, N.Y.	Bi 282,838		360,/½ col.				C
Wall Street Journal........	44 Broad St., New York, N.Y.	Daily 798,169	7.29/L/14	7.29/L/14				C
Wallace's Farmer..........	1912 Grand Ave., Des Moines 5, Iowa	SemiMo 238,603	.30/10	2.80/L/7				C
Washington Grange News....	3104 Western Ave., Seattle, Wash.	SemiMo 33,428	.15/10	.54/L/14				C
Washington Star Sunday Magazine	Washington 3, D.C.	Wk 313,112		1.35/L		Mail Order		P
Western Livestock Journal...	4511 Produce Plaza, Los Angeles 58, Calif.	Mo 51,716	.12/9	12.75/N				C
Western Farm Life.........	Box 299, Denver 1, Colo.	BiWk 142,056	.22	1.65/L/7				C
Western Farmer............	201 Elliott Ave. W., Seattle 99, Wash.	Mo 42,724	.15/20	8.20/N				C
Western Horseman..........	3850 N. Nevada Ave., Colorado Springs, Colo.	Mo 138,717	.50/10	33./N	Yes	Shoppers Corral		C
Westways..................	2601 S. Figueroa St., Los Angeles 54, Calif.	Mo 249,764		2.80/L/14				C
Whisper...................	730 3d Ave., New York 17, N.Y.	Bi —		1./L/14				C
Whitestone Detective Annuals	67 W. 44th St., New York 36, N.Y.	An —		1./L			True Police Yearbook Startling Detective Yearbook Best Detective Cases	C

Name	Address	Circulation	If classified, cost per word	Display cost per line (L) or inch (N)	Free editorial shopping section?	Paid shopping section	Magazines in group	Source of basic data
Winter Sports	Box 7858 Denver 15, Colo.	Qt	.20/17	.42/L	Yes			C
Wisconsin Farm News	115 S. Carroll St. Madison 1, Wis.	88,403 Mo	*	.55/L/14				C
Wisconsin REA News	Box 686 Madison 1, Wis.	88,621 Mo		57.50/L/14				C
Woman's Day	67 W. 44th St. New York 36, N.Y.	6,169,084 Qt						
Woman's National Magazine		7,381				The Grapevine		
Women's Circle	P. O. Box 591 Lynn, Mass.	75,000 Mo	.12/10	.75/L/14				O
Woodmen Circle Tidings	3d & Farnam Omaha 31, Nebr.	112,355 Mo		1./L/3				C
Woodmen of the World Magazine	638 Insurance Bldg. Omaha 2, Nebr.	332,119 Mo	.75/10	2.50/L/5				C
Wool/Sack	306 4th St. Brookings, S. Dak.	47,484 Mo	.20/10	.40/L				C
Workbasket	543 Westport Rd. Kansas City 11, Mo.	1,211,245 Bi	1.75/10	12.35/L/14	Yes	Shoppers Section		C
Workbench	543 Westport Rd. Kansas City 11, Mo.	341,293 Mo	.90/10	4./L/14	Yes	Shoppers Showcase		C
World Outlook	3818 Chestnut St. Philadelphia 4, Pa.	123,685 Mo	.25	1.20/L/14				C
Writer's Digest	22 E. 12th St. Cincinnati 10, Ohio	51,150 Mo		21./N				C
Wyoming Stockman-Farmer	110 E. 17th St. Cheyenne, Wyo.	14,404	.37/L	.37/L/14				C

Name	Address	Freq./Circ.		Rate		
Yankee..........	Dublin, N.H.	Mo 102,849	.30	1.25/L/14		C
The Young Calvinist........	2365 Nelson Ave. S.E. Grand Rapids, Mich.	Mo 22,600				A
Young Catholic Messenger...	38 W. 5th St., Dayton 2, Ohio	Wk 869,258		8.20/L/7		C
Your Future............	730 3d Ave. New York 17, N.Y.	An 170,000		95./L/7		O
Your New Baby.........	52 Vanderbilt Ave. New York 17, N.Y.	Mo 698,165		13.10/L	Yes	C
Your Romance Group........	32 W. 22d St. New York 10, N.Y.	Qt 228,595		2./L/14		C Your Romance Thrilling Confessions
Ziff Davis Fiction Group......	1 Park Ave. New York 16, N.Y.	Mo 102,460	.35/10 (comb.) .25/10	20./L/14 (1 mag) 32./L/14 (comb.)		C Amazing Stories Fantastic Stories of Imagination Fact & Science Fiction

Look them up in the "Business Publication" section of *Standard Rate & Data*. This column should be up to date as of the publication date of this book. But magazine formats change. You yourself should keep the list up to date, and you should obtain the names of the shopping-section editors so that you can write to them personally.

CODE:

L	cost per line	SemiMo	semimonthly
N	cost per inch	Wk	weekly
An	annually	Mo	monthly
Bi	bimonthly	Qt	quarterly

Classified Rate: .14/12, to be read: 14¢ per word, 12-word minimum.
Display Rate: $1.50/L/14, to be read: $1.50 per line, 14-line minimum.

A *N. W. Ayer & Sons Directory*
B *Standard Rate & Data* (Business Publications)
C *Standard Rate & Data* (Consumer Magazines & Farm Publications)
P *Standard Rate & Data* (Newspapers)
O Other sources

* Write to Rural Electric Consumer Publications, Shoreham Building, 15th and H Sts., N.W., Washington 5, D.C., for rates.

Types of Successful Mail-Order Businesses

The purpose of this appendix is to list and describe for you a good many *specific* lines of mail-order businesses which it might be profitable for you to compete with.

It is very important for you to understand that this appendix is not about mail-order *items*. There are literally millions of items sold by mail order, but very few of these items are a business in themselves. What I am trying to describe in this appendix are *lines of items,* or *lines* of business, that will constitute a real business year in and year out.

Let me try to explain the difference. One of the most successful mail-order items in recent years was the flat-tire inflator can. It still sells by mail and will continue to sell, but in the catalogs of a dozen different firms. It may still be an entire business to its manufacturer, but it is only one item in a line of items for mail-order firms that sell it. The *line of items* may be automotive accessories, or novelties. We shall talk only about *lines of items*.

Of course, many items do constitute a business all by themselves; e.g., correspondence courses.

Here are some other examples of *products* that sell well by mail order, but are not likely to constitute a business unless you combine them with a line of similar goods. Note how many of them appear in novelty catalogs, sooner or later.

Blackhead remover	Confederate money
Cuckoo clock	One-way-glass formula
Address labels	Shrunken heads
Closet organizer	Magnets
Cleaning cloths	Supermarket cost counter
Huge balloon	Hand vacuum cleaner
Needle threader	Pocket calculator
Paper playhouse	

This appendix is far from inclusive. If it even scratches the surface, I shall be satisfied. Where I describe one firm, there may be twenty. You will have to do most of the searching for yourself. These are some places to look:

1. The advertising media. Chapter 3 gives you full instructions about how and where to look.

2. The lines of products listed in mail-order list brokers' catalogs. Chapter 15 tells about those catalogs.

3. B. Klein's *Directory of Mail-order Firms* gives some information on what firms sell.

4. The *Standard Advertising Register* and *McKittrick's* at your local library or a nearby advertising agency. Look under "Mail-order," "Books," "Correspondence courses," and similar listings.

5. Lee Mountain, Pisgah, Alabama, issues a catalog of books and correspondence courses he sells by mail. This is a helpful source of ideas.

It is often helpful to have some idea of the size of firms in a business you are interested in. It is difficult to find out the size of a business. Publishers' Information Bureau gives data on the amount that firms spend on advertising in the major consumer magazines. But in most cases, mail-order firms spend most or all of their advertising appropriation in direct mail or unlisted display media.

There is no special reason for the order of the listings in this appendix. I have tried to keep similar lines somewhere near each other. But you may find the same line or product popping up in several different places.

AGENT-SOLD PRODUCTS

Look through any of the salesmen's opportunity magazines to see perhaps 500 different lines in a single issue. We shall mention some of them when we list particular classes of products.

FOOD AND DRINK

Most of the food and drink that is sold by mail is gourmet stuff—special delicacies that are not easily obtainable in nearby stores, or very high-quality foods that gourmets are willing to pay a premium for.

There have been exceptions, but generally it is not possible to sell ordinary-quality foods by mail, even if you offer special price inducements. The cost of shipping is too high relative to the weight of the food to make it possible to offer real bargains.

Liquors, on the other hand, can be offered on a price basis under special circumstances, as we shall see.

There are many mail-order food ads in *Diners' Club* and similar magazines, especially before Christmas.

Meat

Fancy steaks are shipped frozen, by the dozen, at fancy prices. Several firms in the Midwest ship all over the country.

Smoked Ham, Smoked Turkey

Fish

For many years the famous Frank Davis Company in Gloucester, Massachusetts, advertised its mackerel and other fish by direct mail and in magazines. What happened to the firm? I don't know. Maybe there is room for someone, or maybe the market is gone.

Lobsters and Sea Food

A professor who got tired of teaching and who wanted to live on Cape Cod sells lobsters by mail order, far and wide.

Cheese

Cheese is a favorite mail-order food item. Distinctive cheeses are a specialty, and they travel well over long distances. Also, the price/weight ratio is good.

There are several firms in the business, selling through different techniques. Some sell direct to the consumer all year long. Others do most of their business in Christmas gifts. Still others sell their cheeses as *business* gifts. And then there is at least one cheese-of-the-month club plan.

Fruit

I am continuously surprised that fruit can be sold successfully by mail order. And yet, it can.

One fruit firm is responsible for a famous headline in a big ad in *Fortune*. It went something like "Imagine Harry and me advertising our pears in *Fortune!*"

Mail-order fruit is usually remarkably large and juicy and commands a stiff price. One firm sells apples by mail for 24 cents each. They're good, but I can't tell them from the extra-special dime apples I can buy in season right here in town.

One of the most famous and successful advertising men of all time started up a mail-order fruit business after he retired from his old job.

Preserves

There's a little old lady in a dingy little store on a side street in New York who makes her own preserves by hand and sells them by mail. She has been written up in several major magazines and gets orders from all over the world.

Fruit Cake

Candy

Sold to organizations for resale to their members and others, as a fund-raising campaign.

Pecans

Sold direct to consumers, and also to organizations for fund raising.

Coffee and Tea

My first mail-order venture was selling fancy coffee by mail. It was an enjoyable business. But it could never be very big, so I turned it over to someone else, who let it run down and die.

Gourmet Foods, Full Line

There are several firms, including one on the West Coast that has a fabulous millionaire customer list, that sell a full line of fancy foods. This is probably not an easy business to enter.

Health Foods

Look at *Organic Farming* and *Prevention* magazines to see the large numbers of firms, large and small, in this line.

Wine and Liquor

In big cities there are very successful liquor dealers who solicit orders by newspapers and direct-mail advertising. A natural for anyone in the liquor business who wants to branch out into mail order.

Duty-free Liquor

These firms solicit tourists before they go abroad. The liquor is delivered in the United States.

SMOKING MATERIALS

Cigarettes

Several years ago several companies in New Jersey did a thriving business selling cartons of cigarettes by mail to people in states that had higher taxes on cigarettes. But after a long fight the U.S. Supreme Court interfered with the practice. Now several of those firms sell other smoking materials by mail.

Cigarette-rolling Equipment

This ad has appeared for years in the classified sections of various men's magazines, sure evidence of a profitable business: "Cigarettes—Make 20 plain or filter-tip for 9¢. Facts free . . . ."

Cigarettes, Imprinted

A New York firm runs a regular 1-inch ad in the *New York Times* and other media offering cigarettes specially imprinted with "Happy Birthday," "Good Luck Joe" or whatever else you want. This is a good example of offering *personalized* goods as mail-order items.

Cigars

Many of the firms that sold cigarettes by mail turned to selling cigars by mail, and several of them are now thriving. They offer bargain offers and free trials in cigar-length one-column ads in various Sunday newspapers and mail-order sections of magazines. Their profit comes in the repeat business over a long period of time. Cigar smokers like to try various types of cigars from time to time, and the firms make their offers to their lists by direct mail.

A customer list of 25,000 to 75,000 should support a very nice business. Connections with manufacturers of cigars are very helpful in entering this business.

Fancy Smoking Articles

At least two old and famous firms in Boston, and one in New York, issue mail-order catalogs of every conceivable article and tobacco a smoker could want.

Pipes

Look for the ad that says, "Don't give up smoking until you try my pipe." It's a great ad and shows what can be done in this line by mail order.

Tobacco

There are several farm-magazine classified advertisers who sell tobacco by the pound, by mail.

Lighters

HEALTH AND MEDICAL PRODUCTS

Health and medical products, and information on these subjects, are great mail-order items. But be careful! Make sure that what you sell has real and scientifically proved value.

An advantage of this field is that most health preparations are easy to manufacture or to buy from a manufacturing chemist. But this advantage is also a disadvantage. Just as it is easy for you to break in, so it is easy for the competition to break in, too, once it is apparent that you have a profitable line on the market.

Vitamins

Vitamins are a classic mail-order item. Fortunes have been made in this field. Large companies and tiny ones, too, have been successful. Again, however, be very careful about making claims for the effect of vitamins which you can't substantiate. (As a matter of fact, I doubt that *any* claim of benefits for vitamins to *any* potential customers is scientifically reasonable. I think it is all quackery except for obvious diseases, and they require medical treatment.)

Nevertheless, people want vitamins and will continue to purchase them by mail—and in large dollar amounts every year.

Vitamins can be purchased wholesale from a variety of places, in bulk or made up into packages. A little shopping will locate suppliers for you.

The usual marketing technique is to offer a bargain rate for a short-term supply—or even free samples.

You will have plenty of competition, for there are probably *hundreds* of firms selling vitamins by mail. But of course that also proves what a good potential business it is.

Disease Cures

Several "clinics" of various healing persuasions offer their wares by mail. I suspect that some or all of these are quackery at its worst, but of course I can't say for sure (at least, not here).

Salve

There is a firm that sells a plain petroleum jelly salve. It advertises in comic books for small-boy agents. The owner nets $100,000 yearly and plays golf most of the day, according to the account given in a recent government investigation, I'm told.

Acne and Pimples

Blackhead Removers

Prescription Drugs

Several firms are already in the business of selling prescription drugs by mail at discount prices. I would guess that this will be a big, important, and respectable mail-order line in the future.

Hearing Aids

Several companies sell their hearing aids by mail, usually with the aid of agents in the field.

Eyeglasses, Prescription

Look for the occasional—but successful—ad of a company in this field. They sell at prices far below neighborhood opticians. I bet there is room for many more such companies than there are now.

Good advertising media are those that go to areas in which many elderly folk live.

Eyeglasses, Magnifying

Simple and cheap magnifying spectacles. A best seller for years. One firm sells a type that clips onto other eyeglasses for further magnification.

False Teeth and Dentures

Dental-plate Repair or Reliner Kit

Foot-care Materials

A New York firm sells an entire line of devices for bunions, hammer toes, etc. Looks like a good field, to me.

Nose-hair Scissors

Sold directly from ads as well as through other firms' novelty catalogs.

Reducing Preparations

If you can help people to reduce, you have a mail-order product. Dozens of different kinds of preparations have been sold. Most of them are clearly phony, and the government cracks down. Some of them have limited use, and are more or less within the law. My advice is that you don't go near this business with a 10-foot pole.

Reducing Books

Some reducing programs have real value, and can be sold honestly. Others cater to the dreams of those who want a miracle way to lose weight fast. The history of mail order is replete with excursions into this field. All I can say is: be careful; don't get sucked in by the lure of a quick buck.

Diets

There is always a market for appetizing but nonfattening meal plans.

Reducing, Exercise Equipment

Mechanical reducing ads range from $1.98 rubber stretch gadgets, to expensive exercycles. Don't try to sell massage equipment as an aid to reducing, because it just doesn't work.

Antismoking Aids

A rash of these items are hitting the market now, in the wake of recent scientific discoveries of tobacco dangers. Just what any drugs can or cannot do to stop or reduce smoking is questionable. You'll have to do a lot of research for yourself on this.

Antismoking Psychological "Programs"

One book on how to stop smoking sold over 300,000 copies. There are several "programs" selling for up to $50.

Sleep

One firm does well with a line of gadgets that help you sleep comfortably, read in bed, keep sound and light out, etc.

Birth-prevention Devices

It is not clear what the law is on selling information or devices to prevent pregnancy. At least one firm is selling prophylactics, through agents, by mail.

A book on the rhythm system has done well, too. Lately, at least one reputable firm has brought out a mail-order book on birth prevention and artificial contraception.

Trusses for Rupture

A classic mail-order item. One firm was already well-established in 1913, and still does well. Its ads have changed little in that time.

Posture Braces, Slimming Garments, and Girdles

Several firms make and/or sell various body braces. One firm sells an entire line of them, and will sell you its catalog and drop-ship for you, if you have a customer list that you can use it for. They also run their own display ads.

Lately the gift catalogs are carrying these devices.

Bedwetting-prevention Systems for Children

Medical Equipment

Stethoscopes and similar small pieces of equipment are sold to laymen through display advertising. Often billed as "surplus."

COSMETICS AND BEAUTY AIDS

You might guess that cosmetics would be an ideal mail-order line. They are high-markup, repeatedly-bought products, easily shipped by mail. But despite these advantages, full-line cosmetics have shown little promise for mail-order —probably because they require demonstration before women will buy them.

However, specialty cosmetics have succeeded in mail order, as have firms that sell through agents. In fact, two firms that sell cosmetics through agents are among the most flourishing mail-order firms.

Hair Removers (Depilatories)

Various methods of removing women's unwanted hair have done well in mail order. One firm that sells an electrolytic device has run practically the same ad for years and years in women's magazines, a sure sign of success. Another firm began in mail order and sold that way for years, before converting its operation mostly to selling through drugstores.

Special Antiperspirant Products

Fingernail Preservatives

Age-spot Removers

Perfume

Sometimes sold in a basket of many small bottles of various scents. Suffers as a mail-order item because women want to try the scent before they buy.

Wigs

Women's wigs sold successfully by mail long before the recent craze hit the nation.

Toupees for Men

A specialized, high-priced, successful mail-order item.

Men's Hair-coloring Preparations

Cosmetics for Negroes

Special preparations, especially for the hair, sell well by mail to Negroes. There is at least one large company, and many small ones, that specialize in this line. Look for their ads in magazines catering to Negroes.

In-shoe Height Raisers

Electric Shavers

Must be at bargain prices.

CLOTHING

Clothing always has been, and always will be, one of the great mail-order lines. But the mail-order offer must be different from clothes offered in local stores, either in type of clothing or in price.

Women's Dresses

A famous Pennsylvania firm offers unbelievable bargains in inexpensive women's dresses by direct mail.

Another huge firm sells frocks through agents that it recruits by a vast campaign of mail-order advertising in magazines and through direct mail.

Several exclusive dress shops sell some of their simpler styles through *The New York Times Magazine* and other media.

Special-size Women's Clothing

These lines are good examples of how and why mail order works. Many women throughout the country do not fit into the standard sizes of clothing offered at local stores. But the demand is not sufficient in most places for the stores to offer the additional sizes. A mail-order firm, however, can cater to the demand of these women all over the country, without having to fight local competition. In addition to dresses, coats and other clothing are sold.

Half sizes.

Extra-large sizes. One major firm also has department stores in the largest cities.

Small sizes.

Maternity sizes.

Uniforms

Many types of uniforms are sold by mail—to nurses, waitresses, etc. Men's uniforms are also a good mail-order line.

Special Brassieres and Lingerie

One firm sells a fantastic assortment of padded, stuffed, and tapered women's underwear that appear to be marvels of engineering genius. The display pictures make your eyes pop out. Some people buy their 25 cent catalog for entertainment.

Other firms sell only special brassieres, not designed to be spectacular.

A girdle firm has a mailing list of over 150,000 mail-order girdle buyers.

Stockings

Two huge firms sell women's hosiery through agents. They claim special long-wearing properties for their products, and they use imaginative and varied merchandising devices.

Women's Shoes, Wide Sizes

Furs

Fur-coat Remodeling

Wigs

Miscellaneous Women's Clothing

Various firms sell various lines of bathrobes, bathing suits, and other occasional clothing. The trick, of course, is to build a list of women who like the styles you sell.

Men's Suits

Several firms take orders for suits custom-made in Hong Kong.

Other firms have sold custom-made men's suits through agents for years and years.

And there are many exclusive (or expensive) men's shops that circularize the people who have formerly bought from them. They send out two or more brochures or catalogs each year, illustrating the styles they carry.

Men's Suit Remodeling

A specialty of at least two firms is cutting down old double-breasted suits into the up-to-date style. If you wanted to go into this business, you might work up an arrangement with a good tailor who wants to expand his business.

Men's Clothes, Large and Tall Sizes

Small sizes probably would not work as a specialty because of male vanity.

Men's Slacks

A famous New Jersey firm sold ties by mail for many years. Now, as far as I can tell, they are concentrating their energies on selling men's slacks. They send swatches of material in the direct-mail pieces, and offer pants made of DuPont material at bargain prices. It was probably their success that convinced Spiegel to jump into this line, in competition.

Men's Ties

One of Amerca's great advertising men had a hand in building a mail-order firm that sold ties made by hand by New Mexico Indians.

Men's Fancy Shirts

Bathing Suits

Men's Shirts, Custom Made

Men's Shoes

Several big companies sell men's shoes through agents. They use direct-mail, match books, space ads, and all other media to recruit salesmen. This is big business.

Men's Shoes, Large and Wide Sizes

Men's Shoes, Imported

A New Jersey fellow sells shoes imported from England. He advertises in classified and small display in *Saturday Review, The New York Times Magazine*, "shelter" magazines, etc.

He also runs a retail store. I've been in there, and it is a nice little business. He sends out a beautiful printed catalog.

Men's Huaraches, Imported

Moccasins

Riding Boots

Men's Uniforms

Some firms sell through agents.

Robes and Gowns

For ceremonial occasions, graduations, and ministers.

Men's Outdoor Clothing and Equipment

There are at least two fine old firms that sell men everything they need to be dry, warm, and good-looking in the outdoors. They also sell related equipment along with it.

Rain Suits

Western Clothing (Men)

Men's Work Clothes, Used

Small ads in lower-class men's magazines sell reconditioned work clothing for an Ohio firm.

Belts

Fabrics

Several firms sell fabrics by the yard to women who sew at home. You probably need to be near a garment center to be in this business, in order to be close to your supplies.

Fabric Remnants

Back in the '20s several firms did well selling remnants in large quantities at low prices. I would think there is still a good market for this proposition.

Wool

A nice little business in Connecticut sells wool to women (and men) who weave at home.

Sewing Accessories

There are a good many firms that sell women everything they need to sew at home. One firm specializes in dress dummies. Others sell a full line of notions. Look in *Workbasket* to see their offers.

JEWELRY

Diamonds

One firm sells by mail and emphasizes the investment aspect of buying diamonds. It advertises in the *Wall Street Journal,* among other media.

Pearls

Diamond Rings

Several outfits specialize in selling to servicemen. Look in *Army Times* to see their ads.

Synthetic Gems

This is a flourishing mail-order business. Just make sure your advertisements tell exactly what you are selling.

Watches

Richard Sears of Sears, Roebuck got his start selling watches by mail, and it's still a good mail-order business. You must offer a bargain, though.

Jewelry-making Hobby Supplies

AUTOS, BOATS, AND ACCESSORIES

Autos

The automobile manufacturers speculate that in the future they may sell a lot of automobiles from catalogs and mail order. But that's not the business for you!

Midget Cars

Trailers and Parts

Motorcycles and Parts

Hot-rod and Custom Car Parts

Auto Parts and Supplies

Several firms issue huge catalogs of accessories for ordinary stock autos. Other firms sell parts for foreign cars, or to the hot-rod set.

There is also at least one tiny mail-order business that sells parts for the Ford Model T.

Tires

For trucks, cars, sports cars—all at prices said to be below wholesale.

Reconditioned Spark Plugs

Also sold through agents.

Wheel Balancers

Auto Seat Covers

One firm solicits new-car buyers by direct mail from rental lists of new-car registrations.

Sun Glasses, Auto

Guaranteed to prevent glare. Sold by direct mail.

Auto Polishing Cloths

A small-town firm sells nothing but this item, with remarkable success. They advertise by direct mail, and in display ads in such places as the garden page of the *New York Sunday Times*. See Fig. 15–2, page 140, which shows their ad to rent their list. It tells you a great deal about the business.

This is an example of what can be done in the mail-order business with a good basic item, or line of items, plus a great deal of mail-order imagination.

Windshield Fog-cleaner Cloth

This is one of the leading items in the line of a firm that sells various auto and home goods through agents.

Boats and Motors

See the outdoor magazines for the full variety of firms in this market.

Boat Equipment

Canoes

Boat Designs (How-to-Do-It)

Airplane Designs (How-to-Do-It)

Engines and Motors for Lawn Mowers

MAGAZINE SUBSCRIPTIONS

Almost every magazine publisher, from *Time* to *American Bee Journal*, is in the mail-order business of selling subscriptions. And these magazines are the biggest single users of third-class mail in the country. There are literally thousands of magazines in the mail-order business in the United States.

Magazines sell subscriptions to their own magazines. But there are also various types of mail-order firms that sell subscriptions essentially as agents for the magazines.

One firm offers fifty different magazines at cut prices direct to consumers. It sells by direct mail and mails millions of pieces per year. It is a huge operation, run by the former circulation director of a major magazine. Reportedly this operation required a large sum of money to organize, and did not become profitable for quite a while. It makes its profits, like the magazines themselves, on reorders rather than on the initial subscriptions.

Other firms make deals with department stores to enclose stuffers advertising the magazines, along with monthly bills, or on the back of return envelopes. These firms have apparently found that they do best when they offer only a few magazines at a time.

Still other firms sell through agents that they recruit by classified or display advertising.

All these operations are drop-ship operations. They handle no merchandise. All they do is solicit orders, collect money, and take out their commission before forwarding the money to the magazines. Naturally they must sell at bargain prices (though never less than half the listed rate, or the magazine does not get credit for the subscription). And they must get bedrock deals from the magazines. Since magazines themselves often expect to spend every cent they get in subscription revenues in soliciting subscriptions, it is likely that these firms are sometimes able to arrange to keep all the subscription revenue they take in.

Magazines and Newspapers, Back Date

Back-date Racing Forms

Binders for Magazines

Some firms sell the binders. Others bind the magazines for the customers.

BOOKS

There is considerable overlap between this section and the sections on Correspondence Courses and Information. Whether a piece of written material is a course or a book depends mostly on the price and the way it is presented. Most correspondence-course material is also sold as books.

Some books that are good mail-order items are also mentioned in our sections on Health, Sports, and others.

Selling books and pamphlets by mail order has many advantages and some disadvantages. Chief among the advantages is that once you know you have a salable product, you can either write the material or have it written for you. This gives you perfect control over your material and perfect independence from the vagaries of suppliers.

If you own the rights to the material, you are in a position to reap the second great advantage, that of selling books at low cost, as low as 2 cents on the sales dollar.

Books and pamphlets go through the mail very cheaply, partly because of their low weight-to-cost ratio, partly because of the preferential postal rates Congress has seen fit to legislate for books. This is one of the reasons that books and courses are the greatest of the classic mail-order items.

The greatest advantage to selling books and information is also its greatest disadvantage: the ease of entering the field. Just as it is very cheap for you to test out a printed product and then go at it full blast, so it also is very easy for competitors to get in and reap part of the profit as soon as it becomes obvious to them (by repetition of your ads) that you have a profitable item. This means that in the field of selling books and information, more than in any other field, the profits will go to the most efficient operator and the best advertiser.

The best source of ideas for salable books is the mail-order ads, of course. The next best source is the catalog of the Little Blue Book Company (including the Big Blue Book catalog) of Girard, Kansas. The founder of "Little Blue Books," Emmanuel Haldeman-Julius, was one of the great mail-order men of all time, and each book in his huge series was selected with an eye to its mail-order sales appeal. The list covers practically every subject that will have mail-order appeal to a mass public. It is a gold mine of ideas, and it is also a source of books to sell while you are still testing and not ready to print your own.

Other sources of cheap books for the mail-order market include the Padell Book Company in New York and Ottenheimer, Stein in Chicago.

Incidentally, Haldeman-Julius wrote a superb book that is a tremendous store of knowledge for all mail-order sellers. It is called *The First Hundred Million*. Unfortunately, the book is out of print.

Another source of ideas for books to sell by mail is the catalog of Lee Mountain, Pisgah, Alabama. Most of the books listed in his catalog, as well as the courses, have been successful mail-order items at one time or another. I'll mention some of the specific titles. These titles should give you a good idea of which types of books will and which won't make good mail-order items.

Sometimes you can find a good mail-order seller that is not outdated, but that has fallen out of copyright. The book is then in the public domain, and you are perfectly free to duplicate it and sell it yourself without anyone's permission. See Appendix E for further information on copyright law.

Sex Books

This class includes books of sexual knowledge, not pornography or fiction. It is a tremendous mail-order field.

One firm that sells a "marriage book" (perfectly respectable, of course) offers to rent its list of 140,000 buyers in 1962, 170,000 buyers in 1961, and 100,000 buyers in 1960. You can figure for yourself how much they gross at $2.95 per copy. And that's only one of several items they sell. Their basic medium is display ads in men's magazines.

Other firms buy books from publishers and offer several books in their ads. Or they arrange with the publishers to drop-ship for them. All you have to do is persuade the publisher that you are a bookseller—several orders will prove that—and he will drop-ship the merchandise to your customers.

How-to-Do-It Books

Even how-to-do-it encyclopedias have sold well by mail.

Travel Books

Books on how to travel cheaply (by freighter, etc.), and how to retire cheaply in little-known places, are particularly good mail-order offers. One firm offers a line of these books.

Health Books

How to Live Long
How to Stop Smoking
How to Reduce
"Science of Keeping Young"
Home Remedies
Home Medical Encyclopedias
"How to Live 365 Days a Year"
"How to Stop Killing Yourself"

Birth Prevention. I think the U.S. Supreme Court ruled in 1937 that it is legal to send birth-control information by mail, though the post office may not think so. Books on the rhythm system have done well.

Inspirational Books

Business and Moneymaking Books

You'll find a raft of these books advertised in classified space in the mechanical and outdoor magazines.

"Get Rich in Spite of Yourself" is a typical, successful title. This one sells at $1 from newspaper reading notices.

Handwriting Analysis (Graphology)
Cartooning
Show Card Writing
Sign Painting
Restaurant Management
Shoe Repairing
"Cash from Sawdust, Coat-hangers, etc."
"990 Bizarre Businesses"
"609 Unusual, Successful Businesses"

Stock-and-bond Record Books

Miscellaneous

One fellow made a nice little business out of just one book—an adult stunt book of 101 best stunts.

Auto-repair Books

Atlases

Maps

Almanacs

Bibles

A great sold-by-agents business. Some Bibles also are sold directly by mail.

Self-help Books

Bashfulness
Sleep learning
Self-hypnosis
Voice and speaking improvement
Dancing
Penmanship. (This was a better seller before typewriters became so common. But one old firm still sells its instructions.)
English

Etiquette
How to Get to Sleep
Mathematics Made Easy
Public Speaking
Conversation Improvement
Horse-race Betting
Shorthand Systems
Fortune Telling
How to Stop Smoking
Foreign Languages. (Also sold as records.)
Beauty for Women
Body Building for Men (Including Isometrics)
Fighting Methods (Karate, Boxing, Wrestling, Judo, etc.)
Memory Improvement
Musical Instruments, especially guitar
Personal Magnetism
Personal Efficiency
"Seven Keys to Popularity"
"Self-mastery"
"The Knack of Remembering Names and Faces"
"Conquest of Fear"
Correct Breathing
Secrets of Strength
Psychology
Yoga
Hypnotism. (At least 15 firms sell books and hypnotic aids.)
Methods of Success
"How to Put the Subconscious Mind to Work"
Personal Finances
Tax Saving
Social Security Benefits
Salesmanship
Handwriting Analysis
"70 Bible Lessons 25¢. Bulletin, Box 87 . . . ." A long-running classified ad.
How to Buy Surplus from the Government. Several firms sell these guides.

Most self-help books are sold one at a time. However, there are several publishers who sell their whole line of books via consolidated ads in magazines. Some of them sell pamphlets at 50 cents (three for a dollar); others sell books at $2.

Textbooks, New and Used

When you think about mail order and books, you should remember that many, if not most, publishers of hard-cover books are in the mail-order business. This is especially true of university presses.

Coin Catalogs and Albums

Photo Albums and Photo Mounting Supplies

Book Clubs

The Book-of-the-Month Club started a business that has burgeoned. Now there is a book club to suit every interest, it seems: intellectuals, mystery lovers, bargain lovers, etc.

The book club business is specialized, however, and as a beginner you won't be attempting it.

Discount Books

On the next-to-last page of the book-review section of *The New York Times* on Sunday, the *Chicago Tribune*, and in other media, you will see the ads for several firms who advertise books at 25 to 30 percent off the list price. These outfits take your order, deduct the difference between your price and the publisher's wholesale price, and send money and your address to the publisher. That's all. No merchandise to carry. No investment. A nice repeat business.

I'm sure these businesses aren't getting rich. And they must be efficient to make money on their small margin.

Book Finders

The only way to buy a book that is out of print is to get it from a secondhand bookstore, or have a book finder get it for you. The book finders use several trade publications to locate the books. I don't know how they work, but I do know that at least ten of them advertise regularly in classified columns of book reveiws and magazines.

Bookbinding

CORRESPONDENCE SCHOOLS

Correspondence schools are another great mail-order product. Tens of millions of Americans have taken courses in the past, and many of them have been helped to live better lives. (Look at the ICS testimonials in their ads!) And millions of Americans are studying hundreds of different subjects at home right now.

Correspondence schools have the major advantage that the course work travels lightly and cheaply by mail. They sell products which often cannot be studied elsewhere, or cannot be studied locally in most areas. They offer real benefits to the student—either a better job, more money, or a richer life.

In addition to the correspondence schools, there are many resident schools that sell their services by mail. The auctioneering schools, for example, require that the student travel to the school, but all the selling is done by mail.

The listing of types of correspondence courses is nowhere near complete. Lee Mountain's catalog (Pisgah, Alabama) contains the fullest listing of past and present courses that I know of. The classified and display section of *Popular Science, Workbasket,* and the various specialized magazines will give you the complete picture of what's on the market now.

Correspondence courses go on and on, year after year. The owner of a correspondence school is not constantly hunting up new items to put into his catalog, or sweating out the latest fad. He will be continuously experimenting with his advertising, year after year, but he can count on a reasonably stable income from sales of his course.

High School Home Study

A big field, and probably getting bigger even though more and more people graduate from high school.

The schools use many and various methods of promotion, including car cards and match books.

Full-line Correspondence Schools

Most correspondence schools offer one or a few courses. Several offer five or ten related courses, such as the foreign-language schools. ICS and LaSalle are unique in offering many, many courses—over 250 by ICS.

"Do you make these mistakes in English?" is one of the most famous, and most effective, headlines ever written. The Sherwin Cody School has tried many other headlines, and many other ads, over a period of several decades. They always go back to using their original ad.

Self-improvement

Handwriting Analysis
Child-rearing for Parents
Horse Training
Art. The art correspondence schools teach many different facets of art: commercial, cartooning, painting, advertising, etc.
Music. One of the schools ran the most famous headline in advertising forty years ago: "They Laughed when I Sat Down at the Piano—But when I Began to Play . . . ."
You can learn any instrument at one or more of the schools. Other outfits offer just a single course. Guitar instruction is a best seller.
English Improvement
Conversation Improvement
Memory Improvement
Voice and Speech Training
Body Building and Muscle Building for Men
Beauty for Women
Ventriloquism
Penmanship
Home Instruction for Children

Technical Courses

There is a wide variety of technical courses sold by mail order, which we shall not discuss here, ranging from navigation to welding. International Correspondence Schools offers many of them, and you can check their catalog. Advertisements in technical magazines will show you others.

Business, Job and Money-making Courses

Bookkeeping. Instructions to set up your own local business. Government manuals, which are in the public domain, probably supply the backbone of at least one of these inexpensive courses.

Accounting
Accident Investigation
Auctioneering
Watchmaking
Gunsmithing
Detective Training. Detection equipment is also sold by the outfits that sell the courses.
Piano tuning
Practical Nursing
Restaurant Management
Swedish Massage
Invisible Mending
Millinery Design
Locksmithing
Woodworking
Typewriter Repair
Television and Radio Servicing
Photograph Coloring
Interior Decoration
Baking
Landscaping
Forestry and Conservation
Doll Making and Repair
Dressmaking
Floristry
Orchid Raising
Accident Claim Investigation
Hotel Management
Watch Repair
Meat Cutting
Taxidermy. One school has been in business over fifty years with little change in its advertising.
Exterminating. This is a course that I have never seen available, but I think it would be a good bet.
Candy Making
Photography
Child Photography
Writing
Civil Service Examination Studies
Commercial Art
Commercial Writing

Law
Metal Plating
Mirror Silvering
Baby-shoe Metallizing
Travel Agency. I'd guess this course would be a specially good bet today, when so many people are traveling abroad.
Cleaning and Pressing
Printing
Real Estate
Insurance
Salesmanship (sometimes with records)
Electrical Appliance Repairing
Upholstering
Credit and Collection
Sign Painting
Silk-screen Process
Flocking
General Business Training for Executives

INFORMATION SERVICES

Information services differ from books and courses in that the information must be *current and timely*, and therefore must constantly be new and up to date. Because of the high cost of gathering information, it is usually sold at a high price to a few subscribers. Information services sell their product for as high as $30,000 per year to a single firm. But most of the information services that we shall mention sell for from $2 to $100 yearly to individual or business subscribers.

Naturally enough, your information must not be easily available elsewhere, or no one will buy your service.

Information services have many similarities to magazines, and in fact, many magazines have started this way.

Stock-market Advisory Services

Look at their ads in the *New York Times* Business Section. Some are very big, some very small. Taken as a whole, this is big business.

Make sure you really are in a position to provide true information. And get clear on the laws that regulate this business.

Business Newsletters

There are several "inside dope" newsletters that provide general tips. At least one of these is a huge business.

Most major industries also have weekly newsletters that collect industry gossip, promotions, hirings, firings, alarms, and anything else of interest to company executives. These letters are generally started by people who have a wide acquaintance in the industry. They have sources of information, and know what executives want to know about.

Economic Information

One firm supplies leads for salesmen on all new businesses opening all over the country. Another tabulates references to economic forecasts made in all the trade magazines. A third, a huge company, provides information on new building permits.

Information Brokers

One firm has developed an interesting trade in bringing together people who need tips on new business, mergers, etc., and people who can supply such information.

Social Security Information

Most of the information sold is extracted directly from uncopyrighted government publications in the public domain.

Retirement Information

Where to live cheaply.

Sermons for Ministers

Dress Patterns

Architect's Plans for Houses

Boat and Airplane Construction Plans

Look for the ads in the mechanics magazines.

Plans for Home-workshop Projects

Employment and Job Information

Directories

Several firms publish directories of various types of business information: names of firms in an industry, names of buyers, names of trade associations, etc.

PHONOGRAPH RECORDS

Records have much in common with books as mail-order products. They are both readily mailable, can be offered as bargains, and often have specialized audiences.

Record Clubs

Most of the clubs are run or controlled by manufacturers, and they have a cost advantage not available to outsiders.

Language Records

Children's Records

Teaching Records for Children

Popular Hit Records

Combinations of the latest hits, on one record, have sold well from radio-advertising. The commercial ties in with the program.

A similar scheme has worked for classical themes on television.

Religious Records

PHOTOGRAPHY

Moving Pictures and Slides

Respectable home movies are sold via catalogs. Also 35-millimeter slides.

Religious Movies and Filmstrip

Photos of Movie Stars

Wallet Photos for Girls

These firms make copies of photographs. At least one firm has a recent list of 95,000 buyers.

Cameras and Equipment

Cameras and Equipment, Secondhand

Correspondence Photography Courses

Photograph Club Plans

One firm worked up a dandy business selling gift subscriptions for children's pictures taken every year on the child's birthday, from age one to age six. Then they franchised the plan to local studios.

Local Studio Photography

Photographers can increase their local business greatly with mail-order techniques.

Baby Pictures

Film Developing

There are a large number of firms that do this work at cut-rate prices by mail. Their gimmick is that they cut out the middleman-drugstores and other pickup places from the economic chain. They advertise everywhere, in heavy volume, in many media.

GARDEN SUPPLIES

Gardeners are good mail-order buyers. See garden magazines and garden sections of Sunday newspapers. Many large and small firms flourish in this field. One firm has a mailing list of 6 *million* customers. Another large firm sells through agents.

Garden-supply Club Plans

A different plant or seed is sent at regular intervals.

HOBBIES

Every year Americans have more free time and more money to spend on their hobbies. The growth of mail-order businesses in this area proves it.

Hobby Correspondence Courses

Taxidermy, Music, Horse Training, and many others.

Hobby Supplies

Guns

Air Rifles

Antique Guns

Gun Accessories and Supplies

Gunsmith Supplies
Hunting Calls

Blank Pistols for Training Dogs

Archery Equipment

Slingshots

Animal Traps

Fishing Tackle

Rods, reels, lures, tackle of all descriptions. Some sell direct from ads, some from catalogs.
Fish lures and Scents
Trophies

Dogs

Dog Equipment

Collars, kennels, shipping crates, "doors" into the house, dog "toys," etc.

Tents

   Sleeping Bags

Golf Equipment, Club Plans

Golf Books

Personalized Golf Balls

Golf Shoes

Golf Supplies

   Ball warmers, hand dryers, club covers, etc.

Pneumatic Swimming Support

   A German patent, brought here. They sell to other mail-order companies, catalogs, etc.

Ski Supplies, Books, and Clothing

Bar Bells

Body-building Books and Courses

Electronic Equipment, High Fidelity

   Tape Recorder Tape and Supplies

Photography

   Photo Travel Slides

Telescopes

Binoculars

   Domestic and Imported

Scientific Hobby Equipment

Kites for Adults and Children

Leatherwork Supplies

Musical Instruments

   See the music magazines for a full display. Accordions, guitars, and chord organs are sold through mass consumer media.

Recorders

   One firm does well selling just this one instrument.

ART

Correspondence Art Courses

Probably the most successful mail-order business in the art field.

Art Supplies

Necessary to have a retail store also, to maintain the necessary stock. Cut-rate special supplies are sold successfully.

Custom Paintings from Photos

Prints and Reproductions and Posters

Over the past few years these lines finally seem to have had some success.

Paintings, Imported

The firms mail out selections on approval, like stamps.

Statue Reproductions

Posters

Antiques

Antique Reproductions

Picture Moldings

Origami Paper

Stamps

This is one of the great mail-order fields. There are far more than 100 firms in the field, many just one man working part-time. A recent issue of *Popular Science* carried ads for seventy outfits. But you'd better know the stamp game before you try this field.

The larger stamp firms use many media, including match books.

Coins

A booming field in the last five years, and will probably continue to boom.

Some firms make a dandy profit on their catalogs alone, but this may not be ethical.

Indian Relics

This is just one tiny example of hundreds or thousands of types of mail-order firms selling little-known and specialized lines at a neat profit. They advertise in out-of-the-way places, and you must really research the field to come up with those that will be good fields for you.

Ship Models

Woodworking Supplies

Jewelry-making Supplies

Braided-rug Supplies

Costume-jewelry Supplies

TOYS

Toys are not a great mail-order item. Yet, under some conditions they do fine. For example, the famous F.A.O. Schwartz Co. uses display advertising to solicit inquiries for its catalog before Christmas, and Penney's sends out a big catalog, too, among others.

Electronic Computer Toys

Science Kits for Children

Dolls, 100 for $1

Huge Balloons

Balloons, 200 for $1

Magic Tricks and Novelties

PRINTING

This is a field of mail order which already thrives mightily, and which will grow even more in the future, I think, for this reason: if you went into a local printer and ordered 500 address labels, he would probably have to charge you $20. He would have to buy special paper, set up a press specially for the job, get them padded, etc. But a firm that makes a business of address labels can make a profit on them at 25 cents. Why? Because they mass-produce them, at a fantastic volume. It's the old American story, as simple as that.

The same idea holds for personal stationery, memo pads, calenders, office forms, envelopes, and a hundred other types of printing.

So, if you find a printed product that people want, and if you can operate efficiently and cut costs, this can be a mighty profitable field of endeavor.

Address Labels

These are often sold as a "leader" to introduce people to a line of gifts or novelties.

Other firms sell them through agents, and through stores and women's clubs as money-raising goods.

Personal Stationery

Two firms sell 100 letters and 50 envelopes, good quality, at the fabulously low price of $1—and apparently make a nice profit. One of them was reported to gross $750,000 last year.

Greeting Cards

Though cards are sold all year round, the major business is for Christmas. This is a big, solid business, done mostly through agents.

Wedding Announcements

Birth Announcements

Greeting Cards for Business

Office and commercial greeting cards for Christmas are a big business. One firm has a list of 110,000 commercial customers, very nice indeed.

Name Stamp, Rubber

Name stamps are sold for pocket use, with the personal signature engraved on them, and also just plain rubber stamps. One firm has a recent customer list of 104,000.

Book Plates

Embossing Machines

Personalized Welcome Mats

Sold direct and through agents.

Personal Signs

Metal and plastic signs are sold for all kinds of purposes: mailboxes, desks, gardens, everything. People like to see their own names in print, and that's why this is such a flourishing mail-order business.

Business Cards

Sold by mail at less than $4 per thousand.

Letterheads

One firm offers to design them and print them, too.

Office Forms

Standard sales forms, invoices, etc. More complicated forms will probably continue to require a salesman. The economies of the mail-order offer are in standardized forms.

Job Printing

One New York firm cuts its own low prices in its direct-by-mail, cash-with-offer deal.

Mimeographing

A Chicago firm even does mimeographing for large firms whose business it solicited by mail, even though I think its work is not outstanding or its prices particularly low.

Envelopes

Mail-order envelope firms offer real economies to large users of envelopes all over the country.

Collection Aids

An entire big business has been built on collection aids and stickers for insurance offices and similar customers.

Memorandum Devices

These are big sellers to businessmen. The *Diners' Club Magazine* is chock-full of large ads for various varieties—especially at the end of the year, of course.

Schedules and Calendars

Advertising Novelties

Many advertising novelties have the advertiser's name imprinted on the novelty.

Tarot Cards (fortune telling)

An example of a small printed novelty that has sold for years. It has probably been too small a line for anyone to challenge, so one firm seems to have the whole market.

Book Matches, Imprinted

Usually sold through agents.

Prepared Circulars and Stuffers

Various firms prepare advertising literature for cleaners, florists, and other businesses, and sell them to one exclusive customer in each area.

Printing Devices

A Connecticut firm has used the identical ad to sell its low-priced printing presses for 70 years. Another firm sells presses and accessories to commercial users. Another sells mimeograph machines through agents. Still a fourth sells a postcard mimeograph machine. And there are lots more.

MONEY

Money has an advantage for mail order: it is light in weight and easily mailable. It also has a disadvantage: the person with whom you are dealing is not close at hand.

Small Loans

For a while small companies had this field to themselves. Recently a mail-order giant tested the field, and jumped in with both feet.

Business Loans

A large commercial lender mails incessantly to supermarkets and other businesses to find prospects who want to borrow money for new equipment and fixtures. They close the sales in person, however.

Life Insurance

Getting bigger every day.

Health and Casualty Insurance

Burial Insurance

Auto Insurance

I am intrigued by the "special offers" to anyone who says he doesn't drink.

Savings and Loan Associations

Dozens of them advertise for you to save with them. Two firms make a business of acting as mail-order broker for many Savings and Loan accounts. Stock-market firms also get into the act. One reported $60,000 in accounts for a $100 ad.

Stocks and Bonds

Investment Advice and Market Letters

Collection of Debts

One firm obtains collection clients through the agents it recruits by mail.

Credit Clubs

Diners Club has done a remarkable mail-order job in obtaining subscribers. It has utilized car cards and take-one advertising of all kinds, among its media.

HOME-BUSINESS EQUIPMENT AND SUPPLIES

Bees and Beekeeping Materials

Squabs

A gentleman named Elmer Rice made a remarkable mail-order success by putting people into the business of raising squabs. He was also the pet account of one of the three largest advertising agencies in the country.

Chicks and Chicken-farming Equipment and Supplies

Years ago everyone thought it was impossible to sell chicks by mail order. Now the mails are full of them!

Fish, Partridges, Rabbits

Vending Machines

Baby-shoe-bronzing Equipment

Electroplating Kits

Rubber-stamp Machine

Tennis-racket-restringing Equipment

Printing Presses and Printing Supplies

Welding Equipment

Saw-sharpening Machines

Plastic Molding

Synthetic Gem Making

Doughnut Machines

Rug-cleaning Equipment

Typically, one firm sells a franchise and marketing program along with the equipment.

Furniture-cleaning Equipment

Wall-cleaning Equipment

Sign-making Machines

SERVICES

When you think about what to sell by mail order, don't concentrate so much on products that you forget about services. There are many things that you can do *for* people and firms, and that can be arranged by mail—far more than you think. So search your own experience to see if you have a special knowledge that you can sell to people for profit, or if you can develop such a skill or knowledge.

Book Finding

Mentioned earlier under "Books."

Vanity Publishing

Blanket Weaving

"Send us wool for blankets. Write . . . ." reads the ad.

Comforter Recovering

Commercial Photography

Advertisement Writing and Consultation

Several hot direct-mail letter writers make a nice living this way, I'm told.

Commercial Artwork

One fellow caters to mail-order firms and does small ad layouts for them and has done it for years.

Collection Agencies

Most of them do their collection entirely by mail. And some solicit all their clients by mail.

List Owners and List Brokers

One of them advertises in foreign newspapers and does a direct-mail business with its catalog.

Patent Search

You must be in Washington to render this service, I would guess.

Invention Marketing

LOCAL SERVICES

Don't get the idea that a mail-order business must be national in scope. Many local businesses are run on mail-order principles, except that the customer calls or comes in person, or that delivery is limited to a small area. For example, a business that advertises firewood could never be national. But it might operate entirely by advertising and telephone orders, and have all the hallmarks of a mail-order business.

Local services are usually part mail-order-type, part straight retail. The two hands wash each other!

I will list only a few examples of the multitude of services that you can run this way.

Window Washing

Auto Mechanic

Rug, Furniture, and Wall Cleaning

Floor Sanding

A dandy little business for some couples. He goes out and does the jobs, while she minds the phone to answer the inquiries they get from newspaper classified advertising.

Duplicating and Photostat Work

Travel Agency

Some travel agents do considerable business by mail outside the local area, too.

Flower Delivery

In one major city two fellows started a successful weekly club plan. And I experimented with the idea in New York under the name "Flowers Every Friday." I gave it up in favor of another scheme at the time, though afterwards I saw that it had excellent prospects.

BUSINESS TO BUSINESSES

For some reason, beginners in mail order always focus on products and services for consumers, ignoring the huge field of mail-order sales to commercial and industrial firms. It will be very educational to have a friend in a small office collect for you the mail the office receives over a short time. You'll be amazed at its volume.

As an example, I will list just a few of the major types of mail-order offers that come into an ordinary insurance agency.

Office Equipment

Office Supplies

Everything from pencils to filing cabinets. One firm mails to a list of 3 million, among whom are a whopping 800,000 buyers.

Specialized Books

Sales Training Bulletins, Programs, and Records

Letterheads

Stationery

Printing

Janitor Supplies
  Ice-melting products, just for one example.

Brushes, Industrial
  Some sell through agents.

Envelopes

Collection Aids

Specialized Magazines

Typewriters, New and Used

Adding Machines and Calculators
  Imported, usually.

Wall Charts and Display Boards

Advertising Novelties

Tables for Institutions

Machinery
  Of every size, shape, and description from chain hoists to printing presses.

HOME FURNISHINGS AND HOMES

Farms

Home Plots in Retirement Areas

Precut (prefabricated) Houses

Roofing, Especially of Aluminum

House Plans (Architectural)

Lumber
  For do-it-yourself builders, especially.

Fuel Oil
  A local business.

Awnings

Hammocks

Wallpaper

Drapery

Burlap for Home Decoration

Custom-made Drapes

Burglar Alarms
Also sold through agents.

Fire Alarms

Pumps for Miscellaneous Uses

Hardware Novelties
Door knockers, switch plates, etc.

Door Checks

Home-workshop Equipment

Tools

Welding Equipment (Do It Yourself)

Rugs

Furniture
Chairs, tables, cabinets, garden furniture, all kinds of furniture.

Furniture Do-It-Yourself Kits

Chair-caning Supplies

Bars

Bar Supplies
Novelty glasses, mixers, bars, etc.

Cabinets and Drawers
One firm that specializes in Old American style reputedly does a large business, all drop-shipped.

Bed Massage Equipment

Long-life Light Bulbs
Sold through agents.

Fire Extinguishers

Cookware

A terrific amount of cookware is sold by agents through home "parties." Other stuff is sold directly through "unbelievable bargain" ads, some of which are phony "surplus" or "liquidation."

China

Silverware

Basketware

Telephones and Telephone Equipment

Plastic Freezer Containers

One firm has a list of 50,000 customers whose average purchase is $15.

Cutlery

Typewriters

Power Mowers

Lawn Markers

Lawn Furniture

Candles, Decorative

Dry Window Cleaner

Through agents.

Fabric Mending Glue

Through agents. Also needle threader, eyeglass cleaner, etc.

Glue

Through agents.

GENERAL MERCHANDISE

Most firms in the mail-order business specialize in one or a few lines of merchandise. And I strongly advise everyone who is interested in mail order to start off with a specialty line, at least at the beginning.

However, there are also a good number of firms that sell a variety of merchandise. These general merchandisers fall into a few major classes that we shall now describe.

Department Store Type of Firm

Everyone is familiar with the Sears, Roebuck type of operation. 'Nuff said, except to mention that at least two new major firms, J. C. Penney and Singer, have entered the field recently, testimony to the vitality of mail-order selling today.

General Agents' Merchandise

There are several prosperous firms that sell a wide variety of merchandise through mail-order-recruited agents.

Novelty and Gift Merchandise

Since World War II there has been a fabulous growth in the firms that offer novelties priced at between 88 cents to $10 through catalogs. They sell knick-knacks that retail stores don't carry, new and gimmicky things that are fun for customers to buy and give away. Some of these firms have been terrific success stories. One of them has a customer list of 2.6 million, and in a short 16 years has grown from nothing to an annual volume of $7 million.

This is not a field for a beginner starting on a shoestring unless you possess considerable merchandising skill and experience. Capital, too.

These firms solicit new customers in one of two ways: (1) Offering a specially attractive bargain leader in space ads. They lose money on the initial order, but make it up in later purchases. (2) Sending their catalogs to lists rented from, or traded with, competitors in the same general field.

Assorted "Bargains" and "Surplus" Specialties

Klein's Directory lists about 3,000 firms, most of whom are in this category. Many of those firms make little or nothing, however, and many are in the business for only a short time.

These firms work in a variety of ways. One method is to develop a customer clientele for real or apparent bargains of all types. The firm ordinarily advertises one or more of these bargains in space advertising, then follows it up with package stuffers and direct-mail flyers of from one to eight pages of similar merchandise.

Some of the merchandise is truly bargain, imported or domestic, the result of good merchandising ability on the part of the firm. Other merchandise is government surplus. Still other firms sell phony bargains and "liquidated" merchandise that can be bought just as cheaply at retail stores.

Some firms really are able to make money with a succession of one-shot items sold directly from space advertising. But such firms are few and far between. Mostly they must depend on repeat sales for profitable volume.

MISCELLANEOUS LINES

Religious Materials

Dog Repellent

Grave Monuments, $14.95
  These tombstones are made of concrete.

Bed and Sleep Furnishings

Tear-gas Guns

Book Plates

Coin-bank Calendar

Novelty Pets
  Includes monkeys, horses, turtles.

Chalk-talk Cartooning

Old Gold Bought

Fortune Telling
  I do not recommend this field.

Flagpoles

Coats of Arms with Family Name
  In pewter or wood shield $7 or $14.50.

Marriage Brokers

Employment Agencies
  Teacher's employment agencies seem to do well by mail.

Transistor Radios

Charm-and-treasure Jewelry

Slide Rules

Plaques and Tablets

Church Furniture

Children's Things
  See mother's magazines.

Ball-point Pens and Refills

Pest-control Supplies

Trading Cards

There is something to be learned about the mail-order business from this example. You would never guess, from the advertising, that one firm, let alone several firms, does a very substantial volume in trading cards (baseball and other sports pictures) sold to children and collectors.

Only a few tiny ads appear each year in a couple of specialized media, accounting for only a tiny advertising budget. And yet I learned about one of these firms—a retired couple, whose large apartment was filled from wall to wall with trays of cards. The business, started as a hobby, was easily worth $25,000, despite the fact that many items were sold for 2 cents or 5 cents.

APPENDIX K

Books and Articles about Mail Order

If you insist on learning your way in the mail-order business by your own experience alone, your future is not so rosy as it might be. Instead, learn by the experience of others. Learn what pitfalls to avoid, which devices will help you sell. The way to gain the experience of others is by reading what they have written about their experiences in mail order.

Of course, there is no law that will force you to read these books listed here. Other men have begun mail-order businesses without ever reading anything. But those men usually wish they had learned before they started. Either they lose a potful of money before getting into the black—money they would not have needed to lose if they had profited by the experience of others—or they make less profit than they could have made with a better grounding in the field.

So take my advice, and invest a little time and money in books before you begin. Twenty dollars in books will be the best investment you ever make. It may save you $50,000 in time.

Also, don't just skim through the books and put them away. Keep them around, and reread them from time to time. You can appreciate the wisdom in these books only after you have gotten into the business.

Scholars who seek an extensive bibliography should refer to Emmett and Jeuck (listed below).

This reading list does not cover all the works listed in the chapter references that follow, or all mail-order books. I have included only those works with which I am familiar, and which I think are particularly useful.

Alexander, Ken (Segal): *How to Start Your Own Mail Order Business*, Stravon Publishers, New York, 1950.

Pretty fair introduction. Worth reading as a refresher.

Asher, Louis E., and Edith Heal: *Send No Money*, Argus, 1942.

Baker, Robert A.: *Help Yourself to Better Mail Order*, Printers' Ink Publishing Co., Inc., New York, 1953.

An excellent book for the small mail-order operator. Covers basic topics in copy, media, and product choice. Also contains excellent check lists and media lists, plus some good mail-order ads.

Bedell, Clyde: *How to Write Advertising That Sells*, 2d ed., McGraw-Hill, New York, 1952.

A top book on mail-order copy, slanted somewhat toward retail.

Bringe, Paul: *Briefs from Bringe*, privately published monthly, Hartford, Wis.

An informative monthly newsletter, written as a house organ by a crack copywriter. Available from Bringe for a nominal buck a year. Write Paul Bringe, First National Bank Building, Hartford, Wis.

Buckley, Earle A.: *How to Sell by Mail*, McGraw-Hill, New York, 1938.

Caples, John: *Tested Advertising Methods*, Harper & Row, New York, 1940.

An excellent book on mail-order copywriting.

Collier, Robert: *The Robert Collier Letter Book*, Prentice-Hall, Englewood Cliffs, N.J., 1950.

Classic book on direct-mail copy.

Cossman, E. Joseph: *How I Made $1,000,000 in Mail-order*, Prentice-Hall, Englewood Cliffs, N.J., 1963.

A few interesting tidbits, plus inspiration. But I think Cossman's advice is exactly wrong for beginners.

Direct Mail (formerly *The Reporter of Direct Mail Advertising*), Garden City, New York.

Often carries articles on mail-order businesses. Its ads are also of interest.

Emmett, Boris, and John Jeuck: *Catalogues and Counters*, University of Chicago Press, 1950.

An excellent book on Sears, Roebuck, contains a large bibliography on the mail-order business.

Ferrara, V. P.: *A Complete Course in the Mail-order Business*, Nelson-Hall, Chicago, 1955.

This is a very sound volume, from which the mail-order beginner can learn a lot, especially about selling books.

Graham, Irvin: *How to Sell through Mail Order*, McGraw-Hill, New York, 1949.

Very competent book on mail-order *advertising*. Extremely useful if you act as your own agency.

Grant, Paul: *L. W. Mail Order Survey*.

A sound course by a real old pro who is especially knowledgeable about correspondence courses.

Haldeman-Julius, Emanuel: *The First Hundred Million*, Simon and Schuster, New York, 1928.

The best source material for a mail-order bookseller, or any other mail-order man, for that matter. Gives you an unparalleled chance to understand what really makes mail-order copy succeed or fail.

Hall, Samuel R.: *Mail-order and Direct Mail Selling*, McGraw-Hill, New York, 1928.

Somewhat outdated.

Hopkins, Claude: *Scientific Advertising*, Moore, New York, 1952.

A classic little book, by the acknowledged greatest of all copywriters. Out of print, unfortunately.

Hotchkiss, G. B.: *Advertising Copy*, 3d ed., Harper & Row, New York, 1949.

A fine book on copywriting in general.

Howard, James E.: *How to Use Mail Order for Profit*, Grosset & Dunlap, New York, 1963.

Skimpy but sound.

Kelley, Pearce C., and Kenneth Lawyer: *How to Organize and Operate a Small Business*, 3d ed., Prentice-Hall, Englewood Cliffs, N.J., 1961.

A good book to have in your library for reference when problems come up.

Kleid, Lewis (ed.): *Mail Order Strategy*, Direct Mail, Garden City, New York, 1956.

A good collection of articles on direct mail in mail order.

Lustig, Edward: *Modern Mechanical Addressing Systems*, Circulation Associates, New York, 1963.

A detailed discussion of addressing.

Melcher, Daniel, and Nancy Larrick: *Printing and Promotion Handbook*, McGraw-Hill, New York, 1956.

Moran, John: *The Mail Order Business*, MBA Business Associates, Syracuse, 1949.

A hodgepodge of very useful material—facts, lists, anecdotes. Good for idea-browsing, but not a text.

Musselman, Henry E.: *Mail Order Dollars*, Publicity Publications, Kalamazoo, 1954.

Contains useful information.

Pratt, Verneur: *Selling by Mail*, 1st ed., McGraw-Hill, New York, 1924.

Covers many topics in mail order, including catalogs and agents. Includes many illustrations. A valuable book, though dated.

Preston, Harold P.: *Successful Mail Selling*, Ronald, New York, 1941.

Competent discussion of mail-order basic topics.

Rheinstrom, Carroll: *Psyching the Ads*, Covici-Friede, New York, 1929.

A compilation of advertising copy tests, the study of which helps you learn to create good ads.

Sawyer, Samuel: *Secrets of the Mail Order Trade*, 1900.

A fine old book, if you can find it. Old, but not dead.

Schwab, Victor O.: "Successful Mail-Order Advertising," in Roger Barton (ed.), *Advertising Handbook*, Prentice-Hall, Englewood Cliffs, N.J., 1950.

The best short article on display copy.

Schwab, Victor O.: *How to Write a Good Advertisement*, Harper & Row, New York, 1962.

Excellent book on copy.

Shryer, William A.: *Analytical Advertising*, Business Service Corporation, Detroit, 1912.

The first great book about mail order or *any* advertising. My favorite, because it gives *facts and figures*.

Simon, Morton J.: *The Law for Advertising and Marketing*, Norton, New York, 1956.

The bible!

Stone, Robert: *Successful Direct Mail Advertising and Selling*, Prentice-Hall, Englewood Cliffs, N.J., 1955.

An excellent book on direct mail in general, and as used in mail order.

Sumner, G. Lynn: *How I Learned the Secrets of Success in Advertising*, Prentice-Hall, Englewood Cliffs, N.J., 1952.

Easy-to-read stories of mail-order successes, plus some basic factual information.

Swan, Carrol J.: *Which Ad Pulled Best?* Printers' Ink Publishing Co., Inc., New York, 1951.

It is good training in copy to study this book.

Swett, Arthur E.: *Principles of the Mail Order Business*, 4th ed., Swett Publishers, 1900.

Almost as useful now as when published sixty-four years ago. Also interesting for its views on patent-medicine advertising, listings, and rates of mail-order media. (The line rate per 100,000 seems to have changed astonishingly little!) Old mail-order ads.

Wadsworth, R. K.: *Handbook of Mail-order Selling and Merchandising*, Dartnell, Chicago, 1928.

A good book, though somewhat outdated.

Whitney, Walter N.: *Building a Mail-order Business*, Alexander Hamilton Institute, no date shown.

Yeck, John D., and John T. Maguire: *Planning and Creating Better Direct Mail*, McGraw-Hill, New York, 1961.

Excellent book on its subject.

References

CHAPTER 1

1. *Establishing and Operating a Mail-order Business*, U.S. Department of Commerce Industrial Small Business Series, no. 46, p. 12.
2. Robert A. Baker, *Help Yourself to Better Mail Order*, Printers' Ink Publishing Co., Inc., New York, 1953, p. 4.
3. Arthur E. Swett, *Principles of the Mail Order Business*, 4th ed., 1900, p. 1.

CHAPTER 2

1. *The World of Advertising*, special issue, *Advertising Age*, Jan. 15, 1963, p. 137.
2. Joseph H. Rhoads, *Selling by Mail with Limited Capital*, U.S. Small Business Administration, Small Business Bulletin, December, 1958, p. 1.
3. *Time*, Dec. 20, 1963, p. 79.
4. *Direct Mail*, January, 1964, p. 52.
5. *Trade Practice Rules, Subscription & Mail Order Book Industry*, Federal Trade Commission, p. 1.
6. Baker (see Appendix K), p. 78.
7. *Mail Order Business Directory*, B. Klein Company, 1961.
8. W. A. Mindak, A. Neibergs, and A. Anderson, "Economic Effects of the Minneapolis Newspaper Strike," *Journalism Quarterly*, Spring, 1963, p. 216.
9. Stanley I. Fishel, "A Review of Mail-order Shopping Sections," *Media/Scope* April, 1962, p. 78.
10. *The World of Advertising* (Ref. 1 above), pp. 137–138.
11. "Armchair Shopping: Mail Order Is a Big and Still Growing Business," *The Economist*, Feb. 27, 1960, pp. 827–829.
12. James Moyer, privately circulated memorandum.

CHAPTER 3

1. Paul Bringe, *Briefs from Bringe*, August, 1962.
2. John A. Howard, *Marketing Management* (Richard D. Irwin, 1957), pp. 242–243.
3. *Time*, Sept. 21, 1962, p. 84.
4. Howard (Ref. 2 above), p. 244.

CHAPTER 4

1. Emanuel Haldeman-Julius, *The First Hundred Million*, Simon & Schuster, New York, 1928.

2. Peter S. Fischer, "The Leslies of Lafayette Hill," *Direct Mail*, September, 1963, pp. 33ff.
3. *Advertising Age*, Feb. 3, 1964, p. 38.
4. John Moran, *The Mail Order Business*, MBA Business Associates, Syracuse, 1949, p. 426.

CHAPTER 5

1. Morton J. Simon, *The Law for Advertising and Marketing*, Norton, New York, 1956.
2. Verneur E. Pratt, *Selling by Mail*, 1st ed., McGraw-Hill, New York, 1924, pp. 50–51.
3. Samuel Sawyer, *Secrets of the Mail Order Trade*, 1900, p. 23.
4. Sawyer (Ref. 3 above).
5. Morton J. Simon, *Advertising Truth Book*, Advertising Federation of America.

CHAPTER 6

1. Paul Grant, *L. W. Mail Order Survey*, no date.

CHAPTER 7

1. Business Information, Inc., pamphlet, date not known.
2. Business Information, Inc.
3. Victor O. Schwab, in Roger Barton (ed.), *Advertising Handbook* (see Appendix K), p. 605.
4. Victor O. Schwab, "What 92 Split-run Ads Tell Us—Part I," *Advertising & Selling*, April, 1948, p. 62.
5. Harold P. Preston, *Successful Mail Selling*, Ronald, New York, 1941, p. 12.
6. Pratt (see Appendix K), p. 377.
7. Baker (see Appendix K), p. 90.
8. *Esquire Mail Order Newsletter*, undated.
9. Schwab, quoted in Moran (see Appendix K), p. 241.
10. Victor O. Schwab, "What 92 Split-run Ads Tell Us—Part II," *Advertising & Selling*, May, 1948, p. 74.
11. Grant (see Appendix K), page not known.
12. Grant (see Appendix K), p. 82.
13. E. H. Barnes, *Barnes on Credit and Collection*, Prentice-Hall, Englewood Cliffs, N.J., 1961.
14. John D. Little, *Complete Credit and Collection Letter Book*, Prentice-Hall, Englewood Cliffs, N.J., 1953.
15. Richard H. Morris, *Credit and Collection Letters*, National Association of Credit Management, Channel Press, Great Neck, N.Y., 1960.

CHAPTER 9

1. Readex survey quoted in Baker (see Appendix K), p. 103.

CHAPTER 11

1. Victor O. Schwab, in Barton (ed.), *Advertising Handbook* (Ref. 3, Chapter 7, above).

2. John Caples, *Tested Advertising Methods*, Harper & Row, New York, 1940.
3. Victor O. Schwab, *How to Write a Good Advertisement*, 1st ed., Harper & Row, New York, 1962.
4. Clyde Bedell, *How to Write Advertising That Sells*, 2d ed., McGraw-Hill, New York, 1952.
5. G. B. Hotchkiss, *Advertising Copy*, 3d ed., Harper & Row, New York, 1949.
6. Baker (see Appendix K), p. 73.
7. Grant (see Appendix K), page not known.
8. S. D. Cates, quoted in Moran (see Appendix K), p. 137.
9. Irvin Graham, *How to Sell through Mail Order*, McGraw-Hill, New York, 1949, pp. 335–337.
10. G. Lynn Sumner, *How I Learned the Secrets of Success in Advertising*, Prentice-Hall, Englewood Cliffs, N.J., 1952, p. 86.
11. H. K. Simon, *Mail Order Profits and Pitfalls*, H. K. Simon Co., 1961.
12. Ken Alexander (pseudonym for Alexander Segal), *How to Start Your Own Mail Order Business*, Stravon Publishers, New York, 1950.
13. Robert Stone, *Successful Direct Mail Advertising and Selling*, Prentice-Hall, Englewood Cliffs, N.J., 1955, p. 50.
14. Sumner (Ref. 10 above), p. 87.
15. Moran (see Appendix K), p. 493.

CHAPTER 12

1. *House Beautiful* Research Service, reported in Baker (see Appendix K), p. 85.
2. H. C. Daych, *Printers' Ink*, May 8, 1953.
3. Baker (see Appendix K), p. 71.
4. Moran (see Appendix K), page not known.
5. *Fate Magazine*, promotional literature, undated.
6. Stone (see Appendix K), p. 59.
7. Grant (see Appendix K), page not known.
8. O. E. McIntyre, Inc., "Best Seasons for Direct Mail," *Media/Scope*, September, 1963, p. 27.
9. William A. Shryer, *Analytical Advertising*, Business Service Corporation, Detroit, 1912, p. 347.
10. Shryer (Ref. 9 above), pp. 82–83.
11. Schwab, in Barton (ed.), *Advertising Handbook* (Ref. 3, Chapter 7, above), p. 612.
12. Moran (see Appendix K), p. 150.
13. Elon Borton, "Tested Facts Produce One Million Sales for LaSalle in 37 years," *Printers' Ink*, Aug. 10, 1945, pp. 19–20.
14. *Esquire Mail Order Newsletter*, undated.

CHAPTER 13

1. Victor O. Schwab, *Advertising & Selling*, May, 1948, p. 38.
2. Preston (see Appendix K), p. 44.
3. Preston (see Appendix K), p. 48.
4. Victor O. Schwab, *Advertising & Selling*, April, 1948, p. 33.
5. Schwab (Ref. 4 above), p. 60 (Ref. 1 above), p. 38.
6. Schwab, in Barton (ed.), *Advertising Handbook* (Ref. 3, Chapter 7, above), p. 598.

7. Moran (see Appendix K), p. 63.
8. Henry E. Musselman, *Mail Order Dollars*, Publicity Publications, Kalamazoo, 1954, p. 174.
9. David Ogilvy, *Confessions of an Advertising Man*, Atheneum, New York, 1963.
10. Schwab (Ref. 4 above), p. 62.
11. Baker (see Appendix K), p. 42.
12. Stanley Rapp, "Mail-order Inserts Increase Sales Four Times," *Media/Scope*, September, 1961, pp. 79–83.
13. Schwab (Ref. 4 above), p. 60.
14. Shryer (see Appendix K), p. 171.
15. Baker (see Appendix K), p. 49.
16. Caples (see Appendix K), pages not known.
17. Baker (see Appendix K), p. 48.
18. D. B. Lucas and S. H. Britt, *Advertising Psychology and Research*, McGraw-Hill, New York, 1950, p. 248.
19. Pratt (see Appendix K), p. 352.
20. Borton (Ref. 13, Chapter 12, above), pp. 19–20.
21. Lucas and Britt (Ref. 18 above), pp. 234–236.
22. Borton (Ref. 20 above), pp. 19–20.
23. Daniel Starch, "Do Inside Positions Differ in Readership?" *Media/Scope*, February, 1962, p. 44.
24. Schwab, in Barton (ed.), *Advertising Handbook* (Ref. 3, Chapter 7, above), p. 610.
25. Personal conversation with forgotten informant.
26. Schwab, in Barton (ed.), *Advertising Handbook* (Ref. 3, Chapter 7, above), p. 611.
27. D. B. Lucas, "The Impression Value of Tried Advertising Locations in *The Saturday Evening Post*," *Journal of Applied Psychology*, vol. XXI, pp. 613–631, 1937, as quoted in Lucas and Britt (Ref. 21 above).
28. Alexander (Segal) (Ref. 12, Chapter 11, above), p. 39.
29. Sumner (see Appendix K), p. 63.

CHAPTER 14

1. Stone (see Appendix K).
2. Robert Collier, *The Robert Collier Letter Book*, Prentice-Hall, Englewood Cliffs, N.J., 1950.
3. John D. Yeck and John T. Maguire, *Planning and Creating Better Direct Mail*, McGraw-Hill, New York, 1961.
4. Robert Stone, "How to Get the Most Out of Your Direct-Mail Advertising Dollar," in Roger Barton (ed.), *Advertising Handbook*, Prentice-Hall, Englewood Cliffs, N.J., 1950, pp. 571–596.
5. Stone, *Successful Direct Mail Advertising and Selling* (see Appendix K), p. 71.
6. Stone (see Appendix K), p. 70.
7. Moran (see Appendix K), p. 418.
8. Stone (see Appendix K), p. 72.
9. Stone (see Appendix K), p. 71.
10. Stone (see Appendix K), p. 70.
11. B. M. Mellinger, *Mail Order Course*, published by its author, Los Angeles, page not known.
12. Pratt (see Appendix K), p. 143.
13. Stone (see Appendix K), p. 71.

14. *Esquire Newsletter,* undated.
15. Stone (see Appendix K), p. 70.
16. Stone (see Appendix K), p. 73.
17. Stone (see Appendix K), p. 71.
18. Preston (see Appendix K), p. 103.
19. Baker (see Appendix K), p. 164.
20. Musselman (see Appendix K), p. 173.
21. Moran (see Appendix K), p. 245.
22. Stone (see Appendix K), p. 71.
23. Stone (see Appendix K), p. 71.
24. Paul Bringe, *Briefs from Bringe,* June, 1962, quoting from Lewis Kleid, Inc., Research Report no. 48.
25. Grant (see Appendix K), page not known.
26. Baker (see Appendix K), p. 73.
27. Alexander (see Appendix K), page not known.
28. Stone (see Appendix K), p. 50.
29. Source unknown.
30. Grant (see Appendix K), page not known.
31. Art Kemble, *Direct Mail,* date not known.

CHAPTER 15

1. Paul Bringe, *Briefs from Bringe,* April, 1963.
2. Business Information, Inc.
3. Stone (see Appendix K), p. 26.
4. Stone (see Appendix K), p. 26.
5. Moran (see Appendix K), p. 63.
6. Fischer (Ref. 2, Chapter 4, above), p. 33.
7. Wendell Forbes, *Direct Mail,* November, 1962, p. 40.
8. *Direct Mail,* June, 1962, p. 5.
9. Stone (see Appendix K), p. 59.
10. Grant (see Appendix K), page not known.
11. Samuel R. Hall, *Mail-order and Direct Mail Selling,* McGraw-Hill, New York, 1928, chap. III, p. 17.
12. Haldeman-Julius, in Moran (see Appendix K), p. 467.

CHAPTER 17

1. Pratt (see Appendix K), p. 251.
2. Borton (Ref. 13, Chapter 12, above), pp. 19–20.
3. Musselman (see Appendix K), p. 66.
4. Shryer (see Appendix K), p. 221.
5. Grant (see Appendix K), page not known.
6. Grant (see Appendix K), page not known.

CHAPTER 18

1. Source not known.
2. Victor O. Schwab, *Advertising & Selling,* April, 1948, p. 33.
3. William A. Doppler, "A Mail Order Test to End All Tests . . . ," *Direct Mail,* September, 1957, p. 40.

4. Robert Schlaifer, *Introduction to Statistics for Business Decisions*, McGraw-Hill, New York, 1961.
5. Lewis Kleid, Inc., *Bulletin*, undated.
6. Orlan Gaeddert, in private communication to author.
7. William Doppler, in Lewis Kleid, Inc., *Lewis Kleid Reports*, March, 1954.
8. Lewis Kleid, report.

CHAPTER 19

1. Amalgamated Lithographers of America, Local 1 of greater New York, 113 University Place, New York, N.Y. 10003, 1963.

CHAPTER 20

1. *Encyclopedia of Associations*, 3d ed., Gale Research Co., 1961.
2. Sawyer (see Appendix K), p. 25.
3. *Esquire Mail Order Newsletter*, undated.
4. Sawyer (see Appendix K), p. 34.

CHAPTER 21

1. Stone (see Appendix K), p. 87.

CHAPTER 22

1. Pearce C. Kelley and Kenneth Lawyer, *How to Organize and Operate a Small Business*, 3d ed., Prentice-Hall, Englewood Cliffs, N.J., 1961.
2. William J. Papp, "Pitfalls to Avoid in Selling Your Mail Order Business," *Direct Mail*, March, 1963, p. 29.

APPENDIX A

1. William Berkwitz, *Encyclopedia of the Mail-order Business*, 1906.

APPENDIX D

1. Federal Trade Commission, Annual Report, 1954.

APPENDIX E

1. Copyright Office notices and instruction sheets, undated.

APPENDIX F

1. Robert J. Wolfson, personal communication.

Index